Springer Series on
SIGNALS AND COMMUNICATION TECHNOLOGY

SIGNALS AND COMMUNICATION TECHNOLOGY

(continued at the end of book)

Edited by
Yingshu Li
My T. Thai
Weili Wu

Wireless Sensor Networks and Applications

 Springer

Yingshu Li
Georgia State University
Atlanta, GA
USA

My T. Thai
University of Florida
Gainesville, FL
USA

Weili Wu
University of Texas at Dallas
Richardson, TX
USA

ISBN   978-1-4419-4319-4   e-ISBN   978-0-387-49592-7

Printed on acid-free paper.

9 8 7 6 5 4 3 2 1

springer.com

This book is dedicated to our families

Contents

SECTION I   Network Design and Network Modelling

SECTION II   Network Management

SECTION III   Data Management

SECTION IV   Security

Contributing Authors

Bassem Alhalabi
Department of Computer Science & Engineering
Florida Atlantic University
Boca Raton, FL 33431
E-mail: alhalabi@fau.edu

Anish Arora
Department of Computer Science & Engineering
Ohio State University
Columbus, OH 43210
E-mail: anish@cse.ohio-state.edu

Raheem Beyah
Department of Computer Science
Georgia State University
Atlanta, GA 30303
E-mail: rbeyah@cs.gsu.edu

Zhipeng Cai
Department of Computing Science
University of Alberta
Edmonton, Alberta, T6G2E8, Canada
E-mail: zhipeng@cs.ualberta.ca

Mihaela Cardei
Department of Computer Science & Engineering
Florida Atlantic University
Boca Raton, FL 33431
E-mail: mihaela@cse.fau.edu

Dechang Chen
Department of Preventive Medicine and Biometrics
Uniformed Services University of the Health Sciences
Bethesda, MD 20814
E-mail: dchen@usuhs.mil

Maggie Cheng
Computer Science Department
University of Missouri
Rolla, MO 65401
E-mail: chengm@umr.edu

Xiuzhen Cheng
Department of Computer Science
George Washington University
Washington, DC 20052
E-mail: cheng@gwu.edu

Fernand S. Cohen
Electrical and Computer Engineering Department
Drexel University
Philadelphia, PA 19103
E-mail: fscohen@coe.drexel.edu

John Copeland
School of Electrical and Computer Engineering
Georgia Institute of Technology
Atlanta, GA 30332
E-mail: jcopeland@ece.gatech.edu

Cherita Corbett
School of Electrical and Computer Engineering
Georgia Institute of Technology
Atlanta, GA 30332
E-mail: cherita@ece.gatech.edu

Jaudelice C. de Oliveira
Electrical and Computer Engineering Department
Drexel University
Philadelphia, PA 19103
E-mail: jau@ece.drexel.edu

Xiaojiang Du
Department of Computer Science
North Dakota State University
Fargo, ND 58105
E-mail: Xiaojiang.Du@ndsu.edu

Kai-Wei Fan
Computer Science and Engineering Department
Ohio State University
Columbus, OH 43210
E-mail: fank@cse.ohio-state.edu

Joshua Goldberg
Electrical and Computer Engineering Department
Drexel University
Philadelphia, PA 19103
E-mail: jbg25@drexel.edu

Sam Hsu
Department of Computer Science & Engineering
Florida Atlantic University
Boca Raton, FL 33431
E-mail: sam@cse.fau.edu

Dong Hua
Department of Computer Science
George Washington University
Washington, DC 20052
E-mail: gwuhua@gwu.edu

Ali Abu-el Humos
Department of Computer Science & Engineering
Florida Atlantic University
Boca Raton, FL 33431
E-mail: aabuel@fau.edu

Aravind Iyer
School of Electrical and Computer Engineering
Purdue University
West Lafayette, IN 47907
E-mail: iyerav@ecn.purdue.edu

Xiao-Hua Jia
Department of Computer Science
City University of HongKong
Kowloon, Hong Kong
Computer School
Wuhan University
Wuhan 430072, China
E-mail: jia@cs.cityu.edu.hk

Bhaskar Krishnamachari
Department of Electrical Engineering-Systems
Viterbi School of Engineering
University of Southern California
Los Angeles, CA 90089
E-mail: bkrishna@usc.edu

Sunil S. Kulkarni
School of Electrical and Computer Engineering
Purdue University
West Lafayette, IN 47907
E-mail: sunilkul@ecn.purdue.edu

Santosh Kumar
Department of Computer Science
University of Memphis
Memphis, TN 38152
E-mail: santosh.kumar@memphis.edu

Ten H. Lai
Department of Computer Science and Engineering
Ohio State University
Columbus, OH 43210
E-mail: lai@cse.ohio-state.edu

Frank L. Lewis
Automation and Robotics Research Institute (ARRI)
University of Texas at Arlington
Arlington, TX 76118
E-mail: lewis@uta.edu

Jianzhong Li
School of Computer Science & Technology
Harbin Institute of Technology
Harbin 150001, China
E-mail: lijzh@hit.edu.cn

Jinbao Li
School of Computer Science & Technology
Harbin Institute of Technology
Harbin 150001, China
E-mail: lijinbao@hit.edu.cn

Dan-Dan Liu
Computer School
Wuhan University
Wuhan 430072, China
E-mail: liudd2004@hotmail.com

Fang Liu
Department of Computer Science
George Washington University
Washington, DC 20052
E-mail: fliu@gwu.edu

Ren-Shiou Liu
Computer Science and Engineering
Ohio State University
Columbus, OH 43210
E-mail: rsliu@cse.ohio-state.edu

Sha Liu
Computer Science and Engineering Department
Ohio State University
Columbus, OH 43210
E-mail: liusha@cse.ohio-state.edu

Yadi Ma
Computer Science Department
University of Missouri
Rolla, MO 65401
E-mail: ym95d@umr.edu

Vivek Mhatre
School of Electrical and Computer Engineering
Purdue University
West Lafayette, IN 47907
E-mail: mhatre@ecn.purdue.edu

Dan O. Popa
Automation and Robotics Research Institute (ARRI)
University of Texas at Arlington
Arlington, TX 76118
E-mail: popa@arri.uta.edu

Catherine P. Rosenberg
Department of Electrical and Computer Engineering
University of Waterloo
Waterloo, ON N2L3G1, Canada
E-mail: cath@ece.uwaterloo.ca

Lifeng Sang
Computer Science and Engineering
Ohio State University
Columbus, OH 43210
E-mail: sangl@cse.ohio-state.edu

Prasun Sinha
Computer Science and Engineering Department
Ohio State University
Columbus, OH 43210
E-mail: prasun@cse.ohio-state.edu

Curt Schurgers
Electrical and Computer Engineering Department
University of California
San Diego, CA 92093
E-mail: curts@ece.ucsd.edu

Weilian Su
Department of Electrical and Computer Engineering
Naval Postgraduate School
Monterey 93943, Canada
833 Dyer Road, Rm. 452, Spanagel Bldg. 232
E-mail: weilian@nps.edu

Jindong Tan
Department of Electrical and Computer Engineering
Michigan Technological University
Houghton, MI 49931
E-mail: jitan@mtu.edu

Yu Wang
Department of Computer Science
University of North Carolina at Charlotte
Charlotte, NC 28223
E-mail: ywang32@uncc.edu

Yang Xiao
Department of Computer Science
University of Memphis
Memphis, TN 38152
E-mail: yangxiao@ieee.org

Preface

Wireless sensor networks are being employed in a variety applications ranging from medical to military, and from home to industry. The principle aim of this book is to provide a reference tool for the increasing number of scientists who depend upon sensor networks in some way. The book is organized into several sections, each including chapters exploring a specific topic.

Wireless sensor networks are attracting great attention and there are many research topics yet to be studied. In this book, the topics covered include network design and modelling, network management, data management, security and applications.

The articles presented in the book are expository, but of a scholarly nature, including the appropriate history background, a review of the state-of-the-art thinking relative to the topic, as well as a discussion of unsolved problems that are of special interest.

The target readers of this book include the researchers in computer science, computer engineering, and applied mathematics, as well as students in these subjects. Specialists as well as general readers will find the articles stimulating and helpful.

Book Organization

The book is organized into five sections. Section I introduces the design and modelling of sensor networks. Chapter 1, by Iyer, Kulkarni, Mhatre, and Rosenberg, presents a taxonomy of wireless sensor networks, based on their application level objectives, traffic characteristics and data delivery requirements. Popa and Lewis in Chapter 2 describe some algorithms for systematic exploration of unknown environments using a mobile wireless sensor network. In Chapter 3, Tan illustrates a distributed graph model for dynamic coverage in a mobile sensor network.

Section II presents some network management techniques. In Chapter 4, Humos, Cardei, Alhalabi, and Hsu address the Medium Access Control protocols in wireless sensor networks. Wang presents in Chapter 5 an overview of various techniques for topology control protocols in wireless sensor networks. Chapter 6 by Liu, Sang and Sinha discusses some recent techniques for detecting boundaries in sensor networks. In Chapter 7, a time-based localization scheme which uses only short-range beacons is presented by Liu, Cheng, Hua, and Chen. Chapter 8 by Schurgers covers three distinct classes of wake-up solutions. Su introduces in Chapter 9 the factors influencing time synchronization and the design challenges encountered in determining guidelines for developing time synchronization protocols. In Chapter 10, Liu and Jia show how to apply the quorum method to some problems including location service, information dissemination and object tracking. In Chapter 11, Kumar, Arora, and Lai present a case study of ExScal — a wireless sensor network deployed to detect and classify intruders of different kinds. Several fine-grained power management techniques are also discussed.

Section III is devoted to data management, which is a very important task as well as a big challenge for sensor networks. Chapter 12, by Li, Cai, and Li, gives a detailed survey of data management in sensor networks. Data aggregation is introduced by Fan, Liu, and Sinha, in Chapter 13. In Chapter 14, Ma and Cheng compare some clustering-based schemes in sensor networks. Cohen, Goldberg, and de Oliveira present in Chapter 15 a new approach to constrained traffic engineering routing. Krishnamachari surveys in Chapter 16 some models for data gathering in sensor networks.

Section IV discusses security issues in sensor networks. In Chapter 17, Du and Xiao summarize the typical attacks on sensor networks and present the current state-of-art of research on sensor network security. Chapter 18 by Corbett, Copeland, and Beyah introduces the use of spectral analysis to differentiate homogeneous sensor nodes from sensors with a different radio interface composition in order to address the problem of unauthorized access.

Acknowledgement

We would like to acknowledge all the contributing authors, who are experts in sensor networks and have done extensive work in this area. We also appreciate the help of the referees who have devoted much time in reviewing the submissions. We are also grateful to the publisher who made this book possible.

Yingshu Li
Department of Computer Science
Georgia State University
Email: yli@cs.gsu.edu

My T. Thai
Department of Computer and Information Science and Engineering
University of Florida
Email: mythai@cise.ufl.edu

Weili Wu
Department of Computer Science
University of Texas at Dallas
Email: weiliwu@utdallas.edu

SECTION I

NETWORK DESIGN AND NETWORK MODELLING

Chapter 1
A Taxonomy-based Approach to Design of Large-scale Sensor Networks

Aravind Iyer[1], Sunil S. Kulkarni[1], Vivek Mhatre[1] and Catherine P. Rosenberg[2*]

[1] School of Electrical and Computer Engineering
  Purdue University, West Lafayette, IN 47907
  {iyerav, sunilkul, mhatre}@ecn.purdue.edu
[2] Department of Electrical and Computer Engineering
  University of Waterloo, Waterloo, ON N2L 3G1, Canada
  cath@ece.uwaterloo.ca

1 Introduction

Networks of wireless sensor devices are being deployed to collectively monitor and disseminate information about a variety of phenomena of interest. A wireless sensor device is a battery-operated device, capable of sensing physical quantities. In addition to sensing, it is capable of wireless communication, data storage, and a limited amount of computation and signal processing. Advances in integrated circuit design are continually shrinking the size, weight and cost of sensor devices, while simultaneously improving their resolution and accuracy. At the same time, modern wireless networking technologies enable the coordination and networking of a large number of such devices. A wireless sensor network (WSN) consists of a large number of wireless-capable sensor devices working collaboratively to achieve a common objective. A WSN has one or more sinks (or base-stations) which collect data from all sensor devices. These sinks are the interface through which the WSN interacts with the outside world.

The basic premise of a WSN is to perform networked sensing using a large number of relatively unsophisticated sensors, instead of the conventional approach of deploying a few expensive and sophisticated sensing modules. The potential advantage of networked sensing over the conventional approach, can be summarized as *greater coverage, accuracy and reliability at a possibly lower cost*. Some of the early works on WSNs [6, 13, 14] motivate and discuss these benefits in detail. The range of potential applications that WSNs are envisaged to support, is tremendous, encompassing military, civilian, environmen-

---

* The names of the authors appear in alphabetical order.

tal and commercial areas [2]. Some examples include networked sensors for military surveillance, smart sensors to monitor and control manufacturing facilities, biosensors for health applications, sensor networks to monitor habitat or weather, and smart sensor environments for home electronics. Designing, manufacturing and networking wireless sensor devices to support such a wide variety of applications is a complex and challenging endeavor. As a result, there has been a lot of research activity in the area of WSNs over the past five years or so.

Research in the area of WSNs has been active at several levels, starting from the *component level*, the *system level*, and all the way up to the *application level*. The component level research focuses on improving the sensing, communication and computation capabilities of an individual sensor device. Research at the system level is concerned with the mechanism of networking and coordinating several sensor devices in an energy-efficient and scalable fashion. Research at the application level is concerned with the processing of the data produced by sensors, depending on the application objectives. Examples of such problems include localization of a target being tracked by using measurements from several sensors, computing the spatial profile of a signal of interest using all the sensor readings, and so on.

In this chapter, we are concerned with research at the system level, in general, and communication and networking protocols, in particular. Our aim is to establish a framework for designing communication protocols for WSN applications, involving the *tetherless* deployment of a *large number* of sensor nodes. By tetherless, we mean not attached to or assisted by any infrastructure. In particular, tetherless sensor nodes have a limited amount of energy which usually cannot be replenished. While there are some WSN applications which require few, possibly tethered, sensor nodes, the design of large-scale, tetherless sensor networks is an important problem from the networking standpoint. In the next couple of subsections, we provide our motivation, scope and a brief outline.

1.1 Motivation and Scope

The principles of traditional network design cannot be directly applied to the design of communication protocols for the WSNs we consider. This is because traditional communication networks aim to support a diverse set of users, each with their *individual objectives*. Hence, there is a need to design the network in a modular, interoperable and generic fashion, leading to a layered protocol architecture. This approach yields a platform that can support *any* new application on top of the existing network. This *multi-service* paradigm has been very much at the core of networking research in the 1980s and 1990s. Such an approach is unsuitable for the WSNs considered in this chapter because of the following characteristic features which differentiate them from traditional communication networks:

1. The *large density* of nodes, which begs for sensors that are cheap to man-
   ufacture and ready to deploy;
2. The *application diversity*, which requires different kinds of application-
   specific sensor devices;
3. The *tight limitations in energy, processing power and memory*, which call
   for highly optimized and lightweight protocols; and,
4. The *collaborative objective* for which all the sensor nodes cooperate with
   one another.

In order to account for all of the above factors, it is necessary to optimize
the communication protocols, to best satisfy the application level objectives.
Any other design considerations, such as protocol layering, are secondary.
Non-traditional design principles like cross-layer integration and application-
specific design, are recommended and even necessary, to make the protocols
lightweight and energy-efficient. In fact, it is neither easy nor cost-effective,
to devise a generic framework to design communication protocols for WSNs.
This is because each WSN application imposes a unique set of goals and
requirements, and also produces a different type of data traffic.

Consider the following two scenarios. First consider an application to monitor the environmental conditions affecting crops and livestock. Now this is a
"data gathering" application. The data traffic it generates is expected to be
more or less uniform, and the latency requirements on its data are expected
to be loose. It is important in this case, to find and maintain energy-efficient
routes to convey all the sensed information to the sink node(s). On the other
hand, a sensor network deployed to detect forest fires is likely to produce data
in rare bursts with severe latency constraints. Here the overhead in maintaining routes or in coordinating the sensor nodes would be too high. Hence, it is
important to route the data promptly, but without undue overheads for route
maintenance.

The two scenarios discussed above are completely different problems from a
networking standpoint. Clearly, there is a need to develop application-specific
protocol solutions. However, the danger in pursuing an application-specific
approach is to end up developing a different protocol for each application. A
careful examination of the tradeoffs involved is necessary to avoid being too
generic or too specific. Towards this end, it is important to be able to *classify*
WSNs based on the following characteristics:

1. The application level objectives,
2. The data delivery requirements, and
3. The traffic characteristics,

Then we can design protocols that are appropriate for each class. We feel
that in order to extract the best possible performance out of a large number
of limited sensor devices, there is a strong need to develop class-specific and
integrated protocol solutions. We do understand that such a classification may
be neither exhaustive nor precise, and may result in partial overlaps between

the application classes. However, such a classification enables us to partition and organize the design space, and allows for a systematic approach to design of flexible architectures and protocols.

1.2 Key Ideas and Outline

Our goal is to try and provide some answers to the generic question, *"How to design a sensor network?"* from a tax-onomy-based perspective. To be precise, we would like to consider simple but representative abstractions of the component level capabilities, and the application level objectives, and provide guidelines to design system level (*i.e.*, communication and networking) protocols. From that standpoint, we address the following key ideas by means of this chapter:

1. We provide a *taxonomy-based perspective* on designing communication and networking protocols for large-scale sensor networks.
2. For this, we first motivate and provide a *taxonomy* of sensor networks based on their application level objectives, data delivery requirements, and traffic characteristics.
3. Then, *for each application class*, we provide a discussion of the different problems associated with designing the communication protocols.
4. We also discuss a few currently *implemented sensor network testbeds*, and highlight the application-specific nature of problems.

There are several significant problems in sensor network design which can be argued to be common to most sensor networks. However in our view, the relative significance of the different problems changes depending on the specific class. Therefore, it becomes important to consider the problems in the context of a given application class. This is in contrast with some other surveys on sensor networks (*e.g.*, [2]) which simply discuss several important problems, but without attributing them to any application class. In another related work [49], the authors provide a taxonomy of sensor network models, but do not discuss any design problems or their relative significance depending on the application class.

The rest of this chapter is organized as follows. In Section 2, we provide a classification of WSN applications, and give some examples for each application class. Section 3 discusses the salient features of, and Section 4 discusses the possible problems for, all sensor networks. In Section 5, we discuss the relative significance of each of those problems, depending on the application class. In Section 6, we discuss some of the currently implemented sensor networks, and again highlight how the applications affect the significant problems. Finally, we conclude the chapter in Section 7, and provide some broad future directions.

2 Classification of Sensor Network Applications

In this section, we provide a classification of WSNs based on their application objectives, traffic characteristics and data delivery requirements. Most of the current WSN applications fall into one of the following broad classes.

2.1 Event Detection and Reporting

Some examples of WSN applications in this class are intruder detection as a part of military surveillance, detecting anomalous behavior or failures in a manufacturing process, and detection of forest fires. The common characteristic of all these applications is the *infrequency* of occurrence of the events of interest. A WSN deployed for such an application is expected to be inactive most of the time, bursting into activity when an event is detected. Then, the WSN has to *promptly* convey an event report to the sink(s). An event report is expected to contain some location information about the event, and a description of the nature of the event. An important problem for such networks, at the application level, is to minimize the probability of *false alarms*. Generally speaking, detection of an event based on consensus between a group of sensors is likely to produce a lower false alarm rate than detection of an event using a single sensor. However, from the point of view of networking, the significant design problem is that of routing the event report on the fly, to the sink, once the process of event detection is over.

2.2 Data Gathering and Periodic Reporting

WSN applications in this class include, monitoring the environmental conditions affecting crops or livestock, monitoring temperature, humidity and lighting in office buildings, and so on. These monitoring modules could even be combined with actuator modules which can control, for instance, the amount of fertilizer in the soil, or the amount of cooling or heating in a building, based on distributed sensor measurements. In these cases, each sensor is expected to constantly produce some amount of data which has to be conveyed to the sink(s). The sink might not be directly interested in the individual measurements, but could require a distributed computation of some function of the sensor readings. The sensor readings also might need to be attached to some sort of location information, if the sink is interested in recreating a spatial profile of the readings.

2.3 Sink-initiated Querying

The monitoring applications mentioned in the previous subsection may also require the additional feature of sink-initiated querying. In this case, rather than each sensor periodically reporting its measurements, the sink could query a set of sensors for their measurements. This enables the sink to extract information at a different resolution or granularity, from different regions in space. For instance, consider an application monitoring a manufacturing process. In case there is any anomalous behavior, the sensors could report such an event to the sink. Then the sink can query some specific set of sensors to obtain more information, possibly to confirm the event. Depending on the sensor readings thus obtained, the sink could trigger the appropriate actuators, or raise an alarm for human intervention. For the underlying communication protocols, we need (for example) effective means to address and route data to and from dynamic sets of sensors.

2.4 Tracking-based Applications

WSNs for tracking have a lot of applications in military or border surveillance where one is interested in tracking an intruder or the movements of a suspicious object. Environmental applications include tracking the movements and patterns of insects, birds or small animals. Intelligent transportation systems are often interested in wide-area tracking of vehicles where the statistics of such information could be used to better design the highway transport infrastructure. WSNs for tracking combine some of the characteristics of the above three classes. For instance, when the target is detected, the sink needs to be notified *promptly*. Then, the sink may initiate *queries* to receive time-stamped location estimates of the target, so that it can calculate the trajectory and keep querying the appropriate sets of sensors. To design communication protocols we have to answer questions like: is it better to query, compute and route on the fly; or is it better to maintain some level of organization or connectivity to streamline the process of tracking; and so on.

3 Salient Features of Sensor Networks

In the previous section we discussed the applications of sensor networks, and a taxonomy of sensor networks based on the characteristic features of these applications. We noted that sensor networks are very diverse due to their broad range of applications. In this section, we study some of the salient features of sensor networks.

3.1 Collaborative Objective

Perhaps the most important aspect of sensor networks that differentiates them from other wireless networks is their *objective*. Typically, the objective of a sensor network is monitoring a certain signal of interest, and informing a central base station or a sink about the activity in the region that is being sensed. Since a sensor network is deployed for achieving a certain system-wide goal, nodes collaborate instead of competing with each other. For example, if the communication range of each node is limited, the nodes may use multi-hop communication to send their data to the sink. This requires a routing strategy that ensures that the battery energy as well as the throughput are optimized in such a way that the duration of the correct functioning of the entire network, *i.e.,* the network lifetime, is maximized. Thus the nodes collaborate to optimize a system-wide objective. This is unlike other wireless networks such as wireless local area networks (wireless LANs) where the nodes (users) are greedy, and their primary objective is maximizing their own gains.

3.2 Network Scale

While some sensor network applications involve a small number of sensors (10-20), most exciting applications require a large number of sensor nodes (100-1000) [2]. The basic premise being that because of redundancy, a network consisting of a large number of sensor nodes is more robust to node failure than a network consisting of a fewer number of nodes. Developments in integrated circuit design technology are expected to make the mass production of sensor devices relatively inexpensive, and hence such large sensor networks are likely to be common. The networks are also expected to have a high *node density* in most cases. Here, node density refers to the number of nodes in the communication range of a single node. High node density makes the system more robust to routing and node failures, since each node has several alternative paths to reach the sink. Thus sensor networks differ from other wireless networks due to the scale at which the nodes are deployed in the network.

3.3 Many-to-one Communication Paradigm

The primary objective of the nodes in a sensor network is to monitor a signal of interest. These observations are then used by a decision-making center (sink or a base station) to decide the future course of action. Thus data flows in two directions in the network; upstream (many-to-one) in which sensor nodes send their measurements to the sink, and downstream (one-to-many) in which the sink sends queries or code-updates to the sensor nodes. However, the majority of the traffic flows from the sensor nodes to the sink. This is unlike the Internet where the traditional client-server communication paradigm results in most of the traffic flowing from a single server to many clients, or in a peer-to-peer network where the traffic flows between any two nodes of the network. Thus, in general, there is no any-to-any communication, *i.e.,* a sensor node does not communicate with an arbitrary sensor node in the network (except during packet forwarding). The many-to-one communication paradigm has an impact on several design choices. For example, the authors in [27] note that in the context of a many-to-one communication paradigm, network connectivity is a function of the routing algorithm being used. This is because, when packets are to be routed towards the sink, the next hop neighbors of a node that are located in the direction away from the sink do not contribute towards the connectivity of the node.

3.4 Nodes with Limited Capabilities

Another important difference between a cellular network or a wireless LAN, and a sensor network is the device hardware. A wireless laptop, PDA or a cell phone are relatively advanced devices as compared to a sensor node. The latter is often restricted by a battery which is limited in energy and usually cannot be replenished (typically a small lithium battery rated at a few hundred mAh), slower computing speeds (about 4MHz), small memory (about 8KB flash memory and 512 bytes of RAM), low data rates (up to 20 Kbps) and limited communication range (10-100 feet) (see [24] and the references therein). These limitations have a direct impact on the functioning of the network as a whole, and the protocols at different layers have to be designed by taking into account these limitations.

3.5 Clustering for Scalability

Since sensor networks consist of a large number of nodes, it is clear that we need distributed protocols for gathering data, and arbitrating the access to the wireless channel, and these protocols should *scale* well as the number of nodes in the network increases. One way to achieve this is to organize the network into smaller sub-networks called clusters. Each cluster can be then managed autonomously. Such a hierarchy results in lower routing overheads, and could also be used for in-network aggregation of the measured data. The clusters themselves could consist of nodes with different hardware capabilities. Within each cluster, the responsibilities of co-ordinating MAC and routing, as well as data aggregation could be assigned to nodes with special hardware [35].

3.6 Node Deployment versus Placement

Depending on the application, sensor nodes could either be deployed randomly over the area of interest (battlefield surveillance, forest fire detection, *etc.*), or the nodes could be placed deterministically at specified locations (temperature and light monitoring in buildings, seismic monitoring of bridges and buildings, *etc.*). When nodes can be placed deterministically, ensuring network connectivity is relatively easy. However, when we do not have control over node locations (random deployment), a certain extent of over-provisioning of nodes is required to ensure network connectivity [21].

3.7 Node Mobility and Dynamic Topology

In many cases, the sensor nodes have very little, or no mobility. However, there are some applications such as monitoring of military personnel and equipment, and wildlife monitoring which involve node mobility. When the nodes are mobile, the topology of the network changes, and it may be necessary to update the routing information of the nodes. In addition to mobility, time varying fading and shadowing due to changes in the surrounding environment may also result in a dynamic network topology, even when the nodes are static. In networks where data updates are to be sent to the sink infrequently, the nodes may turn off their radio circuitry to save battery power, and enter a sleep state. When one or more nodes enter a power saving mode, the topology of the network changes. Network topology also changes due to node failures. Thus sensor networks often have a dynamic topology due to node mobility, time varying channel, node failures, and radio duty-cycling. If the nodes are highly mobile, then the node mobility has a stronger impact on the network topology than the other factors. This has to be taken into account in designing communication protocols.

4 Common Design Problems in Sensor Networks

Although sensor networks have different characteristics in terms of their applications and requirements, there are certain design problems that are common to most of the sensor networks. These problems are as follows:

4.1 Communication versus Computation

Communicating information over the wireless channel is orders of magnitude more energy-intensive than computing [2]. In several sensor network applications, it is possible to perform local signal processing within the network to compress or aggregate the gathered data. Any form of in-network data aggregation can reduce the amount of data that is actually sent to the sink, and this results in considerable energy savings. However, the extent of in-network data aggregation that is possible, depends on the spatio-temporal correlation of the signal of interest, and the nature of application.

In-network data aggregation itself has overheads due to energy spent on computations. For example, in [23], the authors consider a clustered sensor network in which measurements of all the nodes in a cluster can be aggregated into a single measurement at the clusterhead. Thus instead of sending multiple measurements, a single aggregated measurement is sent to the sink. However this aggregation process requires extensive signal processing computations at the clusterhead. The larger the number of nodes in a cluster, the higher the extent of aggregation, and consequently, the higher the energy savings on communication between the sensor nodes and the sink. However, the larger the number of nodes in a cluster, the larger the energy spent on data aggregation computations. Thus there is an inherent tradeoff between communication and computation, and this tradeoff is a characteristic feature of many sensor networks.

4.2 Many-to-one Routing

As discussed in the previous section, sensor networks are characterized by the many-to-one communication paradigm where all the sensor nodes wish to send their data to a single sink node. This provides a sense of directionality to the flow of data in the network, and results in ease of routing. However, as noted in [35, 33], the many-to-one data flow also results in a non-uniform energy drainage pattern in the network causing the nodes in certain regions of the network may exhaust their battery energy earlier than other nodes due to excessive relaying burden. Hence the routing algorithm has to be designed to mitigate this problem.

4.3 Power-saving Algorithms for the Radio

Since a sensor network consists of a large number of nodes, each having a limited communication range, the nodes may have to use multi-hop communication to reach the sink. This requires using the neighboring nodes as relays. However, if the relay nodes do not know the exact time instant at which they are going to receive a packet for forwarding, they have to keep the receiver circuitry of their radios on. This is referred to as idle listening. Keeping the receiver circuitry on has battery energy overheads [44], and hence if the node stays in idle mode for too long, the node battery drains out rapidly. In order to reduce idle mode energy expenditure, the nodes can turn off their receiver circuitry periodically. This is referred to as duty-cycling. Nodes going to sleep causes changes in the network topology, and this may impact the routing algorithm. Also, the fraction of the time for which a node is in the sleep mode will have an impact on end-to-end latency of packet forwarding. Thus designing power-saving algorithms to meet the delay and energy requirements of a given application is an important design problem, and this problem has been addressed in [26, 57].

4.4 Localization and Synchronization

The objective of sensor nodes is to report their measurements to the sink. Hence it is important for the sink to know the locations at which these measurements were taken so that future actions can be taken accordingly. This requires a localization scheme so that the nodes can determine their current location. Since sensor nodes are small, energy constrained, and often deployed indoors, GPS-based solutions are not suitable for them. Hence it is necessary to devise other means for localization. Time synchronization is also required so that the measurements can be time-stamped. Synchronization is also useful in scheduling sleep-wake patterns of the nodes in power-saving algorithms. However, both localization and synchronization have communication overheads associated with them, and these tradeoff issues have been addressed in several works such as [41, 18, 19].

4.5 Connectivity and Coverage in Unfriendly Terrain

In many sensor network applications, the user does not have complete control over the placement of each node. Consequently, once the nodes have been deployed, some of them could end up in locations that are wireless-unfriendly due to shadowing. Even for applications where the user has control over node deployment, the nodes could experience bad fades due to changes in the surrounding environment. Sometimes, nodes could experience temporary or permanent hardware failure due to changing environmental conditions such as heat and humidity, and this may impact the network connectivity. Hence it is necessary to dimension the number of nodes in the network and their communication range, and also design routing protocols so that sensing coverage of the entire region of interest is assured. Works in [22, 42] contain results on network connectivity and sensing coverage in large sensor networks with random node deployment and/or under possible node failures. Effects of shadowing at the wireless physical layer on network connectivity for a network with randomly deployed nodes are studied in [4].

5 Class-specific Problems in Sensor Networks

The approach taken by previous survey papers on sensor networks, such as [2], has been that of discussing the design problems in sensor networks on a per-problem basis. Ours is the first work that systematically classifies these networks based on the application characteristics, and then discusses the problems faced by each class of applications. In what follows, we discuss the past work that focuses on problems pertaining to each application class.

5.1 Event Detection and Reporting

The objective of sensor networks in this application class is to detect rare events, such as forest fires or intrusions, and to promptly communicate a report of such an event to the sink. Due to the infrequency of the events of interest, the driving design principle in this case is to minimize the energy consumption due to all the activities other than event reporting. Issues such as packet collisions or link-layer fairness are not very important, due to the low traffic load. However it is important to curb the energy expenditure due to (i) idle-listening in MAC protocols, and due to (ii) the control message exchanges for the routing and MAC protocols. Also, for such networks, it is reasonable to assume that there would be no data destined for an individual sensor device. As discussed in Subsection 3.3, there might be a need for the sink to communicate with all the sensors for reconfiguration. But due to the infrequency of sensor events, the volume of this traffic is expected to be very low, if at all. Following are some of the important design challenges for this class of applications:

Lightweight Addressing

In general, there is a need for addressing in a sensor network for the following three purposes: (i) MAC, (ii) routing, and (iii) location information to tag the data. The traditional mechanism for addressing is to use a unique per-node identifier which can be mapped and used at all the three levels. However, owing to the large number of nodes in many sensor networks, using strict per-node addressing is wasteful. Not only would the size of an address be large, but also these addresses would need to be allocated and exchanged at different layers of the protocol stack. Besides, as noted in Subsection 3.3, sensor networks follow the many-to-one paradigm of communication. So it is unlikely that any two sensors would want to communicate with each other. Therefore, it is important to find smart and efficient ways to allocate MAC, routing and location identifiers to sensor nodes, without relying on strict per-node addressing, except when there is a need to communicate with an individual sensor node.

As an example, consider Geographic Adaptive Fidelity (GAF) with Manhattan routing [55]. Here, a network of sensor nodes is divided into cells in a grid-like fashion, with each cell being assigned a location identifier. Thus, every node belonging to a particular cell shares the same location identifier. These location identifiers are used in conjunction with a geographic routing protocol (Manhattan routing), where packets are routed from one cell to another regardless of the actual identity of the nodes in both the cells. Thus, all nodes in a particular cell also share the same routing address. Another example can be found in AIMRP [26], where nodes use randomly chosen addresses on a per-packet transmission attempt basis, rather than using their hardware MAC identifiers, to distinguish between one another at the MAC layer. The length of these random addresses can be much smaller than the length of MAC identifiers, and these random addresses can be shared over time by all the nodes.

Routing Overheads

There are generally two types of routing mechanisms that a network can use: proactive and reactive. In proactive routing, the status of routing paths is periodically updated through control message exchanges between neighboring nodes. On the other hand, reactive routing schemes obtain routing information on demand. In other words, there is no periodic control information that is exchanged between the nodes. Reactive routing is more suitable for event detection, since the data transfer from the sensors to the sink takes place relatively infrequently. Also, due to the many-to-one nature of the data flow, it is possible to use smart mechanisms to route the data to the sink. For example, [26] uses an address-light, integrated MAC and routing protocol (AIMRP), in which the nodes do not maintain any dynamic routing information. Each node simply keeps track of its "tier-id" (a measure of its distance from the sink in terms of number of hops). Whenever a node detects an event, its report is forwarded towards the sink by a node with a lower tier-id. Thus, it is possible to exploit the many-to-one nature of the data flow to reduce the addressing and routing overheads.

Idle-listening and Power-saving Algorithms

As noted in Subsection 4.3, a considerable amount of energy is consumed by the radio in idle-listening. This can have a significant impact on the network lifetime. Due to the fact that the sensor events are rare, the sensor nodes spend very little time in actually communicating information. It would be reasonable to turn the radio module of these nodes off, and only keep the sensing module on. However, most sensor networks require the use of multi-hop communication, since the communication range of an individual sensor could be much smaller than the size of the region. Hence, it is important for the sensor nodes to remain awake for some time, in order to be ready to relay the data from the other sensor nodes.

One way to curb the energy-expenditure due to idle-listening, is for the nodes to use a power saving mode [26, 57]. In such schemes, nodes turn off their radios periodically either independently [26] or in a co-ordinated fashion [57]. This enables the node to save battery energy for the duration for which its radio is turned off. In [57], the authors propose a scheme called S-MAC in which nodes are organized into small groups called virtual clusters. All the nodes in a virtual cluster have their sleep-wake schedule synchronized. Thus multi-hop forwarding within the same virtual cluster, can take place without requiring to wait for the next-hop node to wake up. The disadvantage of using such a scheme is that the co-ordination of the sleep-wake cycles requires some communication between the nodes, which in turn amounts to additional protocol and energy overheads.

The power saving mode presented in [26] does not require the nodes to co-ordinate their sleep-wake cycles. Nodes are assumed to execute their sleep-wake cycles independent of each other. The per-hop latency of communication then depends on the frequency of these sleep-wake cycles, and the spatial density of the sensor nodes. The authors provide tight bounds on the average latency of end-to-end packet delivery. Other ways to reduce idle mode energy consumption include, for instance, using an additional low power radio just for channel sensing [20].

5.2 Data Gathering and Periodic Reporting

Data gathering and periodic reporting sensor networks form the class of sensor networks in which the objective of the network is to send periodic updates to the sink. Thus there is regularity in terms of data gathering phases, and there is a steady flow of data from the sensor nodes to the sink. In-network data aggregation is useful in such applications because measurements of neighboring nodes are likely to be correlated, and could be used to reduce the amount of data that needs to be communicated to the sink. This in turn reduces communication energy expenditure of the nodes, and prolongs the *lifetime* of the network. Depending on the nature of application, lifetime could mean the time duration after which: the first node in the network exhausts its battery; a certain fraction of the nodes in the network exhaust their batteries; or network connectivity or coverage falls below a certain percentage; or some other appropriate event.

Since the correlation in measurements is primarily due to the proximity of the neighboring nodes, clustering could be used as a means of aggregation. In clustered sensor networks, nodes are organized into smaller groups called clusters. A clusterhead is associated with each cluster for co-ordinating MAC and routing, as well as for aggregating the data collected by the nodes in that cluster. Nodes may use multi-hopping to send their data to the cluster head. Instead of using clustering, it is possible to have a hierarchy in which the nodes send their measured data directly to the sink using multi-hopping, and the intermediate nodes aggregate the data on a per-hop basis. Clustering offers a natural way of gathering information over smaller regions, and aggregating the information by exploiting the spatial correlation. On the other hand a flat hierarchy allows for hop-by-hop aggregation of data as it travels toward the sink. A network may use either of the two approaches. Following are some of the design problems and their corresponding solutions as have been proposed in the recent literature. Except for the problem of energy-efficient routing discussed in Subsection 5.2, the rest of the problems pertain mainly to networks that use clustering. Energy-efficient routing is an important problem whenever multi-hop communication is used in the network. Hence we first focus on energy-efficient routing.

Energy-efficient Routing

In periodic data gathering sensor networks, data flows regularly from sensor nodes to the sink during the lifetime of the network. For typical wireless transceivers, the majority of the battery energy expenditure is on communication. Hence it is important to choose routing paths in such a way that the lifetime of the network is maximized. This problem was first studied in

[7]. The authors study the problem of determining the optimal routing strategy in a multi-hop sensor network where the objective is to maximize the time until the first battery expires. The authors associate a fixed amount of energy expenditure for each packet reception as well as transmission. They then note that choosing a route with minimum total energy expenditure as in [3, 12, 15, 17, 39, 40, 43, 45] does not necessarily maximize the network lifetime. This is because such a strategy repeatedly uses routing paths with low total energy expenditure, and consequently the nodes along those paths run out of battery. Hence in [7], the authors propose using a routing scheme that performs some form of load balancing. In other words, the originating data from the source node is spread over several different routing paths so that no single path is over-burdened. The authors also propose a distributed algorithm that each sensor node must execute to determine the exact fraction of incoming data that it must forward over all its links. They use tools from network flow analysis [1] to solve this problem. The above work mainly focuses on energy-efficiency in routing without taking into account any bandwidth constraints. In [59], the authors study the lifetime-maximization problem under an additional constraint of limited bandwidth over each link.

None of the above works takes into account the possibility that the forwarding nodes could aggregate the data that they forward towards the sink. In [5], the authors use a network flow framework identical to the one used in [8, 59], and formulate a network flow optimization problem by taking into account the possibility of data aggregation along intermediate hops. Using this framework, the authors determine upper bounds on the lifetime of a sensor network. No distributed scheme is proposed in [5] to implement this optimal routing and data aggregation policy, but the results could be used as a guideline to determine the upper bound on the network lifetime.

Load Balancing

We saw in the previous sub-section that routing can be designed to exploit load-balancing to ensure a more uniform energy drainage pattern across the entire network. This in turn improves the network lifetime.

The principle of load-balancing can also be used for sharing the energy burden in clustered sensor networks. In [23], the authors propose a protocol, LEACH, that can be used in data gathering scenarios in homogeneous clustered sensor networks. A homogeneous sensor network is a network in which all the nodes have identical hardware capabilities. The clusterheads are responsible for collecting data from the other nodes in the cluster, performing data aggregation computations, and sending the aggregated data to the remotely located sink. Thus the energy expenditure of the clusterheads is much higher than the rest of the nodes. Hence to ensure load balancing, and a uniform energy drainage pattern across over the entire network, the authors propose rotating the role of a clusterhead periodically and randomly. The authors determine the optimum number of clusters required in the network, and also propose distributed protocols for clusterhead election. Other data gathering schemes such as PEGASIS [29] and M-LEACH (Multi-hop LEACH) [34] also use the principle of randomized role rotation for load balancing.

Node Heterogeneity

While role rotation is useful for load balancing, it also requires that each node in the network be capable of performing the functions of a clusterhead. This requires sophisticated clusterhead hardware in *all* the nodes. If the network consists of a large number of nodes, this could result in a high overall *cost* of the network. Motivated by this, the authors in [35] consider a heterogeneous sensor network consisting of two types of nodes; sensor nodes that have simple hardware and low battery energy, and clusterhead nodes that have sophisticated hardware and higher battery energy required for performing complex computations and long range communication. Thus the expensive functionality is embedded in only a few nodes, and the overall network cost is lowered. However, role rotation is no longer possible in such heterogeneous networks. In [33, 34], the authors present a cost-based comparison of homogeneous and heterogeneous networks, and provide guidelines to choose the most cost-optimal architecture for a given scenario.

Mode of Communication

In a clustered sensor network, in order to communicate with their respective clusterheads, the sensor nodes can either use single hop or multi-hop mode of communication. The problem of determining the optimum mode of communication has been studied in [33]. The authors also propose a hybrid mode of communication that the sensor nodes can use if they have power control capabilities. This hybrid mode of communication is a combination of single-hop and multi-hop modes, and results in a more uniform energy drainage pattern across the network. In [33, 34], the authors also determine the optimum communication range when multi-hopping is used within the clusters.

5.3 Sink-initiated Querying

In several application classes, the sink is not interested in data updates from all the nodes in the network. The sink may want updates from different regions at different times. Thus, requiring all the nodes to send their data to the sink at all times amounts to wastage of energy on communication as well as computation. In such cases, the sink selectively queries a set of sensor nodes located in the region of interest. This results in a more energy-efficient use of resources. Following are some of the important design issues in such sink-initiated querying sensor networks.

Addressing Requirements

Since the sink is interested in disseminating queries to a subset of sensor nodes, a node-addressing strategy should be in place. It may not be necessary for the sink to be aware of addresses of all the nodes in the network. In most cases, it is sufficient if the node-addressing is tied to the node locations, because typically the sink is interested in querying a subset of nodes located in a *specific region*.

Selective Querying

In order that the sink be able to query a subset of sensor nodes selectively, it is also necessary to have a routing infrastructure that allows for limited broadcasting in the selected region [56, 11]. For this, a routing broadcast must use information about node locations. Hence it is necessary to have a reliable transport protocol such as PSFQ [54] for dissemination of control messages from the sink to the sensor nodes. There is also a need for performing data aggregation within the selected region to avoid sending the raw data to the sink. This could be achieved via clustering and/or hop-by-hop aggregation.

Querying Language

Since querying of sensor nodes for data is identical to the paradigm of querying in databases, selective querying sche-mes use an SQL-based querying language for query-based communication between the sink and the sensor nodes. Such a querying language enables the sink to advertise its interest using the meta attributes of data such as FROM, WHERE, SAMPLE PERIOD, HAVING AVG(), HAVING MAX(), *etc.* [30].

Reprogrammability of Sensor Nodes

In query-based sensor networks, the sensor nodes can be activated or deactivated selectively by the messages from the sink. Besides this, the functioning of the sensor nodes such as frequency of data updates, type of data updates, criteria for sending data updates are to be controlled by the sink. Hence it is required that most of the hardware settings of the sensor nodes be controllable through the software.

5.4 Tracking-based Applications

Tracking-based WSN applications are interested in detecting, localizing and tracking targets, and conveying the relevant information to the sink, in a timely fashion. They combine some of the characteristics of the three application classes discussed earlier, and consequently some of the problems for tracking-based applications are similar to the ones discussed earlier. For example, when the target is detected the sensors need to promptly route its location estimates to the sink, while minimizing the routing overheads. Also, the sink may be interested in querying the sensors for their location estimates of the target, so that it can compute the trajectory of the target. Following are some of the important problems faced by tracking-based applications:

Target Detection and Classification

This is actually an application-level problem. However, it is important to understand the mechanism of target detection and classification, in order to better design communication protocols for such applications. For example, Li, *et. al.*, [28, 37] argue that in order to facilitate the distributed detection of a target, the routing of the data should be based on the geographical location of the sensor nodes, rather than their hardware identities. The detection of the target could be done either based on some *a priori* knowledge about the sensor signals that the target produces, or it could be done simply based on thresholding the energy of the sensor signals. The former approach is more useful in detecting multiple targets and in classifying and maintaining target identities. Some of these approaches are suggested and studied in [9, 31, 32].

Chen, *et. al.*, [9] provide an overview of the issues involved in using beamforming techniques to detect a target. They also make a case for using collaborative signal processing among sensors, in order to accurately localize the target. In [31, 32], the problem of target detection and classification is considered at two levels. Firstly, each sensor can use signal processing techniques based on the signals obtained from all of its physical sensing elements, and secondly, sensors can also collaborate with neighboring sensors. While target detection could be performed using a single sensing element, for target classification, collaboration both within and amongst sensors is very useful. Once multiple targets are detected and classified, each target identity needs to be tracked. Sensors get activated and could form dynamic clusters on detecting a target identity. These clusters could then be used to perform target localization. In the following subsections, we look at these problems.

Location determination

Location determination is an important problem for almost all WSN applications. However, it becomes particularly important in case of tracking-based applications, since the whole objective of the sensor network is to *track* a particular target. In this case, the problem of location determination is at two levels. Firstly, the sensor nodes themselves need to determine their location at an appropriate level of granularity. Secondly, the sensors have to localize the target, at various time instants. The two desirable features of any such location determination scheme are (i) robustness [38] and (ii) energy-efficiency [58, 36]. By robustness, we mean that the scheme should be able to produce an accurate location estimate of the target in spite of variations in the radio channel, or changes in topology due to node failures or duty-cycling. By energy-efficiency, we mean that the localization should be done at the desired level of resolution, at the minimum possible cost in terms of energy consumption. There is an inherent conflict and tradeoff between the energy expenditure and accuracy of the target localization. This is explored in [36].

Dynamic clustering

The problem of formation and maintenance of dynamic clusters (sets of sensors), which can collaborate on target localization and report time-stamped location estimates of the target to the sink, is considered in [16, 10]. [16] considers a simple application where one is interested in counting the number of targets in the region monitored by the sensor network. The authors consider a simple model in which the target can be detected as a signal by each sensor, the amplitude of which decays with the distance to the target. The spacing of the sensors, and the attenuation profile of the target signal determines the accuracy of target localization, and the ability to distinguish between targets that are close to one another. Sensors participate in forming clusters based on the signal levels they sense. [10] considers an acoustic target tracking application, for which a heterogeneous network with two kinds of nodes (sensors and clusterheads), is deployed. The issues addressed are how the clusterheads collaborate so that the one closest to the target is active, and how sensors collaborate so that a small but sufficient number of sensors respond with their measurements to the activated clusterhead.

6 Sensor Network Implementations

In the previous section, we have looked at some of the important design problems in WSNs, from a taxonomy-based perspective. However, it may not be possible to identify all the significant problems of an application through such an approach. As we shall see in the next few subsections, there are certain implementation specific design problems which are also significant. Such problems become apparent when we examine case studies of practical sensor network deployments and experiments. In what follows, we describe three sensor network projects, and illustrate the above issues.

6.1 The Great Duck Island Experiment

Objective

Intel Research Laboratory at Berkeley, in cooperation with the College of the Atlantic at Bar Harbor, and the University of California at Berkeley, deployed on the Great Duck Island, Maine a sensor network consisting of over

150 sensor nodes [48, 50, 47]. The sensor network was designed to collect the data at nesting burrows used by Leach's Storm Petrel, a particular species of duck. The main objective of developing this sensor network was to study in a non-intrusive way, (i) the occupancy of the burrows by these ducks, and (ii) the role of the micro-climatic factors in their habitat selection. Two sets of experiments were carried out, one in summer 2002 and another in summer 2003. We focus our attention on the details of the experiments from summer 2003. However we also note some important observations made from the experiments in summer 2002.

Node Architecture

The experiment used several Mica2Dot sensor nodes, running the TinyOS operating system [52]. The Mico2Dot is a repackaged Mica2 sensor node developed by Crossbow Inc. [53]. The Mica2Dot uses an ATmega128 microcontroller at 4MHz with 512 KB of memory, and a 433 MHz radio with a data rate of 40Kbps. All the sensing elements, namely, the photoresistive light sensor, the digital temperature sensor, the capacitive humidity sensor, the digital barometric pressure sensor, and the infrared detector, were integrated into a single sensor board. The digital sensors were interfaced directly using a serial interface, while the analog sensors used an Analog-to-Digital Converter for interfacing. Two types of sensor nodes were designed: burrow nodes for detecting occupancy and weather nodes for monitoring the surface microclimates. The body of the sensor nodes was sealed, but the sensing elements were exposed to the environment. The nodes were deployed manually, burrow nodes being inserted unobtrusively into the burrows of the storm petrels, and weather nodes being deployed on the ground surface. The nodes were powered with lithium batteries, and were expected to have a lifetime of around 100 days. The nodes were not expected to have significant mobility.

Network Architecture

A multi-level, hierarchical, data-gathering sensor network architecture was used in this experiment. At the lowest level in the hierarchy, a group of closely spaced sensor nodes would communicate with a gateway node using either a direct transmission or multi-hop relaying. The gateway nodes, which form the next level of the hierarchy, were programmed to communicate with a remote sink located about 350 feet away, through a local transmit network. The sink provided a database service and a satellite Internet connection, so that the sensor data could be analyzed remotely. The gateway node is nothing but a relay node with a high gain directional Yagi antenna.

The entire sensor network was divided into two parts, a single-hop based network, and a multi-hop based network, in order to experimentally compare and contrast the two modes of communication. The first part, which was a single-hop network, consisted of nodes which sampled the sensory data every five minutes, and communicated the data with the gateway using direct (single-hop) communication. There were no routing issues in this network because of the direct single-hop communication. The second part, which was a multi-hop network, consisted of nodes which sampled the data every twenty minutes. These nodes employed adaptive multi-hop routing to route the data packets to the gateway. A sleep and wake duty cycle of 2.2% was fixed to maximize the node lifetime. The gateway sent routing beacons periodically to initiate the network discovery process.

Observations

Following are some of the important observations made from both the experiments.

1. **Overhearing and Node Lifetime:** Severe weather conditions (Hurricane Isabel) forced the base station to shut down for a month affecting the lifetime and correct operation of the overall network. Also the observed sensor node lifetime was considerably smaller than expected. It was concluded that the shortened lifetime of the multi-hop nodes was a result of the high overhearing. Long preambles (designed to work with the sleep and wake cycles of sensor nodes) coupled with the availability of many neighboring nodes for multi-hop routing resulted in a high degree of overhearing. The power consumption observations indicated that the overhearing consumed nearly eight times more power than the power consumed in the packet transmission. This demonstrated that designing an energy efficient MAC protocol in a multi-hop setting is still an important issue, even with low volumes of traffic.

2. **Reliable Packet Delivery:** As the sensory data was oversampled by a factor of three, no link layer retransmissions were employed to guarantee successful data delivery. Hence in the case of a single-hop network, the packet delivery rate met expectations. However in the case of a multi-hop network, the packet delivery rate was smaller than expected. The collisions and the congestion was not a major factor, as the nodes used a CSMA MAC protocol and the total network utilization was small. It was concluded that the single-hop packet loss rate along with the correlated node failures lead to substantial packet losses that increased exponentially with the number of hops. This suggested that even a communication protocol that employs only link layer retransmissions, but ignores wider network outages, may not be sufficient for reliable packet delivery. Hence end-to-end transfer approaches are necessary for reliable packet delivery.

3. **Node Failures:** During the first set of experiments in summer 2002, significant packet collisions were observed for some nodes even though the expected network utilization was very low. Some of the collisions could have been triggered due to clock skew, however it was concluded that the

sustained collisions were caused by the faulty node behavior due to severe environmental conditions. It was observed that because of the node failures, the network size reduced over time. Even though this improved the packet losses by reducing the packet collisions, smaller network size compromised the objective of deploying a sensor network. Hence a proper sensor node packaging to protect from harsh weather conditions is necessary.

4. **Node Reclamation:** Due to the environmental impact and sensor node costs, it was necessary to recollect the sensor nodes deployed in the field. However only half of the deployed sensor nodes could be recollected. The rest of the nodes were unrecoverable and might have been moved by animals. As the sensor networks become larger and more prevalent, node reclamation would become an important issue in the design of the wireless sensor networks, due to pollution and cost concerns.

Thus these experiments provided valuable insights into the functioning of an unmanaged sensor network. Specifically, it showed that the problems of MAC and end-to-end reliability are important issues for a data gathering sensor network even with low traffic density. The importance of these issues could not have been foreseen without these experiments. Details of these experiments can be found in [47, 48].

6.2 The Shared Wireless Infostation Model (SWIM)

Objective

The SWIM architecture [46] was developed to study the impact of natural and man-made environmental conditions on the behavior and mobility patterns of whales and large marine mammals. As many of these species are endangered, they are of particular interest to researchers, environmentalist groups, lawmakers, and to the general public. Successful sensor network implementation to study these large mammals would be of immense help in gathering the necessary data to study the environmental impacts of human activities.

Node Architecture

A SWIM node consists of a Texas Instruments microprocessor, MSP430, with 60 KB of flash memory, and a 32 KHz quartz crystal reference for maintaining the clock. The radio transmitter of the node uses a Silicon Labs Si4112 Phase Lock Loop that is controlled by the MSP430 processor, and can generate a carrier frequency of 62 MHz to 1GHz. The node can implement pulse interval coding or frequency shift keying, for data communication. Various sensors such as pressure, light, and temperature sensors, accelerometers, and electrodes can be controlled through the microprocessor. The microprocessor has a small dormant power consumption, and to minimize the energy consumption, the node can employ duty-cycling.

Node Mobility and Network Architecture

The total area spanned by the whales, or equivalently the range and the area that needs to be monitored, is very large, possibly covering thousands of square kilometers of deep sea. However, the high mobility of the whales provides an elegant solution to this problem. In SWIM, a sensor node is directly attached to the body of a whale. Thus, instead of deploying sensors over a large area, the nodes are directly attached to the objects of interest, *i.e.*, the whales. The nodes then use their sensors to measure the quantities of interest, and report these measurements to one or more sinks that are located in the sea.

Design Problems

The above network architecture presents several unique design problems due to high node mobility, some of which are as follows.

1. **Sink Deployment:** Since the whales have very high mobility, it is not possible to ensure that the whales are always in the communication range of a sink. However, it is important to note that there is no stringent delay requirement in this application. Hence the sensor nodes may store the measured data for a long duration before they are able to communicate with a sink. Thus, if the sinks are placed at a few locations that the whales are expected to visit often, then only a small number of sinks are required. Hence, in SWIM, sinks are placed on floating devices (buoys) at common food habitat of the whales, and along the paths frequently traveled by the whales. Since the sensor nodes have to store the data until they come within the communication range of a sink, the number of sinks required depends on factors such as the data storage capacity of a node, and the frequency with which the whales come within the communication range of a sink. The sinks can also be mobile for systematic and periodic survey (*e.g.*, on a dedicated ship), or can be placed on seabirds.

2. **Data Gathering Protocol:** The sensors gather various data related to the whales, and store the information as a time-tagged packets in their memory. Whenever a whale comes in proximity of a sink, *i.e.*, the sink is within the communication range of the sensor, the gathered data is transmitted to the sink using single-hop transmissions. To reduce the potentially large delay due to high whale mobility and limited number of sinks, the sensor nodes share their measured data with each other. In other words, when two sensor nodes come within communication range of each other, some or all of the packets of each of the sensor nodes are replicated on the other sensor node via single-hop communication. When a node is able to communicate with a sink, it offloads *all* the data it has gathered, *i.e.*, its own measurements, and the measurements replicated from other nodes. Thus, with a higher number of nodes, the data measured by a node will be replicated on more nodes, and consequently, the delay in reporting this measurement to the sink is reduced.

3. **Packet Replication and Buffer Dimensioning:** While packet replication reduces delays, it results in increased storage requirements at each node. A naive way to replicate packets would be for two nodes to exchange *all* their measurements with each other. However this would require considerable storage at each node, since a node may potentially visit every other node before reaching the sink. Other packet replication strategies that are proposed in [46] are: (i) replicating packets with a certain probability, (ii) maintaining a record of packets that have already been offloaded to the sink, so that these packets need not be reacquired from other nodes, (iii) maintaining a record of offloaded packets, and also informing other nodes about these packets, so that they can safely erase these packets from their memory, etc. See [46] for details on the packet replication and erasure strategies.

4. **Packet Replication and Energy Expenditure:** Besides affecting the packet delivery delays, the packet replication strategy also impacts the energy expenditure of the sensor nodes. For example, consider a packet replication strategy that is aggressive in terms of erasing redundant information, *i.e.,* information that is already conveyed to the sink. Such a scheme results in lower storage requirements at each node. However, it also requires additional communication between the sensor nodes so that all the nodes are aware of all the packets that have already been delivered to the sink. This additional communication results in higher battery energy expenditure for all the nodes.

Thus, we note that the solution of tagging the whales with sensor nodes to monitor them presents several interesting and challenging design problems. For details, see [46].

6.3 The ZebraNet Wildlife Tracker

Objective

The ZebraNet architecture [25] was developed with the objective of gathering data on a range of species of terrestrial animals, in order to understand their interactions and influence on one another. The goal was also to understand the migration patterns of such wild animals, and how they may be affected by changes in the weather patterns and other influences like human development into wilderness. The architecture is currently being deployed to study the behavior of zebras, at the Sweetwaters Reserve in central Kenya.

Node Architecture

The ZebraNet system uses sensor nodes which are referred to as collars in the ZebraNet literature since these nodes are placed around the animal's neck. Due to the availability of solar energy, the nodes in the ZebraNet system can be equipped with a solar array to power their batteries. A ZebraNet collar consists of a miniature GPS receiver (GPS-MS1E from μBlox), an integrated microprocessor (Hitachi-SH1, 20MHz), I/O support, and 1MB of flash RAM. It is also equipped with two radios: (i) a short-range, Linx Technologies SC-PA radio which offers a range of 100 meters, with low power consumption, and (ii) a long-range Tekk data radio which offers up to 8 km in communication range, though with a low data rate. A simple TDMA-like MAC protocol controlled by the microprocessor, is used with the short-range radio. Lithium Ion Polymer cells are used as batteries, and a solar array is used for powering the Lithium Ion cells.

Application-specific Requirements

Some of the main design requirements of the ZebraNet project, as per the wildlife biologists are as follows:

1. GPS position samples should be taken every three minutes, and detailed activity logs for three minutes should be taken every hour. The latency of this data is not important, however the packet delivery rate to the sink should be almost 100%.
2. There should be no direct human intervention for at least one year.
3. The architecture should not have any fixed sinks, and must cover a wide range of open land.
4. The weight of the ZebraNet collar should not be more than 5 lbs. For animals smaller than the zebra, the weight restrictions may be lower.

Design Problems

Based on the requirements stated above, the ZebraNet project can be considered to be a data gathering or a wide-area tracking application. The collection and delivery of the data is of primary importance, while packet delay is not such an important concern. Also, the vast habitat of the zebras has to be monitored in a non-intrusive fashion. These application-specific constraints motivate the following design issues:

1. **Data Gathering Protocol:** The objectives of the ZebraNet project are similar to those of the SWIM project. Hence, the ZebraNet collars use a data gathering protocol similar to that used in SWIM. The nodes forward and replicate the collected information among several nodes, until one of them is able to deliver the information to the sink node. Two kinds of approaches are possible, either (i) a flooding-based approach, or (ii) a history-based approach. In the flooding-based approach, every data packet at any node is forwarded to, and replicated at, all the nodes that come into its communication range. In the history-based approach, each node is assigned a hierarchy level based on its past success in forwarding the data to the sink. This hierarchy level is nothing but the routing state

of the node. Whenever a node comes close to a sink, its hierarchy level is increased, and its hierarchy level is decreased over time whenever it remains out of the range of the sink. Nodes forward packets to a neighbor with the highest hierarchy level in their communication range. This is similar to the tier-based routing scheme in [26].

2. **Dual Radio Design:** In order to monitor the vast habitat of the zebras, the field researchers use a mobile sink (or base station) which can be driven around the area non-intrusively. In order to avoid direct human contact, the ZebraNet collars use long-range radios to communicate with the mobile sink, so that the data can be collected from afar. However a long-range radio requires considerably more power than a short-range radio. So the short-range radio is exclusively used by the collars for communicating with one another. This dual radio design enables the non-intrusive collection of data using a few long-range communications, and also reduces energy consumption of the nodes by using short-range, low power communications most of the time.

Thus, we see how application-specific requirements lead to some unique and challenging design problems. The ZebraNet sensor network is currently under deployment at the Mpala Research Center, in the Sweetwaters Reserve in central Kenya. The Mpala Research Center is a biology field station administered by Princeton University along with the Kenya Wildlife Service, the National Museums of Kenya, the Mpala Wildlife Foundation, and the Smithsonian Institution. Further details of this project can be found in [51].

7 Conclusions and Future Directions

In this section, we provide a summary of the ideas discussed in the chapter, and discuss a few broad directions for future work.

Wireless sensor networks are anticipated to play a key role in observing, collecting and disseminating relevant information about a variety of interesting phenomena. The performance of these networks depends heavily on the design of the underlying communication protocols. In order to collaboratively network and coordinate a large number of sensor devices with limited capabilities, it is necessary to apply non-traditional design principles such as cross-layer integration and application-specific design, in order to develop lightweight and integrated protocol solutions. Towards this end, we motivate and provide a taxonomy of WSN applications, based on their objectives, data delivery requirements and traffic characteristics. Such a classification enables us to partition and organize the design space, and to achieve the right mix of generality and specificity in our designs. However, there are some significant problems which surface only during experimental studies. Therefore it is necessary to use the taxonomy-based approach, in conjunction with the lessons learnt from sensor network experiments. We have provided a brief survey of some of the significant problems in WSNs, in both the above contexts. Such an approach also enables us to identify future directions for research, some of which we list below.

1. **Event Detection and Reporting:** As mentioned in Subsection 5.1.1, addressing is a major cause of overheads in an event-detecting sensor network. So it is important to devise smart and scalable addressing schemes, for the MAC and routing protocols in a WSN. Now, for localizing an event or a target, the authors in [28, 37] argue that nodes need to exchange information about their geographical location with their neighbors. Devising and using addressing schemes based on geographical location, at an appropriate level of granularity, so that they can be used for MAC, routing and localization of the event, is an important problem.

2. **Data Gathering and Periodic Reporting:** Although the problem of energy-efficient routing has been studied extensively, there are other important issues such as overhearing at MAC layer which results in significant energy expenditure, and the lack of end-to-end reliability which results in high packet loss. This was particularly observed in the implementation of the Great Duck Island Experiment [47] (see Subsection 6.1). Thus, besides routing, issues such as overhearing, link scheduling, and end-to-end reliability are important problems that need to be addressed.

3. **Sink-initiated Querying:** For the sink to be able to selectively query sensor nodes in a certain region, there is a need for designing energy-efficient broadcasting schemes. A naive approach is to flood the entire network with the query from the sink. Except for the nodes of interest, the remaining nodes ignore the query. However, such network-wide flooding has considerable energy overheads. Besides, if the nodes use duty-cycling, then the broadcast mechanism has to ensure that even the nodes that are temporarily asleep receive the sink query in a timely fashion. A more energy-efficient way to disseminate queries is to organize the network into smaller clusters, and then selectively flood the query in the clusters located in the region of interest. This gives better granularity, and results in a more energy-efficient flooding. However, clustering has energy overheads of its own, and thus there is a tradeoff involved. Studying this tradeoff is an interesting future problem.

4. **Tracking-based Applications:** In this case, [16, 10] study the problem of dynamic clustering where sensor nodes form clusters dynamically, to collaborate on localizing the target being tracked. Such sensor networks are anticipated to use some form of duty-cycling or other power-saving schemes. The accuracy and coverage of detection and tracking improves with more sensor nodes being awake. However, the energy consumption will be higher if more sensor nodes are awake more often. Thus, there is a tradeoff between the accuracy and coverage, and the energy-efficiency. This represents another direction for future work.

By means of this chapter, we have motivated and provided a taxonomy-based framework to design communication protocols for WSNs. We have provided a brief survey of the literature, and a sampling of some problems for future research. The discussion of the various issues considered in this chapter is by no means exhaustive or complete. There are several other factors and design considerations to be tackled, before we can design and deploy large-scale, reliable and efficient sensor networks.

References

1. R. K. Ahuja, T. L. Magnanti, and J. B. Orlin. *Network Flows*. Prentice Hall, 1993.
2. I. F. Akyildiz, W. Su, Y. Sankarasubramaniam, and E. Cayirci. Wireless sensor networks: A survey. *Computer Networks (Elsevier) Journal*, pages 393–422, March 2002.
3. D. J. Baker and A. Ephremides. The architectural organization of a mobile radio network via a distributed algorithm. *IEEE Transactions on Communications*, COM-29(11):56–73, Jan 1981.
4. C. Bettstetter and C. Hartmann. Connectivity of wireless multihop networks in a shadow fading environment. In *MSWiM'03, San Diego, CA*, Sep 2003.
5. M. Bhardwaj, T. Garnett, and A. P. Chandrakasan. Upper bounds on lifetime of sensor networks. In *IEEE International Conference on Communications (ICC'01)*, June 2001.
6. A. Chandrakasan, R. Amirtharajah, S. Cho, J. Goodman, G. Konduri, J. Kulik, W. Rabiner, and A. Wang. Design considerations for distributed micro-sensor systems. In *Proceedings of the IEEE 1999 Custom Integrated Circuits Conference*, pages 279–286, May 1999.
7. J. Chang and L. Tassiulas. Routing for maximum lifetime in wireless ad-hoc networks. In *37th Annual Allerton Conference on Communication, Control and Computation*, Sep 1999.
8. J. Chang and L. Tassiulas. Energy conserving routing in wireless ad-hoc networks. In *IEEE INFOCOM, Tel Aviv, Israel*, Mar 2000.
9. J. C. Chen, K. Yao, and R. E. Hudson. Source localization and beamforming. *IEEE Signal Processing Magazine*, March 2002.
10. W.P. Chen, J.C. Hou, and L. Sha. Dynamic clustering for acoustic target tracking in wireless sensor networks. In *Proceedings of the 11th IEEE International Conference on Network Protocols (ICNP'03)*, November 2003.
11. M. Demirbas and H. Ferhatosmanoglu. Peer-to-peer spatial queries in sensor networks. In *Third International Conference on Peer-to-Peer Computing (P2P 2003)*, Sep 2003.
12. A. Ephremides, E. J. Wieselthier, and D. J. Baker. A design concept for reliable mobile radio networks with frequency hopping signaling. *Proceedings of IEEE*, 75(1):56–73, Jan 1987.
13. D. Estrin, L. Girod, G. Pottie, and M. Srivastava. Instrumenting the world with wireless sensor networks. In *Proceedings of the International Conference on Acoustics, Speech and Signal Processing (ICASSP 2001)*, May 2001.

14. D. Estrin, R. Govindan, J. Heidemann, and S. Kumar. Next century challenges: Scalable coordination in sensor networks. In *Proceedings of the ACM MobiCom '99*, pages 263–270, 1999.

15. M. Ettus. System capacity, latency and power consumption in multihop-routed ss-cdma wireless networks. In *IEEE Radio and Wireless Conference (RAWCON) 98, Colorado Springs, CO*, pages 55–58, Aug 1998.

16. Q. Fang, F. Zhao, and L. Guibas. Counting targets: Building and managing aggregates in wireless sensor networks. *Xerox Palo Alto Research Center (PARC) Technical Report*, P2002-10298, June 2002.

17. R. G. Gallager, P. A. Humblet, and P. M. Spira. A distributed algorithm for minimum weight spanning trees. Technical Report Technical Report LIDS-P-906-A, Laboratory of Information Decision Systems, Massachusetts Institute of Technology, Oct 1979.

18. S. Ganeriwal, R. Kumar, and M. B. Srivastava. Timing-sync protocol for sensor networks. In *SenSys'03, Los Angeles, California, USA*, Nov 2003.

19. J. V. Greunen and J. Rabaey. Lightweight time synchronization for sensor networks. In *WSNA'03, San Diego, California, USA*, Sep 2003.

20. C. Guo, L.C. Zhong, and J.M. Rabaey. Low power distributed mac for ad hoc sensor radio networks. In *IEEE GLOBECOM*, volume 5, pages 25–29, 2001.

21. P. Gupta and P. R. Kumar. Critical power for asymptotic connectivity in wireless networks. *Stochastic Analysis, Control, Optimization and Applications: A Volume in Honor of W. H. Fleming (W. M. McEneany, G. Yin and Q. Zhang, eds.)*, 1998.

22. P. Gupta and P. R. Kumar. The capacity of wireless networks. *IEEE Transactions on Information Theory*, IT-46(2):388–404, March 2000.

23. W. Heinzelman, A. Chandrakasan, and H. Balakrishnan. An application-specific protocol architecture for wireless microsensor networks. *IEEE Transactions on Wireless Communications*, 1(4), October 2002.

24. J. Hill, R. Szewcyk, A. Woo, D. Culler, S. Hollar, and K. Pister. System architecture directions for networked sensors. In *ASPLOS*, 2000.

25. P. Juang, H. Oki, Y. Wang, M. Martonosi, L. Peh, and D. Rubenstein. Energy-efficient computing for wildlife tracking: Design tradeoffs and early experiences with zebranet. In *Proceedings of ASPLOS-X*, October 2002.

26. S. Kulkarni, A. Iyer, and C. P. Rosenberg. An address-light, integrated mac and routing protocol for wireless sensor networks. *IEEE/ACM Transactions on Networking*, 14(4):793–806, August 2006.

27. S. S. Kulkarni, A. Iyer, C. Rosenberg, and D. Kofman. Routing dependent node density requirements for connectivity in multi-hop wireless networks. In *IEEE Globecom 2004, Dallas, TX*, Dec 2004.

28. D. Li, K. D. Wong, Y. H. Hu, and A. M. Sayeed. Detection, classification, and tracking of targets. *IEEE Signal Processing Magazine*, 19(2):17–29, March 2002.

29. S. Lindsey and C. Raghavendra. Pegasis: Power efficient gathering in sensor information systems. In *Proceedings of IEEE International Conference on Communications (ICC'01)*, June 2001.

30. S. Madden, M. Franklin, J. Hellerstein, and W. Hong. Tinydb: An acquisitional query processing system for sensor networks. *ACM Transactions on Database Systems*, 30(1):122–173, March 2005.

31. D. McErlean and S. Narayanan. Distributed detection and tracking in sensor networks. In *Proceedings of the Asilomar Conference on Signals, Systems and Computers*, volume 2, Nov 2002.

32. C. Meesookho, S. Narayanan, and C. S. Raghavendra. Collaborative classification applications in sensor networks. In *Proceedings of the Sensor Array and Multichannel Signal Processing Workshop, 2002*, Aug 2002.

33. V. Mhatre and C. Rosenberg. Design guidelines for wireless sensor networks: Communication, clustering and aggregation. *Ad Hoc Networks Journal, Elsevier Science*, 2(1):45–63, 2003.

34. V. Mhatre and C. Rosenberg. Homogeneous vs heterogeneous sensor networks: A comparative study. In *Proceedings of International Conference on Communications (ICC 2004)*, June 2004.

35. V. Mhatre, C. Rosenberg, D. Kofman, R. Mazumdar, and N. Shroff. A minimum cost surveillance sensor network with a lifetime constraint. *IEEE Transactions on Mobile Computing*, 4(1):4–15, January 2005.

36. S. Pattem, S. Poduri, and B. Krishnamachari. Energy-quality tradeoffs for target tracking in wireless sensor networks. In *Workshop on Information Processing in Sensor Networks (IPSN '03)*, April 2003.

37. P. Ramanathan. Location-centric approach for collaborative target detection, classification, and tracking. In *Proceedings of the IEEE CAS Workshop on Wireless Communication and Networking*, September 2002.

38. S. Ray, R. Ungrangsi, F.D. Pellegrini, A. Trachtenberg, and D. Starobinski. Robust location detection in emergency sensor networks. In *Proceedings of the IEEE INFOCOM 2003*, volume 2, March-April 2003.

39. V. Rodoplu and T. H. Meng. Distributed network protocols for wireless communication. In *1998 IEEE Symposium on Circuits and Systems, ISCAS'98, Monterey, CA*, volume 4, pages 600–603, June 1998.

40. V. Rodoplu and T. H. Meng. Minimum energy mobile wireless networks. In *1998 IEEE International Conference on Communications, ICC'98, Atlanta, GA*, volume 3, pages 1633–1639, June 1998.

41. C. Savarese, J. M. Rabaey, and J. Beutel. Locationing in distributed ad-hoc wireless sensor networks. In *ICASSP*, May 2001.

42. S. Shakkottai, R. Srikant, and N. Shroff. Unreliable sensor grids: Coverage, connectivity and diameter. In *Proceedings of the IEEE INFOCOM*, 2003.

43. T. Shepard. Decentralized channel management in scalable multihop spread spectrum packet radio networks. Technical Report Technical Report MIT/LCS/TR-670, Massachusetts Institute of Technology Laboratory for Computer Science, July 1995.

44. E. Shih, S. Cho, N. Ickes, R. Min, A. Sinha, A. Wang, and A. Chandrakasan. Physical layer driven protocol and algorithm design for energy-efficient wireless sensor networks. In *Seventh Annual ACM Conference on Mobile Computing and Networking (ACM MOBICOM'01), Rome, Italy*, Jul 2001.

45. S. Singh, M. Woo, and C. S. Raghavendra. Power-aware routing in mobile ad hoc networks. In *Fourth Annual ACM/IEEE International Conference on Mobile Computing and Networking, Dallas, TX*, Oct 1998.

46. T. Small and Z. J. Haas. The shared wireless infostation model – a new ad hoc networking paradigm. In *Proceedings of ACM MOBIHOC*, June 2003.

47. R. Szewczyk, A. Mainwaring, J. Polastre, and D. Culler. An analysis of a large scale habitat monitoring application. In *Second ACM Conference on Embedded Networked Sensor Systems (SenSys)*, Nov 2004.

48. R. Szewczyk, J. Polastre, A. Mainwaring, and D. Culler. Lessons from a sensor network expedition. In *Proceedings of 1st European Workshop on Wireless Sensor Networks (EWSN '04)*, January 2004.

49. S. Tilak, N. B. Abu-Ghazaleh, and W. Heinzelman. A taxonomy of wireless sensor network communication models. *Mobile Computing and Communication Review*, 6(2), April 2002.
50. www.greatduckisland.net. Habitat Monitoring on Great Duck Island.
51. www.princeton.edu/ mrm/zebranet.html. The ZebraNet Wildlife Tracker.
52. www.tinyos.net. TinyOS Community Forum, An open-source OS for the networked sensor regime.
53. www.xbow.com. Crossbow Technology Inc.: Inertial and Gyro Systems, Wireless Sensor Networks, Smart Dust and Advanced Sensors.
54. C.Y. Wan, A.T. Campbell, and L. Krishnamurthy. Psfq: A reliable transport protocol for wireless sensor networks. In *WSNA'02, Atlanta, Georgia, USA*, Sep 2002.
55. Y. Xu, J. Heidemann, and D. Estrin. Geography-informed energy conservation for ad hoc routing. In *Proceedings of International Conference on Mobile Computing and Networks MOBICOM*, 2001.
56. Y. Yao and J. Gehrke. The cougar approach to in-network query processing in sensor networks. *SIGMOD Record*, 31(1), Mar 2002.
57. W. Ye, J. Heidemann, and D. Estrin. An energy-efficient mac protocol for wireless sensor networks. In *IEEE INFOCOM, New York, NY*, Jun 2002.
58. Y. Zou and K. Chakrabarty. Energy-aware target localization in wireless sensor networks. In *Proceedings of the IEEE International Conference on Pervasive Computing and Communications (PerCom'03)*, March 2003.
59. G. Zussman and A. Segall. Energy efficient routing in ad hoc disaster recovery networks. In *Proceedings of IEEE INFOCOM*, April 2003.

Chapter 2
Algorithms for Robotic Deployment of WSN in Adaptive Sampling Applications

Dan O. Popa and Frank L. Lewis

Automation and Robotics Research Institute (ARRI)
University of Texas at Arlington
Arlington, TX 76118
popa@arri.uta.edu, lewis@uta.edu

1 Introduction

Recently, there has been renewed interest in using mobile robots as sensor-carrying platforms in order to perform hazardous tasks, such as searching for harmful biological and chemical agents, search and rescue in disaster areas, or environmental mapping and monitoring [9, 25, 31, 36]. Even though mobility introduces additional degrees of complexity in managing an untethered collection of sensors, it also expands the coverage and fault tolerance of a sensor network. When considering mobile sensor nodes, many important issues regarding the deployment architecture have yet to be fully addressed, including tradeoffs between node size, cost, and coverage, the selection of appropriate information measures to quantify the data collection performance of the mobile wireless sensor network (MWSN), distribution of communication and computation, etc.

Developing robust deployment algorithms for mobile sensor units requires simultaneous consideration of several optimization problems that have traditionally been addressed separately. One problem is related to the quality and usefulness of the collected sensor information (e.g., choosing optimal locations in space where environmental samples are taken by the robotic system), another is related to the robot team behavior for goal attainment (e.g., how does the robot team accomplish the sampling objectives), and a third is related to routing and congestion control in the ad-hoc wireless network formed by the robots (e.g., how do we reposition the robots to increase the communication bandwidth).

The analysis of MWSN can make use of many results from prior robotics research on cooperative mobile robots [7, 30, 34, 46] including methods to estimate robot position (localization) using SLAM [12, 15, 33, 49], attain area coverage [50], environment mapping [47], and flight formation [13]. Many of these algorithms are based on stochastic estimation techniques using the Extended Kalman Filter that integrates navigational information with external sensor information in a recursive algorithm [28]. Examples of robot team tasks have been investigated on a variety of hardware platforms, for example foraging, ant colony behavior, robotic soccer, map making, area searching, mine sweeping, etc [2]. Examples of relevant sensor deployment scenarios considered in the past are the distributed algorithm for odor localization in [20], battery charging behaviors for a mobile robot team in [32], object tracking [8, 56, 57], target classification [30], distributed control [48], and sensor validation [1].

While multiple vehicle localization and sensor fusion are classic problems in robotics, the problem of distributed field variable estimation is typically relevant to charting and prediction in oceanography and meteorology [4, 13, 14, 17]. The typical inverse modeling approach involves finding a partial differential equation and corresponding boundary conditions to express the evolution of the field variables in the 4D position-time space, based on a set of observation samples. In this context, measurement uncertainty has also been addressed using Kalman-filter estimation [3].

Some mobile robot navigation research has been addressed using potential fields. Obstacle avoidance or goal attainment schemes often use penalty functions to bend feasible paths around obstacles, or to reposition holonomic or nonholonomic wheeled robots at an end point attractor, such as it was originally presented in [26] and [24]. Path planning algorithms for mobile robots now routinely employs potential fields [27, 44, 45]. In [31], an artificial repelling field is used to reposition mobile sensor nodes within an area of interest. In [59] robot group uniformity is maintained through the use of artificial potentials. In Robocup 2002, the Sony legged league was won using a heuristic algorithm with shared potential functions [52]. The potentials are formed from estimates of the environment together with control forces, and local stability analysis is provided using Lyapunov functions. As with many optimization schemes, only convergence to a local minima can be guaranteed [23, 38, 51].

Extensive research has also been done in the context of ad-hoc sensor networks, in particular in finding heuristic solutions for network routing [19], deployment [22, 29], and congestion control [35, 55]. Routing in ad-hoc sensor networks has been usually addressed as a discrete optimization problem with optimality criteria related to node energy minimization, time-delay through the network, bandwidth maximization [18, 52, 54], etc. Congestion control is a relatively new research topic for sensor networks, but has been investigated extensively in the context of static (wired) network protocols. The congestion control problem consists of setting both the source and link controls of the network to ensure that the data rates and node buffers remain stable and stabilize to their optimal values. Various feedback schemes such as the primal (dynamic source rates, static link rates), dual (static source rates, dynamic link rates), and primal-dual (dynamic source rates, dynamic link rates) algorithms have been proposed [35]. A general passivity framework is proposed in [55] as a superset solution for flow control.

Several wireless network protocols have been proposed and implemented using many of the above concepts, such as IEEE 802.11a,b, Bluetooth and PAMAS, and some of them specifically apply to sensor networks, such as PI-CONET and SMAC [11, 52, 54]. There are significant differences between wireless protocols for distributed sensors, and wireless protocols used for telecom or computer networking. For example, concepts such as bandwidth fairness between users do not apply in the sensor network case. In fact, one would like the sensor nodes with "interesting" sensor information to be allocated more bandwidth than others. Defining what constitutes "interesting" sensor information is entirely dependent on the sensor network task. For example, it could be the detection of a single event that produces sensor readings above a certain level, or it could be continuous high bandwidth video feed from a camera that has captured an event of interest.

2 Problem Formulation

A number of fundamental issues arise in the coordination of multiple mobile sensor nodes used to sample a space-time field distribution, subject to a set of constraints. First, one would like to maximize the sensor information acquired through planning and control of the vehicles' paths and their sampling locations. At the same time, communications pathways are utilized and may have limited bandwidth constraints between vehicles that vary with location, and also energy expenditure must be monitored in order to complete tasks and plan reachable deployments.

These elements of distributed sensor coordination with mobile nodes are depicted in Figure 1 for an underwater deployment scenario. Several prior papers from Popa and Stephanou [39], Popa and Sanderson [40], and Popa and Lewis [41] describe basic aspects of the deployment scenario using potential fields for communication and navigation, and information measures for determining the location of optimal sampling locations. This chapter combines the following fundamental aspects of the deployment problem:

- *Combined navigation and estimation of robot nodes.* As robots move in the 3D sampling space and acquire sensory information, the uncertainty in their localization will affect the sensor maps generated. A combined localization-sensor field estimation problem is formulated. Robot navigation will be driven by uncertainty measures such as the norm of Kalman filter covariance matrices. The algorithms described here combine the uncertainty in localization as well as in the sensor measurements to achieve effective adaptive sampling. Both of these uncertainties are especially relevant for underwater vehicles, since position estimates are often inaccurate due to navigational errors from dead-reckoning [5].
- *Robot navigation for maximizing the amount of raw data streamed from the sensor nodes.* Communication rates in sensor nets deteriorate as the

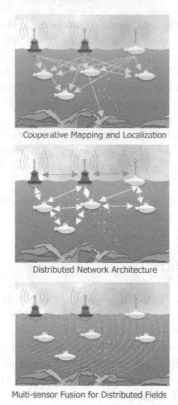

Cooperative Mapping and Localization

Distributed Network Architecture

Multi-sensor Fusion for Distributed Fields

Fig. 1. Schematic diagram of fundamental problems related to adaptive sampling.

receiver moves away from the transmitter. Obviously, mobile sensor nodes will require continuously changing path lengths, leading to variable data rates. In some applications, such as underwater robotics, stringent communication constraints are made much worse by interference in a common broadcast space. Network capacity is addressed in the context of congestion control with variable link rates.

- *Robot navigation for minimizing the amount of energy expended through motion and communication.* Both repositioning robots, as well as robot node communication, requires energy expenditure. The energy expenditure by robot motion can in some cases be a lot more significant than the one required by communication.

- *Combining communication constraints, sensor fusion requirements, energy constraints, navigation limitations, and adaptive sampling into a distributed, scalable deployment algorithm.* A scalable way to combine the results of communication, navigation, and information optimization problems is via the potential fields method. MWSN nodes move according to forces calculated from network, navigation and information "energy-like" functions.

3 Communication Models

We can formulate the network model of the mobile sensor nodes based on results from congestion control. The flow control problem through an ad-hoc sensor network can be separated into two problems:

- The "routing problem" is similar to a "ravelling salesman" NP-hard problem in that it aims to select data routes ("hops") with minimal cost between the wireless nodes forming a graph. The "cost" can be defined in terms of geographical distance, energy consumed, or time delay through the network.
- The "congestion control problem" consists of finding and regulating the optimal flow rates between the network nodes in the presence of network capacity constraints. This problem can be further decomposed into a static optimization problem (finding the optimal flow) and a dynamic stabilization problem (converging to the optimal flow)

Solutions to both the routing and congestion control problems are differentiators between different network protocols, but we will assume that the communication hardware provided to the robot nodes has been a-priori chosen.

We focus on creating a robot/sensor architecture that combines navigation and communication. Specifically, we would like to control individual robot location (r_i), and its sensor data rate (x_i) over time in order to maximize a combined network utility function, subject to a set of capacity constraints that vary with distance:

$$max_{x \geq 0} \sum_{i=1}^{N} U_i(x_i) \ subject \ to \ R_x \leq c(r_i) \qquad (1)$$

where U_i is a strictly concave utility function, R is the routing matrix for the network, and $c(r)$ is a position dependent link capacity function. The concave/convex requirement for U_i, combined with a full row rank condition of the routing matrix R are sufficient (but not necessary) conditions to ensure that there exists a unique minimum solution to the associated constrained optimization problem (1). Various utility functions are used for different network models, for example $arctan(x_i)$ for TCP Reno and $log(x_i)$ for TCP Vegas [35].

As a reflection of the network mobility, however, we assume that the link capacity constraints can vary with the distance between network nodes. This is consistent with Shannon's theorem that predicts that the maximum achievable data rate between two nodes is given by:

$$C = W log_2 \left(1 + \frac{K}{W N_o} \frac{P_t}{d^\alpha} \right) \tag{2}$$

where P is the power, d is the distance between nodes, W is the bandwidth, α is the path loss coefficient, F is the fading margin, K' is the propagation constant dependent on the medium, and $K = K'F$ [42]. Eq. (2) breaks down as d decreases to 0, since communication rates are limited by on-board processing capabilities. We use a different capacity model:

$$C = \begin{cases} c_0(\frac{1}{d^\alpha} - \frac{1}{r_{zone}^\alpha}), & r_{min} < d < r_{zone} \\ c_0(\frac{1}{r_{min}^\alpha} - \frac{1}{r^\alpha}), & d \le r_{zone} \\ 0, & d > r_{zone} \end{cases} \tag{3}$$

with a profile shown in Figure (2-a). Because the data rate varies with distance between nodes, the optimal utility function value will also vary with node location, as the solution of an unconstrained optimization problem using Lagrange multipliers:

$$U^*(r_{i=1,N}) = min_{p_l > 0} max_{x_i > 0} (\sum_{i=1}^{N} w_i U(x_i) + \sum_{l=1}^{L} p_l(c_l(r_i) - y_l)).$$

In a classical network formulation, the utility functions of each node are equally weighed. By using different but non-zero, positive weights w_i (to maintain convexity), we can assign levels of importance to nodes in the network.

3.1 Example: Capacity in a four-node network

Consider the four node network shown in Figure (2-b). The flow optimization problem using logarithmic utility functions can be reduced to finding the optimal flow vector $x^* = (x_1^*, x_2^*, x_3^*)^T$, solution of a 3D constrained optimization problem. If the location of the nodes can vary, the maximum capacities will also vary similarly with the graph in Figure 2. Assuming that the location of nodes 1, 3, and 4 is fixed, but the second node is allowed to move in a 2D plane, the resulting optimal utility function can be calculated numerically, and is shown in Figure 3.

4 Sampling of Parametrized Fields based on Closed-form Information Measures

We describe the problem of adaptive sampling, e.g., the problem of reconstructing a parametrized field model from observations taken using mobile robot nodes. If the parametric form of a measurement field is known, as might

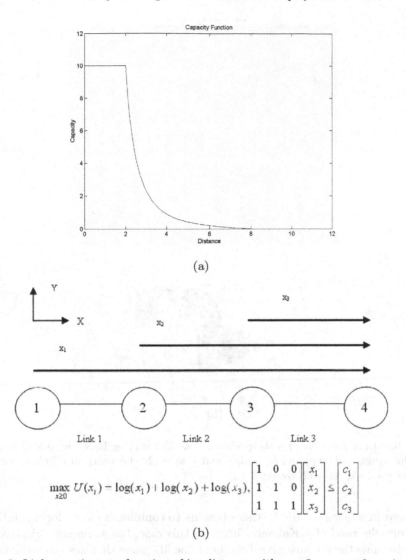

(a)

(b)

$$\max_{x \geq 0} U(x_i) - \log(x_1) + \log(x_2) + \log(x_3), \begin{bmatrix} 1 & 0 & 0 \\ 1 & 1 & 0 \\ 1 & 1 & 1 \end{bmatrix} \begin{bmatrix} x_1 \\ x_2 \\ x_3 \end{bmatrix} \leq \begin{bmatrix} c_1 \\ c_2 \\ c_3 \end{bmatrix}$$

Fig. 2. Link capacity as a function of its distance with $\alpha = 2$, $r_{zone} = 8$, $rmin = 2$ (a), and the optimization problem for a simple four-link network configuration (b).

be the case, for example, with a bottom profile or systematic variations in temperature or salinity, the field estimation can be integrated with localization in order to improve these estimates. Given uncertainty models for the field measurements and the location where the samples are taken, determining optimal sampling points can be based on minimizing information measures. An example of such measures is the state covariance estimates of the Kalman Filter. Furthermore, certain simple assumptions, such as that the field distribution

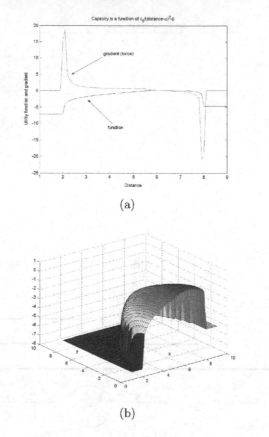

(a)

(b)

Fig. 3. Utility function with the position of node 2 varying between nodes 1 and 3 on the x axis (1d - top) and on both x and y axes (2d - bottom) for a link capacity model with =2, rmin=2, rzone=8.

is linear in a given region, further allow us to compute a closed form solution without the need of a Kalman Filter. In this case, the sampling objective is to determine the unknown coefficients of the 3D plane that describes the field variable, given a known localization uncertainty described by the robot dynamic model. As an example, consider navigation in a shallow region (lake or coastal region) where smooth changes in depth provide a linear field model measured as altitude by the vehicle.

4.1 Closed-form estimation for a field without localization uncertainty

Let's first assume that we are estimating a field distribution that is known to be linear in its parameters. For instance, the field can represent dissolved oxygen in a body of water that varies linearly with the location of the sample point in the (x, y) direction, and quadratically with the sample point depth (z). Or it can represent a general field distribution that has been approximated through a finite number of coefficients using a polynomial, Fourier or Wavelet basis. The linear-in-parameters form allows us to compute a closed form solution for the information measure used by the sampling algorithm. Since there is no uncertainty in the vehicle localization, the unknown field coefficient covariance can be calculated directly using a simple least-square estimation. After n measurements taken at location x_i, the field model depends linearly on the coefficients a_j via position-dependent functions, and we can directly estimate the unknown coefficients from the least-square solution:

$$z_1 = a_0 + a_1 g_1(x_1) + \cdots + a_m g_m(x_1)$$
$$z_2 = a_0 + a_1 g_1(x_2) + \cdots + a_m g_m(x_2)$$
$$\vdots$$
$$z_n = a_0 + a_1 g_1(x_n) + \cdots + a_m g_m(x_n)$$

$$\hat{A}_n = (1 \quad g_i(x_j))^+_{i \leq m, j \leq n} \begin{pmatrix} X_1 \\ \vdots \\ X_n \end{pmatrix} = M_n^+ \begin{pmatrix} Z_1 \\ \vdots \\ Z_n \end{pmatrix}. \tag{4}$$

In equation (4) $g_i(x)$ are nonlinear basis functions that depend on the sample location x, while the field variables z_i represent the field model at location x_i. Because the pseudo-inverse of the matrix $M_n = (1 \ g_i(x_j))_{i \leq m, j \leq n}$ can be directly calculated from $M_n^+ = (M_n^T M_n)^{-1} M_n^T$, we obtain a closed-form solution for the covariance of the unknown parameters a_j:

$$\hat{A}_n = \left(\sum_{j=1}^{n} (1 \cdots g_i(x_j) \cdots g_m(x_j)) \begin{pmatrix} 1 \\ \vdots \\ g_i(x_j) \\ \vdots \\ g_m(x_j) \end{pmatrix} \right)^{-1} \sum_{j=1}^{n} Z_j \begin{pmatrix} 1 \\ \vdots \\ g_i(x_j) \\ \vdots \\ g_m(x_j) \end{pmatrix}. \tag{5}$$

The covariance matrix of $\hat{A}_n$ can now be related directly to the (constant) measurement uncertainty as: $var(\hat{A}_n) = var(z_i)(M_n^T M_n)^{-1}$, and the adaptive sampling algorithm will move the vehicle from location x_n to x_{n+1}, such that the following p-norm is maximized over the search space $\ominus$:

$$m(x) = \left\| \begin{pmatrix} 1 \\ \vdots \\ M_n^T \ g_i(x) \\ \vdots \\ g_m(x) \end{pmatrix} \left(1 \cdots g_i(x) \cdots g_m(x) \right) \right\|,$$

$$m(x_{n+1}) \geq m(x), (\forall)x \in \ominus. \qquad (6)$$

A summary of the deployment algorithm using closed-form variance estimation is shown below:

Closed-Form Adaptive Sampling Algorithm (AS-1)

Assumptions: The field model is linear in the parameters, field model functions g_j are known, sampling locations x_j belong to a discrete sampling space $\ominus$ and do not have uncertainty. The sample measurements have constant uncertainty $\sigma_z^2 = var(z_i)$. The sampling space $\ominus$ can be a grid. Constants $\varepsilon > 0$, $p \geq 1$ are given.

Step1 (initialize): Sample at least $n_0 \geq m$ initial locations, where m is the number of field model basis functions g_j. These initial sampling locations could be randomly chosen close to a starting robot location. Remove these sampling points from $\ominus$. Denote the remaining sampling space as $\ominus_{n_0}$. After Step1, the robot will be at location x_{n_0}.

Step2: For $n \geq n_0$ form measurement vector $Z = (z_j)_{i \leq j \leq n}$ after n samples. Form basis function matrix M_n as shown in equation (4).

Step3: For all sampling points x in the parameter space $\ominus_n$, calculate $m(x)$ using equation (6). Select the next sampling location to be x_{next} for which $m(x)$ is minimal.

Step4: Command the robot to move from location x_n to location x_{next}. While in transit, sample at k discrete locations $x_{n+1}, x_{n+2}, ..., x_{n+k} = x_{next}$. The number k can be chosen depending on the length of travel. Remove these points from $\ominus_n$ to form $\ominus_{n+k}$.

Step5: Calculate the parameter uncertainty measure

$$var(\hat{A}_n) = \sigma_z^2 ||(M_n^T M_n)^{-1}||_p.$$

If $\ominus_{n+k}$ is empty (the whole space has been sampled), or if $var(\hat{A}_n) \leq \varepsilon$ (the parameter uncertainty measure is below a threshold), exit. Otherwise, set n to be $n + k$ and repeat Step2.

For a 2D spatially distributed field variable, a particularly common basis that can be used to approximate the field is a sum of Gaussians (SOG) distribution. If the Gaussian centers and variance are known, then the unknown SOG coefficients a_j can be estimated using equations 4-6 above. If, however, the centers and variances of the Gaussians are unknown, then the field to be estimated becomes nonlinear-in-parameters. For $m = 2$, the measurement equations are: $y = a_0 + a_1 e^{-\frac{(x-x_1)^2+(y-y_1)^2}{2\sigma^2}} + a_2 e^{-\frac{(x-x_2)^2+(y-y_2)^2}{2\sigma^2}}$, and we are estimating $a_0, a_1, a_2, x_1, y_1, x_2, y_2, \sigma$. Instead of the linear least-square solution (6), we can use a numerical nonlinear least-square solution provided by MATLAB's fmincon, however, we cannot obtain a closed form measure of uncertainty for the whole parameter vector.

4.2 Example: Monte-Carlo simulations with a SOG field

We have run simulations using a 2D nonlinear field (though still linear in the parameters), consisting of a sum of two Gaussian distributions:

$$G(x,y) = a_0 + a_1g_1(x,y) + a_2g_2(x,y), g(x,y) = e^{-\frac{\sqrt{(x-x_0)^2+(y-y_0)^2}}{2\sigma^2}}.$$

First, we assume that the centers of Gaussians and the covariance for $g_1(x,y)$, $g_2(x,y)$ are known, and they are located at $(30,30)$, $(65,45)$, $\sigma = 10$. The sampling sequences generated are shown in Figure 4 (a)$-$(d). The second sampling sequence is obtained for a SOG field assuming that the location of the Gaussian centers are not known. In this case we use a numerical constrained optimization solver from MATLAB (fmincon) to obtain the sampling sequence. Assuming nominal values of $a_0 = 1$, $a_1 = 4$, $a_2 = -5.5$, $(x_1,y_1) = (30,30)$, $(x_2,y_2) = (35,65)$, we first divide the Gaussian center's search space into an $N \times N$ grid. We constrain our nonlinear optimization routine to searching inside all grid pairs where the centers are located (in order to avoid local minima results). The optimal location of the grid center moves according to the graphs shown in Figure 5. The figure also shows the convergence of the three linear field coefficients to their actual values. For the simulation results in Figure 5, $N = 2$, and the search space was $a_0, a_1, a_2 = [-10 \ 10]$, (x_1,y_1), (x_2,y_2) in random subsquare pairs.

Because we cannot use the LSE estimate to find all the unknown parameters, the sampling algorithm used is different than (AS-1) and summarized below:

Numerical Gradient Search Adaptive Sampling Algorithm (AS-2)

Assumptions: The field model is nonlinear but parametric, sampling locations x_j belong to a discrete sampling space $\ominus$ and do not have uncertainty. The field depends linearly on parameter set A, and nonlinearly on parameter set B (in the previous example these are the centers and variance of the Gaussian functions). The sample parameter set B is part of a discrete coarse grid in its own q-dimensional space. The sample measurements have constant uncertainty $\sigma_z^2 = var(z_i)$. The sampling space $\ominus$ can be a grid. Constants $\varepsilon > 0$, $p \geq 1$ are given.

Step1 (initialize): Sample at least $n_0 \geq m$ initial locations, where m is the number of field model basis functions g_j. These initial sampling locations could be randomly chosen close to a starting robot location. Remove these sampling points from $\ominus$. Denote the remaining sampling space as $\ominus_{n_0}$. After Step1, the robot will be at location x_{n_0}.

Step2: Pick a starting guess for the parameter set B, and denote that set as $\hat{B}_{n_0}$.

Step3: For $n \geq n_0$ form measurement vector $Z = (z_j)_{1 \leq j \leq n}$ after n samples. Form basis function matrix M_n as shown in equation (4), using the current parameter set B estimate.

Step4: For all sampling points x in the parameter space $\ominus_n$ calculate $m(x)$ using equation (6). Select the next sampling location to be x_{next} for which $m(x)$ is minimal.

Step5: Command the robot to move from location x_n to location x_{next}. While in transit, sample at k discrete locations $x_{n+1}, x_{n+2}, ..., x_{n+k} = x_{next}$. The number k can be chosen depending on the length of travel. Remove these points from $\ominus_n$ to form $\ominus_{n+k}$.

Step6: Using a nonlinear iterative root solver (such as *fmincon* in MAT-LAB) solve the constrained nonlinear equation

$$
\begin{aligned}
z_1 &= a_0 + a_1 g_1(x_1, B_{n+k}) + \cdots + a_m g_m(x_1, B_{n+k}) \\
z_2 &= a_0 + a_1 g_1(x_2, B_{n+k}) + \cdots + a_m g_m(x_2, B_{n+k}) \\
&\vdots \\
z_n &= a_0 + a_1 g_1(x_n, B_{n+k}) + \cdots + a_m g_m(x_n, B_{n+k})
\end{aligned}
\quad ,
$$

to find $\hat{A}_{n+k} = (a_0, a_1...a_m)$, $\hat{B}_{n+k} = (b_1, ..., b_q)$. Constrain the nonlinear root-finding problem by having B located inside a cubic element inside its coarse grid from the q-dimensional space.

Step7: Calculate the parameter uncertainty measure

$$
var(\hat{A}_n) = \sigma_z^2 ||(M_n^T M_n)^{-1}||_p.
$$

If $\ominus_{n+k}$ is empty (the whole space has been sampled), or if $var(\hat{A}_{n+k}) \leq \varepsilon$, and $||\hat{B}_{n+k} - \hat{B}_n|| \leq \varepsilon$ (the parameter uncertainty measure is below a threshold, and the parameter estimates B do not change), go to Step8. Otherwise, set n to be $n + k$ and repeat Step3.

Step8: If the residual error between the measurement vector Z and the parametric field $g(A, B)$ is smaller than ε exit. Otherwise, pick another starting guess for the parameter set B from its coarse grid and repeat Step2.

4.3 Closed-form estimation for a linear field with localization uncertainty

Previously, we used a numerical "closed-form" calculation of the parameter variance, in the absence of state uncertainty. The parameter variance calculation relies on calculating the pseudo-inverse of a matrix whose entries are assumed to be known. These entries depend on the position at the point where measurements are taken, and in the context of MWSNs, this location is not known exactly. Let's consider a very simple one-dimensional sampling example, in which we add localization uncertainty. We set $m = 2$ and $g(x) = x$ in order to obtain an algebraic closed-form solution of the parameter variance. If the set of measurements is given by:

$$
\begin{aligned}
y_1 &= a_1 + a_2 x_1 \\
y_2 &= a_1 + a_2 x_2 \\
&\vdots \\
y_n &= a_1 + a_2 x_n
\end{aligned}
\quad ,
\begin{bmatrix} y_1 \\ y_2 \\ \vdots \\ y_n \end{bmatrix}
=
\begin{bmatrix} 1 & x_1 \\ 1 & x_2 \\ \vdots \\ 1 & x_n \end{bmatrix}
\begin{bmatrix} a_1 \\ a_2 \end{bmatrix}
, Y_n = M_n A,
$$

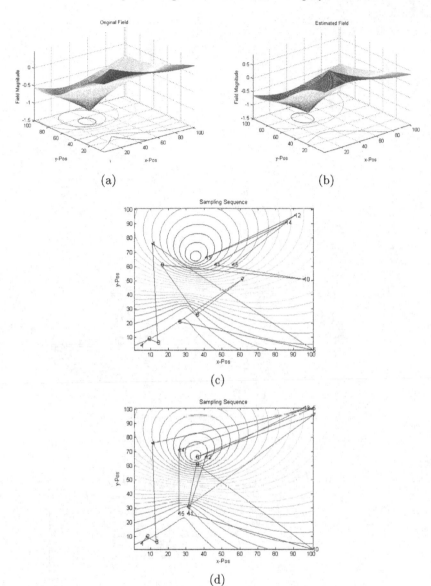

(a)

(b)

(c)

(d)

Fig. 4. Sampling sequence for a Gaussian field distribution (original - (a), estimated -(b)) is generated to minimize error variance using the infinity norm (c), and the 2-norm (d). First fifteen sampling locations are shown.

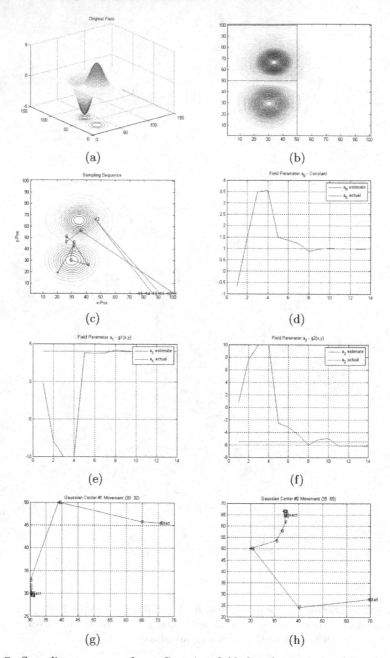

Fig. 5. Sampling sequence for a Gaussian field distribution where the Gaussian centers are unknown, generated using fmincon and the 2-norm of the linear field parameters. Convergence of all parameters, including the Gaussian centers to their true values is observed.

in which Y_n is the measurement vector after n samples, M_n is the basis function matrix from equation (4), and A is the vector of unknown parameters. Note that the measurement values y_i are the corresponding measurement values z_i in equation (4). The least-square estimate of 'A' after n measurements will be: $\hat{A} = M_n^+ Y_n = (M_n^T M_n)^{-1} M_n^T Y_n$,

$$\hat{A} = \left\{ \begin{bmatrix} 1 & 1 \cdots 1 \\ x_1 & x_2 \cdots x_n \end{bmatrix} \begin{bmatrix} 1 & x_1 \\ 1 & x_2 \\ \vdots \\ 1 & x_n \end{bmatrix} \right\}^{-1} \begin{bmatrix} 1 & 1 \cdots 1 \\ x_1 & x_2 \cdots x_n \end{bmatrix} \begin{bmatrix} Z_1 \\ Z_2 \\ \vdots \\ Z_n \end{bmatrix},$$

$$\Rightarrow \hat{A} = \frac{1}{n \sum_{i=1}^n x_i^2 - (\sum_{i=1}^n x_i)^2} \begin{bmatrix} \sum_{i=1}^n y_i \sum_{i=1}^n x_i^2 - (\sum_{i=1}^n x_i y_i) \sum_{i=1}^n x_i \\ -\sum_{i=1}^n y_i \sum_{i=1}^n x_i + n(\sum_{i=1}^n x_i y_i) \end{bmatrix}$$

$$= \frac{1}{f_0(x)} \begin{bmatrix} f_1(x,y) \\ f_2(x,y) \end{bmatrix} = \begin{bmatrix} F_1(x,y) \\ F_2(x,y) \end{bmatrix}.$$

The variance of $\hat{A}$ can now be calculated based on the variance of (x,y) through Jacobians:

$$var(\hat{A}) = \left(\frac{\partial \hat{A}}{\partial (x,y)} \right) var(x,y) \left(\frac{\partial \hat{A}}{\partial (x,y)} \right)^T,$$

where the Jacobian is given by

$$\frac{\partial \hat{A}}{\partial (x,y)} = \begin{bmatrix} \frac{\partial F_1}{\partial x_i} & \frac{\partial F_1}{\partial y_i} \\ \frac{\partial F_2}{\partial x_i} & \frac{\partial F_2}{\partial y_i} \end{bmatrix}, \quad and$$

$$\frac{\partial F_1}{\partial x_j} = \frac{f_0 \frac{\partial f_1}{\partial x_j} - f_1 \frac{\partial f_0}{\partial x_j}}{f_0^2}, \quad \frac{\partial F_2}{\partial x_j} = \frac{f_0 \frac{\partial f_2}{\partial x_j} - f_2 \frac{\partial f_0}{\partial x_j}}{f_0^2},$$

$$\frac{\partial f_1}{\partial x_j} = (\sum_{i=1}^n y_i) \cdot 2x_j - (\sum_{i=1}^n x_i y_i) - (\sum_{i=1}^n x_i) \cdot y_j,$$

$$\frac{\partial f_0}{\partial x_j} = 2nx_j - 2\sum_{i=1}^n x_i, \quad \frac{\partial f_2}{\partial x_j} = -(\sum_{i=1}^n y_i) + ny_j.$$

Similarly,

$$\frac{\partial F_1}{\partial y_j} = \frac{1}{f_0} \frac{\partial f_1}{\partial y_j} = \frac{1}{f_0} \{ (\sum_{i=1}^n x_i^2) - (\sum_{i=1}^n x_i) \cdot x_j \},$$

$$\frac{\partial F_2}{y_j} = \frac{1}{f_0} \frac{\partial f_2}{\partial y_j} = \frac{1}{f_0} \{ -(\sum_{i=1}^n x_i) + nx_j \}.$$

Even though we obtained closed-form algebraic solutions for the unknown parameter covariance, we can see that introducing localization uncertainty to our sampling problem makes it hard to obtain closed-form solutions for a large number of parameters, or for nonlinear fields. Using closed-form variance solutions to determine optimal sampling locations is only feasible if no localization uncertainty is considered.

5 Adaptive Sampling using the Extended Kalman Filter

Due to difficulties in estimating the combined parametric and localization uncertainty using closed-form solutions, we employ an iterative estimation approach to select optimal sampling points. Let x_k denote the 3D position of one of the mobile robots at sample number k. A model for the mobile node is usually nonlinear, and describes the state evolution as:

$$x_{k+1} = x_k + Tf(x_k, u_k) + Tw_k$$

where T is the sampling rate, u_k is the control input to the vehicle and w_k is state measurement noise, assumed to be white, with zero mean, and covariance matrix Q_k^1. Additional navigation measurements are then given by:

$$y_k = h(x_k) + \xi_k.$$

The field measurements depend on the state, as well as a set of parameters which are unknown:

$$z_k = g(x_k, a_k) + \varsigma_k.$$

If the set of unknown coefficients is constant or slow time-varying, we add the vector a to the overall system state, with an evolution governed by $a_{k+1} = a_k + v_k$. The noise covariances are given by $E[\xi_k \xi_k^T] = R_k^1$, $E[\varsigma_k \varsigma_K^T] = R_k^2$, and $E[v_k v_K^T] = Q_k^2$. A simultaneous sampling and navigation estimation problem is formulated using the extended Kalman Filter (EKF), using an overall state vector $X_k = (x_k, a_k)$, a measurement vector $Z_k = (y_k, z_k)$:

$$X_{k+1} = F(X_k, u_k) + p_k, \ Z_k = H(X_k) + n_k, \tag{7}$$

$$E[p_k p_k^T] = \begin{pmatrix} T^2 Q_k^1 & 0 \\ 0 & Q_k^2 \end{pmatrix} = Q_k, \ E[n_k n_k^T] = \begin{pmatrix} R_k^1 & 0 \\ 0 & R_k^2 \end{pmatrix} = R_k. \tag{8}$$

The Extended Kalman Filter Equations from nonlinear functions F and H, could be written using the Jacobians $F_X(.) \equiv \frac{\partial F}{\partial X}(.)$, $H_X(.) \equiv \frac{\partial H}{\partial X}(.)$:
Time Update:

$$\hat{X}_{k+1}^- = F(\hat{X}_k, u_k), \tag{9}$$

$$\hat{Z}_{k+1}^- = H(\hat{X}_{k+1}^-), \tag{10}$$

$$P_{k+1}^- = F_X(\hat{X}_k, u_k) P_k F_X^T(\hat{X}_k, u_k) + Q. \tag{11}$$

Measurement Update:

$$(P_{k+1})^{-1} = (P_{k+1}^-)^{-1} + H_X^T(X_{k+1}^-) R^{-1} H_X^T(X_{k+1}^-) \tag{12}$$

or

$$P_{k+1} = \frac{P_{k+1}^- - P_{k+1}^- H_X(X_{k+1}^-)H_X^T(X_{k+1}^-)P_{k+1}^-}{H_X^T(X_{k+1}^-)P_{k+1}^- H_X(X_{k+1}^-) + R}, \tag{13}$$

$$\hat{X}_{k+1} = \hat{X}_{k+1}^- + P_{k+1}H_X^T(\hat{X}_{k+1}^-)R^{-1}(Z_{k+1} - \hat{Z}_{k+1}^-). \tag{14}$$

The EKF provides a recursive method for computing the state covariance, and can be utilized as an information measure. The sampling algorithm will choose the next locations in space to sample such that the covariance norm is minimized. Note that in the time and measurement updates, no measurement is needed to be taken for the covariance updates. The measurement Z_{k+1} is *only* needed for the estimate measurement update (14).

This means that the equations (11) and (12) are covariance updates available *before* the measurement is taken at time $k+1$. They can be used to predict the usefulness of the measurement at time $k + 1$ before it is ever taken.

Also, they show the effect not only of the measurement Z_{k+1} in reducing the error covariance, they also show the cost of moving to the estimated position $\hat{X}_{k+1}^-$ needed to take the measurement Z_{k+1} in terms of uncertainty injected due to the motion uncertainty (e.g., covariance increase in (11)). This aspect may avoid long distance movements as appear in [40], where we are jumping to far corners of the map to take the next measurements, and has added benefits in that the EKF linear approximation becomes less accurate as we move long distances. The nonlinearity can be offset by predicting the states using the time update (9) and using the predicted states in (11). Finally, in order to choose the next sampling location, we use the following algorithm:

EKF-Based Adaptive Sampling Algorithm (AS-3)

Assumptions: The field model is nonlinear but parametric, sampling locations x_j belong to a discrete sampling space $\ominus$ and can have uncertainty. The robotic vehicle model, the sampling model is of form (7), and its uncertainty covariances are given by (8). The sampling space $\ominus$ can be a grid. Constants $\varepsilon > 0$, $p \geq 1$ are given.

Step1 (initialize): Assume a starting robot location X_0. Pick an initial covariance estimate P_0, and unknown parameter guess estimate a_0. Remove the starting sampling points from $\ominus$. Denote the remaining sampling space as $\ominus_0$.

Step2: For each iteration step k starting at $k = 0$, and for each possible control vector Uk, propagate the time update equations (9)−(11) estimates of the robot position and the current parameter guesses. Propagate the P matrix measurement update using equation (13).

Step3: Pick the control input Uk that minimizes the p-norm of P_{k+1}.

Step4: Command the robot using the Uk found in Step3. Update the robot position and the parameter estimates using equation (14) by utilizing aposteriori measurements of the robot states and the sampling data while the robot is in transit.

Step5: If the uncertainty measure becomes "small" enough, $||P_{k+1}|| \leq \varepsilon$, exit, otherwise set $k = k + 1$ and repeat Step2.

It is apparent that the algorithm AS-3 is a more systematic way to reposition the robot and estimate the parametric field than algorithms AS-1 and AS-2.

5.1 EXAMPLE: Kalman Filter estimation for a parameter-linear field

Instead of using the closed form numerical or algebraic solutions from Section 4.1, sampling measures can be obtained for parameter-linear fields by using a Kalman Filter to set up the recursive equations. A similar simple case appears in [28, pp.137]. First, if there is no localization uncertainty, the state and output equations can be written as:

$$A_{k+1} = A_k, \ Z_k = G_k A_k + v_k, \ where$$

$$G_k = (1 \cdots g_i(X_k) \cdots g_m(X_k)), \ E[v_k v_k^T] = R.$$

Because of the simple state update equation, the error covariance update can be reduced to:

$$A_0 \sim (\bar{A}_0, P_{A_0}), \ P_0 = P_{A_0}, \ P_{k+1}^{-1} = P_k^{-1} + G_{k+1}^T R^{-1} G_{k+1},$$

$$\hat{A}_{k+1} = \hat{A}_k + P_{k+1} G_{k+1}^T R^{-1}(Z_{k+1} - G_{k+1}\hat{A}_k).$$

The error covariance is similar to the least squares solution, and can be directly calculated by $P_k = (P_o^{-1} + \sum_{j=1}^{k} G_j^T R^{-1} G_j)^{-1}$.

Because the field is linear in the parameter form, we don't have to use the Taylor series expansion in the EKF, even in the presence of localization uncertainty:

$$\begin{pmatrix} X_{k+1} \\ A_{k+1} \end{pmatrix} = \begin{pmatrix} X_k \\ A_k \end{pmatrix} + \begin{pmatrix} I \\ 0 \end{pmatrix} U_k + \begin{pmatrix} w_k \\ 0 \end{pmatrix} = \begin{pmatrix} X_k \\ A_k \end{pmatrix} + BU_k + \vartheta_k,$$

$$\begin{pmatrix} Y_k \\ Z_k \end{pmatrix} = \begin{pmatrix} I & 0 \\ 0 & (1 \ g(X_k^T)) \end{pmatrix} \begin{pmatrix} X_k \\ A_k \end{pmatrix} + \lambda_k,$$

where

$$E[\vartheta_k \vartheta_k^T] = Q = \begin{pmatrix} Q_1 & 0 \\ 0 & 0 \end{pmatrix}, E[\lambda_k \lambda_k^T] = R = \begin{pmatrix} R_1 & 0 \\ 0 & R_2 \end{pmatrix}$$

are the white noise covariances of the state and output. The nonlinear Kalman filter equations become:

$$P_{k+1}^- = P_k + Q, \ \begin{pmatrix} X_{k+1}^- \\ A_{k+1}^- \end{pmatrix} = \begin{pmatrix} \hat{X}_k \\ \hat{A}_k \end{pmatrix} + BU_k, \ P_{k+1} = \frac{1}{\frac{1}{P_{k+1}^-} + H_{k+1}^T \frac{1}{R} H_{k+1}},$$

$$H_k = \begin{pmatrix} I & 0 \\ 0 & (1 \;\; g(X_k^T)) \end{pmatrix}, \;\; \begin{pmatrix} X_{k+1}^- \\ A_{k+1}^- \end{pmatrix} = \begin{pmatrix} X_k \\ A_k \end{pmatrix} + BU_k,$$

$$\begin{pmatrix} \hat{X}_{k+1} \\ \hat{A}_{k+1} \end{pmatrix} = \begin{pmatrix} X_{k+1}^- \\ A_{k+1}^- \end{pmatrix} + P_{k+1} H_{k+1}^T R^{-1} (\begin{pmatrix} Y_{k+1} \\ Z_{k+1}^- \end{pmatrix} - H_{k+1} \begin{pmatrix} X_{k+1}^- \\ A_{k+1}^- \end{pmatrix}).$$

If however, the parametrized field is nonlinear, such as in the case of the sum of Gaussians (SOG) with unknown centers or variance, the recursive equations need to be set up using the Taylor series expansion of H.

A set of simulations was performed for the case of simultaneous vehicle localization and linear parameter field estimation. In a 1D case (a linear field with two unknowns − intercept and slope), we considered data sets generated under Gaussian noise assumptions, using nominal coefficient values $a_0 = 2$, $a_1 = 0.5$ (intercept and slope), and measurement noise covariance of 0.5, state measurement noise covariance of 0.1, and state transition noise covariance of 0.1. The convergence of the coefficient estimates to their nominal values is shown in Figures 6 (a)−(d) for two different sampling sequences. For Figures 6(a) and (c), the sampling sequence is the default one (1,2,), while Figures 6(b) and (d) were obtained by minimizing the error covariance, e.g., the adaptive sampling algorithm moves the vehicle from location X_n to X_{n+1}, such that the following infinity norm is maximized over the search space $\ominus$:

$$m(X) = ||P_n||_\infty, \;\; m(X_{n+1}) \geq m(X), \;\; (\forall) X \in \ominus.$$

Note that the slope estimate of the second sampling sequence converges faster to its nominal value. The optimal sampling sequence is similar to the one in Figure 2(a) because the localization error is still smaller than the measurement error. The optimal sampling sequences are identical to the ones reported in [40] using the closed-form parameter variance.

6 Potential Fields

In the context of robot navigation, the potential field method creates a vector field representing a navigational path based on a potential function. These vectors then act as artificial forces upon the nodes resulting in motion through a dynamic equation of motion. Given a scalar potential field function $U(r)$ that depends on the robot position, one can calculate forces governing the robot motion based on the gradient of the scalar potential field $F = -\nabla U(\vec{r})$. Similar approaches for MWSN deployment have been described by others in [21, 31, 58], but in their case the potential field forces are not based on actual measures of communication or information. For a MWSN, we consider the following actuation forces:

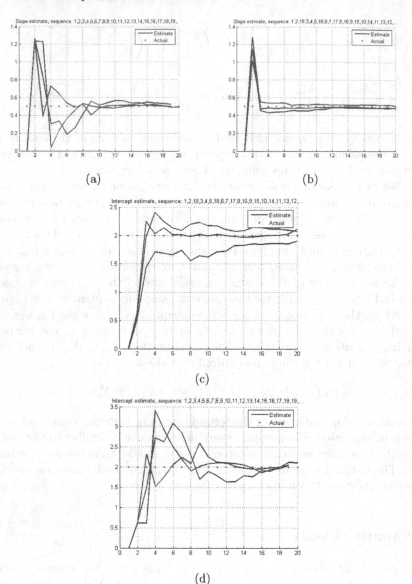

Fig. 6. The convergence of slope and intercept in a combined KF field estimation and localization problem for the default (a,c) and optimal (b,d) 1D sampling sequence.

- Attractive forces towards goals, which are defined as locations in space where the sensor nodes need to sample next, based on adaptive sampling criteria: $F_{goal} = -w_g(r - r_{goal})$.
- Repulsive forces given by obstacles and other robots, in particular rolling down a potential "hill" around the object:

$$F_{obs} = \begin{cases} \eta(\frac{1}{D(r)} - \frac{1}{Q})\frac{\nabla D(r)}{D^2(r)}, & D(r) \le Q \\ 0, & D(r) > 0 \end{cases}$$

where Q is area of influence of the obstacle and $D(r)$ is the Euclidean distance from the obstacle to the robot.

- Attractive forces based on maximizing communication capacity between nodes: $F_{comm} = -\frac{\partial U^*}{\partial r}$, where U^* is the optimal value of the communication utility function. For each MWSN node, the gradient is computed along each separate data route going through the node, and the resultant force is computed by superposition as in [39].
- Attractive "restoring" forces based on penalties for exceeding the maximum allowable communication distance between two nodes i and j: $F_{restore}(i, j) = u_{ij}(r_j - r_i)$.
- Information forces that depend on the gradient of the uncertainty measure, $F_{inf} = -\frac{\partial \|P_k^T(r)P_k(r)\|}{\partial r}$, where $P_k(r)$ is the uncertainty measure for sampling calculated via the closed form or the Kalman Filter.

After the force calculation, the equation of motion for the i-th MWSN node will be given by integrating a simple mass-damper model over time: $m_i\ddot{r}_i + v_i\dot{r}_i = F_i$, where m and v are mass and damping terms respectively. These coefficients have no physical meaning, but they are used to define a dynamic equation of motion for the system in the direction of the gradient of a global potential field function consisting of obstacles, goal locations, network utility, and information gain. At each adaptive sampling step, the motion of the robots stops when a minimum potential configuration is reached. A summary of the potential field deployment algorithm is shown below:

Potential Field Sensor Node Repositioning Algorithm (POT-1)

Assumptions: The bandwidth between two nodes in the network is governed by a known path-loss model. The N sensor nodes are positioned within a 2D or 3D spatial domain $\ominus$ and do not have positional uncertainty. We assume that an ad hoc WSN routing algorithm is available. Constant $\varepsilon > 0$ is given, and a fixed number of iterations N_0 is chosen.

Step1 (initialize): Assume starting mobile sensor locations X_0. Assume that a table look-up is available and stored for the forces generated by optimal network flow in the 3 and 4 node network models shown in section 3.1. This table look-up contains information on the potential field force acting on a "middle" node or an "end" node in these two simple networks, given the relative location of the nodes. Examples of look-up tables for the 3 and 4 node networks are shown in Figures 7(a), (b).

Step2: Increase the iteration count $k = k + 1$.

Step3: For each node I, do:

- Consider each of the routes J passing through it that connects a sensor node to the network sink.
- If node I is not a terminal node:
  - Consider the nodes $I1$ — preceding I along the route, and $I2$ — following node I along the same route.
  - Calculate the node force acting on I based on a previously computed $I1 - I - I2$ middle node network model.
- If node I is a terminal node (first node along the route):
  - Consider the node $I2$ — following node along route J.
  - Calculate the node force acting on I based on a previously computed $I - I2$ end node network model.
- Add all the forces resulting from routes passing through node I to determine the overall communication force F_{commI}.

Step4: For each node I the forces generated by the goals, obstacles, restoring forces, and information forces to find the overall force acting on node I.

Step5: For each node I Update the mobile position I based on a discretized version of mass-damper model differential equations.

Step6: If iteration number k is a multiple of No, perform a global rerouting to reflect the fact that the protocol may change the routing scheme as the sensor nodes reposition.

Step7: If the node positions change by less than the positive "small" scalar ε, exit, otherwise repeat Step2.

6.1 Considerations of energy consumption

Considerations of energy minimization are important in ensuring the maximum lifetime of the MWSN. In a typical mobile robot equipped with a wireless radio, the node energy consumption due to computation is measured in the microwatt range, to communication in mW to hundreds of mW range, and to motion in hundreds of mW to tens of W range. The larger the size of the robot, the more likely it is for the motion energy expended to exceed the energy required by communications, and vice-versa. One way to reduce the energy consumption is by making the node damping coefficients vary with the amount of energy expended:

$$v_i(t) = v_0(1 + k_{v_i} E_i(t)), E_i(t) = \int_0^t F_i(\tau)\dot{r}_i(\tau)d\tau. \tag{15}$$

If the robot node damping increases with expended motion energy, or alternatively, it decreases with the amount of on-board energy available, the robot speed decreases accordingly. As a result the node can remain useful as a network node.

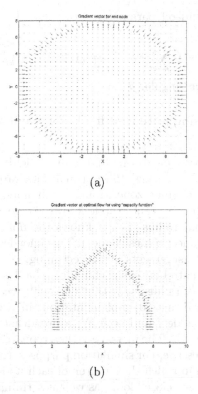

(a)

(b)

Fig. 7. 2D force fields indicating communication forces on the end-node for a simple 3-node network (a), and on the "middle" node for a simple 4-node network. The plots were obtained for $\alpha = 2$, $r_{min} = 2$, $r_{zone} = 8$ in equation (3) by numerically solving the capacity optimization problem and differentiating to obtain the force.

We can also tie the cost of node movement with the information measures while sampling by noting that the covariance measure P_k behaves like an energy. Suppose that battery usage is proportional to the distance moved according to a spring constant such as $F = W\triangle x$. Then more energy is used as $(x_{k+1} - x_k)$ increases. Therefore, define predicted work needed to go to the next predicted state as:

$$\hat{M}_{k+1} = (\hat{X}_{k+1}^- - X_k)^T W (\hat{X}_{k+1}^- - X_k) \qquad (16)$$

where stiffness weighting matrix W can be used to select only the vehicle states x_k and not the parameters a_k, which do not contribute to motion energy needed. We can then move to the state that minimizes the weighed cost

$$E_{k+1} = \alpha \hat{M}_{k+1} + (1 - \alpha) tr(P_{k+1}^T P_{k+1})$$

with α a weighting tradeoff parameter. Note that if the SVD of P is $P = U \sum V^T$, then

$$tr(P^T P) = tr(V \sum {}^2 V^T) = tr(VV^T \sum {}^2) = tr(\sum {}^2),$$

which is the sum of the singular values.

6.2 EXAMPLE: Using potential fields for navigation and communication

Simulations of navigation based on the potential fields were run using Zone Routing Protocol (ZRP) routing [19], optimal data rates, and attractive 2D goals. ZRP creates a circular zone around each node of radius parameter r_{zone}. Within each zone, the center node knows the geographical topology of the network within that radius (i.e., it knows the nodes located inside that perimeter and the distance to these nodes). This knowledge could be based on triangulation range measurements, dead reckoning, cooperative localization, etc. Finding a routing path between each node and a destination node is based on overlapping circles of radius r_{zone} that eventually lead to the discovery of the destination node. In actual implementation, in order to determine the routing path between node I and node N, a broadcast message is sent from node I within its own r_{zpne}. The message is then repeated until the destination node N receives the message. For simulation purposes, routes are chosen based on a depth first search in which the children of each node are the nodes inside r_{zpne}, and by not allowing closed loops as well as terminated routes with more than m ($m = 8$) hops to destination.

Figure 8(a) shows the beginning of a 20-node simulation run, generated after the nodes have been placed randomly and the routing completed, but before goals have been selected, with node 20 being a network sink, or data collection node. In figure 8(b), a goal location of (7,8) is selected and a $T = 0.01$ Euler-step discretization of the potential field equations is to run for 100 iterations. The nodes within communication range of the goal are being attracted to the goal location in order to collect samples at that location. A bar graph records the energy consumed by each node. The simulation results show that:

• Rerouting, forced after a limited number of iterations ($No = 10$), significantly alters the network routes if the nodes are moving.

• The nodes that are not involved with goal attainment or routing of sensory data from the robots near the goal will drift towards the terminating node (node 20 at located at (0,0)), unless they are assigned different sampling missions.

• The damping coefficient affects goal attainment as well as the individual energy consumption per node. Small damping values will lead to high energy consumption rates, while high damping values will prevent nodes from reaching the goals. A trade-off value of damping was found experimentally to provide the final configuration in Figure 8(b).

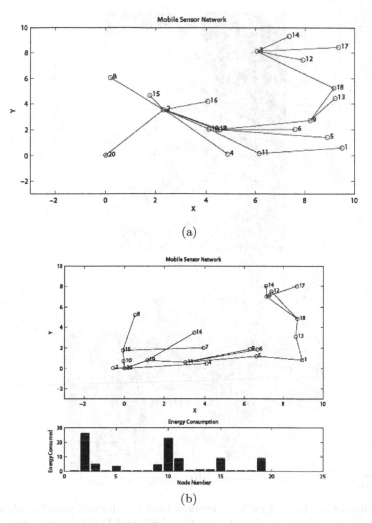

(a)

(b)

Fig. 8. Motion of a 20 node network after 100 iterations, under a potential field that optimizes the data rate through the network and repositions to sample at goal location (7.8).

7 Conclusions and Future Work

The algorithms described in this chapter, in particular the EKF (AS-3) and potential fields (POT-1), provide a strategy for systematic exploration of unknown environments using MWSN. The robot nodes are directed to sample at locations that most reduce the uncertainty in our knowledge of the field distribution. At the same time, they are constrained by attractive potentials to maintain a network with optimized data rates. Future work includes experimental work to validate the proposed algorithms on nonlinear and time-

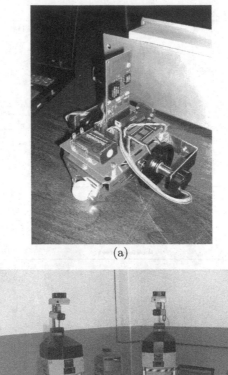

(a)

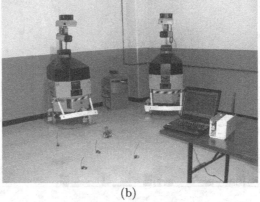

(b)

Fig. 9. Inexpensive Rover Unit for color-based indoor adaptive sampling algorithm validation testbed (top) and CyberGuard SR2/ESP, and MICA Xbow motes on the lab floor at ARRI's WSN Lab(bottom).

varying field distributions, using proper kinematic and dynamic vehicle models, multiple vehicles, and secondary optimization objectives such as energy resources and communication bandwidth. The research described here is coordinated with larger efforts in environmental sensing and monitoring related to rivers, and coastal areas [40]. Furthermore, a fleet of several inexpensive mobile sensor network nodes is currently being operated at ARRI's WSN lab, as part of a larger testbed composed of larger CyberGuard SR2/ESP robots and wireless Xbow motes to study WSN deployment algorithms using mobile robots (Figure 9).

References

1. P. Aarabi, Self-localizing dynamic microphone arrays, IEEE Transactions on Systems, Man and Cybernetics, Part C, Vol. 32, pp. 474−484, Nov., 2002.
2. Ronald C. Arkin, Behavior-Based Robotics (Intelligent Robotics and Autonomous Agents), MIT Press, May 22, 1998.
3. A. Bennet, Inverse Modeling of the Ocean and Atmosphere, Cambridge Press, 2002.
4. Brink, K.H., Observational coastal oceanography, Advances and Primary Research Opportunities in Physical Oceanography Studies, (APROPOS) Workshop, NSF-sponsored workshop on the Future of Physical Oceanography, 15–17 December, 1997.
5. D. R. Blidberg, The development of autonomous underwater vehicles (AUV); a brief summary, in Proceedings of the IEEE International Conference on Robotics and Automation (ICRA), Seoul, Korea, May, 2000.
6. W. Burgard, M. Moors, D. Fox, R. Simmons, and S. Thrun., Collaborative multi-robot exploration, in Proc. of IEEE International Conferenceon Robotics and Automation, volume 1, pages 476–81, 2000.
7. Y. Cao, A. Fukunaga, and A. Kahng, Cooperative mobile robotics: Antecedents and directions, Autonomous Robots, vol. 4, pp. 7–27, 1997.
8. J. Chen, L. Yip, J. Elson, H. Wang, D. Maniezzo, R. Hudson, K. Yao, D. Estrin, Coherent acoustic array processing and localization on wireless sensor networks, in Proceedings of the IEEE, vol. 91, pp. 1154–1162, August, 2003.
9. J. Cortes, S. Martinez, T. Karatas, and F. Bullo, Coverage control for mobile sensor networks, in IEEE Trans. On Robotics and Automation, 2002.
10. Curtin, T.B., J.G. Bellingham, J. Catipovic and D. Webb, Autonomous ocean sampling networks, Oceanography, 6(3), pp. 86–94, 1993.
11. D. Estrin, et al. Embedded Everywhere, a Research Agenda for Networked Systems of Embedded Computers. Landover, MD: Computer Science and Telecommunications Board, National Research Council, National Academy Press, 2001.
12. J. Fenwick, P. Newman, and J. Leonard, Cooperative concurrent mapping and localization, in Proc. IEEE Int. Conf. On Robotics and Automation, pp. 1810–1817, Washington, D.C., May, 2002.
13. D. W. Gage., Command control for many-robot systems, in AUVS-92, the Nineteenth Annual AUVS Technical Symposium, pages 22-24, Hunstville Alabama, USA, June 1992. Reprinted in Unmanned Systems Magazine, Fall 1992, Volume 10, Number 4, pp. 28–34.
14. Glenn, S.M., G.Z. Forristall, P. Cornillon and G. Milkowski, 1990. Observations of Gulf Stream Ring 83-E and Their Interpretation Using Feature Models, Journal of Geophysical Research, 95, 13,043–13,063.
15. J. Cox, An experiment in guidance and navigation of an autonomous robot vehicle, IEEE Transactions on Robotics and Automation, vol. 7, pp. 193–204, April, 1991.
16. H. F. Durrant-Whyte, Sensor models and multisensor integration, Int. J. Robotics Research, vol. 7, pp. 97–113, 1988. [17] Creed, E.L., S.M. Glenn and R. Chant, "Adaptive Sampling Experiment at LEO-15", 1998.
17. P. Gupta, and P.R. Kumar, The Capacity of Wireless Networks, in IEEE Transactions on Information Theory, vol. 46, No.2, March 2000.
18. Z. J. Haas, A new routing protocol for the reconfigurable wireless networks, in IEEE International Conference on Universal Personal Computing, 1997.

19. A. T. Hayes, A. Martinoli, and R. M. Goodman Distributed Odor Source Lo-
    calization, in IEEE Sensors Journal, Vol. 2, No. 3, June 2002.
20. A. Howard, M. J. Mataric, and G. S. Sukhatme, An incremental Self-Deployment
    Algorithm for Mobile Sensor Networks, in Autonomous Robots 13, pp. 113–126,
    2002.
21. N. Hutin, C. Pegard, E. Brassart, A Communication Strategy for Cooperative
    Robots, in Proc. 1998 IEEE/RSJ Int'l Cong. On Intelligent Robots and Systems",
    Oct. 1998.
22. Y. Koten and J. Borenstein Potential Field Methods and Their Inherent Lim-
    itations for Mobile Robot Navigation, in Proc. Of International Conference on
    Robotics and Automation, 1991.
23. O. Khatib Real-time obstacle avoidance for manipulators and mobile robots, in
    Proc. Of International Conference on Robotics and Automation, 1985.
24. V. Kumar G. A. S. Pereira, A. K. Das and M. F. M. Campos, Decentralized
    motion planning for multiple robots subject to sensing and communications con-
    straints, in Proceedings of the Second Multi Robot Systems Workshop, 2003.
25. B. H. Krogh, A generalized potential field approach to obstacle avoidance con-
    trol, in Robotics Research: The Next Five Years and Beyond, Society of Manu-
    facturing Engineers, 1984.
26. J. Latombe, Robot Motion Planning, Kluwer Academic Publishers, MA, 1991.
27. F.L. Lewis, Optimal Estimation with an Introduction to Stochastic Control
    Theory, John Wiley and Sons, New York, 1986.
28. D. Li, K. Wong, Y. Hu, A. Sayeed, Detection, classification, and tracking of
    targets, IEEE Signal Processing Magazine, pp. 17–29, March, 2002.
29. M. Mataric, Issues and approaches in the design of collective autonomous agents,
    Robotics and Autonomous Systems, vol. 16, pp. 321–331, December, 1995.
30. M. J. Mataric A. Howard and G. S. Sukhatme, Mobile sensor network deploy-
    ment using potential fields: A distributed, scalable solution to the area coverage
    problem, in Proceedings of the 6th Int'l Symposium on Distributed Autonomous
    Robotics Systems, 2002.
31. F. Michaud and E. Robichaud, Sharing charging stations for long-term activity
    of autonomous robots, in Proc. IEEE International Conference on Intelligent
    Robots and Systems, 2002.
32. P. Newman, On The Structure and Solution of the Simultaneous Localisation
    and Map Building Problem. PhD thesis, University of Sydney, Australian Centre
    for Field Robotics, 1999.
33. R. Chatila and J.-P. Laumond, Position referencing and consistent world mod-
    eling for mobile robots., in Proc. IEEE Int. Conf. Robotics and Automation, pp.
    138–145, 1985.
34. F. Paganini S.H. Low and J. C. Doyle, Internet congestion control, in IEEE
    Control Systems Magazine, 2002.
35. L. E. Parker, B. Kannan, X. Fu, and Y. Tang, Heterogeneous Mobile Sensor
    Net Deployment Using Robot Herding and Line-of-Sight Formations, in Proc. of
    IEEE International Conference on Intelligent Robots and Systems, 2003.
36. S. Poduri and G. S. Sukhatme, Constrained Coverage for Mobile Sensor Net-
    works, in Proc. IEEE Int. Conf. Robotics and Automation, New Orleans, LA,
    April, 2004.
37. D. Popa, J. Wen, Nonholonomic Path-Planning with Obstacle avoidance, in
    Proc. Int'l Conference in Robotics and Automation, Minneapolis, April 1996.

38. D. Popa, C. Helm, H. E. Stephanou, A. Sanderson, Robotic Deployment of Sensor Networks using Potential Fields, in Proc. Of International Robotics and Automation Conference, April-May 2004.

39. D. Popa, A. Sanderson, R. Komerska, S. Mupparapu, R. Blidberg, S. Chappel, Adaptive Sampling Algorithms for Multiple Autonomous Underwater Vehicles, in Proc. of 2004 Workshop on Underwater Vehicles, Sebasco Estates, ME, June 2004.

40. D. Popa, K. Sreenath, and F.L. Lewis, Robotic Deployment for Environmental Sampling Applications, in Proc. Int'l Conf. on Control Applications, Budapest, June 2005.

41. A. Pandya, A. Kansal, G. Pottie, and M. Srivastava, "Bounds on the Rate Distortion of Multiple Cooperative Gaussian Sources", Center for Embedded Networked Sensing (CENS) Technical Report 0027, Sept. 2003.

42. M. Rahimi, R. Pon, W. J. Kaiser, G. S. Sukhatme, D. Estrin, and M. Srivastava, Adaptive Sampling for Environmental Robotics, Proc. IEEE Int. Conf. Robotics and Automation, New Orleans, LA, April, 2004.

43. J. Ren and K. A. McIsaac, A Hybrid-Systems Approach to Potential Field Navigation for a Multi-Robot Team, in Proc. Of International Conference on Robotics and Automation, Taipei, Taiwan, 2003.

44. E. Rimon, D. Koditscheck, Exact Robot Navigation using Artificial Potential Functions, in IEEE Trans. On Robotics and Automation, Vol. 8, No. 5, October 1992.

45. A. C. Sanderson, Multirobot navigation using cooperative teams, Distributed Autonomous Robotic Systems 2, Berlin, Springer-Verlag, Asama et al., eds., pp. 389–400, 1998.

46. R. Simmons, D. Apfelbaum, W. Burgard, D. Fox, M. Moors, S. Thrun, and H. Younes, Coordination for multi-robot exploration and mapping, in Proc. of the Seventeenth National Conference on Artificial Intelligence (AAAI-2000), pages 852–858, 2000.

47. B. Sinopoli, C. Sharp, L. Schenato, S. Schaffert, S. Shastry, Distributed control applications within sensor networks, in Proceedings of the IEEE, vol. 91, pp. 1225–1246, August, 2003.

48. R. Smith and P. Cheeseman, On the estimation and representation of spatial uncertainty, Int. J. Robotics Research, vol. 5, Winter, 1987.

49. J. Tan, N. Xi, W. Sheng, and J. Xiao, Modeling Multiple Robot Systems for Area Coverage and Cooperation, in Proc. IEEE Int. Conf. Robotics and Automation, New Orleans, LA, April, 2004.

50. P. Vandakkepat, K.C. Tan, et.al., Evolutionary Artificial Potential Fields and Their Applications to Real-Time Robotic Path-Planning, in Proc. Of IEEE Congress on Evolutionary Computing, 2000.

51. D. Vail and M. Veloso, Dynamic Multi-Robot Coordination, Multi-Robot Systems, Kluwer 2003.

52. W. Ye, J. Heindemann, D. Estrin, An Energy-Efficient MAC Protocol for Wireless Sensor Networks, in Proc. of INFOCOM 2002.

53. Y. Yu, R. Govindan, D. Estrin, Geographical and energy aware routing: a recursive data dissemination protocol for wireless sensor networks, UCLA CS Department Technical Report, CSD-TR-01-0023, May, 2001.

54. J. T. Wen and M. Arcak, A unifying passivity framework for network control, IEEE Trans. on Automatic Control, vol.2, pp. 1156–1166, March, 2003.

55. F. Zhao, J. Liu, J. Liu, L. Guibas, J. Reich, Collaborative signal and information processing: an information-directed approach, in Proceedings of the IEEE, vol. 91, pp. 1199–1209, August, 2003.
56. F. Zhao, J. Shin, J. Reich, Information-driven dynamic sensor collaboration, IEEE Signal Processing Magazine, pp. 61–72, March, 2002.
57. Y. Zou and K. Chakrabarty, Sensor Deployment and Target Localization Based On Virtual Forces, in Proc. of IEEE INFOCOMM, 2003.
58. R. Bachmayer and N. E. Leonard, Vehicle Networks for a Gradient Descent in a Sampled Environment, in Proceedings of the 41st IEEE Conference on Decision and Control, December 2002.

Chapter 3
A Scalable Graph Model and Coordination Algorithms for Mobile Sensor Networks

Jindong Tan

Department of Electrical and Computer Engineering
Michigan Technological University, Houghton, MI 49931
jitan@mtu.edu

1 Introduction

A mobile sensor network consists of a collection of wireless connected mobile robots equipped with a variety of sensors, as shown in Figure 1. In such a system, each mobile robot has sensing, computation, communication, and locomotion capabilities. The mobile robots spread out across certain areas and share sensory information through an ad hoc wireless network. A mobile sensor network is therefore a wireless sensor network with reconfigurable sensing capabilities [14], [22]. Mobile sensor networks have a myriad of civilian and military applications ranging from foraging, surveillance, search and rescue to mobile target tracking. A mobile sensor network can be rapidly deployed in hostile environments, inaccessible terrains or disaster relief operations for sensing and reconnaissance tasks, where a task is generally achieved by coordination of the robots' activities. The variety of task specifications and the ever-changing environment require the control algorithms of the reconfigurable mobile sensor network to be flexible, scalable and adaptive. This chapter presents a distributed model and algorithms for locally optimized control of mobile sensor networks. Multi-robot coordination and formation control is addressed to the continuous reconfiguration of the mobile robots for varying task requirements and changing environments.

A mobile sensor network augments the capacity of a sensor network with motion, which enhances its collaborative sensing, coverage, reliability and flexibility. A number of mobile sensor deployment algorithms have been proposed, such as the incremental deployment approach [22], potential field approach [23], [38], constrained coverage [34], and Voronoi based approach with known distributions [14]. A reactive approach discusses the deployment of mobile sensors in response to dynamic events [10]. A control strategy for mobile sensor networks to track sensing gradient to is discussed in [30]. Among others, mobile sensor networks have found applications in exploration [3] and network maintenance [13], [12]. On the interaction between sensor networks and mobile robots, robot task allocation and navigation have recently been discussed [5], [4], [11], [26].

A mobile sensor network is simultaneously a multi-robot system. Based on the vision that multiple robots have the potential to perform a task faster, and more efficiently than a single robot [32], cooperation and formation control of multiple robots has been emerging as an important research area [20], [24], [32]. Robot control structures for cooperation of multiple robots, such as the subsumption structure [7], reactive control and hybrid control [9], and behavior-based control [2], [28] have been proposed in the literature. Behavior based robotics [2] coordinates multiple robots based on a collection of behaviors, which are processes or control laws that achieve and/or maintain goals. Sophisticated cooperative behavior based on both perception and symbolic communication, which is common in primates, has also drawn researchers' attention in the cooperation of mobile sensor networks. Pheromone robotics utilizes the biologically inspired pheromone phenomena to coordinate the actions of a large number of robots [33]. Our previous work addresses the integrated task planning, sensing and control of robot systems based on a perceptive reference frame approach [36].

The combination of graph theory and decentralized control for cooperation of multiple robots is receiving more attention [15], [17]. A wireless network of mobile robots can be modeled as an undirected graph or a directed graph [37], [19], [17]. Graph theory has also been used in the network coverage and sensor deployment for static sensor networks [29]. Mobile robot sensor deployment based on graph theory for area coverage has also been discussed [22], [23]. In [30], the cooperative control of a vehicle network is discussed using virtual bodies and artificial potentials. In [15] and [21], a controlled graph is presented for a group of mobile robots to organize themselves into and to maintain a desired formation shape. In [10], an event based approach is discussed for dynamic coverage of a mobile sensor network. This work is also motivated by [14] in which a deployment algorithm based on Voronoi diagrams is discussed. The approach proposed in this work uses the Delaunay triangulation as the data structure which avoids the computation of Voronoi diagrams. A mobile robot coordinates with only its one-hop neighbors, defined by the Delaunay triangulation, but a global objective can be achieved. The topology of the mobile sensor network is subject to change with respect to different environments and task specifications.

One of the objectives for a mobile sensor network is to reconfigure the robot position and maximize sensing capabilities in both constrained and unconstrained areas. Area coverage and sensor deployment problems have been discussed in a variety of static sensor networks, such as [8], [29]. However, only limited work has been published on sensor deployment approaches for coordinated area coverage problems of mobile sensor networks [10], [22]. This chapter suggests a distributed graph model for dynamic coverage in a mobile sensor network. The graph model defines the geographical relationship using Delaunay triangulation where the motion of a robot is only related to its immediate one-hop neighbors and its environment. Based on this distributed model, virtual potential field method [23], [25] is combined with the Delaunay triangulation to develop the distributed autonomous deployment algorithm for a multiple robots system. The algorithms are proven to be globally convergent

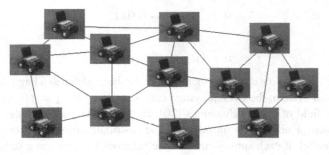

Fig. 1. In a mobile sensor network, each mobile robot is equipped with sensing, communication, computation capabilities for a wireless mobile sensor network.

and robust to robot failures. The algorithms are extended to the tracking control of nonholonomic robot systems. Formation control of the mobile sensor network is further discussed. The formation control algorithms allow a mobile sensor network to sweep larger areas along specified paths.

2 Distributed Graph Model

2.1 Mobile Robot Model

The mobile sensor network in this chapter is given by n mobile robots, as shown in Figure 1. The mobile robots, denoted by $\mathcal{R} = \{R_1, R_2, \cdots, R_n\}$, are deployed on a planar space. The configuration of robot R_i is denoted by $\mathbf{q}_i(t) = [x_i, y_i, \theta_i]$, $i = 1, 2, \ldots, n$. where x_i and y_i are the coordinates of robot R_i and θ_i is the orientation of the robot with respect to its local coordinate system. The dynamics of mobile robot R_i can be described by $\dot{\mathbf{q}}_i = f_i(\mathbf{q}_i, \mathbf{u}_i)$, where $\mathbf{u}_i$ is the control input of subsystem R_i.

In this chapter, the discussion is based on both the holonomic model and the nonholonomic model of a mobile robot. The holonomic model of the robot can be described as:

$$
\begin{aligned}
\dot{x}_i &= v_{ix}, \\
\dot{y}_i &= v_{iy}, \\
\dot{v}_{ix} &= u_{i1}, \\
\dot{v}_{iy} &= u_{i2},
\end{aligned}
\tag{1}
$$

where v_{ix} and v_{iy} are the translational velocities along x and y direction in its local coordinate system, respectively. In this model, the control input $\mathbf{u}_i$ is defined as: $\mathbf{u}_i = \{u_{i1}, u_{i2}\}^T$.

2.2 Delaunay triangulation and network model

The configuration and control input of the entire system can then be denoted by

$$q = \{q_1, q_2, \ldots, q_n\}^T$$

and

$$u = \{u_1, u_2, \ldots, u_n\}^T$$

respectively. The multiple robotic vehicle system can be modeled as a large-dimensional interconnected system, the overall system can be denoted by $\dot{q} = f(q, u)$, where f is the vector field of system dynamics [20]. In the chapter, a distributed model for the mobile sensor network is introduced. The distributed model has two parts: the dynamical model of each subsystem, and the relationship between a subsystem and its neighboring robots.

To facilitate the definition of a global objective of the mobile sensor network, $\tilde{p}_i = \{\tilde{x}_i(t), \tilde{y}_i(t)\}^T$ is defined as the position of the robot R_i in a unified inertial coordinate system, and $\tilde{p} = \{\tilde{p}_1, \tilde{p}_2, \ldots, \tilde{p}_n\}^T$ is the position of the mobile sensor network in a unified inertial coordinate system. We further define that $p_i = \{x_i(t), y_i(t)\}^T$ is the coordinate frame of robot R_i in its local coordinate frame.

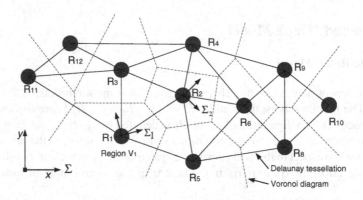

Fig. 2. Delaunay triangulation and Voronoi diagram.

The neighborhood relationship between robot nodes is defined by two graphs, a Delaunay tessellation and a Voronoi diagram [16], as shown in Figure 2. Given an open set $\Omega \subseteq \mathbb{R}^n$, the Delaunay tessellation is a triangulation of the space based on a set of points $\tilde{p} = \{\tilde{p}_1, \tilde{p}_2, \ldots, \tilde{p}_n\}^T$ [14], [29]. The Delaunay triangulation with a set of nodes $\tilde{p}$ is defined such that any additional edge between any two nodes intersects one of the existing edges. The robot R_i is also called a *generator*. The Voronoi diagram and the Delaunay triangulation are dual to each other in a planar space.

In the graph, the nodes that are directly connected to node R_i are called the one-hop neighbors of R_i. The Delaunay triangulation defines the link properties between one-hop neighbors, which are defined by a set of edges $E = \{d_{i\text{-}j}(t), i, j = 1, 2, \ldots, n, i \neq j\}$. The distance between one-hop neighbors, $d_{i\text{-}j}$, can be estimated by using local positioning systems or global positioning systems.

In a large scale system, a huge amount of communication and computation is required to calculate the Delaunay Triangulation. In a distributed system, it is desirable to use a localized algorithm for the graph model [1], [27], [35]. Each robot calculate its own local Delaunay Triangulation by communicating only with the nodes within its communication range. The robots may construct different Delaunay triangulation locally because of the limited visibility or communication ranges. The union of local Delaunay triangulations is a superset of the Delaunay triangulation. A robot communicates with other robots to eliminate the inconsistent edges. A circumcircle test by communicating with neighboring robots will eliminate the inconsistency edges and generate a Partial Delaunay Triangulations(PDT). As shown in Figure 3, some edges are lost in partial Delaunay triangulation due to the visibility of communication. In [35], a simple test is used to generate partial Delaunay triangulation locally. Instead of using a circumcircle formed by the three robots on a triangle, a circumcircle formed by the two robots on each edge of a triangle is used. This approach uses a stricter test and yields a subset of edges of the Delaunay triangulation. Note that this test is scalable because it can be accomplished with just one-hop communication. Figure 3 shows the Delaunay Triangulation and its corresponding partial Delaunay Triangulation based on the test in [35]. Correspondingly, a robot R_i's one-hop neighbor are the robots that are directly connected to R_i in PDT. All the following discussion and algorithms are applicable for both Delaunay triangulation and partial Delaunay triangulation.

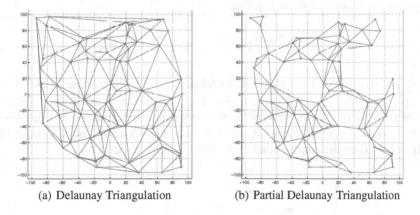

(a) Delaunay Triangulation   (b) Partial Delaunay Triangulation

Fig. 3. Comparison of Delaunay Triangulation and partial Delaunay Triangulation for the same set of generators.

Motivated by the adjacency matrix for a mobile sensor network [19], an *adjacency matrix*, $A(t)$, is defined to specify the connectivity of the Delaunay tessellation. $A(t)$ is a square matrix which is uniquely defined by the Delaunay triangulation. Here $A_{ij} = d_{i\_j}$ if R_i and R_j are one-hop neighbors, otherwise $A_{ij} = 0$. The ith column of $A(t)$, denoted by $\mathbf{d}(t) = \{d_{i\_1}, d_{i\_2}, \ldots, d_{i\_n}\}^T$, defines the link properties of R_i and its one-hop neighboring robots. For example, robot R_2 in Figure 2 has six neighbors, which form subgraph of the Delaunay triangulation. For a cooperation task, the motion of robot R_2 is only affected by its immediate one-hop neighbors.

The robot model considering its one-hop neighbors can be described as:

$$\dot{\mathbf{q}}_i = f_i(\mathbf{q}_i, \mathbf{u}_i),$$
$$\mathbf{u}_i = h_i(\mathbf{p}_{i1}, \mathbf{p}_{i2}, \ldots, \mathbf{p}_{ik}), \tag{2}$$

where $\mathbf{p}_{i1}, \mathbf{p}_{i2}, \ldots, \mathbf{p}_{ik}$ are the positions of the one-hop neighbors $R_1, R_2, \ldots, R_k \in K_i \subseteq R$ in the coordinate frame of robot R_i, Σ_i.

3 Self-deployment Algorithm

3.1 Autonomous Deployment

In a mobile sensor network, the robot can cooperate to perform spatially distributed tasks such as distributed sensing or cooperative manipulation. One of the objectives of robot cooperation in such a system is to maximize the coverage area of the network, for example, an incremental approach and a potential field approach have been introduced [22]. In the present paper, a distributed self-deployment algorithm is proposed based on both the potential field method and the Delaunay triangulation.

For a mobile robot R_i in the mobile sensor network, a performance index(candidate Lyapunov function) is defined as follows:

$$V_i = \frac{1}{2} \sum_{j=1}^{m_i} k_i(\|\mathbf{p}_{ij}\| - c_{i\_j})^2 + \frac{1}{2} k_{iv} \|\mathbf{v}_i\|^2, \tag{3}$$

where $\mathbf{p}_{ij}$ is a vector from robot R_i to robot R_j in the coordinate frame of R_i, and $\|\mathbf{p}_{ij}\| = \sqrt{(x_i - x_j)^2 + (y_i - y_j)^2}$ and c_{i_j} are the actual and desired distance between the two robots respectively. m_i is the total number of the one-hop neighbors of R_i. k_i and k_{iv} are parameters for the virtual potential energy and kinetic energy of the robot. Then the control input of the robot R_i is derived by:

$$
\begin{aligned}
\mathbf{u}_i &= -\frac{\partial V_i}{\partial \mathbf{p}_i} - \frac{\partial V_i}{\partial \mathbf{v}_i} \\
&= -\sum_{j=1}^{m_i} k_i(\|\mathbf{p}_{i\_j}\| - c_{i\_j})\frac{\mathbf{p}_{i\_j}}{\|\mathbf{p}_{i\_j}\|} - k_{iv}\mathbf{v}_i \\
&= -F_i - k_{iv}\mathbf{v}_i,
\end{aligned} \tag{4}
$$

where $F_i = \{F_{ix}, F_{iy}\}$ is the virtual potential force generated by the one-hop neighbors of R_i. Here

$$F_i = \sum_{j=1}^{m_i} k_i(\|\mathbf{p}_{i\_j}\| - c_{i\_j})\frac{\mathbf{p}_{i\_j}}{\|\mathbf{p}_{i\_j}\|}. \tag{5}$$

If all the other robots but R_i are static, it is easy to prove that the above controller is globally convergent. Considering the mobile sensor network as a single system, the performance index in terms of the total kinetic and virtual potential energy of the system can be described as

$$V = \sum_{i=1}^{n} V_i = \frac{1}{2} \sum_{i=1}^{n} \sum_{j=1}^{m_i} k_i (\|\mathbf{p}_{ij}\| - c_{i\_j})^2 + \frac{1}{2} \sum_{i=1}^{n} \|\mathbf{v}_i\|^2. \tag{6}$$

The control input vector $\mathbf{u}$ of the mobile sensor network is derived based on the total energy function V. The virtual force F_i of robot R_i considering the entire system is derived by:

$$\frac{\partial V}{\partial \mathbf{p}_i} = \frac{\partial V_i}{\partial \mathbf{p}_i} + \sum_{j=1}^{m_i} \frac{\partial V_j}{\partial \mathbf{p}_i}$$

$$= \frac{\partial V_i}{\partial \mathbf{p}_i} + \sum_{j=1}^{m_i} k_j (\|\mathbf{p}_{j\_i}\| - c_{j\_i}) \frac{-\mathbf{p}_{j\_i}}{\|\mathbf{p}_{j\_i}\|}$$

$$= \frac{\partial V_i}{\partial \mathbf{p}_i} + \sum_{j=1}^{m_i} k_i (\|\mathbf{p}_{i\_j}\| - c_{i\_j}) \frac{\mathbf{p}_{i\_j}}{\|\mathbf{p}_{i\_j}\|}$$

$$= 2 \frac{\partial V_i}{\partial \mathbf{p}_i}.$$

Here we assume $k_i = k_j$. The control input for robot R_i considering the entire system can then be derived by:

$$\mathbf{u}_i = -\frac{\partial V}{\partial \mathbf{p}_i} - \frac{\partial V}{\partial \mathbf{v}_i}$$

$$= -\sum_{j=1}^{m_i} 2 k_i (\|\mathbf{p}_{i\_j}\| - c_{i\_j}) \frac{\mathbf{p}_{i\_j}}{\|\mathbf{p}_{i\_j}\|} + k_{iv} \mathbf{v}_i. \tag{7}$$

Since k_i is a control gain parameter, it is seen that the distributed controller eq. (4) and eq. (7) of robot R_i are essentially the same. We have therefore proved the global convergence of the mobile sensor network controller based on the virtual potential field and Delaunay triangulation method. The distributed controller of robot R_i based on its one-hop neighbors leads to the global convergence of the entire system.

3.2 Convergence Analysis with Topological Events

In a dynamic Delaunay triangulation, the location of the *generators* varies with respect to time. The shape of the triangulation is continuous with respect to the motion of the robots until *topological events* occur [31]. A topological event for a robot occurs when it loses a neighbor or gains a new neighbor. Four *generators* are cocircular [31] when a topological event occur. As shown in Figure 4, points A, B, C

and D are co-circular. Sufficiently small continuous changes of point A will lead to topological changes in the Delaunay triangulation. However, the topological changes only involve the swap of the triangles $\triangle ABD$ and $\triangle BCD$ to triangles $\triangle ABC$ and $\triangle ACD$. The perimeter of the polygon $ABCD$ is not changed, and the topological event does not affect the rest of the topological structure.

According to the definition of the virtual potential function, the continuity of V_i for a robot vehicle depends on the number of its neighbors. A drastic change occurs when it loses or gains a neighbor. The continuity of the virtual force is therefore affected by the topological events. The virtual potential energy and force have an abrupt change during the motion, which results in discontinuous motion trajectories. It can be explained by using Figure 4. Assuming the position of node A' and A'' are in a sufficiently small region of node A. The potential energy for node A' and A'' is denoted by $V_{A'}$ and $V_{A''}$ respectively. The link $A''C$ may significantly change the value of $V_{A''}$ and therefore the virtual force on node A. The stability of node A should be analyzed when a topological event occurs. In the following analysis, $V_{A'}$ and $V_{A''}$ represent the candidate Lyapunov functions for the left and right topology structure of Figure 4, which are denoted as topology A' and A'' respectively.

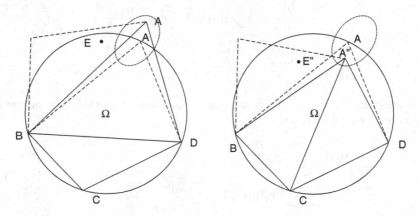

Fig. 4. A *topological event* occurs when a node loses or gains a neighbor.

In the following analysis, the co-circular region is denoted by Ω, the region outside of the circle is denoted by $\bar{\Omega}$. The two equilibrium points for candidate Lyapunov functions $V_{A'}$ and $V_{A''}$ are denoted by E' and E'' respectively. We have shown that the point A will converge to an equilibrium if there is no topological event. Node A will converge to E' under a controller derived by $V_{A'}$; it will converge to E'' under a controller obtained by $V_{A''}$, as shown in Figure 4. We further define a region δ which includes both equilibrium points E' and E'', as shown in Figure 5. Based on the definition of the candidate Lyapunov function (eq. 3) and the controller $\mathbf{u}_i$ in (eq. 4), it is seen that

$$\frac{\partial V_{A'}}{\partial t} < 0, \quad \frac{\partial V_{A''}}{\partial t} < 0; \quad \forall \, \mathbf{p}_i \in \Omega \cup \bar{\Omega} \backslash \delta. \tag{8}$$

In other words, for $\mathbf{p}_i, \mathbf{p}_j \in \Omega \cup \bar{\Omega}\backslash\delta$, if potential energy at point $\mathbf{p}_i$ is smaller than the potential energy at point $\mathbf{p}_j$ for topology A', i.e., $V_{A'}(\mathbf{p}_i, t) < V_{A'}(\mathbf{p}_j, t)$, then it is also true for topology A'', i.e., $V_{A''}(\mathbf{p}_i, t) < V_{A''}(\mathbf{p}_j, t)$.

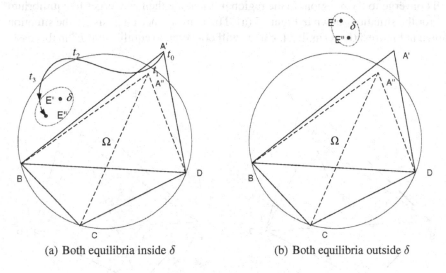

(a) Both equilibria inside δ (b) Both equilibria outside δ

Fig. 5. Convergence analysis with topological events.

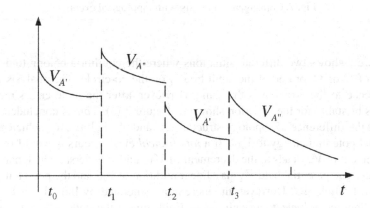

Fig. 6. Candidate Lyapunov functions in a switching system.

The location of the equilibrium is partially determined by the desired distance between neighboring nodes. Figure 5 shows two possible situations: both equilibria are inside or outside of the circular region Ω. For the situation shown in Figure 5 (a), we assume a candidate trajectory of the node which incurs topological events three times at time instance t_1, t_2 and t_3 respectively. $V_{A'}$ and $V_{A''}$ govern the motion of the node alternatively during the topological changes, as shown in Figure 6. It can be concluded that $V_{A''}(t_2^-) < V_{A''+}(t_1)$ and $V_{A'}(t_2^+) < V_{A'}(t_1^-)$. According to the multiple Lyapunov function method, the switching system is stable [6]. The node will converge to the δ region. In the region δ, the node then converges to equilibrium E'' for the situation shown in Figure 5 (a). The convergence analysis for the situation shown in Figure 5 (b) is similar, the node will converge to equilibrium E' in this case.

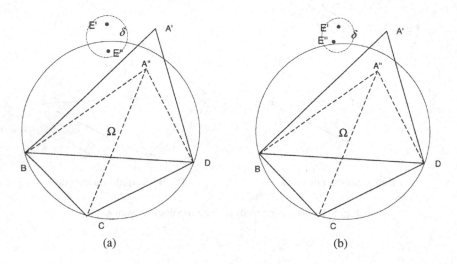

(a)   (b)

Fig. 7. Convergence analysis with topological events.

Figure 7 shows two different situations where the equilibria belong to different regions of Ω or $\bar{\Omega}$, or one of the equilibria is on the co-circle. The analysis for the convergence to the δ region is the same. However, after the node enters region δ, then it is bi-stable for the situation shown in Figure 7 (a). This is concluded by the fact that the difference of topology structure A' and A'' is link AC, which adds to additional potential energy to $V_{A''}$. If a *topological event* occurs inside of region δ, the increment of $V_{A'}$ leads to the decrement of $V_{A''}$ and vice versa, which may cause resonance. The potential field $V_{A''}$ is a linear addition of $V_{A'}$ and the potential energy generated by link AC. However, the increment generated by link AC is bounded, thus the *topological event* can only occur finite times; the node will enter a small region around E' or E'' and then converge. Depending on the initial position in region δ, it may converge to either equilibria. For the situation shown in Figure 7 (b), the equilibrium on the circle is an unstable equilibrium. The node will converge to another equilibrium. In summary, the convergence of the controller is guaranteed even with topological events.

3.3 Obstacles and Constrained Environments

The Delaunay triangulation-based, virtual potential field method can incorporate with constrained environments and dynamic obstacles. For an environment such as shown in Figure 8, additional links are added based on the sensor information of the robots. The additional links are used to define the virtual energy function for robot R_i. The energy of the system with obstacles can be described as:

$$V_i = \frac{1}{2} \sum_{j=1}^{m_i} k_{ij}(\|\mathbf{p}_{ij}\| - c_{i\_j})^2$$

$$+ \frac{1}{2} \sum_{l=1}^{m_o} k_{il}(\|\mathbf{p}_{i\_l}\| - c_{i\_l})^2,$$

where k_{il} is a parameter, m_o is the total number of obstacles in the sensing range of robot R_i, $\|\mathbf{p}_{i\_l}\|$ and c_{i_l} are the actual and the desired distance between the robot and an obstacle. It is worthing noting that the definition is still distributed. A robot R_i consider its one-hop neighbors and the obstacles in its own sensing range.

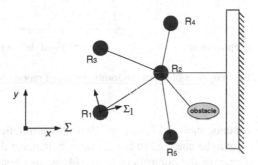

Fig. 8. Delaunay Triangulation in a constrained environment.

The virtual potential force of node R_i can then be derived as:

$$F_i = \frac{\partial V_i}{\partial \mathbf{p}_i} = \sum_{j=1}^{m_i} k_{ij}(\|\mathbf{p}_{i\_j}\| - c_{i\_j})\frac{\mathbf{p}_{i\_j}}{\|\mathbf{p}_{i\_j}\|} \tag{9}$$

$$+ \sum_{j=1}^{m_o} k_{il}(\|\mathbf{p}_{i\_l}\| - c_{i\_l})\frac{\mathbf{p}_{i\_l}}{\|\mathbf{p}_{i\_l}\|}.$$

The robot controller in the constrained environment can be developed based on the new virtual force.

4 Simulation Results

To test the effectiveness of the proposed distributed model and the algorithms, simulations in various situations have been conducted. This section discusses the simulation results of the proposed algorithms.

4.1 Autonomous deployment in open space

A group of seven mobile robots are randomly deployed in an open space. Figure 9 (a) shows the initial configuration of the system. Applying the distributed robot control in eq. (4) to each robot in the group, the system autonomously deploys itself. It is worth noting that the shape of the Delaunay triangulation changes during the deployment process. Some nodes gain neighbors and some lose neighbors.

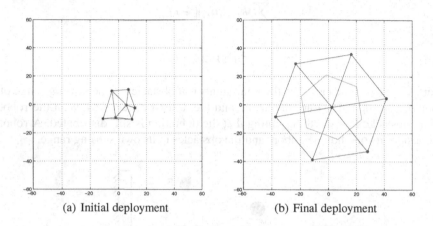

(a) Initial deployment   (b) Final deployment

Fig. 9. Self-Deployment of seven randomly deployed mobile robots.

In all these experiments, $k_i = 0.25$, $c_{i\_j} = 40$ in the simulation shown in Figure 9. The value of c_{i_j} can be changed to congregate or disperse the mobile sensor network. The convergence of the controllers in eq. (4) is also tested using a large number of robot nodes. Figure 11 shows the initial deployment and the configuration after the self-deployment. It is seen that the area of coverage by the system is greatly enlarged. The performance of the coverage under the distributed control law is evaluated using a centroidal Voronoi diagram. Figure 4.1 shows both the Delaunay triangulation and the Voronoi diagram. It is shown that the Voronoi diagram is a centroidal Voronoi diagram [18]. The centroidal Voronoi diagram is used for the quantization of planar space and evaluation of the coverage area [14], [18].

If the mobile robots are sparsely deployed in an open space, the algorithm can be used to congregate the mobile robots to cover a certain area. Figure 10 shows the deployment results when the mobile robots use Delaunay triangulation and partial Delaunay triangulation topological structure respectively, applying the controller in eq. (4). Both of these two topology structures can congregate the mobile robots to form a pattern similar to Figure 11(b). Thus, using the proposed algorithm, the mobile sensor network can either disperse or congregate the mobile robots in responding to the task requirements. When the partial Delaunay triangulation is used to define the topological structure, the final pattern is more dependent on the initial deployment because each robot considers only the positions of the robots within its communication range and some neighbors in Delaunay triangulation may not be counted when employing the algorithm.

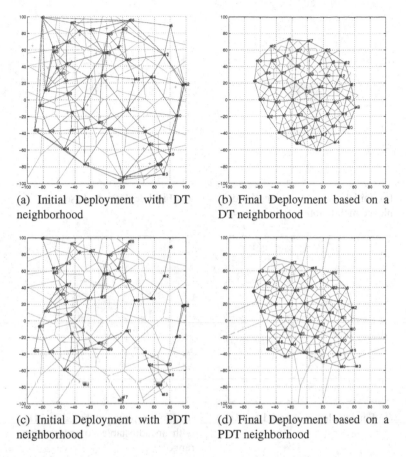

(a) Initial Deployment with DT neighborhood

(b) Final Deployment based on a DT neighborhood

(c) Initial Deployment with PDT neighborhood

(d) Final Deployment based on a PDT neighborhood

Fig. 10. Self-deployment of 50 mobile robots in an open space. Neighborhoods of the mobile robot are defined by DT and PDT respectively. The robots congregate into a small area to enhance the sensing capabilities.

In an initial deployment where the robots are aggregated within a small area, there are too many robots within each other's communication range, such as the situation in Figure 11(a). It introduces a significant computation and communication overhead to calculate a robot's Delaunay neighbors locally. To avoid this undesirable situation, each robot can adjust its own visibility of communication to reduce the overhead. As a matter of fact, a robot need only consider the closest robots in calculating its partial Delaunay triangulation. The simulation results for the algorithms based on a centralized Delaunay triangulation and a partial Delaunay triangulation with fixed communication range are shown in Figures 11(b) and (c). Figure 11(d) shows the simulation of the algorithm while the partial Delaunay triangulation is calculated when a small number of closest neighbors are considered.

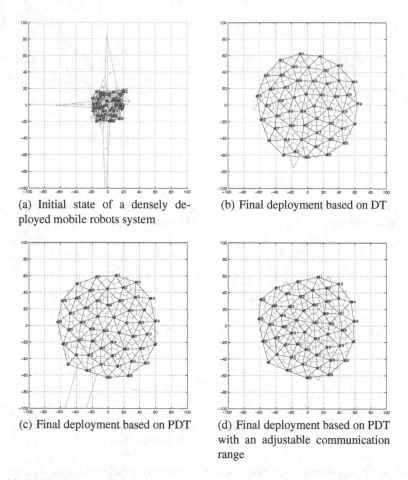

(a) Initial state of a densely deployed mobile robots system

(b) Final deployment based on DT

(c) Final deployment based on PDT

(d) Final deployment based on PDT with an adjustable communication range

Fig. 11. Self-deployment of 50 mobile robots in an open space; the robots disperse into a larger area based on DT, PDT and PDT with an adjustable communication range.

All the above simulations assume continuous communication among robots. However, in a real system, robots communicate with each other in a discrete and asynchronous fashion, i.e., they communicate only at certain rates. In this situation, robots can only execute the proposed algorithm in a discrete way. In the interval of two communications, the Delaunay triangulation may not be updated and therefore the controller defined in eq. (6) will not be updated. Figure 12 shows the simulation results under this condition with different definitions of topological structure. The initial deployment is the same with the one in Figure 10 (a). The final deployment patterns of the whole system are very similar to the ones shown in Figure 10(b) and

Figure 10(d) respectively. Note that if the communication interval is too long, the deployment algorithm may go unstable. The proposed algorithm can be employed in a real mobile sensor network with a carefully chosen communication rate which is proportional to robot velocity.

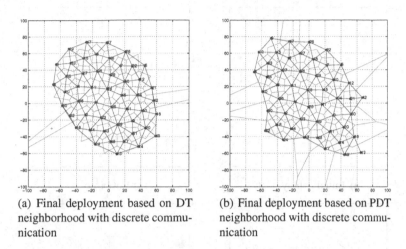

(a) Final deployment based on DT neighborhood with discrete communication

(b) Final deployment based on PDT neighborhood with discrete communication

Fig. 12. Final deployment of mobile robots with discrete communication.

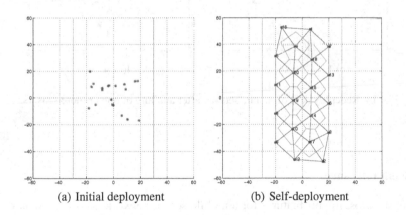

(a) Initial deployment   (b) Self-deployment

Fig. 13. Autonomous deployment of 20 mobile robots in a corridor.

4.2 Autonomous deployment in constrained space

Generally a mobile sensor network works in unstructured environments. Figure 13 shows an initial deployment of 20 mobile robots in a corridor and the final configuration of the system after the redeployment. Using the distributed controller, each robot in the group computes its virtual potential force based on its own neighbors and sensing of the obstacles.

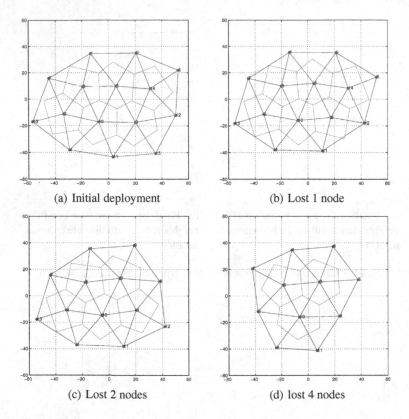

(a) Initial deployment   (b) Lost 1 node

(c) Lost 2 nodes   (d) lost 4 nodes

Fig. 14. Redeployment of mobile sensors after a failure of one or more sensors.

4.3 Fault tolerance

One of the most import features for a mobile sensor network is its redundancy and fault tolerance. If one or more robots fail, the other robots can redeploy their positions according to the requirement of the task. Figure 14 shows the validity of the deployment algorithm for this situation. Starting with a system configuration shown in Figure 14(a), Figures 14(b), (c) and (d) show the adjustment of the system after 1, 2, and 4 nodes are lost respectively. Under the deployment algorithm, the system can reorganize itself if some nodes fail. Figure 14 shows the Delaunay triangulation and Voronoi diagram after the redeployment.

5 Conclusion

This chapter presents a distributed model for mobile sensor network based on graph theory, which uniquely defines the relationship of one robot with its neighbors. Based on this model, autonomous deployment algorithms are proposed to redeploy the robots to cover a larger area. The algorithm integrates graph theory with the virtual potential field approach. The paper simulated all the proposed algorithms. The simulation results have shown the efficacy and validity of the algorithms.

References

1. F. Araujo and L. Rodrigues. Fast localized delaunay triangulation. In *Proceedings of the 8th International Conference on Principles of Distributed Systems (OPODIS)*, Grenoble, France, December 2004.
2. T. Balch and R. Arkin. Behavior-based formation control for multirobot teams. *IEEE Transactions on Robotics and Automation*, 14(6):926–939, 1998.
3. M. Batalin and G. S. Sukhatme. Coverage, exploration and deployment by a mobile robot and communication network. *Telecommunication Systems Journal, Special Issue on Wireless Sensor Networks*, 26(2), 2004.
4. M. Batalin and G. S. Sukhatme. Using a sensor network for distributed multi-robot task allocation. In *IEEE International Conference on Robotics and Automation*, pages 158–164, New Orleans, Louisiana, Apr 2004.
5. M. Batalin, G. S. Sukhatme, and M. Hattig. Mobile robot navigation using a sensor network. In *IEEE International Conference on Robotics and Automation*, pages 636–642, New Orleans, Louisiana, Apr 2004.
6. M. S. Branicky. Multiple lyapunov functions and other analysis tools for switched and hybrid systems. *IEEE Transactions on Automatic Control*, 43(4):475–482, 1998.
7. R. Brooks. A robust layered control system for a mobile robot. *International Journal of Robotics and Automation*, 2(1):14–23, 1986.
8. N. Bulusu, J. Heidemann, and D. Estrin. Adaptive beacon placement. In *Twenty-first International Conference on Distributed Computing Systems (ICDCS)*. IEEE Computer Society, April 2001.
9. R. Burridge, A. Rizzi, and D. Koditschek. Sequential compostion of dynamically dexterous robot behaviors. *The International Journal of Robotics Research*, 18(6):534–555, 1999.
10. Z. Butler and D. Rus. Event-based motion control for mobile sensor networks. *IEEE Pervasive Computing*, 2(4):34–43, 2003.
11. P. Corke, R. Peterson, and D. Rus. Networked robots: Flying robot navigation using a sensor net. In *Proceedings of the 11th International Symposium of Robotics Research*, 2003.
12. P. I. Corke, S. E. Hrabar, R. Peterson, D. Rus, S. Saripalli, and G. S. Sukhatme. Autonomous deployment and repair of a sensor network using an unmanned aerial vehicle. In *IEEE International Conference on Robotics and Automation*, pages 3602–3609, Apr 2004.
13. P. I. Corke, S. E. Hrabar, R. Peterson, D. Rus, S. Saripalli, and G. S. Sukhatme. Deployment and connectivity repair of a sensor net with a flying robot. In *International Symposium on Experimental Robotics*, 2004.

14. J. Cortes, S. Martinez, T. Karatas, and F. Bullo. Coverage control for mobile sensing networks. *IEEE Transactions on Robotics and Automation*, 20(2):243–255, 2004.

15. A. Das, J. Spletzer, V. Kumar, and C. Taylor. Ad hoc networks for localization and control. In *Proceedings of the 41st IEEE Conference on Decision and Control*, pages 2978–2983, December 2002.

16. M. de Berg, M. van Kreveld, M. Overmars, and O. Schwarzkopf. *Computational Geometry Algorithms and Applications*. Springer, 2000.

17. J. P. Desai, J. P. Ostrowski, and V. Kumar. Modeling and control of formations of nonholonomic mobile robots. *IEEE Transactions on Robotics and Automation*, 17(6):905–908, 2001.

18. Q. Du, V. Faber, and M. Gunzburger. Centroidal voronoi tessellations: Applications and algorithms. *SIAM Review*, 41(4):637–676, 1999.

19. J. A. Fax. *Optimal and Cooperative Control of Vehicle Formations*. Dissertation of California Institute of Technology, Pasadena, California, 2002.

20. J. F. Feddema, C. Lewis, and D. A. Schoenwald. Decentralized control of cooperative robotic vehicles: Theory and application. *IEEE Transactions on Robotics and Automation*, 18(5):852–864, 2002.

21. R. Fierro, A. K. Das, R. V. Kumar, and J. P. Ostrowsk. Hybrid control of formations of robots. In *Proceedings of IEEE International Conference on Robotics and Automation*, pages 157–162, 2001.

22. A. Howard, M. J. Mataric, and G. S. Sukhatme. An incremental self-deployment algorithm for mobile sensor networks. *Autonomous Robots*, 13:113–126, 2002.

23. A. Howard, M. J. Mataric, and G. S. Sukhatme. Mobile sensor network deployment using potential fields: A distributed, scalable solution to the area coverage problem. In *Proceedings of the 6th International Conference on Distributed Autonomous Robotic Systems*, pages 299–308, Fukuoka, Japan, 2002.

24. A. Jadbabaie, J. Lin, and A. Morse. Coordination of groups of mobile autonomous agents using nearest neighbor rules. *IEEE Transactions on Automatic Control*, 48(6):988–1001, 2003.

25. O. Khatib. Real-time obstacle avoidance for manipulators and mobile robots. *The International Journal of Robotics Research*, 5(1), 1986.

26. Q. Li, M. De Rosa, and D. Rus. Distributed algorithms for guiding navigation across a sensor network. In *Proceedings of the 9th annual international conference on Mobile computing and networking*, pages 313–325. ACM Press, 2003.

27. X.-Y. Li, G. Calinescu, P.-J. Wan, and Y. Wang. Localized delaunay triangulation with application in ad hoc wireless networks. *IEEE Transactions on Parallel and Distributed Systems*, 14(10):1035–1047, 2003.

28. M. J. Mataric. Behavior-based robotics as a tool for synthesis of artificial behavior and analysis of natural behavior. *Trends in Cognitive Science*, 2(3):82–87, 1998.

29. S. Meguerdichian, S. Slijepcevic, V. Karayan, and M. Potkonjak. Localized algorithms in wireless ad-hoc networks: location discovery and sensor exposure. pages 106–116, Long Beach, CA, July 2001.

30. P. Ogren, E. Fiorelli, and N. E. Leonard. Cooperative control of mobile sensor networks: Adaptive gradient climbing in a distributed environment. *IEEE Transactions on Automatic Control*, 49(8):1292–1302, 2004.

31. A. Okabe, B. Boots, K. Sugihara, and S. N. Chiu. *Spatial Tessellations*. John Wiley and Sons, 1999.

32. L. E. Parker. Distributed algorithms for multi-robot observation of multiple moving targets. *Autonomous Robots*, 12:231–255, 2002.

33. D. Payton, M. Daily, R. Estkowski, M. Howard, and C. Lee. Pheromone robotics. *Autonomous Robots*, 11(3):319–324, 2001.

34. S. Poduri and G. S. Sukhatme. Constrained coverage for mobile sensor networks. In *IEEE International Conference on Robotics and Automation*, pages 165–172, New Orleans, LA, May 2004.

35. P. Sander, D. Peleshcuk, and B. Grosz. A scalable, distributed algorithm for efficient task allocation. In *Proceedings of the First Joint Conference on Autonomous Agents and Multi-agent Systems*, pages 1191–1198, Bologna, Italy, July 2002.

36. J. Tan, N. Xi, A. Goradia, and W. Sheng. Coordination of human and mobile manipulator formation in a perceptive reference frame. In *Proceedings of IEEE International Conference on Robotics and Automation*, 2003.

37. A. Winfield. Distributed sensing and data collection via broken ad hoc wireless connected networks of mobile robots. *Distributed Autonomous Robotic Systems 4, ed. L. E. Parker, G. Bekey, J. Barhen, Springer-Verlag*, pages 273–282, 2000.

38. Y. Zou and K. Chakrabarty. Sensor deployment and target localization based on virtual forces. In *Proceedings of the Twenty-Second Annual Joint Conference of the IEEE Computer and Communications Societies*, pages 1293–1303, April 2003.

SECTION II
NETWORK MANAGEMENT

Chapter 4
Medium Access Control Protocols for Wireless Sensor Networks

Ali Abu-el Humos, Mihaela Cardei, Bassem Alhalabi, and Sam Hsu

Department of Computer Science & Engineering
Florida Atlantic University, Boca Raton, FL 33431
{aabuel@, mihaela@cse., alhalabi@, sam@cse.}fau.edu

1 Introduction

Recent improvements in affordable and efficient integrated electronic devices have a considerable impact on advancing the state of wireless sensor networks (WSNs), which constitute the platform of a broad range of applications related to national security, surveillance, military, health care, environmental monitoring, smart spaces, inventory tracking, and recently industrial controls.

A WSN is a collection of a large number of wireless nodes deployed to measure and report certain parameters such as temperature, pressure, humidity, etc. Each node consists of sensing, processing, power and radio units [1]. Sensor nodes are usually deployed to serve one application and are configured to operate as a multi-hop network. A WSN contains one or more sinks that relay data between users and sensor nodes. The main functions of a sensor node are to sense the surrounding environment and to participate in data forwarding. Additionally, a sensor node might perform data aggregation in order to reduce the bandwidth consumption, power consumption for communication, and media access delay. The two important operations of a WSN are data dissemination (send data/queries from sinks to sensor nodes) and data gathering (send sensed data from sensor nodes to the sinks).

There are two types of sensor data collection: event-driven and demand-driven. In the event-driven type, the reporting process is triggered by one or more sensor nodes which detect an event and report it to the monitoring station. In the demand-driven type, the reporting process is initiated by the monitoring station and sensor nodes send their data in response to an explicit request. A forest fire monitoring system is event-driven, whereas an inventory control system is demand-driven. A hybrid system can operate on both types, event and demand-driven.

Although WSNs share some characteristics with traditional wireless networks (such as cellular, Bluetooth and ad hoc networks), they differ from them in the following aspects:

1. Energy conservation is of primary interest in WSNs. Sensors are battery powered, and their batteries are usually neither replaceable nor rechargeable. Energy resources might not be the main concern in the other networks, where maintaining a certain Quality of Service (QoS) might be, for example, the primary goal.

2. Sensor nodes might not have unique identifiers. Communication is data-centric, where queries might be addressed to sensors satisfying certain properties or to other sensors sensing certain parameter values. For example, the user might be interested in all locations where temperature exceeds a certain threshold. In contrast, ad hoc networks are address-centric, where communication is performed between two nodes, with unique addresses.

3. WSNs use multi-hop communication to relay data between sensors and sinks. Each node, besides sensing its surrounding environment, has to be able to forward data coming from other sensor nodes. In contrast, single-hop communication is dominant in other wireless networks. For example, the nodes responsible for data forwarding are the base stations in cellular communication, and the master nodes in a Bluetooth piconet.

4. In WSNs, nodes are usually densely deployed, in large numbers (thousands or millions), while in other networks the number of nodes varies from several nodes to several hundreds. For example, Bluetooth piconets can support up to eight nodes, while ad hoc wireless networks have usually less than a hundred nodes.

5. In WSNs, data generated at one node is typically highly correlated with the data generated by its neighbor nodes and all the nodes in a WSN tend to serve one application. In traditional wireless networks, however, data is generated by one node and is independent from the data generated by neighboring node. Furthermore, nodes may be running different applications.

6. In WSNs, sensor nodes might perform data aggregation, by combining local measurements with data received from neighbors. In this case, only the combined, assembled results are forwarded toward the sink.

This chapter addresses the topic of Medium Access Control (MAC) protocols in WSNs. A MAC protocol has the important role to control access to a shared communication medium. The specific characteristics of WSNs trigger the main requirements of a MAC protocol running in such an environment. A careful design of the MAC protocol is required for an optimal performance and increased lifetime of the network. Thus, it becomes critical to design MAC protocols that are energy-efficient, distributed, and scalable. Depending on the application, additional parameters such as latency might be required as well.

This chapter describes the main characteristics of MAC protocols in WSNs and surveys MAC protocols recently proposed in the literature.

The rest of this chapter is structured as follows. In Section 2 we present the requirements, classification and main design challenges of a MAC protocol in WSNs. We continue with a description of the representative MAC protocols. We classify them as scheduled-based protocols and contention-based protocols, depending on the mechanism used to dictate the access to the communication medium. Section 3 presents scheduled-based MAC protocols and Section 4 describes representative contention-based MAC protocols. In Section 5, we briefly point-out a deficiency of the current implementation of the energy model in NS2 [24] network simulator. We end our presentation with conclusions in Section 6.

2 Characteristics of MAC Protocols in WSNs

A MAC protocol is mainly responsible for providing a mechanism that controls access to the shared communication medium. The specific characteristics of a WSN determine the requirements of the MAC protocol. It is impractical to use the MAC protocols designed for other wireless network types. New MAC protocols have to be designed, specifically tailored for the characteristics of WSNs. Next, we present the main requirements of MAC protocols for WSNs and their classification, followed by a discussion of energy-efficient design of MAC protocols.

2.1 Requirements of MAC Protocols in WSNs

The main requirements of a traditional wireless network MAC protocol are per-node fairness, low delay and high throughput. Network lifetime is not considered critical, as batteries might be replenished, although power efficient schemes are recommended.

In contrast, for a WSN, an energy-efficient design is considered as the top priority. The design should also be scalable, in order to accommodate large networks. Latency and bandwidth utilization become secondary goals, while per-node fairness is not considered a critical parameter. The main requirements of a MAC protocol for WSNs can be summarized as follows [16, 17]:

1. **Energy efficiency**. The most important requirement of a MAC protocol is to be energy-efficient. Power consumption is a critical issue in WSNs, since sensor nodes are battery operated and replacing or recharging the battery is usually infeasible.
2. **Scalability**. A MAC protocol should adapt and run properly in a dynamic and scalable topology. The WSN is expected to contain a large number of sensor nodes. Additionally, nodes may be added, die or move to different locations.

3. **Latency**. Depending on the application served, some latency delay can be tolerated in general. The latency and energy conservation are two conflicting attributes in the MAC layer design for WSN. Choosing the shortest path without considering the current energy level of intermediate nodes might prematurely deplete power resources of some nodes and trigger network partition.

4. **Fairness**. Usually, fairness is not considered to be a critical parameter since all the nodes in a WSN serve the same application. For example, when nodes in the same vicinity have similar data to transmit to the upper stream, unfairness among nodes in the same vicinity is acceptable.

5. **Bandwidth utilization**. Designing a MAC protocol that efficiently uses the bandwidth is a desirable factor to enhance the WSN performance.

2.2 Classification of MAC protocols in WSNs

MAC protocols can be divided into two main categories [16, 17]: *scheduled-based protocols* and *contention-based protocols*.

Scheduled-based protocols are basically Time Division Multiple Access (TDMA) protocols. In TDMA protocols a centralized (master) node distributes the transmission schedule among other nodes in the network during the initialization period. After the initialization period, no overhead control packets (RTS or CTS) are required. TDMA protocols are collision free and perform best in single-hop networks. They require strict synchronization among nodes in order to coordinate node transmission slots. TDMA based protocols are not adaptive. Once the transmission schedule is distributed, it cannot be modified to accommodate newly added nodes. TDMA protocols are not scalable. They cannot support a large number of nodes because latency increases significantly with the number of nodes. We present some scheduled-based MAC protocols in Section 3.

Contention-based protocols are basically Carrier Sense Multiple Access (CSMA) protocols [12]. In CSMA, wireless nodes are able to sense the communication medium and defer their transmission while the channel is busy. CSMA protocols can easily accommodate newly added nodes (adaptive), do not require strict synchronization among nodes, and can support a large number of sensor nodes (scalable). Multi-hop communication is easier to handle in CSMA protocols than in TDMA ones. Several contention-based MAC protocols are described in more detail in Section 4.

2.3 Energy-Efficiency in WSNs MAC Protocols

Wireless sensor nodes are energy constrained and therefore they require energy-efficient protocol designs in order to prolong network lifetime. Power awareness is prominent in all aspects of WSNs ranging from the hardware design to algorithms and protocols designed at all layers of the network architecture.

The main sources of energy consumption are sensing, data processing and communication. Among these, communication is the major power consumer. For example, the communication to computation power usage ratio is between 1500 and 2700 for Rockwell's WIN sensor nodes [9].

In general, radios can operate in four distinct modes of operation: transmit, receive, idle and sleep. When a node is not sending or receiving packets, it is in the idle mode, with power consumption nearly as high as in the receiving mode. The highest power consumption is in the transmit mode and the lowest in the sleep mode, when a node turns off its transceiver. For example, the power consumption for Rockwell WINS seismic sensors [9] for transmit:receive:idle:sleep modes is (0.38–0.7W):(0.36W):(0.34W):(0.03W), while the sensing power is 0.02 W.

Based on these results, an important method to save power resources is to have sensor nodes enter the sleep mode whenever they are not actively participating in data transmission or reception. This way they avoid large energy consumption in idle states. This energy saving method is actually used extensively by the current MAC protocols for sensor nodes, and such mechanisms are further detailed in the following sections.

For the scheduled-based protocols, since nodes know ahead of time when they will be active, they can go to sleep mode for the rest of the time when they are inactive.

Four major sources of energy waste in contention-based schemes are identified [16, 17]:

1. **Collisions.** If node A starts transmitting a message to node B and B is within the communication range of another transmitting node C, then there will be collisions at node B. Collisions require retransmission of data, which results in waste of energy resources.
2. **Overhearing.** This happens when a node hears a transmission intended to other nodes. As a result, the node consumes energy even if the packet was not intended for it.
3. **Control packet overhead.** Control packets such as RTS, CTS and ACK used for example in IEEE802.11 MAC protocol, consume energy when transmitted and received, and consequently reduce the network bandwidth available for data packets.
4. **Idle listening.** If a wireless sensor node is not transmitting or receiving, it is in idle mode. Idle listening is a major energy waste in WSNs. It usually consumes 50–100% of the energy required for receiving [11, 4].

Designing MAC protocols that avoid or reduce these energy waste sources are of critical importance and will have a direct impact on prolonging network lifetime.

3 Scheduled-based MAC Protocols

Scheduled-based schemes assign collision free channels to each node, using Time Division Multiple Access (TDMA), Frequency Division Multiple Access (FDMA) or Code Division Multiple Access (CDMA). The preferred scheduling technique in WSNs is TDMA, since it does not require a complex hardware design and allows inactive nodes to enter the sleep state. In this section we present two schedule-based MAC protocols, LEACH and Bluetooth.

3.1 Low-Energy Adaptive Clustering Hierarchy (LEACH) Protocol

In LEACH [3], the network topology contains a single sink node and many sensor nodes that sample the environment at a constant rate and send their data to the sink. The network has a hierarchical organization. The network is divided into clusters, and each cluster has associated a cluster head node. Each node in the cluster sends its sensed data to the cluster head where it belongs. The cluster head aggregates the data packets received into a single packet, which is transmitted to the sink. For this operation, a perfect correlation among the received data packets is assumed.

The network activity is organized into rounds, where each round has two phases: initialization phase and steady-state phase. During the initialization phase, clusterheads are elected and new clusters are formed. For each round, new nodes act as cluster heads in order to evenly distribute the energy consumption among network nodes, so that nodes will die randomly at approximately the same rate. Each cluster head coordinates the activity of the sensors in its cluster and establishes the TDMA schedule. This schedule is then broadcasted to all the nodes in the cluster. During the steady-state phase, all nodes transmit their sensed data according to the TDMA schedule. Thus, each node transmits during its allocated time slot and enters the sleep mode otherwise.

While TDMA prevents collisions within each cluster, it does not prevent collisions between clusters. Nodes in neighbor clusters might transmit at the same time, resulting in collisions. In order to prevent collisions, LEACH uses the CDMA mechanism and assigns to each cluster a unique CDMA code.

LEACH is a distributed and localized protocol. It achieves energy savings by having inactive nodes enter the sleep state, by using cluster head rotations, and by using data aggregation at the cluster head. The main disadvantage of this protocol is that it uses CDMA to resolve interferences between adjacent clusters. This may not be always feasible and may result in poor bandwidth utilization.

3.2 Bluetooth

Bluetooth (IEEE 802.15.1) [19] is a wireless technology intended to connect different wireless devices such as telephones, notebooks, PDAs, printers, computers and so on to form a Piconet as shown in Figure 1. Piconets can be

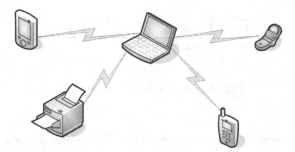

Fig. 1. Bluetooth Piconet.

combined together to form a Scatternet, where the slave node in one Piconet may act as the master for the adjacent Piconet. Bluetooth devices are low power devices with a transmission range of approximately 10 m. Frequency-hopping spread spectrum is used to avoid interference with other devices or other networks. Bluetooth operates in the 2.4 GHz ISM band which is divided into 79 channels of 1 MHz each, with a bit rate of 1 Mbps. A Bluetooth network can have at most eight nodes, one master and seven slaves. This small number of nodes disqualifies Bluetooth technology from being used in WSNs.

4 Contention-based Protocols

The IEEE 802.11 Distributed Coordination Function (DCF) [23] is a contention-based MAC protocol used in Mobile Ad hoc Networks (MANETs). This protocol was intended for single-hop networks. Energy waste due to idle listening is not a serious problem in MANETs. However, IEEE 802.11 provides an option where nodes can switch to Power Save (PS) mode and turn off their radios to conserve energy. Even if this option is enabled, the IEEE 802.11 may still not be able to properly maintain node synchronization in the network [17]. However, the IEEE 802.11 PS mode was further exploited in the design of MAC layer protocols for WSNs and is usually considered as a point of comparison in simulations.

There is a rich literature addressing contention-based MAC protocols in sensor nodes. We describe next several of the most representative such protocols.

4.1 Sensor-MAC (SMAC) Protocol

SMAC protocol [16] considers energy efficiency as the most important factor, while latency and fairness are regarded as secondary criteria. Since most of the time a wireless node will be in idle listening, SMAC turns off the node's transceiver periodically. This will introduce some latency in the system. Fairness among nodes in the same vicinity can be tolerated since all these nodes

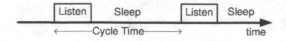

Fig. 2. Periodic listen and sleep.

are expected to serve the same application. Therefore, a node with a long data message will not give up the medium to other nodes until its whole data message is transmitted. Thus, shorter messages waiting on the queues of neighboring nodes might have to wait longer to get access to the medium. This can be justified considering that in WSNs, application level latency is usually favored over the per-node fairness.

The SMAC protocol has the following four features:

1. Periodic Listen and Sleep
Each node in the network turns off its transceiver (sleeps) and wakes up to listen to the medium periodically, as shown in Figure 2. The parameter that governs the percentage of the wake-up period to the sleep period is called the *duty cycle* and is given by :

$$Duty\ cycle = listen\ time/cycle\ time$$

2. Synchronization
SMAC introduces a new packet type (SYNC) to accomplish the synchronization task. At the deployment time, all nodes keep listening to the medium until one node broadcasts a SYNC packet containing its schedule (the time left to sleep). Neighboring nodes, upon receiving this packet, will set their schedule to the new schedule and broadcast a SYNC packet to their neighbors as well. However, this process does not guarantee that all nodes in the network will follow the same schedule. This might happen because two or more nodes outside of each other's transmission range could start broadcasting their schedules simultaneously. Nodes at the border of two different schedules will adopt both schedules and therefore will sleep less than other nodes. However, border nodes may choose to adopt one schedule and only wake up on the other schedule if they have data to transmit. Note that, by using this choice, broadcast messages are transmitted twice, once for each adopted schedule. There is still a possibility that neighbor nodes may not discover each other if they adopt different schedules. To enable nodes to discover their neighbors, nodes discovery process is initiated periodically (every 50 cycles for example). In order to maintain synchronization with neighboring nodes, every node transmits a SYNC packet periodically (every 10 cycles for example). The listen period in SMAC is divided as shown in Figure 3. When a node wants to transmit a SYNC packet, it must contend for the medium before transmitting. If a node has data to transmit, it has to contend for the medium before transmitting

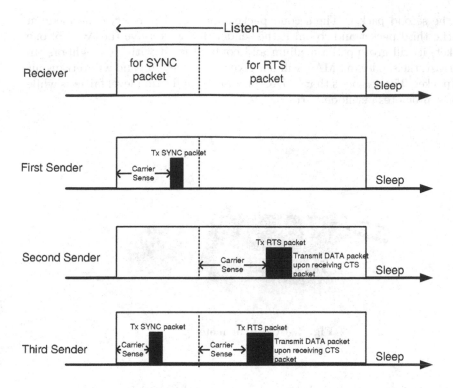

Fig. 3. Listen period in SMAC for three senders and a receiver.

the RTS packet as well. Upon receiving a CTS packet, the node can start transmitting its data and go back to sleep after receiving the ACK packet.

3. Collision and Overhearing Avoidance
SMAC protocol uses a mechanism similar to the IEEE 802.11 for medium access contention (fixed contention window) and hidden terminal avoidance (use of RTS/CTS packets). All immediate nodes of both the sender and receiver will go to sleep upon receiving RTS or CTS packets.

4. Message Passing
Transmitting a long message as a whole typically uses only one RTS/CTS and ACK packets. However, if some bits are not received properly, this will require retransmission of the whole packet, which will cause energy waste. On the other hand, dividing a message into smaller packets and transmitting them independently will increase the overhead. The IEEE 802.11 protocol avoids this overhead by using only one RTS/CTS packet exchange to reserve the medium for the first packet. The first packet and its ACK reserve the medium

for the second packet. The second packet and its ACK reserve the medium for the third packet and so on. If the sender did not receive the ACK of one packet, it will give up the medium and contend for it with its neighbors. In contrast, the sender in SMAC will not give up the medium and will retransmit the packet. The reason is that SMAC promotes application level fairness while 802.11 promotes per-node fairness.

Fig. 4. UCB Rene motes [21].

The performance of SMAC was tested using the UCB Rene Motes shown in Figure 4. The authors compared the energy consumption performance of the SMAC with full features and SMAC with message passing and overhearing avoidance but without periodic sleep, against a simplified version of the IEEE 802.11 Distributed Coordination Function (DCF) protocol. At light traffic, SMAC outperforms IEEE 802.11 because idle listening is the major source of energy consumption in IEEE 802.11 at light load. SMAC reduces the energy consumption during idle listening through periodic sleep. However, in heavy traffic, idle listening is not expected to happen frequently and SMAC achieves its energy savings through avoiding message overhearing and transmitting long massages using message passing technique. On the other hand, some intermediate nodes which are involved in packet routing may show better energy savings using the IEEE 802.11 than using SMAC during heavy traffic. This is because of the synchronization overheard (SYNC packets) associated with SMAC and due to the latency introduced by SMAC due to the periodic sleep.

4.2 Timeout-MAC (TMAC) Protocol

TMAC protocol [13] tries to enhance energy savings in SMAC by further reducing the idle listening. A node in the listen mode will go back to sleep after time TA, as shown in Figure 5, if there is no activation event (start of

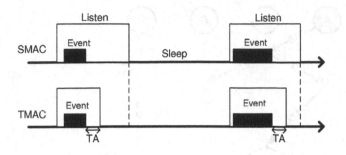

Fig. 5. Every node turns its transceiver off if there is no activity for a time duration TA.

listen period, receiving any packet, etc). The choice of TA is critical for the performance of TMAC. The following equation defines the minimum value of TA:

$$TA > CW + TxRTS + T$$

where CW is the contention window size, $TxRTS$ is the the transmission time of the RTS packet and T is the turn-around time after the end of the RTS packet and the arrival of the CTS packet. A static value of TA is chosen to be 1.5 times the minimum value of TA.

The early sleeping problem is noticed by the TMAC authors in unidirectional source to sink communication. Figure 6 explains this problem. Node C is aware of node A transmission to B, however node D is not and will go to sleep after TA seconds. When A transmission to B is over, C cannot transmit its data to D since D is sleeping. The *future request to send packet* technique is proposed to overcome the early sleeping problem. When node C overhears the CTS packet coming from node B, it will immediately send a Future Request To Send (FRTS) packet to inform node D to wake up when A's transmission to B is finished. In oder to avoid collision at node B between the data packet coming from node A and the FRTS packet coming from node C, node A first transmits a Data-Send (DS) packet of size equal to the FRTS packet, but this DS packet contains no useful information. After sending the DS packet, node A starts transmitting its data packet to node B. The *future request to send packet* technique, however, may result in more energy loss during heavy traffic, which is undesirable in WSNs.

TMAC performance is compared against the performance of SMAC and CSMA protocols using OMNeT++ simulator [14]. TMAC energy savings are better than SMAC, however, TMAC throughput (bytes per node per second) is less than SMAC at heavy traffic due to the early sleeping problem. A limited version of TMAC was implemented on the EYES hardware [13] with all the

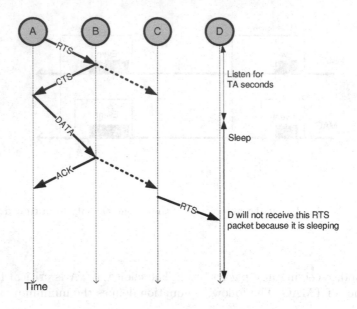

Fig. 6. The early sleeping problem occurs at the node D.

nodes adopting the same schedule, and within the transmission range of each other. TMAC shows excellent energy savings because nodes enter sleep mode (rather idle listening) after TA seconds of no activity during the listen period.

4.3 SMAC with Coordinated Adaptive Sleeping

Periodic sleep introduces a serious latency problem in SMAC especially at very low duty cycle. Figure 7 shows a three-hop communication scenario where a packet is to be transmitted from A to D. We assume that the duration of listen period is long enough to transmit only one packet. In order for the packet to reach D, it requires three time frames. If an adaptive listening feature is added to the SMAC protocol as proposed in [17], then node C will wake up when the transmission from A to B is completed and B can start transmitting its data to C as shown in Figure 8. However, node C should wait until the beginning of the next frame to transmit its data to D, since D was not aware of B's transmission to C (D was sleeping).

It is proven that in an N-linear hop network, SMAC with adaptive listening can reduce the latency of traditional SMAC (without adaptive listening) by almost 50% under light traffic conditions. This improvement can reach more than 50%, since nodes two hops away from the transmitting node might

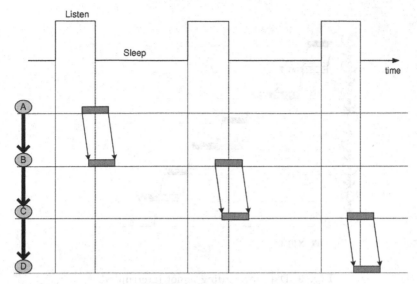

Fig. 7. SMAC without adaptive listening.

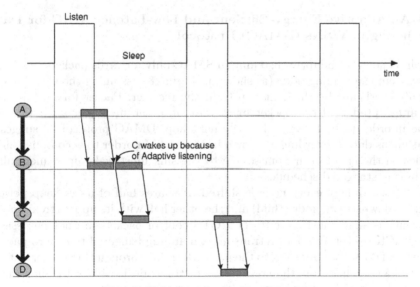

Fig. 8. SMAC with adaptive listening.

become aware of its transmission due to various wireless communication propagation modes (paths).

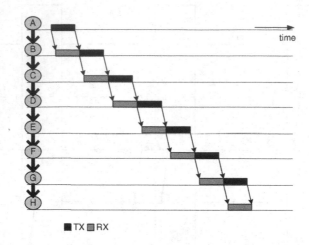

Fig. 9. Data forwarding is not interrupted.

4.4 An Adaptive Energy-Efficient and Low-Latency MAC for Data Gathering in WSNs (DMAC) Protocol

Within one cycle, adaptive listening in SMAC only forwards packets two hops away from the sending node (as shown in Figure 8) assuming the CTS packet is only overheard by the next hop from the receiver. Packet forwarding will be interrupted, and the packet must wait until the next scheduled wakeup time in order to be forwarded to the next hop. DMAC protocol [6] suggests continuous data forwarding as shown in Figure 9. In order to accomplish this, nodes on the chain path from source to the sink must wake up sequentially, by having staggered schedules.

The schedule of every node is shifted. It shares half of its wakeup period with its downstream node (child) and the other half with its upper stream node (parent) as shown in Figure 9. RTS/CTS control packets are not necessary. Only ACK packet and data retransmission are implemented to ensure packet delivery. DMAC adapts itself to the network traffic through three schemes: (1) First, if a node has more than one packet to transmit, it will set the more data flag in the MAC header to request its parent node to extend its wakeup time (e.g., node 9 in Figure 10), (2) Second, if two or more nodes have the same parent node (e.g., nodes 3 and 4 in Figure 10), the parent node will extend its wakeup time to allow all its child nodes to transmit their data to it. This is called a data prediction scheme in DMAC, and (3). Third, if two interfering nodes at the same tree level have different parent nodes (e.g., nodes 7 and 8 in Figure 10), then one of them can use the More-To-Send packet to request its parent node to extend its wakeup time.

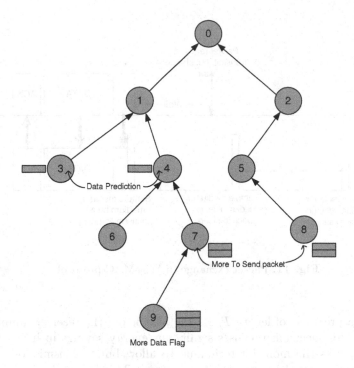

Fig. 10. DMAC wakeup times in data gathering tree.

DMAC is only efficient in data gathering tree scenario where traffic is unidirectional from source node to sink node. SMAC is a more general and more efficient protocol under different communication scenarios.

4.5 Wireless Sensor MAC (WiseMAC) Protocol

In WiseMAC protocol [2], all the nodes in the network wake up periodically (with period Tw) to check for any activity of the medium, as shown in Figure 11. Nodes are not synchronized to wake up simultaneously and this reduces the synchronization overhead. On the other hand, since a receiving node turns its radio on for a short period of time($\ll Tw$) when it samples the medium, the transmitting node should transmit along a preamble signal of size equal to Tw, in order to ensure that the receiving node will be awake to receive the data packet which follows the preamble. After receiving the data packet, the receiving node will reply with an ACK packet to confirm the reception of the data packet and to inform the transmitting node about its next sampling time. Thus, next time the transmitting node has data to send to this node, it

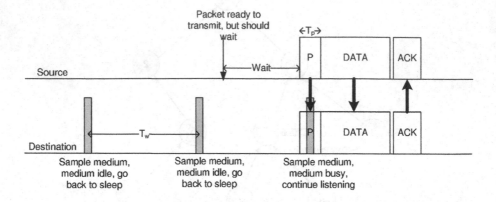

Fig. 11. Packet exchange in WiseMAC protocol.

will send a preamble of length $Tp \ll Tw$ just before the receiver samples the medium. This mechanism causes significant energy savings in heavy traffic. WiseMAC uses the more bit technique to allow burst transmission of data (transmitting more than one packet at a time). This feature is similar to the message passing technique used in SMAC.

Unfortunately, WiseMAC does not solve the interruption in forwarding data packets over multiple hops. This is because nodes on the next hop are not aware of the data transmission of the downstream hop since their wakeup times are random (not synchronized).

4.6 Energy and Latency Control in Low Cycle MAC Protocols

In SMAC-like protocols, all nodes follow the same schedule or they may follow different schedules. Nodes following the same schedule form a virtual cluster and nodes on the borders of two or more virtual clusters are called border nodes (see Figure 12). Although it is thought that there are usually only few such border nodes in the network, experiment shows that more than 40% of the nodes in the network adopt two or more schedules. This is because of the unexpected radio propagation paths [15, 18]. Having multiple schedules is undesirable in a WSN since border nodes must wake up during the listen times of all adopted schedules. Consequently, border nodes will die much faster than other nodes in the network.

SMAC tries to reduce the number of schedules in the network through singleton schedule elimination technique. After a node broadcasts its schedule, it will not adopt this schedule until it learns that other nodes have adopted it

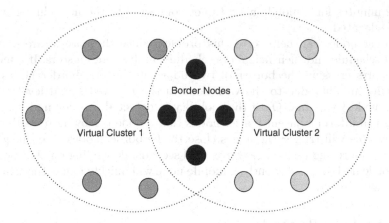

Fig. 12. Virtual clusters and border nodes in SMAC.

as well. This will help in eliminating the schedules broadcast by newly added nodes into an existing network but does not guarantee all nodes to follow the same schedule.

To solve this problem, the Global Schedule Algorithm technique was proposed [5]. If a node receives a schedule different than its own schedule, it will switch to this schedule if it is older than its own schedule. If the received schedule has the same age as the node's schedule, the one with the lower ID will be adopted. This node will update its neighboring nodes of any change on its schedule, so that all nodes in the network will eventually converge to follow the same schedule. The Fast Path Algorithm was introduced to reduce the latency in SMAC, provided that all nodes in the network follow the same schedule and the path from the source node to the sink node is known. Coordinated wake-ups are inserted on the path from source to sink such that each node wakes up when its downstream node is ready to send its data. This technique is very close to the work done in DMAC. Fast Path Algorithm is, however, more general than DMAC which only works under the assumption of having one sink in the network. Additionally, Fast Path Algorithm is verified using UCB Motes.

4.7 Mobile Sensor MAC (MS-MAC) Protocol

SMAC was originally designed for static WSNs. MS-MAC [8] protocol provides a mechanism for mobile nodes to quickly follow the schedule of the cluster it is moving to. SMAC neighbor discovery mechanism enables nodes to discover newly added nodes to the network. This mechanism will also help discover nodes moving from one cluster to another. During neighbor discovery, nodes keep listening to the medium for 10 seconds every 2 minutes. Thus, it could take 2 minutes for a mobile node to get connected to the new cluster where it has relocated.

Border nodes can help solve this problem since they are aware of their cluster schedule and their neighbors schedule on different clusters. If a mobile node starts crossing the border of two adjacent clusters, border nodes will detect its mobility due to the variations in the received signal level at the border nodes' antenna. Once the mobility is detected, border nodes in one cluster will inform adjacent border nodes that a node is moving towards their cluster. This will trigger the nodes close to the border nodes to do neighbor discovery more aggressively (say every 30 seconds, depending on the speed of the mobile node). Consequently, a mobile node will quickly follow the schedule of the new cluster.

4.8 Two Radio Protocols

The concept of having two radios, one for signaling and the other for data, was first introduced in PAMAS protocol [10]. PAMAS used this idea to overcome the problem of overhearing among neighboring nodes, thus reducing the energy consumption. On the other hand, PAMAS did not consider idle listening as a source of energy waste and, furthermore, it assumed that idle listening consumes zero power.

The work in [7] uses the two-radio architecture introduced by PAMAS, but tries to solve the idle listening problem. It uses a low power (with very low duty cycle) wakeup radio and a primary radio for data transmission. Both the sender and receiver try to adapt their wakeup times depending on the network traffic. If the traffic is high, both sender and receiver will wake up more often. Otherwise, they will spend a longer time sleeping. To adapt their wake up times to the network traffic, nodes must use a fixed size packet queue and should have pre-knowledge of the number of neighbor nodes. Although this work shows considerable energy savings in single-hop and multi-hop scenarios, latency is not improved in multi-hop scenarios due to the lack of coordinated wake-ups between nodes on different hops. In addition, so far there is no real implementation for the two-radio architecture in sensor networks.

4.9 A Transmission Control Scheme for Media Access in Sensor Networks

The goal of this protocol introduced in [15] is to achieve node fairness while maintaining efficient energy consumption and bandwidth utilization. It follows the same data transmission sequence as the IEEE 802.11 protocol (RTS/CTC/DATA/ACK). However, in order to account for the fact that traffic generated by sensor nodes is highly correlated, a random delay (where the node keeps its radio off) followed by a constant listen period are added before starting the data transmission. This will lead to efficient energy usage and will alleviate the collision problem. Simulation results show that backoff with a fixed window size or binary exponential decrease in window size are more suitable to achieve proportional fairness.

In order to control packet injection into the network, to prevent congestion, and to maintain acceptable bandwidth utilization level, an adaptive rate control (ARC) scheme is proposed. Each node determines to increase or decrease its traffic injection into the network independently, without the need to exchange any traffic control packets with other nodes in the network. ARC is computationally simple and gives preference to route-through traffic over the traffic generated from the sensor node application. This will ensure that nodes closer to the sink node are not favored over nodes far away from it.

Unlike SMAC, ARC does not provide any periodic listen/sleep mechanism. Moreover, this protocol accentuates per-node fairness while SMAC trades it off for further energy savings.

4.10 ZigBee and the Industry Standard IEEE 802.15.4 Protocol

The 802.15.4 standard [22] is a simple packet data protocol for very low duty cycle wireless networks. It is a CSMA with collision avoidance and optional time slotting protocol. The ZigBee technology is based on the IEEE 802.15.4 protocol. Its applications vary from home and industrial automation to remote control and medical monitoring. It uses a wide range of frequencies: sixteen channels in the 2.4 GHz ISM band with a bit rate of 250 kbps, one at 868 MHz with a bit rate of 20 kbps, and ten at the 916 MHz ISM band with bit rate of 40 kbps. It can accommodate up to 2^{64} nodes in the network.

Three types of devices are defined (see Figure 13): Network Coordinator, Full Function Device, and Reduced Function Device. Network Coordinator (Master node) is aware of all the nodes in the network. Full Function Device supports full 802.15.4 functionality, and it has additional memory and computing power which makes it ideal for a network router. Reduced Function Device has limited functionality to prolong its battery life time and is usually deployed at the network edges. While Bluetooth supports moderate duty cycle with short life battery time, ZigBee on the other hand, supports very low duty cycle, and long life battery time. Bluetooth has a moderate bit rate with a very high QoS and low latency. In contrast, ZigBee has a lower bit rate with an optional low latency. However, while the maximum number of nodes in Bluetooth Piconet is eight, the maximum number of nodes can reach up to 2^{64} in ZigBee network. We should remember that ZigBee technology was developed to serve different applications than Bluetooth, which results in significant reduction in power consumption. ZigBee applications are still in the development phase.

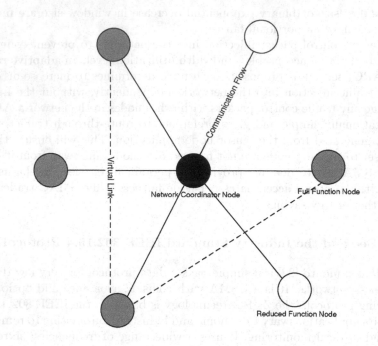

Fig. 13. Node types in ZigBee.

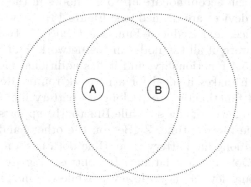

Fig. 14. Two node setup to test NS2 energy model.

5 Short Note on the Energy Model in NS2 Network Simulator

In this section we briefly mention a deficiency of the current implementation of the Energy Model in NS2 [24] network simulator. We ran a simple simulation

Event	Event duration (s)	No. times event occurred	Total event time (s)	Event power (W)	Total event energy (J)
SYNCPktTX	0.0102	4	0.0408	2	0.0816
SYNCPktRX	0.0102	3	0.0306	1	0.0306
RTSPktTX	0.011	1	0.011	2	0.022
RTSPktRX	0.011	1	0.011	1	0.011
CTSPktTX	0.011	1	0.011	2	0.022
CTSPktRX	0.011	1	0.011	1	0.011
DATAPktTX	0.043	2	0.086	2	0.172
DATAPktRX	0.043	1	0.043	1	0.043
ACKPktTX	0.011	1	0.011	2	0.022
ACKPktRX	0.011	1	0.011	1	0.011
Sleep	0.1432	9	0	0	0
Idle	NA	NA	9.733599	1	9.733599
TOTAL			**9.999999**		**10.159799**

Table 1. Simulation results that ignore the sleep time at node A.

to test the validity of the Energy Model implemented in NS2, using a simple topology comprised of two nodes A and B, as illustrated in Figure 14. Both nodes are within the transmission range of each other. We choose the transmit, receive and idle powers of 2 W, 1 W, and 1 W respectively.

Event	Event duration (s)	No. times event occurred	Total event time (s)	Event power (W)	Total event energy (J)
SYNCPktTX	0.0102	4	0.0408	2	0.0816
SYNCPktRX	0.0102	3	0.0306	1	0.0306
RTSPktTX	0.011	1	0.011	2	0.022
RTSPktRX	0.011	1	0.011	1	0.011
CTSPktTX	0.011	1	0.011	2	0.022
CTSPktRX	0.011	1	0.011	1	0.011
DATAPktTX	0.043	2	0.086	2	0.172
DATAPktRX	0.043	1	0.043	1	0.043
ACKPktTX	0.011	1	0.011	2	0.022
ACKPktRX	0.011	1	0.011	1	0.011
Sleep	0.1432	9	1.2888	0	0
Idle	NA	NA	8.529939	1	8.529939
TOTAL			**10.085139**		**8.956139**

Table 2. Simulation results that account the sleep time at node A.

Although these values are exaggerated for the radio of a sensor node, it will emphasize the energy problem we experienced in NS2.

Our simulations indicate about five seconds needed for node synchronization. At time equal to eight seconds, a packet is generated from node A destined to node B. Table 1 shows the simulation statistics gathered at node A. Note that, although we have generated only one data packet from node A to node B, the table indicates two data packets generated by node A. The second packet is the Address Resolution Protocol (ARP) packet. If the time required to transmit and receive all packets is added to the idle time, the result equals the total simulation time. This means that NS2 code does not account for the sleep time!

To confirm this conclusion, we calculated the total energy consumed by node A. The total energy adds up to 10.1598 J which is found to be the same value the NS2 energy model produces. It is clear that the NS2 energy model does not account for the sleep time, and yet considers it as an idle time.

To overcome this problem, we performed the Energy Model modifications in NS2 [20]. To verify the correctness of our modification, we performed the same test as above when setting the sleep power to 0, and we obtained the results in Table 2.

The total event time column adds up to 10.085139 seconds which is equal to the total simulation time. The idle time in Table 2 is less than that of Table 1. This is because the sleep time is taken into consideration in our simulation this time. From Table 2, the total energy consumed at node A is calculated to be 8.956139 which is equal to the same value obtained by the simulation. This verifies that our code produces the desired energy results.

6 Conclusion

Wireless Sensor Networks (WSNs) are large collections of tiny nodes that sense the surrounding environment and communicate with each other via wireless links. WSNs are constrained on power, processing, storage and size that make them more difficult than traditional wireless networks to design and build practical applications.

Different MAC layer protocols are proposed for WSNs. TDMA-based protocols provide excellent energy savings, but are not scalable and are not adaptive to the dynamic changes of the number of nodes in the network. TDMA protocols also require strict synchronization among nodes in the network. CSMA-based protocols are adaptive to the changes in the network dynamics and can accommodate a large number of nodes in the network without requiring strict node synchronization, but still suffer from idle listening and collision problems.

The IEEE 802.11 DCF protocol is not suitable for use in WSNs since it is not originally designed for multi-hop networks and suffers from the idle listening problem which is a major source of energy waste.

SMAC exploits the IEEE 802.11 DCF power save mode and tries to adapt it to the unique characteristic of a WSN. SMAC introduces a periodic listen/sleep cycle to reduce energy waste in idle listening. On the other hand, periodic listen/sleep cycles cause a latency problem. SMAC with adaptive listening, TMAC, and DMAC try to solve the latency problem in SMAC while keeping the energy consumption at low level. WiseMAC achieves more energy savings over SMAC by exploiting the preamble sampling technique, but does not provide better latency results than SMAC. Two-radio architecture protocols achieve excellent energy savings, but require complex hardware.

Protocol	Advantages	Disadvantages	Testing platform	Comments
LEACH [3]	- Nodes are turned off when not in use - Simple to implement	- Requires strict synchronization among nodes - Not scalable, not adaptive to dynamic changes in the network - Using DSSS for interference avoidance is not a feasible solution all the time	- Simulation using MATLAB	- TDMA based protocol - Hierarchical clustering network architecture
Bluetooth [19]	- Same as LEACH	- Strict synchronization among nodes - Limited number of nodes (7 slaves and 1 master node)	- Industrial standard	- TDMA based protocol - Designed to interconnect different wireless devices - Up to 1 Mbps bit rate
IEEE 802.11 DCF [23]	- Scalable and adaptive to dynamic changes in the network - Synchronization is not a problem	- Idle listening - Suitable for single hop networks	- Industrial standard	- CSMA based protocol - Has optional PS energy saving mode - Promotes per node fairness
SMAC [16]	- Less strict synchronization requirement - Scalable and adaptive to dynamic changes in the network - Reduces idle listening - Suitable for multi hop communications	- High latency - Multiple schedules in the network	- UCB motes	- CSMA based protocol - Promotes application level fairness over per node fairness
TMAC [13]	- Same as SMAC with better energy savings and latency performance	- Same as SMAC, latency is better, but still a problem - Throughput is less than SMAC at heavy traffic due to early sleeping problem	- OMNeT++ simulator - Partially implemented with EYES hardware	- CSMA based protocol
SMAC with adaptive listening [17]	- Same as SMAC with better energy savings and better latency performance (at least 50% improvement during light load	- Same as SMAC, latency is better than SMAC, but still a problem	- UCB motes	- CSMA based protocol
DMAC [6]	- Same as SMAC with better energy savings and minimal latency	- Same as SMAC, latency is not a problem any longer - Only suitable for data gathering with unidirectional traffic, from source node to the sink - More complex than SMAC	- NS2 network simulator	
WiseMAC [2]	- Same as SMAC with better energy savings	- Latency is not better than SMAC	- GloMoSim simulator	- Based on the Preamble Sampling Technique
SMAC with Global Scheduling and Fast Path Algorithm [5]	- Same as SMAC with only one schedule in the network, better energy savings and minimal latency - More general than DMAC	- More complex than SMAC	- UCB motes	- CSMA based protocol
MS-MAC [8]	- Same as SMAC - Provides a solution for nodes moving between clusters in the network	- Same as SMAC	- No implementation is observed	- CSMA based protocol
Two-radio MAC with Rate Estimation and Triggered Wakeups [7]	- Same as SMAC but nodes can sleep longer in light traffic and wakeup more during heavy traffic	- Complex hardware, with two radios - Latency is still a problem	- NS2 network simulator	- CSMA based protocol
Transmission Control Scheme for Media Access in Sensor networks [15]	- A CSMA most suitable for WSNs applications: random delay, constant window listen time with fixed or exponential decreased back off window - Easy computable, adaptive traffic rate control	- Does not address idle listening	- UCB motes - Simple UNIX simulator	- Does not address data aggregation in WSNs
ZigBee [22]	- Can accommodate a huge number of nodes (up to 2^{64}) - Supports very low duty cycle and long lifetime for battery powered sensor nodes	- Lower bit rate than Bluetooth - More complicated network structure	- Industrial standard	- CSMA based protocol with optional time slotting - Suitable for low bit rate applications

Table 3. Comparison and summary of different wireless MAC protocols.

The Automatic Rate Control (ARC) technique provides a simple and easy-to-compute scheme to control traffic generation and routing in WSNs. The ZigBee technology is built on the IEEE 802.15.4 standard. Its applications are similar to the applications targeted by WSNs and expected to become a dominant industry protocol for WSNs. In Table 3 we compare and summarize the main features of the MAC protocols discussed in this chapter.

We have also discussed a deficiency of the current implementation of the Energy Model problem in the NS2 network simulator, and showed an example where sleep mode in SMAC is not counted for, being treated as idle listening mode. We modified the NS2 code [20] to solve this problem and provided some exemplifying simulation results.

As future work for WSNs, more emphasis has to be put on cross-layer designs, including aspects at different layers such as physical, MAC, and routing layers. In order to validate the protocols through simulations, there is a high need for a reliable sensor network simulator, that correctly accounts for wireless sensor network characteristics, such as a large number of nodes (e.g., hundreds of thousands of sensor nodes) and various energy models. Finally, protocol characteristics and performances should be validated through experimentations, using a real wireless sensor network environment (e.g., using Crossbow MICA motes [21]).

References

1. I. F. Akyildiz, W. Su, Y. Sankarasubramaniam, and E. Cayirci, A Survey on Sensor Networks, *IEEE Communications Magazine*, Vol 40, No 8, (Aug. 2002), pp. 102–116.
2. A. El-Hoiydi and J. Decotignie, WiseMAC: An Ultra Low Power MAC Protocol for Multi-hop Wireless Sensor Networks, In *Algorithmic Aspects of Wireless Sensor Networks: First International Workshop (ALGOSENSORS'04)*, Springer, (Jul. 2004).
3. W. Heinzelman, A. Chandrakasan, and H. Balakrishnan, Energy-Efficient Communication Protocols for Wireless Microsensor Networks, *Proc. of the Hawaii International Conference on Systems Sciences (HICCS 2000)*, (Jan. 2000).
4. O. Kasten, Energy Consumption, Eldgenossische Technische Hochschule Zurich, http://www.inf.ethz.ch/~kasten/research/bathtub/energy_consumption.html.
5. Y. Li, W. Ye, and J. Heidemann, Energy and Latency Control in Low Duty Cycle MAC Protocols, *IEEE Wireless Communications and Networking Conference (WCNC'05)*, (Mar. 2005).
6. G. Lu, B. Krishnamachari, and C. Raghavendra, An Adaptive Energy-Efficient and Low-Latency MAC for Data Gathering in Sensor Networks, In *Workshop on Energy-Efficient Wireless Communications and Networks (EWCN '04)*, (Apr. 2004).
7. M. Miller and N. Vaidya, Minimizing Energy Consumption in Sensor Networks using a Wakeup Radio, *IEEE WCNC'04*, (Mar. 2004).

8. H. Pham and S. Jha, Ms-MAC: An Adaptive Mobility-Aware MAC Protocol for Sensor Networks, *The 1st IEEE International Conference on Mobile Ad-hoc and Sensor Systems*, (Oct. 2004).

9. V. Raghunathan, C. Schurgers, S. Park, and M. B. Srivastava, Energy-Aware Wireless Microsensor Networks, *IEEE Signal Processing Magazine*, Vol 19, No 2, (Mar. 2002), pp. 40–50.

10. S. Singh and C.S. Raghavendra, PAMAS: Power Aware Multi-Access Protocol with Signaling for Ad Hoc Networks, *ACM Computer Communication Review*, Vol 28, No 3, (Jul. 1998), pp. 5–26.

11. M. Stemm and R. Katz, Measuring and Reducing Energy Consumption of Network Interfaces in Hand-Held Devices, *IEICE Transactions on Communications*, Vol E80-B, No 8, (Aug. 1997), pp. 1125–1131.

12. A. Tanenbaum, Computer Networks, 4th ed., *Prentice Hall*, 2003.

13. V. Tijs and K. Langendoen, An Adaptive Energy-Efficient MAC Protocol for Wireless Sensor Networks, In *Proc. of the First ACM Conference on Embedded Networked Sensor Systems*, (Nov. 2003), pp. 171–180.

14. A. Varga, The OMNeT++ Discrete Event Simulation System, In *European Simulation Multiconference (ESM'01)*, (Jun. 2001).

15. A. Woo and D. Culler, A Transmission Control Scheme for Media Access in Sensor Networks, in *Proc. ACM/IEEE Int. Conf. Mobile Computing and Networking*, (Jul. 2001), pp. 221–235.

16. W. Ye, J. Heidemann, and D. Estrin, An Energy-efficient MAC Protocol for Wireless Sensor Networks, *Proc. IEEE INFOCOM 2002*, (Jun. 2002), pp. 1567–1576.

17. W. Ye, J. Heidemann and D. Estrin, Medium Access Control with Coordinated Adaptive Sleeping for Wireless Sensor Networks, *IEEE, ACM Transactions on Networking*, Vol 12, No 3, (Jun. 2004), pp. 493–506.

18. J. Zhao and R. Govindan, Understanding Packet Delivery Performance in Dense Wireless Sensor Networks, In *Proceedings of the First ACM Conference on Embedded Networked Sensor Systems*, (Nov. 2003), pp. 1–13.

19. Bluetooth SIG Inc., Specification of the Bluetooth System, http://www.bluetooth.org.

20. Fixing Energy Model in NS2, http://student.cse.fau.edu/~AABUEL.

21. Wireless MICA motes, http://www.xbow.com/.

22. IEEE Computer Society, Wireless LAN Medium Access Control (MAC) and Physical Layer (PHY) Specifications for Low-Rate Wireless Personal Area Networks (LR-WPANs), IEEE, New York, NY, USA, 2003.

23. LAN MAN Standards Committee of the IEEE Computer Society, Wireless LAN Medium Access Control (MAC) and Physical Layer (PHY) Specification, IEEE Std. 802.11-1997 Edition, 1997.

24. The Network Simulator ns-2, http://www.isi.edu/nsnam/ns.

Chapter 5
Topology Control for Wireless Sensor Networks

Yu Wang

Department of Computer Science
University of North Carolina at Charlotte, Charlotte, NC 28223
ywang32@uncc.edu

1 Introduction

Due to its potential applications in various situations such as battlefield, emergency relief, environment monitoring, and so on, wireless sensor networks have recently emerged as a premier research topic. Sensor networks consist of a set of sensor nodes which are spread over a geographical area. These nodes are able to perform processing as well as sensing and are additionally capable of communicating with each other. With coordination among these sensor nodes, the network together will achieve a larger sensing task both in urban environments and in inhospitable terrain. The sheer numbers of these sensors, the limited resources on each sensor, and the expected dynamics in these environments present unique challenges in the design of wireless sensor networks.

Topology control is one primary challenge in these scenarios. Unlike the wired networks that typically have fixed network topologies, each sensor node in a sensor network can potentially change the network topology by adjusting its transmission range and/or selecting specific nodes to forward its messages, thus, controlling its set of neighbors. The primary goal of topology control in wireless sensor networks is to maintain network connectivity and optimize network lifetime and throughput. In this chapter, we will survey various techniques used for topology control in wireless sensor networks from a theoretical perspective. First, we will discuss how to use geometrical position information to design power-efficient network topologies, such as geometrical spanners (which are power-efficient for routing) and geometrical low-weight structures (which are power-efficient for broadcasting). Then, we will review methods to build hierarchical structures, virtual backbones, efficiently for sensor networks. Finally, we will also briefly introduce other research issues on topology control such as fault tolerance, interference, transmission power assignment and power management. Due to the space limit, we can not cover all research issues and methods in topology control. Thus, we will mainly focus on how to build geometric structures and virtual backbones for wireless sensor networks.

1.1 Network Models and Assumptions

In the literature, people usually use a *unit disk graph* to model a sensor network. Consider a sensor network consisting of a set V of n wireless sensor nodes distributed in a two-dimensional plane. Each wireless sensor node has an omni-directional antenna, so that a single transmission of a node can be received by all nodes within its vicinity which, we assume, is a disk centered at the node. We call the radius of this disk the *transmission range* of this sensor node. By a proper scaling, we assume that all nodes have the maximum transmission range equal to one unit. Two nodes within each other's transmission ranges can communicate directly, while two far away nodes can communicate through multi-hop wireless links by using intermediate nodes to relay the message. These wireless sensor nodes define a *unit disk graph* UDG(V) in which there is an edge between two nodes if and only if their Euclidean distance is at most 1. See Figure 1(a) for illustrations. Hereafter, we always assume that $UDG(V)$ is a connected graph. We call all nodes within a constant k hops of a node u in the unit disk graph as the k-local nodes (or k-hop neighbors) of u, denoted by $N_k(V)$. It is clearly impossible to collect up-to-date neighborhood information for large k efficiently, therefore, k is usually a small integer such as 1 or 2 in sensor networks. The size of the unit disk graph could be as large as the square order of the number of sensor nodes, such as the example shown in Figure 1(b). So in topology control protocol, we try to construct a subgraph for the unit disk graph $UDG(V)$ so that the subgraph is sparse and can be constructed locally in an efficient way.

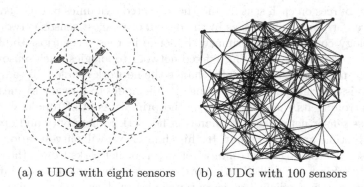

(a) a UDG with eight sensors   (b) a UDG with 100 sensors

Fig. 1. Examples of unit disk graphs.

Notice that a unit disk graph is not a perfect model for practical sensor networks, since the transmission ranges of sensor nodes could be different and not be perfect disks. In [1], Zhou *et al.* studied the impact of radio irregularity on wireless sensor networks. Recently, many other more practical models have been proposed, such as *quasi unit disk graph* [2] and *mutual inclusion graph* [3].

However, since the unit disk graph has its theoretical simplicity, we still use it to model the sensor network in our chapter.

We also assume that all wireless sensor nodes have distinctive identities (denoted by ID hereafter). Some topology control protocols use position information. For these protocols, it always assumes that each node knows its position information either through a low-power Global Position System (GPS) receiver or some other way (such as location service and localization algorithms in [4–6]). With the position information, we can apply computational geometry techniques to solve some challenging questions in sensor networks.

Energy conservation is a critical issue in sensor network for the node and network life, as the nodes are powered by batteries only. Each sensor node typically has a portable set with transmission and reception processing capabilities. In the most common power-attenuation model, the power to support a link uv is assumed to be $\|uv\|^\beta$, where $\|uv\|$ is the Euclidean distance between u and v, β is a real constant between 2 and 5 depending on the wireless transmission environment.

1.2 Localized Algorithms vs Centralized Algorithms

For algorithm design, there are two types of algorithms. *Centralized methods* usually give better results, but have huge communication costs. *Distributed methods* or *localized methods* can achieve weaker results but use less communication costs. In sensor networks, the large numbers of sensors and the expected dynamics present unique challenges in the design of network protocols. We believe there are significant robustness and scalability advantages to designing protocols using *localized algorithms* — where sensors only interact with other sensors in a restricted vicinity, but nevertheless collectively achieve a desired global objective (such as spanner or low weight). Since in the localized algorithms each node communicates only with other nodes in some neighborhood, the communication overhead scales well with increase in network size. For a similar reason, these algorithms are robust to network partitions and node failures. Specifically for topology control, it is preferred that the underlying network topology can be constructed in a localized manner. Here a distributed algorithm constructing a graph G is a *localized algorithm* if every node u can exactly decide all edges incident on u based only on the information of all nodes within a constant hop of u.

1.3 Organization

The rest of the chapter is organized as follows. In Section 2, we survey several geometry spanners that can be used as power-efficient topology for wireless sensor networks. In Section 3, we review several low-weight structures that are suitable for broadcasting in wireless sensor networks. In Section 4, state of the art of constructing virtual backbone for sensor networks is reviewed. As there are many heuristics proposed in this area, we concentrate on the ones that have theoretic performance guarantees. Section 5 describes some other related research issues on topology control for sensor networks. Finally, the chapter concludes with Section 6.

2 Geometrical Spanners

As we mentioned before, when each node knows its geometrical position, the geometry techniques can be applied in protocol design for sensor networks to achieve better performance. Specifically for topology control, many geometrical structures have been proposed to be used as the power efficient topologies for sensor networks. Remember, we use a unit disk graph to model the communication graph for sensor networks. Not every connected subgraph of the unit disk graph are suitable to be a network topology. One of the perceptible requirements of topology control is to construct a subgraph such that the shortest path connecting any two nodes in the subgraph is not much longer than the shortest path connecting them in the original unit disk graph. This aspect of path quality (power efficiency of the path) is captured by the *stretch factor* of the subgraph. A subgraph with constant stretch factor is often called a *spanner* and a spanner is called a *sparse spanner* if it has only a linear number of links. In this subsection, we study how to construct a sparse spanner (as the network topology) efficiently for a set of static sensor nodes.

Spanners have been studied intensively in recent years [7–13]. Let $G = (V, E)$ be a geometric graph defined on an n-vertex set V with edge set E. The distance in G between two vertices $u, v \in V$ is the total length (or weight) of the shortest path between u and v and is denoted by $d_G(u, v)$. A subgraph $H = (V, E')$, where $E' \subseteq E$, is a *t-spanner* of G if for every $u, v \in V$, $d_H(u, v) \leq t \cdot d_G(u, v)$. The value of t is called the *stretch factor*. For sensor networks, the communication graph G is modelled by a unit disk graph. Consider any unicast $\Pi(u, v)$ in G from a node $u \in V$ to another node $v \in V$: $\Pi(u, v) = v_0 v_1 \cdots v_{h-1} v_h$, where $u = v_0$, $v = v_h$. Here h is the number of hops of the path Π. The total *transmission power* $p(\Pi)$ consumed by this path Π is defined as

$$p(\Pi) = \sum_{i=1}^{h} \|v_{i-1} v_i\|^{\beta}.$$

Let $p_G(u, v)$ be the least energy consumed by all paths connecting nodes u and v in G. Let H be a subgraph of G. The *power stretch factor* of the graph H with respect to G is then defined as

$$\rho_H(G) = \max_{u,v \in V} \frac{p_H(u, v)}{p_G(u, v)}.$$

If G is a unit disk graph, we use $\rho_H(V)$ instead of $\rho_H(G)$. If the $\rho_H(V)$ is bounded by a constant for all unit disk graphs, we call the graph H a *power spanner*. Similarly, we can define the length stretch factors $\ell_H(G)$ and

$\ell_H(V)$ by setting $\beta = 1$. And we say a graph H is a *length spanner* if the $\ell_H(V)$ is bounded by a constant. It is not difficult to show that, for any $H \subseteq G$ with a length stretch factor δ, its power stretch factor is at most δ^β for any graph G. In particular, a graph with a constant bounded length stretch factor must also have a constant bounded power stretch factor, but the reverse is not true. Finally, the power stretch factor has the following monotonic property: If $H_1 \subset H_2 \subset G$, then the power stretch factors of H_1 and H_2 satisfy $\rho_{H_1}(G) \geq \rho_{H_2}(G)$.

Several geometrical spanners have been studied recently both by computational geometers and network engineers. In this section, we review the definitions and properties of some geometrical spanners which could be used in wireless sensor networking applications.

2.1 Planar Spanners

A network topology is preferred to be planar (no two edges crossing each other in the graph) to enable some localized routing algorithms work correctly and efficiently, such as Greedy Perimeter Stateless Routing (GPSR) [14], Greedy Face Routing (GFG) [15], Adaptive Face Routing(AFR) [16]. and Gready Other Adaptive Face Routing (GOAFR) [17]. Notice that with planar network topology as the underlying routing structure, these localized routing protocols guarantee the message delivery without using a routing table: each intermediate node can decide which logical neighboring node to forward the packet to, using only local information and the position of the source and the destination. We then review several planar structures which have been used in sensor networks as routing topologies.

Relative Neighborhood Graph and Gabriel Graph

The *relative neighborhood graph*, denoted by RNG(G), is a geometric concept proposed by Toussaint [18,19]. It consists of all edges $uv \in E$ such that there is no point $w \in V$ with edges uw and wv in E satisfying $\|uw\| < \|uv\|$ and $\|wv\| < \|uv\|$. Thus, an edge uv is included if the intersection of two circles centered at u and v and with radius $\|uv\|$ do not contain any vertex w from the set V such that edges uw and wv exist in E. See Figure 2 (a) for an illustration. Let $disk(u,v)$ be the disk with diameter uv. Then, the *Gabriel graph* [20] GG(G) contains an edge uv from G if and only if $disk(u,v)$ contains no other vertex $w \in V$ such that there exist edges uw and wv from G. See Figure 2 (b) for an illustration. When G is a unit disk graph, we use RNG(V) and GG(V) to denote the graphs instead of RNG(G) and GG(G).

Both RNG(V) and GG(V) are planar graphs (that is, no two edges cross each other), which also implies their sparseness: $|RNG(V)| \leq 3n$ and $|GG(V)| \leq 3n$, where n is the number of vertices. It is easy to show that RNG(V) is a subgraph of GG(V). For an undirected and connected graph

G, both $GG(G)$ and $RNG(G)$ are connected and contain the minimum spanning tree of G. In other words, if the $UDG(V)$ is connected, the constructed $RNG(V)$ and $GG(V)$ are connected too. This insures the connectivity of the sensor networks. Another important property they have is that they can be constructed easily using localized methods. From the definitions, each node only needs information from its one-hop neighbors to construct the $RNG(V)$ and $GG(V)$.

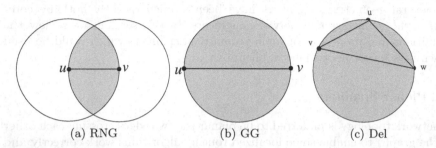

(a) RNG   (b) GG   (c) Del

Fig. 2. The definitions of RNG, GG and Del on a point set. The shaded area is empty of nodes inside. (a): The lune using uv is empty for RNG. (b): The diametric circle using uv is empty for GG. (c): The circumcircle of uvw is empty for Del.

A Gabriel graph was used as a planar subgraph in the face routing protocol [15, 21] and the GPSR routing protocol [14] that guarantee the delivery of the packet. A relative neighborhood graph was used for efficient broadcasting (minimizing the number of retransmissions) in the one-to-one broadcasting model in [22]. However, the same analysis by Bose *et al* [9] implied that the length stretch factor of $RNG(V)$ is at most $n-1$ and the length stretch factor of $GG(V)$ is at most $\frac{4\pi\sqrt{2n-4}}{3}$. Recently, Wang *et al* [23] showed that the length stretch factor of $GG(V)$ is precisely $\sqrt{n-1}$ actually. Li *et al.* [24] first studied and analyzed the power stretch factors of $RNG(V)$ and $GG(V)$. They showed that the power stretch factor of $RNG(V)$ is actually $n-1$ by constructing an example, and proved that the power stretch factor of any Gabriel graph is 1. Therefore, in summary, $RNG(V)$ is not a power/length spanner, while $GG(V)$ is a power spanner but not a length spanner. For unicast routing in sensor networks, a Gabriel graph is power efficient when a relative neighborhood graph is not.

Delaunay Triangulation and Its Relatives

While Gabriel graphs and relative neighborhood graphs are not length spanners, *Delaunay triangulation* is a well-known length spanner. Assume that there are no four vertices of V that are co-circular. A triangulation of V is a *Delaunay triangulation*, denoted by $Del(V)$, if the circumcircle of each of its triangles does not contain any other vertices of V in its interior. A triangle is called the *Delaunay triangle* if its circumcircle is empty of vertices of V. See Figure 2 (c) for an illustration.

Dobkin *et al.* [25] first proved the Delaunay Triangulation is a length spanner with length stretch factor bounded by $\frac{1+\sqrt{5}}{2}\pi$. Then Keil and Gutwin [26] improved the constant to be $\frac{2\pi}{3\cos(\frac{\pi}{6})} = \frac{4\sqrt{3}}{9}\pi \approx 2.42$. Notice that the Gabriel graph is a subgraph of the Delaunay triangulation and the power stretch factor of a Gabriel graph is 1. Thus, the power stretch factor of Delaunay triangulation is also one, due to the monotonic property of the power spanner.

Given a set of points V, let UDel(V) be the graph obtained by removing all edges of $Del(V)$ that are longer than one unit, i.e., $UDel(V) = Del(V) \cap UDG(V)$. Li *et al* [27] considered the *unit Delaunay triangulation* UDel(V) for planar spanner of UDG and proved that UDel(V) is a $\frac{4\sqrt{3}}{9}\pi$-spanner of UDG(V).

Though Delaunay triangulation (or unit Delaunay triangulation) is a well-known planar spanner, it is not appropriate to require the construction of the Delaunay triangulation in the wireless communication environment because of the possible massive communications it requires. Notice that the circumcircle of a triangle can be very large (much larger than the transmission range of a sensor node), therefore it may need global information to build the Delaunay triangulation. Several published results [27–30] were proposed to build Delaunay triangulation or its relatives in a localized way.

Localized Delaunay Triangulation

Li *et al* [27, 28] gave a localized algorithm that constructs a sequence of graphs, called a *localized Delaunay* $LDel^{(k)}(V)$, which are supergraphs of UDel(V). We begin with some necessary definitions before reviewing the algorithm. Triangle $\triangle uvw$ is called a *k-localized Delaunay triangle* if the interior of the circumcircle of $\triangle uvw$ does not contain any vertex of V that is a k-neighbor of u, v, or w; and all edges of the triangle $\triangle uvw$ have length no more than one unit. The *k-localized Delaunay graph* over a vertex set V, denoted by $LDel^{(k)}(V)$, has exactly all Gabriel edges in UDG and edges of all k-localized Delaunay triangles.

The localized algorithm for the construction of $LDel^{(k)}(V)$ goes as follows. Each node u first gathers the location information of its k-hop neighbors $N_k(u)$ and computes the Delaunay triangulation $Del(N_k(u))$ of its k-neighbors $N_k(u)$, including u itself. Each node u marks all *Gabriel edges uv* incident on u, which will never be deleted. Each node u finds all triangles $\triangle uvw$ from $Del(N_k(u))$ such that all three edges of $\triangle uvw$ have length at most one unit. If angle $\angle wuv \geq \frac{\pi}{3}$, node u broadcasts a message proposal(u, v, w) to form a k-localized Delaunay triangle $\triangle uvw$ in $LDel^{(k)}(V)$, and listens to the messages from other nodes. When a node u receives a message proposal(u, v, w), u accepts the proposal of constructing $\triangle uvw$, if $\triangle uvw$ belongs to the Delaunay triangulation $Del(N_k(u))$, by broadcasting message accept(u, v, w); otherwise, it rejects the proposal by broadcasting message reject(u, v, w). A node u adds the edges uv and uw to its set of incident edges if the triangle $\triangle uvw$ is in the Delaunay triangulation $Del(N_k(u))$ and both v and w have sent either accept(u, v, w) or proposal(u, v, w).

It was proved that the graph constructed by the above algorithm is $LDel^{(k)}(V)$. Indeed, for each triangle $\triangle uvw$ of $LDel^{(k)}(V)$, one of its interior angles is at least $\pi/3$ and $\triangle uvw$ is in $Del(N_k(u))$, $Del(N_k(v))$ and $Del(N_k(w))$. So one of the nodes among $\{u, v, w\}$ will broadcast the message proposal(u, v, w) to form a k-localized Delaunay triangle $\triangle uvw$. As $Del(N_k(u))$ is a planar graph, and a proposal is made only if $\angle wuv \geq \frac{\pi}{3}$, node u broadcasts at most six proposals. And each proposal is replied to by at most two nodes. Therefore, the total communication cost (except messages for gathering the information of k-hop neighbors) is $O(n)$ messages.

As shown in [27, 28], the graph $LDel^{(1)}(V)$ may contain some edges intersecting while $LDel^{(k)}(V)$ is a planar graph for any $k \geq 2$. Although $LDel^{(1)}(V)$ is not a planar graph, [27] proved $LDel^{(1)}(V)$ has thickness 2 which implies it is sparse. Since $UDel(V) \subseteq LDel^{(k)}(V)$, which is proved in [27,28], $LDel^{(k)}(V)$ is also a length spanner.

For sensor networks, we can construct $LDel^{(2)}(V)$, which is guaranteed to be a planar spanner of $UDel(V)$, but it is difficult to collect the 2-hop neighbors for every node in $O(n)$ messages. A total communication cost of a simple broadcast approach to collect 2-hop information is $O(m)$ messages, where m is the number of edges in $UDG(V)$ and could be as large as $O(n^2)$. Recently, Călinescu [31] proposed an approach (using $O(n)$ messages total) which is based on the specific connected dominating set introduced by [32]. Using this approach, we can build $LDel^{(2)}$ in $O(n)$ messages, however the constant behind it is still large. There was such an algorithm proposed in [33]. In order to reduce the total communication cost to $O(n)$ messages, [27, 28] do not construct $LDel^{(2)}(V)$, and they extract a planar graph $PLDel(V)$ out of $LDel^{(1)}(V)$ instead. They provided a novel algorithm to make $LDel^{(1)}(V)$ planar using linear communications after building it. The final graph still contains $UDel(V)$ as a subgraph. Thus, it is a spanner of the unit-disk graph. For detailed algorithm and proofs, refer to [27, 28].

Restricted Delaunay Graph

Gao *et al* [29] also proposed another structure, called a *restricted Delaunay graph* RDG and showed that it has constant stretch factor properties and can be maintained locally. A restricted Delaunay graph of a set of points in the plane is a planar graph and contains all the Delaunay edges with length at most 1. In other words, they call *any* planar graph containing $UDel(V)$ a restricted Delaunay graph. They described a distributed algorithm to construct an RDG such that at the end of the algorithm, each node u maintains a set of edges $E(u)$ incident to u. Those edges $E(u)$ satisfy that (1) each edge in $E(u)$ has length at most one unit; (2) the edges are consistent, i.e., an edge $uv \in E(u)$ if and only if $uv \in E(v)$; (3) the graph obtained is planar; (4) The graph $UDel(V)$ is in the union of all edges $E(u)$.

The algorithm works as follows. First, each node u acquires the position of its 1-hop neighbors $N_1(u)$ and computes the Delaunay triangulation $Del(N_1(u))$ on $N_1(u)$, including u itself. In the second step, each node u sends $Del(N_1(u))$ to all of its neighbors. Let $E(u) = \{uv \mid uv \in Del(N_1(u))\}$. For each edge $uv \in E(u)$, and for each $w \in N_1(u)$, if u and v are in $N_1(w)$ and $uv \notin Del(N_1(u))$, then node u deletes edge uv from $E(u)$.

When the above steps are finished, the resulting edges $E(u)$ satisfy the four properties listed above. However, unlike the local Delaunay triangulation, the computation cost and communication cost of each node needed to obtain $E(u)$ is not optimal within a small constant factor.

2.2 Bounded-Degree Spanners

Besides the sparseness and spanner properties, it is also desirable that the node degree in the constructed topology is small and bounded from above by a constant. A small node degree reduces the MAC-level contention and interference also may help to mitigate the well-known hidden and exposed terminal problems. Therefore, we now review some bounded degree spanners. Notice that all of the planar structures mentioned in the previous subsection do not have bounded node degree. An example of such node configuration is shown in Figure 3(a) [24].

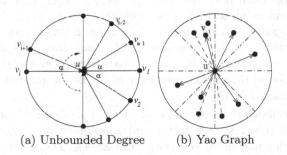

(a) Unbounded Degree   (b) Yao Graph

Fig. 3. (a) Node u has degree (or in-degree) $n - 1$. (b) Illustration of Yao graph: bound out-degree by Yao structure. Here $k = 8$.

Yao Graph and θ-graph

The *Yao graph* [13] with an integer parameter $k \geq 6$, denoted by $\overrightarrow{YG}_k(G)$, is defined as follows. At each node u, any k equally-separated rays originated at u define k cones. In each cone, choose the shortest edge uv among all edges from u, if there is any, and add a directed link $\overrightarrow{uv}$ (as shown in Figure 3(b)). Ties are broken arbitrarily. The resulting directed graph is called the Yao graph. If we add the link $\overrightarrow{vu}$ instead of the link $\overrightarrow{uv}$, the graph is denoted by

$\overleftrightarrow{YG}_k(G)$, which is called the *reverse* of the Yao graph. Some researchers used a similar construction named θ-graph [34, 45], the difference is that, in each cone, it chooses the edge which has the shortest projection on the angular bisector of the cone instead of the shortest edge.

Applying Yao structure on $UDG(V)$ to bound node degree is a very natural idea. Hereafter, we use $\overrightarrow{YG}_k(V)$ to denote $\overrightarrow{YG}_k(UDG(V))$. The Yao graph $\overrightarrow{YG}_k(V)$ has length stretch factor $\frac{1}{1-2\sin\frac{\pi}{k}}$. Thus, its power stretch factor is no more than $(\frac{1}{1-2\sin\frac{\pi}{k}})^\beta$. Li *et al* [24] proved a stronger result: the power stretch factor of the Yao graph $\overrightarrow{YG}_k(V)$ is at most $\frac{1}{1-(2\sin\frac{\pi}{k})^\beta}$.

Li *et al* [35] also proposed to apply the Yao structure on top of the Gabriel graph structure (the resulting graph is denoted by $\overrightarrow{YGG}_k(V)$), and apply the Gabriel graph structure on top of the Yao structure (the resulting graph is denoted by $\overrightarrow{GYG}_k(V)$). These structures are sparser than the Yao structure and the Gabriel graph structure and they still have a constant bounded power stretch factor. These two structures are connected graphs if the UDG is connected, which can be proved by showing that RNG is a subgraph of both structures. A similar idea is proposed in the two-phased approach by Wattenhofer *et al* [36] which consists of a variation of the θ-graph followed by a variation of the Gabriel graph.

Li *et al* [37] proposed a structure that is similar to the Yao structure for topology control. Each node u finds a power $p_{u,\alpha}$ such that in every cone of degree α surrounding u, there is some node that u can reach with power $p_{u,\alpha}$. Then the graph G_α contains all edges uv such that u can communicate with v using power $p_{u,\alpha}$. It was proved in [37] that, if $\alpha \leq \frac{5\pi}{6}$ and the UDG is connected, then graph G_α is a connected graph. On the other hand, if $\alpha > \frac{5\pi}{6}$, they showed that the connectivity of G_α is not guaranteed by giving some counter-examples [37].

Note that although the directed graphs $\overrightarrow{YG}_k(V)$, $\overrightarrow{GYG}_k(V)$ and $\overrightarrow{YGG}_k(V)$ have a bounded power stretch factor and a bounded out-degree k for each node, some nodes may have very large in-degrees. The node configuration given in Figure 3(a) will result in a very large in-degree for node u. Bounded out-degree gives us advantages when we apply several routing algorithms. However, unbounded in-degree at node u will often cause large overhead at u. Therefore it is often imperative to construct a sparse network topology such that both the in-degree and the out-degree are bounded by a constant while it is still power-efficient.

Sink Structure

Arya *et al* [7] gave an ingenious technique to generate a bounded degree graph with constant length stretch factor. In [24], Li *et al* applied the same technique to construct a sparse network topology with a bounded degree and a bounded power stretch factor from $\overrightarrow{YG}_k(V)$. The technique is to replace the directed star consisting of all links toward a node u in $\overrightarrow{YG}_k(V)$ by a directed tree $T(u)$ of a bounded degree with u as the sink. Tree $T(u)$ is constructed recursively. The algorithm is as follows. First, construct the graph $\overrightarrow{YG}_k(V)$. Each node u will have a set of in-coming nodes $I(u) = \{v \mid \overrightarrow{vu} \in \overrightarrow{YG}_k(V)\}$. For each node u, use the following method (called $\mathsf{Tree}(u, I(u))$) to build tree $T(u)$. First, node u chooses k equal-sized cones centered at u: $C_1(u), C_2(u),$ $\ldots, C_k(u)$ to partition the unit disk centered at u. Node u finds the nearest node $y_i \in I(u)$ in $C_i(u)$, for $1 \leq i \leq k$, if there is any. Link $\overrightarrow{y_i u}$ is added to $T(u)$ and y_i is removed from $I(u)$. For each cone $C_i(u)$, if $I(u) \cap C_i(u)$ is not empty, recursively call $\mathsf{Tree}(y_i, I(u) \cap C_i(u))$ and add the created edges to $T(u)$. Figure 4 (a) illustrates a directed star centered at u in $\overrightarrow{YG}_k(V)$ and Figure 4 (b) shows the directed tree $T(u)$ constructed to replace the star with $k = 8$. The union of all trees $T(u)$ is called the *sink structure* $\overrightarrow{YG}_k^*(V)$.

Notice that node u constructs the tree $T(u)$ and then broadcasts the structure of $T(u)$ to all nodes in $T(u)$. Since the total number of edges in the Yao structure is at most $k \cdot n$, where k is the number of cones divided, the total number of edges of $T(u)$ of all nodes u is also at most $k \cdot n$. Thus, the total communication cost of broadcasting the $T(u)$ to all its neighbors is still at most $k \cdot n$.

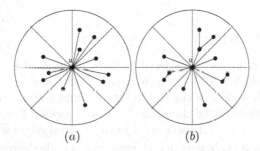

(a)   (b)

Fig. 4. (a) Star - links toward to u. (b) Directed tree $T(u)$ sinked at u.

The algorithm uses a directed tree $T(u)$ to replace the directed star for each node u. Therefore, if nodes u and v are connected by a path in $\overrightarrow{YG}_k$, they are also connected by a path in $\overrightarrow{YG}_k^*$. It is already known that $\overrightarrow{YG}_k$ is strongly connected if UDG(V) is connected, so is $\overrightarrow{YG}_k^*$. In [24], the authors also proved that the power stretch factor of $\overrightarrow{YG}_k^*(V)$ is at most $(\frac{1}{1-(2\sin\frac{\pi}{k})^\beta})^2$ and the maximum degree of $\overrightarrow{YG}_k^*(V)$ is at most $(k+1)^2 - 1$.

Sparsified Yao Graph

Another Yao-based algorithm is proposed by Li *et al* [35] that constructs a sparser and bounded-degree topology. The basic idea is to apply reverse Yao structure on $\overrightarrow{YG}_k$ to bound the in-degree. Node u chooses a node v from each cone, if there is any, so the directed link $\overrightarrow{vu}$ has the smallest length among all directed links $\overrightarrow{wu}$ in $\overrightarrow{YG}_k$ in that cone. The union of all chosen directed links is the final network topology, denoted by $\overrightarrow{YY}_k(V)$. Notice that in [38,39], they reinvestigate $\overrightarrow{YY}_k(V)$ structure, and call it a *Sparsified Yao graph* or *Yao Yao graph*.

In [35], the authors proved $\overrightarrow{YY}_k(V)$ is strongly connected if UDG(V) is connected and $k > 6$. It was proved in [40] that $\overrightarrow{YY}_k(V)$ is a spanner in civilized unit disk graphs (also called λ-precision unit disk graphs [41]). Here a unit disk graph is a civilized graph if the distance between any two nodes in this graph is larger than a positive constant λ. Notice that the sensor devices in wireless sensor networks can not be too close or overlapped. Thus, it is reasonable to model the sensor network as a civilized unit disk graph. The experimental results by Li *et al* [35,40] showed that this sparse topology has a small power stretch factor in practice. They [35, 40] conjectured that $\overrightarrow{YY}_k(V)$ also has constant-bounded length and power stretch factors theoretically in any unit disk graph. Recently Jia *et al* [42] and Schindelhauer *et al* [43] proved that $\overrightarrow{YY}_k(V)$ has a constant bounded power stretch factor theoretically. However, it is still an open problem whether it is a length spanner.

Symmetric Yao Graph

In [30, 40, 44], Li *et al* also considered another undirected structure, called a *symmetric Yao graph* $YS_k(V)$, which guarantees that the node degree is at most k. Each node u divides the region into k equal angular regions centered at the node, and chooses the closest node in each region, if any. An edge uv is selected to graph $YS_k(V)$ if and only if both directed edges $\overrightarrow{uv}$ and $\overrightarrow{vu}$ are in the $\overrightarrow{YG}_k(V)$. Then it is obvious that the maximum node degree is k. In [30,44], the authors proved that $YS_k(V)$ is strongly connected if UDG(V) is connected and $k \geq 6$. The experiment in [30,40,44] also showed that it has a small power stretch factor in practice. However, it was shown in [38] recently that $YS_k(V)$ is not a spanner theoretically. They constructed a counter example to show that $YS_k(V)$ may have large stretch factor.

2.3 Bounded-Degree Planar Spanners

The structures discussed so far either have bounded degree, or are planar, or are spanners, but none of the structures has all these three properties together. We then review one recent result [33] that can construct a bounded degree planar spanner in a localized manner. Their method rigorously combines localized Delaunay triangulation $LDel^{(2)}(V)$ and the ordered Yao structure [45].

Algorithm 1 CONSTRUCT BOUNDED-DEGREE PLANAR SPANNER

1. First, compute the planar localized Delaunay triangulation $LDel^{(2)}(V)$ (using the method in [31] to collect the location information of $N_2(u)$), so that every node u knows all its neighbors $N_{LDel^{(2)}}(u)$ and its node degree $d(u)$ in $LDel^{(2)}(V)$. Assume a synchronized method is used to collect $N_{LDel^{(2)}}(u)$ for every node u.

2. Build a local order π of V as follows: (Every node u initializes $\pi_u = 0$, i.e., unordered.)

   a) If node u has $\pi_u = 0$ and $d(u) \leq 5$, then u queries each node v, from its unordered neighbors, the current degree $d(v)$. If node u has the smallest ID among all unordered neighbors v with $d(v) \leq 5$, node u sets

   $$\pi_u = \max\{\pi_v \mid v \in N_{LDel^{(2)}}(u)\} + 1,$$

   and broadcasts π_u to its neighbors $N_{LDel^{(2)}}(u)$.

   b) If node u receives a message from its neighbor v saying that $\pi_v = k$, it updates its $d(u) = d(u) - 1$ and also updates the order π_v stored locally. So $d(u)$ represents how many neighbors are not ordered so far. If node u finds that $d(u) \leq 5$ and $\pi_u = 0$, it goes to Step 2 (a). When node u finds that $d(u) = 0$ and $\pi_u > 0$, it can go to step 3.

3. Build structures based on local order π as follows: (Initialize all nodes unprocessed)

   a) If an unprocessed node u has the highest local order in its unprocessed neighbors N_u in $LDel^{(2)}(V)$, let k be the number of processed neighbors of u in $LDel^{(2)}(V)$ (at most 5 since graph $LDel^{(2)}(V)$ is planar). Assume that $v_1, v_2, \ldots, v_k$ be the processed neighbors of u in $LDel^{(2)}(V)$. Node u divides its transmission range into k *open* sectors cut by the rays from u to these processed neighbors. Then divide each sector into a minimum number of *open* cones of degree at most α with $\alpha \leq \pi/3$. For each cone, let $s_1, s_2, \ldots, s_m$ be the ordered unprocessed neighbors of u in $N_{LDel^{(2)}}(u)$. For this cone, node u first adds an edge us_i, where s_i is the nearest neighbor among $s_1, s_2, \ldots, s_m$. Node u then tells $s_1, s_2, \ldots, s_m$ to add all the edges $s_j s_{j+1}$, $1 \leq j < m$. Node u marks itself processed, and tells all nodes in $N_{LDel^{(2)}}(u)$ that it is processed.

   b) If an unprocessed node v receives a message for adding edge vv' from its neighbor u, it adds edge vv'.

4. When all nodes are processed, the final network topology is denoted by $BPS(V)$.

Notice that in the algorithm we use *open* sectors, which means that in the algorithm we do not consider adding the edges on the boundaries (any edge involved previously processed neighbors). In other words, the open cones do not include any edges uv_i. This guarantees the algorithm does not add any edges to node v_i after v_i has been processed. This approach bounds the node degree. In [33], the authors proved that the maximum node degree of the graph

$BPS(V)$ is at most $19 + \lceil \frac{2\pi}{\alpha} \rceil$. For example, when $\alpha = \pi/3$, the maximum node degree is at most 25. Note that the ordering computed by this method is not a global ordering. Some nodes may have the same order. However, no two neighboring nodes in $LDel^{(2)}(V)$ receive the same order. Thus, after all nodes are ordered, the algorithm will process all nodes. Observe that the algorithm does not process two neighboring nodes at the same time. Assume that there are two nodes, say u and v, processed at the same time. Remember that we process a node only if it has the highest ordering among its unprocessed neighbors. Thus, nodes u and v must receive the same order, i.e., $\pi_u = \pi_v$, which is impossible in the ordering method. In [33], the authors also proved that graph $BPS(V)$ is a planar t-spanner, where $t = \max\{\frac{\pi}{2}, \pi \sin \frac{\alpha}{2} + 1\} \cdot C_{del}$. Hereafter, we use C_{del} to denote the length stretch factor of the Delaunay triangulation. The proofs of the planar and spanner properties are much more complex; refer to [33] for details. In addition, Algorithm 1 uses at most $O(n)$ messages, where each message has $O(\log n)$ bits. However, the hidden constant could be as high as several hundreds since the method needs to collect the 2-hop information for every node.

Remember that a Gabriel graph is a planar power spanner. To reduce the total communication cost, Song *et al* [46] proposed a new method by applying the ordered Yao structures on a Gabriel graph to bound node degree. The idea is similar with the above method in [33]. The major differences are in [46]: (1) they only use one-hop information instead of two-hop information, which reduces communication cost significantly; (2) they use a Gabriel graph instead of the localized Delaunay triangulation, which makes the localized method much simpler and more efficient.

The algorithm is as follows. First, each node self-constructs the Gabriel graph GG locally. Let $N_{GG}(u)$ be the neighbor's set of node u in GG. Then, each node u decides its order π locally using the same method in [33]. After that, all nodes self-form the final topology based on local order π as follows. Initially, all nodes are marked with WHITE color, i.e., unprocessed. Let $N_{OYGG}(u)$ be the set of neighbors of u in the final topology, which is initialized as $N_{GG}(u)$. If node u is unprocessed (marked WHITE), and it has the largest order $\pi[u]$ among all its WHITE neighbors in $N_{GG}(u)$, it divides its transmission range (which is a unit disk centered at the node u) into k equal-sized cones, keeps one nearest WHITE neighbor $v \in N_{OYGG}(u)$ (if available) in each cone and deletes others. Node u marks itself BLACK, i.e., processed, and notifies all nodes in $N_{GG}(u)$ of the deleted edges through a broadcasting message UPDATEN. The message UPDATEN includes all unselected neighbors. Once the node u receives the message UPDATEN for deleting edge vu from its neighbor v, it deletes the node v from its local list $N_{OYGG}(u)$. When all nodes are processed, all the remaining edges $\{uv | v \in N_{OYGG}(u)\}$ form the final network topology $OrdYaoGG$.

It is proved in [46] that $OrdYaoGG$ is a bounded-degree planar power spanner. The power stretch factor is at most $\frac{1}{1-(2\sin\frac{\pi}{k})^\beta}$ while the node degree is bounded from above by a positive constant $k+5$ where $k > 6$ is an adjustable parameter. Moreover, by assuming that the node ID and its position can be represented in $O(\log n)$ bits each for a sensor network of n nodes, they showed that the structure can be constructed using at most $24n$ messages, where each message is $O(\log n)$ bits.

Furthermore, Song et al. [46] proposed another method to build a degree-bounded planar power spanner, which can be constructed easier and demands less communication cost during construction.

Algorithm 2 CONSTRUCT DEGREE-k PLANAR POWER SPANNER

1. First, each node self-constructs the Gabriel graph GG locally.
2. All nodes together self-form the final topology as follows. Initially, each node u is marked with WHITE, i.e., unprocessed, and initializes $N_{SYGG}(u)$ as the set of all the neighbor nodes in GG.

   a) If a WHITE node u has the smallest ID among its WHITE neighbors in GG, it divides its transmission range into k equal-sized cones where $k > 8$ is an adjustable parameter. In each cone, node u checks whether there are some BLACK nodes in $N_{SYGG}(u)$ within the same cone:

      i. Yes. Node u keeps the closest BLACK neighbor $v \in N_{SYGG}(u)$ among them and deletes all the other links in the cone;

      ii. No. Node u keeps a closest WHITE neighbor $v \in N_{SYGG}(u)$ (if available) among them and deletes all the other links in the cone.

      After processing all k cones, node u marks itself BLACK, i.e., processed, then notifies each deleted neighboring node v in GG by a broadcasting message UPDATEN.

   b) Once a WHITE node v receives the message UPDATEN from a neighbor u in GG, it checks whether it itself is in the nodes set for deleting: if so, it deletes the sending node u from $N_{SYGG}(v)$, otherwise, marks u as BLACK in its local list $N_{SYGG}(v)$.

   c) Once a BLACK node v receives the message UPDATEN from a neighbor belonging to $N_{SYGG}(v)$, it checks whether it itself is in the nodes set for deleting: if so, it deletes the sending node u from $N_{SYGG}(v)$, otherwise, marks u as BLACK in its local list $N_{SYGG}(v)$.

3. When all nodes are processed, all selected edges $\{uv | v \in N_{SYGG}(u)\}$ form the final network topology, denoted by $SYaoGG$.

Algorithm 2 further reduces the communication cost during constructing a degree-bounded planar power spanner to $3n$ messages, because it does not demand the local ordering before construction. It also reduces the degree bound to k, and keeps all other nice properties, except that the theoretical power stretch factor is relaxed to $\frac{\sqrt{2}^\beta}{1-(2\sqrt{2}\sin\frac{\pi}{k})^\beta}$, where $k > 8$ is an adjustable parameter.

Notice that both $OrdYaoGG$ and $SYaoGG$ are degree-bounded planar power spanners, but they are not length spanners. However, $BPS(V)$ is a degree-bounded planar length spanner. The summary of properties of all spanners reviewed is given in Table 1.

Table 1. Summary of the geometric spanners

	Power-Spanner	Length-Spanner	Bounded-Degree	Planar	Built-Locally
RNG	no	no	no	yes	yes
GG	yes	no	no	yes	yes
Del	yes	yes	no	yes	no
$LDel$	yes	yes	no	yes	yes
RDG	yes	yes	no	yes	yes
YG	yes	yes	no	no	yes
YG^*	yes	yes	yes	no	yes
YY	yes	open	yes	no	yes
YS	no	no	yes	no	yes
BPS	yes	yes	yes	yes	yes
$OYAOGG$	yes	no	yes	yes	yes
$SYAOGG$	yes	no	yes	yes	yes

3 Geometrical Low-Weight Structures

The power stretch factor we previously discussed is defined for unicasting communications. However, in practice, we also have to consider broadcast or multicast communications. Wan *et al* [47] showed that the minimum energy cost of broadcasting or multicasting is related to the total energy cost of all links in the Euclidean minimum spanning tree *MST*. The *minimum spanning tree* of G, denoted by MST(G), is the tree belong to E that connects all nodes and whose total edge length is minimized. MST(G) is obviously one of the sparsest connected subgraphs. Wan *et al* [47] proved that a broadcasting method based on the Euclidean minimum spanning tree rooted at the sender uses energy no more than 12 times the minimum energy cost of any broadcasting scheme. Therefore, we want the network broadcast topology to be a low-weight structure. Given a structure G over a set of points, let $\omega(G)$ be the total length of the links in G and $\omega_\beta(G)$ be the total power needed to support all links in G, i.e., $\omega_\beta(G) = \sum_{uv \in G} \|uv\|^\beta$. Then, a structure G is called *low weight* if $\omega(G)$ is within a constant factor of $\omega(MST)$.

Unfortunately, the total weight of any graph structures mentioned above could be arbitrarily larger than MST theoretically [35, 48]. In [35, 48], an instance of a wireless network with n nodes is given, and the total weight of the relative neighborhood graph on the network could be n times the $\omega(MST)$. In addition, all other graph structures described previously contain RNG as a subgraph for that node configuration. It then implies our previous claim.

In this section we will discuss how to design algorithms achieving low weight, and (possibly) in addition to some other properties such as spanner, bounded degree, and planar.

3.1 Localized Low-Weight Structures

Notice that it is well-known that the communication complexity of constructing a minimum spanning tree of an n-vertex graph G with m edges is $O(m + n \log n)$; while the communication complexity of constructing MST for UDG is $O(n \log n)$ even under the local broadcasting communication model in wireless networks. It was shown in [49] that it is *impossible* to construct a low-weight structure using only one hop neighbor information. Recently, Li *et al* [48–50] proposed three localized structures which are low weight, planar and have bounded node degree. Building these low weight structures uses partial 2-hop information for each node.

Low-Weight Structure Based on RNG'

In [49], Li proposed the first localized method to construct a structure H with weight $O(\omega(MST))$ using total $O(n)$ local-broadcast messages. The method is based on a modified relative neighborhood graph. Traditionally, the relative neighborhood graph will always select an edge uv even if there is some node on the boundary of $lune(u, v)$. Thus, RNG may have unbounded node degree, e.g., the example in Figure 3(a). Notice that for the sake of lowering the weight of a structure, the structure should contain as few edges as possible without breaking the connectivity. Li [49] then naturally extended the traditional definition of RNG as follows. The *modified relative neighborhood graph* consists of all edges uv such that (1) the *interior* of $lune(u, v)$ contains no point $w \in V$ and, (2) there is no point $w \in V$ with $ID(w) < ID(v)$ on the boundary of $lune(u, v)$ and $\|wv\| < \|uv\|$, and (3) there is no point $w \in V$ with $ID(w) < ID(u)$ on the boundary of $lune(u, v)$ and $\|wu\| < \|uv\|$, and (4) there is no point $w \in V$ on the boundary of $lune(u, v)$ with $ID(w) < ID(u), ID(w) < ID(v)$, and $\|wu\| = \|uv\|$. Li called such a structure RNG'. Obviously, RNG' is a subgraph of a traditional RNG and it still can be constructed using n messages. It was proved in [49] that RNG' has a maximum node degree 6 and still contains a MST as a subgraph. However, RNG' is still not a low-weight structure.

The localized algorithm given in [49] that constructs a low-weight structure using only two-hops information is as follows. First, all nodes together construct the graph of RNG' in a localized manner. Each node u locally broadcasts its incident edges in RNG' to its one-hop neighbors. Assume node u received a message informing existence of edge $xy \in RNG'$ from its neighbor x. For each edge $uv \in RNG'$, if uv is the longest among uv, xy, ux, and vy, node u removes edge uv. Ties are broken by the label of the edges. Here assume that $uvyx$ is the convex hull of u, v, x, and y. Let H be the final structure formed by all remaining edges in RNG'.

Obviously, if an edge uv is kept by node u, then it is also kept by node v. Li [49] proved that the total edge weight of H is within a constant factor of that of the minimum spanning tree. This was proved by showing that the edges in H satisfy the *isolation property* (defined in [51]). He also showed that the final structure contains MST of UDG as a subgraph and the communication cost of the algorithm is at most $7n$. The computational cost could be high since for each link $uv \in RNG'$, node u has to test whether there is an edge $xy \in RNG'$ and $x \in N_1(u)$ such that uv is the longest among uv, xy, ux, and vy. Then [48, 50] presents some new algorithms that improve the computational complexity of each node while still maintaining low communication costs.

Low-Weight Structure Based on LMST

The new method in [48, 50] uses a structure called *local minimum spanning tree*. It was first introduced by Li, Hou and Sha [52]. Each node u first collects its one-hop neighbors $N_1(u)$. Node u then computes the minimum spanning tree $MST(N_1(u))$ of the induced unit disk graph on its one-hop neighbors $N_1(u)$. Node u keeps a directed edge uv if and only if uv is an edge in $MST(N_1(u))$. They call the union of all directed edges of all nodes the *local minimum spanning tree*, denoted by $LMST_1$. They prove that the graph is connected, and has bounded degree 6. In [48, 50], Li *et al* further showed that graph $LMST_1$ is actually planar but not low weight. Then they extend the definition to k-hop neighbors, the union of all edges of all minimum spanning trees $MST(N_k(u))$ is the k *local minimum spanning tree*, denoted by $LMST_k$.

For example, the two local minimum spanning trees can be constructed as follows. Each node u collects its two-hop neighbors' information $N_2(u)$. Each node u computes the Euclidean MST $MST(N_2(u))$ of all nodes $N_2(u)$, including u itself. For each edge $uv \in MST(N_2(u))$, node u tells node v about this directed edge. Node u keeps an edge uv if $uv \in MST(N_2(u))$ or $vu \in MST(N_2(v))$. Let $LMST_2^+$ be the final structure formed by all edges kept. Another option is to keep an edge uv only if both nodes u and v want to keep it. Let $LMST_2^-$ be the structure formed by such edges.

In [50], they proved that structures $LMST_2$ ($LMST_2^+$ and $LMST_2^-$) are connected, planar, low-weight, and have bounded node degree at most 6. In [48], they generalized the results to a k local minimum spanning tree. They proved that (1) $LMST_k$ is connected, for all $k \geq 1$; (2) $LMST_k$ are planar graphs and with bounded node degree at most 6, for all $k \geq 1$; and (3)$LMST_k$ is low-weight, for all $k \geq 2$.

Although the constructed structure $LMST_2$ has several nice properties such as being of bounded degree, planar, and low-weight, the communication cost of the algorithm could be very large to save the computational cost of each node. The large communication costs are from collecting the two-hop neighbors' information $N_2(u)$ for each node u.

Low-Weight Structure Based on Combining RNG' and LMST

We could improve the communication cost of collecting $N_2(u)$ by using a subset of two hop information without sacrificing any properties. Define $N_2^{RNG'}(u) = \{w \mid vw \in RNG' \text{ and } v \in N_1(u)\} \cup N_1(u)$. The modified algorithm [48, 50] works as follows.

All nodes together construct the graph RNG'. Each node u locally broadcasts its incident edges in RNG' to its one-hop neighbors. Each node u computes the Euclidean MST $MST(N_2^{RNG'}(u))$ of all nodes $N_2^{RNG'}(u)$, including u itself. For each edge $uv \in MST(N_2^{RNG'}(u))$, node u tells node v about this directed edge. Node u keeps an edge uv if $uv \in MST(N_2^{RNG'}(u))$ or $vu \in MST(N_2^{RNG'}(v))$. Let $IMRG^+$ be the final structure formed by all edges kept. Similarly, the final structure is called $IMRG^-$ when edge $uv \in RNG'$ is kept iff $uv \in MST(N_2^{RNG'}(u))$ and $uv \in MST(N_2^{RNG'}(v))$. Here IMRG is the abbreviation of *Incident MST and RNG Graph*.

In the algorithm, node u constructs the local minimum spanning tree $MST(N_2^{RNG'}(u))$ based on the induced UDG of the point sets $N_2^{RNG'}(u)$. It is obvious that its communication cost is at most $7n$. In [48, 50], Li *et al* showed that structures $IMRG^+$ and $IMRG^-$ are still connected, planar, of bounded degree, and low-weight. Clearly, the constructed structures are a supergraph of the previous structures, i.e., $LSMT_2^+ \subseteq IMRG^+$ and $LSMT_2^- \subseteq IMRG^-$, since this algorithm uses less information than the algorithm of $LMST_2$ in constructing the local minimum spanning tree.

3.2 Low-Weight Spanners

Notice that all above localized low-weight structures are not spanners. The spanner property and low-weight property are not easy to be achieved at the same time. Intuitively, the spanner property requires one to keep more links, while the low-weight property requires one to keep fewer links from the original graph. As of now there is no efficient distributed algorithm that can achieve all following desirable features: bounded degree, planar, low weight and spanner.

Arya *et al* [7, 8] gave a centralized algorithm to construct a spanner with bounded node degree and the total edge length is no more than a constant factor of that of MST. However, it is very complicated to transform their algorithms to a distributed algorithm and their spanners are not planar.

Recently, Bose *et al* [53] proposed the first centralized algorithm which constructs a bounded-degree and low-weight planar spanner for a given point set V. The basic steps of their algorithm is as follows. First, compute the Delaunay triangulation of V, $Del(V)$, and a degree-3 spanning subgraph $BDS(V)$ of $Del(V)$ that includes the convex hull $CH(V)$ of V. This graph $BDS(V)$ partitions $CH(V)$ into (possibly degenerate) simple polygons, such that each node of V is on the boundary of at most three polygons. For each polygon P in the above partition, their algorithm first orders the nodes according to a geometry based breadth-first search, and processes the nodes of P in increasing order. It prunes this part of the Delaunay triangulation (edges inside or on the boundary of P) such that each node of P has low degree. The resulting graph is a planar spanner for the nodes of P in the sense that any two nodes u and v of P are connected by a path whose length is at most a constant times the length of a shortest path between u and v that is *completely contained* in P. By combining all the spanners for each of the polygons, they get a planar spanner of bounded degree. Finally, they Run a greedy algorithm in [54] on the planar spanner with bounded degree to bound the total weight from the weight of $MST(V)$. They show that the length stretch factor of the final graph is $((\pi + 1)C_{del})^2 \cdot (1 + \epsilon)$, node degree is at most 27 and the total weight is at most a constant times the weight of MST. The running time of their algorithm is $O(n \log n)$.

Borrowing some ideas from Bose *et al*'s method, in [55], the authors proposed another simpler centralized method for constructing a low weight bounded degree planar spanner with better bounds. Their algorithm is similar to the one in [33]. It first computes the Delaunay triangulation of a set V of n nodes, $Del(V)$. Then, it finds an order π of V by removing the node with smallest degree in $Del(V)$ (tie broken by ID). The first removed node has the highest order in π. Repeat this procedure until only the last node is left, and it has the lowest order in π. Since the graph is always a planar graph and we know that the smallest node degree is at most 5. Then, in ordering π, node u has at most 5 edges to its predecessors in $Del(V)$. Let E be the edge set of $Del(V)$, and let E' be the edge set of the desired spanner. Initialize E' to be the empty set and all nodes in V are marked as *unprocessed*. Then, for each node u in V, following the increasing order of π, run the third step in Algorithm 1 to add some edges from E to E'. Until all nodes are processed, the final graph is formed by edges E'. Finally, run the greedy spanner algorithm by Gudmundsson *et al* [54] to bound the weight of the graph. Li *et al* [55] proved that given a set V of n points in a two-dimensional plane, the above $O(n \log n)$-time algorithm constructs a graph (1) that is planar; (2) that is a t-spanner, for $t = (\max\{\frac{\pi}{2}, \pi \sin \frac{\alpha}{2} + 1\} \cdot C_{del})^2 (1 + \epsilon)$; (3) in which each point of V has degree at most $19 + \lceil \frac{2\pi}{\alpha} \rceil$; (4) and whose total edge weight is bounded from above by a constant factor[1] of the weight of the Euclidean minimum spanning tree of V. Here $0 < \alpha < \pi/2$ is an adjustable parameter. The time complexity of the algorithm is $O(n \log n)$, the same as the method by Bose *et al* [53]. However, it has smaller bounded node degree, and it has potential to become a localized version for wireless sensor networks application. The only problem here is the last step — a greedy method can not be performed in a local way.

Most recently, Li *et al* [56] proposed the first *distributed* method to construct a new bounded degree planar spanner which is also low-weighted. They first proposed a new bounded degree planar power-spanner called $S\Theta GG$, which is similar with $SYaoGG$ [46] except using a new concept of θ-dominating region instead of the fixed cones. Then, they described a novel distributed algorithm to build a low-weight structure from $S\Theta GG$ by removing some of its edges. The removing process is carefully designed so that it does not destroy the spanner property and other nice properties. For the detailed algorithm and proofs, refer to [56]. The authors also claimed they could build a bounded degree planar length-spanner by using $LDel$ instead of GG in their method.

---

[1] Here the constant factor depends on ϵ.

4 Virtual Backbones

While all the geometric structures discussed so far are flat structures, another set of structures, called hierarchical structures, is used in wireless sensor networks as network topologies. Instead of all nodes being involved in relaying packets for other nodes, the hierarchical routing protocols pick a subset of nodes that serve as the backbone routers, forwarding packets for other nodes. The notion of establishing a subset of nodes which perform the routing has been proposed in many routing algorithms [57–60]. These methods often construct the virtual backbone by using the connected dominating set, which is often constructed from a dominating set or a maximal independent set.

A subset S of V is a *dominating set* if each node u in V is either in S or is adjacent to some node v in S. Nodes from S are called dominators, while nodes not in S are called dominatees. A subset C of V is a *connected dominating set* (CDS) if C is a dominating set and C induces a connected subgraph. Consequently, the nodes in C can communicate with each other without using nodes in $V - C$. A dominating set with minimum cardinality is called a *minimum dominating set*, denoted by MDS. A connected dominating set with minimum cardinality is denoted by *minimum connected dominating set* (MCDS). A subset of vertices in a graph G is an *independent set* if for any pair of vertices, there is no edge between them. It is a *maximal independent set* if no more vertices can be added to it to generate a larger independent set. It is a *maximum independent set* (MIS) if no other independent set has more vertices.

4.1 Connected Dominating Set

The structure used to build virtual backbone is usually the connected dominating set. The problem of finding a minimum CDS for a general network is proved to be NP-complete [61]. Even for a unit disk graph, such a problem is also NP-complete [62]. Therefore, many heuristics and approximation algorithms have been proposed.

Centralized Methods

Guha and Khuller [63] studied approximation of the connected dominating set problem for general graphs. They gave two different approaches, both of which guarantee an approximation ratio of $\Theta(H(\Delta))$, where H is the harmonic function and Δ is the maximum node degree. Their approaches are for general graphs and thus do not utilize the geometry structure if applied to wireless sensor networks. One approach is to grow a spanning tree that includes all nodes. The internal nodes of the spanning tree are selected as the final connected dominating set. This approach has approximation ratio $2(H(\Delta) + 1)$. The other approach is first approximating the dominating set and then connecting the dominating set to form a connected dominating set. They [63] proved that this approach has approximation ratio $\ln \Delta + 3$.

One can also use the Steiner tree algorithm to connect the dominators. This straightforward method gives approximation ratio $c(H(\Delta) + 1)$, where c is the approximation ratio for the unweighted Steiner tree problem. Currently, the best ratio is $1 + \frac{\ln 3}{2} \simeq 1.55$, due to Robins and Zelikovsky [64].

Hunt *et al* [41] and Marathe *et al* [62] also studied the approximation of the maximum independent set and the minimum dominating set for unit disk graphs. They gave the first PTASs for MDS in UDG. The method is based on the following observations: a maximal independent set is always a dominating set; given a square Ω with a fixed area, the size of any maximal dominating set is bounded by a constant C. Assume that there are n nodes in Ω. Then, we can enumerate all sets with size at most C in time $\Theta(n^C)$. Among these enumerated sets, the smallest dominating set is the minimum dominating set. Then, using the shifting strategy proposed by Hochbaum [65], they derived a PTAS for the minimum dominating set problem.

Since we have PTAS for minimum dominating set and the graph $VirtG$ connecting every pair of dominators within at most 3 hops is connected [66], we have an approximation algorithm (constructing a minimum spanning tree $VirtG$) for MCDS with approximation ratio $3 + \epsilon$. Notice that, Berman *et al* [67] gave a $\frac{4}{3}$ approximation method to connect a dominating set and Robins *et al* [64] gave an $\frac{4}{3}$ approximation method to connect an independent set. Thus, we can easily have an $\frac{8}{3}$ approximation algorithm for MCDS. Recently, Cheng *et al*. [68] designed a PTAS for MCDS in UDG. However, it is difficult to distributize their method efficiently.

Distributed Methods

Many distributed clustering (or dominating set) algorithms have been proposed in the literature [69–74]. This subsection is devoted to the distributed methods that approximate the minimum dominating set and the minimum connected dominating set for a unit disk graph. In the rest of this subsection, we will interchange the terms clusterhead and dominator. The node that is not a clusterhead is also called *dominatee*.

Clustering without Geometry Property

For general graphs, Jia *et al* [75] described and analyzed some randomized distributed algorithms for the minimum dominating set problem that run in polylogarithmic time, independent of the diameter of the network, and that return with high probability a dominating set of size that falls within a logarithmic factor from the optimum. Their best algorithm runs in $O(\log n \log \Delta)$ rounds with high probability, and every pair of neighbors exchange a constant number of messages in each round. The computed dominating set is within $O(\log \Delta)$ in expectation and within $O(\log n)$ with high probability. Their algorithm works for weighted dominating set also.

The method proposed by Das *et al* [57,76] contains three stages: approximating the minimum dominating set, constructing a spanning forest of stars, expanding the spanning forest to a spanning tree. Here the *stars* are formed by connecting each dominatee node to one of its dominators. The approximation method of MDS is essentially a distributed variation of the centralized Chvatal's greedy algorithm [61] for set cover. Notice that the dominating set problem is essentially the set cover problem which is well-studied. It is then no surprise that the method by Das *et al* [57,76] guarantees an $H(\Delta)$ for the MDS problem, where H is the harmonic function and Δ is the maximum node degree.

While the algorithm proposed by Das *et al* [57,76] finds a dominating set and then grows it to a connecting dominating set, the algorithm proposed by Wu and Li [60,77] takes an opposite approach. They first find a connecting dominating set and then prune out certain redundant nodes from the CDS. The initial CDS $\mathcal{C}$ contains all nodes that have at least two non-adjacent neighbors. A node u is said to be *locally redundant* if it has either a neighbor in $\mathcal{C}$ with larger ID which dominates all other neighbors of u, or two adjacent neighbors with larger ID which together dominate all other neighbors of u. Their algorithm then keeps removing all locally redundant nodes from $\mathcal{C}$. They showed that this algorithm works well in practice when the nodes are distributed uniformly and randomly, although no theoretical analysis is given by them either for the worst case or for the average approximation ratio. However, it was shown by Alzoubi *et al* [69] that the approximation ratio of this algorithm could be as large as $\frac{n}{2}$.

Stojmenovic *et al* [59] proposed several synchronized distributed constructions of a connecting dominating set. In their algorithms, the connecting dominating set consists of two types of nodes: clusterhead and border-nodes (also called gateway or connectors elsewhere). The clusterhead nodes are just a maximal independent set, which is constructed as follows. At each step, all white nodes which have the lowest *rank* among all white neighbors are colored black, and the white neighbors are colored gray. The ranks of the white nodes are updated if necessary. Here, the following rankings of a node are used in various methods: the ID only [72,73], the ordered pair of degree and ID [78], and an ordered pair of degree and location [59]. After the clusterhead nodes are selected, border-nodes are selected to connect them. A node is a border-node if it is not a clusterhead and there are at least two clusterheads within its 2-hop neighborhood. It was shown by [69] that the worst case approximation ratio of this method is also $\frac{n}{2}$, although it works well in practice.

Clustering with Geometry Property

Notice that none of the above algorithm utilizes the geometry property of the underlying unit disk graph. Recently, several algorithms were proposed with a constant worst case approximation ratio by taking advantage of the geometry properties of the underlying graph. These methods typically use two messages similar to lamDominator and lamDominatee, and typically have the following procedures: a white node claims itself to be a dominator if it has the smallest ID among all of its white neighbors, if there are any, and broadcasts IamDominator to its 1-hop neighbors. A white node receiving IamDominator message marks itself as dominatee and broadcasts IamDominatee to its 1-hop neighbors. The set of dominators generated by the above method is actually a maximal independent set. Here, we assume that each node knows the IDs of all its 1-hop neighbors, which can be achieved by asking each node to broadcast its ID to its 1-hop neighbors initially. This approach to constructing MIS is well-known. For example, Stojmenovic *et al* [59] also used this method to compute the MIS.

The second step of backbone formation is to find some *connectors* (also called *gateways*) among all the dominatees to connect the dominators. Then the connectors and the dominators form a *connected dominating set*. Recently, Wan, *et al* [80] proposed a communication efficient algorithm to find connectors based on the fact that there are only a constant number of dominators within k-hops of any node. The following observation is a basis of several algorithms for CDS. After clustering, one dominator node can be connected to many dominatees. However, it is well-known that a dominatee node can only be connected to at most *five* dominators in the unit disk graph model. Generally, it was shown in [66, 80] that for each node (dominator or dominatee), there are at most a constant number $\ell_k < (2k+1)^2$ of dominators that are at most k units away. Let $VirtG$ be the graph connecting all pairs of dominators within at most three hops. As shown in [66], $VirtG$ is connected. Then it is natural to form a connected dominating set by finding connectors to connect any pair of dominators if they are connected in $VirtG$. This strategy is also adopted by [80]. Notice that, in the approach by Stojmenovic *et al* [59], they set any dominatee node as the connector if there are two dominators within its 2-hop neighborhood. This approach is very pessimistic and results in a very large number of connectors in the worst case [69]. Instead, Alzoubi *et al* [32] suggested looking for only one unique shortest path to connect any two dominators that are at most three hops away. Wang and Li [66] and Wan *et al* [80] discussed in detail some approaches to optimize the communication cost and the memory cost.

In [32, 66, 81], they proved the number of connectors found by their algorithms is at most ℓ_3 times the minimum and the size of the connected dominating set found is within a small constant factor of the minimum. It was also shown in [32, 66, 81] that the constructed CDS is a sparse spanner in terms of both hops and length with factors 3 and 6, meanwhile CDS has a bounded node degree $\max(\ell_3, 5 + \ell_2)$. See [81] for detailed proofs.

4.2 Low-Weight Connected Dominating Set

All of the above methods try to minimize the number of clusterheads, i.e., the number of nodes in the backbone. However, in many applications of wireless sensor networks, minimizing the size of the backbone is not sufficient. For example, different sensor nodes may have different costs for serving as a cluster-head, due to device differences, power capacities, and information loads to be processed. Therefore, in this subsection, we assume that each wireless node u has a *generic cost* (or *weight*) $c(u)$. The cost may also represent the *fitness* or *priority* of each node to be a clusterhead. The lower cost means higher priority. Then a connected dominating set C is called a *weighted connected dominating set* (WCDS). A subset C of V is a *minimum weighted connected dominating set* (MWCDS) if C is a WCDS with minimum total cost. It is clear that MWCDS is an NP-hard problem. Guha and Khuller [82] studied centralized algorithms for a weighted minimum connected dominating set in general graphs; by combining a weighted set cover approximation algorithm and a node-weighted Steiner tree approximation algorithm they achieve approximation ratio $3 \ln n$. In [83], they further improved the approximation ratio to $1.35 \ln n$ which is the best known ratio.

Recently, many proposed clustering algorithms [79, 84–90] also considered different weights as a *priority criterion* to decide whether a node will be a clusterhead. Notice, the ultimate goal of the majority protocols is still to minimize the size of the cluster (or backbone), not the total weight of the cluster (or backbone). For example, methods in [79, 86, 89] considered the stability or mobility of each node as the weight. In [85], a combined weight metric was considered in their clustering algorithm; it takes into account several system parameters like the node-degree, transmission power, mobility and the battery power of the nodes. Most of these proposed weighted clustering algorithms applied the simple greedy algorithms where the nodes with highest priority (lowest cost) become clusterheads. For example, the cluster method in [85] selects a node with the lowest cost among its unchosen neighbors to serve as a clusterhead. These greedy heuristics work well in practice, but Wang *et al* [91] showed that they may generate a backbone with a high cost compared with the optimum. Some of these methods [87, 88] are randomized algorithms and nodes become clusterheads randomly with a weighted election probability. In [84], Turgut proposed a genetic algorithm to optimize cluster processing. None of these cluster methods guarantee any approximation ratio of the weighted cluster compared with the optimum.

In [91], Wang *et al* first studied how to approximate the minimum weighted connected dominating set problem using distributed algorithms. They first showed that many classical greedy methods [57, 61, 66, 85, 90, 92] may produce dominating sets with arbitrarily larger weight than the optimum solution. Then they proposed a new distributed method of constructing a dominating set whose total cost is comparable with the optimum solution. Their method first constructs a maximal independent set (MIS) using node weight as selection criterion. Then for each node v in MIS, they run a local greedy set cover method (like in [57, 61, 92]) on *local neighborhood* $N_2(v)$ to find some nodes $GRDY_v$ to cover all one-hop neighbors of v. If $GRDY_v$ has a total cost smaller than v, then they use $GRDY_v$ to replace v, which will further reduce the cost of MIS. In [91], Wang *et al* proved that their algorithm constructs a dominating set whose total cost is no more than $\min(18\log Delta, 4\delta + 1)$ times the optimum for networks modelled by UDG. Here δ is the maximum ratio of costs of two adjacent wireless nodes and Δ is the maximum node degree in the communication graph. The second step of weighted connected dominating set formation is to find some *connectors* (also called *gateways*) among all the dominatees to connect the dominators. Their new connector selection method for a weighted connected dominating set is similar to those in [32, 66, 81]. First, let two dominators u and v be *neighboring dominators* if they are at most three hops away, i.e., they are neighbors in the graph $VirtG$. For every pair of neighboring dominators u and v, their method will find the shortest path with at most three hops to connect them. To bound the total weight, they also run a distributed algorithm to build a MST on graph $VirtG$. The nodes on this shortest path in the MST will be assigned a role of connector. For the detailed algorithm, refer to [91]. Then they proved that the connectors selected by their algorithm have a total cost no more than 10 times the optimum for networks modelled by UDG. Therefore, the constructed weighted connected dominating set has total cost no more than $\min(18\log\Delta, 4\delta+1)+10$ times of the optimum. The advantage of this WCDS is that the total cost is small compared with the optimum when either the costs of wireless nodes are smooth, i.e., two neighboring nodes' cost differ by a small constant factor, or the network density is low.

5 Others

For geometric structures, besides the spanner and low-weight properties, there are many other research issues and challenges. For example, *fault tolerance* is one of the central challenges in designing the wireless sensor networks. A sensor node may be battery constrained or subject to hostile environments, so individual node failure will be a regular or common event. To make fault tolerance possible, first of all, the underlying network topology must have multiple disjoint paths to connect any two given sensor devices. Recently, applying stochastic geometry, Penrose [93, 94], Bettstetter [95], Li *et al* [96] studied how to set the transmission radius to achieve the k-connectivity with certain probability for a network when wireless nodes are uniformly and randomly distributed over a two-dimensional region. Levcopoulos *et al* [97], Lukovszki [34], and Li *et al* [96] proposed some methods to construct a spanner that can sustain k-nodes or links failures. How to find a small transmission range (power) for each node such that the resulted communication graph is k-connected is also studied in [98, 99]. Another important issue affecting the throughput of the network topology is *interference*. Jia, Rajaraman and Scheideler [42] studied the interference analysis of sparsified Yao graph ($YY_k(V)$) recently. They established an upper bound on the interference number of $YY_k(V)$ for a random node distribution. Martin Burkhart *et al* [100] provided a concise and intuitive definition of interference and proposed connectivity-preserving and spanner constructions that are interference-minimal.

One problem related to topology control is *transmission power assignment*. In the previous sections, we have assumed that the transmission power of every node is equal and is normalized to one unit. However, in practice, each node can adjust its transmission power according to its neighbors' positions. This will also change the underlying topology of the network. A natural question is then how to assign the transmission power for each node such that the wireless sensor network is connected (or with other nice properties) with optimization criteria minimizing the maximum (or total) transmission power assigned. Much research has been done in this area [98, 99, 101–105].

Another related problem is *power management* in sensor networks. Remember that power is the critical issue in sensor networks, therefore network lifetime can be prolonged by using smart power management techniques. The most common power management technique is turning off the radio of the inactive sensor node to save power. However, sensor networks require nodes to forward packets for other nodes. Therefore, there is a tradeoff between energy conservation and network performance. The goal of power management is turning off as many nodes as possible without significantly diminishing the capacity or connectivity of the network. Several power management protocols [106–108] have been proposed. The main assumption of all these power management protocols is high density of sensors.

Due to the various applications of sensor networks, the topology control design is also various. For example, Pan *et al* [109] considered a two-tiered wireless sensor network consisting of sensor clusters deployed around strategic locations and base-stations (BSs) whose locations are relatively flexible. Within a sensor cluster, there are many small sensor nodes (SNs) that capture relevant information from the designated area, and there is at least one application node (AN) that receives raw data from these SNs, creates a comprehensive local view, and forwards the composite bit-stream toward a BS. In practice, both SN and AN are battery-powered and energy-constrained, and their node lifetimes directly affect the network lifetime of sensor networks. In [109], they focused on the topology control process for ANs and BSs, which constitute the upper tier of a two-tiered sensor network. They proposed approaches to maximize the topological network lifetime, by arranging BS location and inter-AN relaying optimally.

6 Conclusion

This chapter presented an overview of various techniques used for topology control protocols in wireless sensor networks. Mainly, two kinds of approaches were reviewed: geometric structures and virtual backbones. We first reviewed several sparse geometric spanners which can be built locally and used as the underlying network topology. Spanner property can guarantee the power efficiency of a unicast route on these spanners. Then, we described three low-weight geometric structures for power efficient broadcasting in sensor networks and gave the localized algorithms to build them. Later, we also surveyed techniques of how to form virtual backbones based on connected dominating sets or weighted connected dominating sets. Finally, we briefly discussed some other research issues in topology control for sensor networks. Due to the space limit, we did not give all of the detailed algorithms, proofs, and simulation results for most protocols reviewed here. For more detail, refer to the references. Though topology control has attracted considerable attention and been heavily studied recently, there are still many open problems and we still believe that the topology control is one primary challenge and plays an important role in research of wireless sensor networks.

Some open problems and potential future work are listed as follows.

1. Though [42, 43] proved the sparsified Yao graph is a power spanner, it is still open whether it is a length spanner for general graphs.
2. Is there a localized method or an easier way than the method in [56] to build a bounded-degree planar spanner with low weight locally?
3. In this chapter, we assumed that the emission power is the major component of the power consumption. However, in many cases, the emission power is at the same level of the power needed for being idle or to receive messages. It is then necessary to design new topologies under the new energy model when the receiving power is not negligible.
4. As we mentioned before, practically, the networks are never so perfect as unit disk graphs. It is very interesting (and hard) to study how to design topology for more complex models than UDG which may consider the impact of radio irregularity.
5. Since the applications of sensor networks are various, the design of network topology should be also applica-tion-oriented. According to different requirements of applications, the topology control protocol could be specifically designed.

References

1. Gang Zhou, Tian He, Sudha Krishnamurthy, and John A. Stankovic, "Impact of radio irregularity on wireless sensor networks," in *Proc. of 2nd international conference on Mobile systems, applications, and services (MobiSys)*. 2004.
2. Fabian Kuhn, Roger Wattenhofer, and Aaron Zollinger, "Ad-hoc networks beyond unit disk graphs," in *Proc. of 1st ACM Joint Workshop on Foundations of Mobile Computing (DIALM-POMC)*, 2003.
3. Xiang-Yang Li, Wen-Zhan Song, and Yu Wang, "Efficient topology control for wireless ad hoc networks with non-uniform transmission ranges," *ACM Springer Wireless Networks (WINET)*, vol. 11, no. 3, pp. 255–264, 2005.

4. Srdjan Capkun, Maher Hamdi, and Jean-Pierre Hubaux, "GPS-free positioning in mobile ad-hoc networks," in *Proc. Hawaii Int. Conf. on System Sciences*, 2001.

5. Jinyang Li, Jannotti Jannotti, Douglas S. J. De Couto, David R. Karger, and Robert Morris, "A scalable location service for geographic ad-hoc routing," in *Proc. of ACM International Conference on Mobile Computing and Networking*, 2000, pp. 120–130.

6. Xiang Ji and Hongyuan Zha, "Sensor positioning in wireless ad-hoc sensor networks with multidimensional scaling," in *IEEE INFOCOM 2004 - The Conference on Computer Communications*, 2004, pp. 2652–2661.

7. Sunil Arya, Gautam Das, David Mount, Jeffrey Salowe, and Michiel Smid, "Euclidean spanners: short, thin, and lanky," in *Proc. 27th ACM STOC*, 1995, pp. 489–498.

8. Sunil Arya and Michiel Smid, "Efficient construction of a bounded degree spanner with low weight," in *Proc. 2nd Annu. European Sympos. Algorithms (ESA), volume 855 of Lecture Notes in Computer Science*, 1994, pp. 48–59.

9. Prosenjit Bose, Luc Devroye, William Evans, and David Kirkpatrick, "On the spanning ratio of Gabriel graphs and Beta-skeletons," in *Proceedings of the Latin American Theoretical Infocomatics (LATIN)*, 2002.

10. Barun Chandra, Gautam Das, Giri Narasimhan, and Jose Soares, "New sparseness results on graph spanners," in *Proc. 8th Annual ACM Symposium on Computational Geometry*, 1992, pp. 192–201.

11. Menelaos I. Karavelas and Leonidas J. Guibas, "Static and kinetic geometric spanners with applications," in *Proceeding of the Twelfth Annual Symposium on Discrete algorithms*, 2001, pp. 168–176.

12. Christos Levcopoulos, Giri Narasimhan, and Michiel Smid, "Efficient algorithms for constructing fault-tolerant geometric spanners," in *Proceedings of the thirtieth annual ACM symposium on Theory of computing*, 1998.

13. Andrew C.-C. Yao, "On constructing minimum spanning trees in k-dimensional spaces and related problems," *SIAM J. Computing*, vol. 11, pp. 721–736, 1982.

14. Brad Karp and H.T. Kung, "GPSR: Greedy perimeter stateless routing for wireless networks," in *Proc. of the ACM/IEEE International Conference on Mobile Computing and Networking (MobiCom)*, 2000.

15. Prosenjit Bose, Pat Morin, Ivan Stojmenovic, and Jorge Urrutia, "Routing with guaranteed delivery in ad hoc wireless networks," *ACM/Kluwer Wireless Networks*, vol. 7, no. 6, 2001.

16. Fabian Kuhn, Roger Wattenhofer, and Aaron Zollinger, "Asymptotically optimal geometric mobile ad-hoc routing," in *Proc. of ACM international workshop on Discrete algorithms and methods for mobile computing and communications (Dial-M)*. 2002, pp. 24–33.

17. Fabian Kuhn, Roger Wattenhofer, and Aaron Zollinger, "Worst-Case Optimal and Average-Case Efficient Geometric Ad-Hoc Routing," in *Proc. 4th ACM Int. Symposium on Mobile Ad-Hoc Networking and Computing (MobiHoc)*, 2003.

18. Jerzy W. Jaromczyk and Godfried T. Toussaint, "Relative neighborhood graphs and their relatives," *Proceedings of IEEE*, vol. 80, no. 9, pp. 1502–1517, 1992.

19. Godfried T. Toussaint, "The relative neighborhood graph of a finite planar set," *Pattern Recognition*, vol. 12, no. 4, pp. 261–268, 1980.

20. K. Ruben Gabriel and Robert R. Sokal, "A new statistical approach to geographic variation analysis," *Systematic Zoology*, vol. 18, pp. 259–278, 1969.
21. Susanta Datta, Ivan Stojmenovic, and Jie Wu, "Internal node and shortcut based routing with guaranteed delivery in wireless networks," *Cluster Computing*, vol. 5, no. 2, pp. 169–178, 2002.
22. Mahtab Seddigh, Julio Solano Gonzalez, and Ivan Stojmenovic, "RNG and internal node based broadcasting algorithms for wireless one-to-one networks," *ACM Mobile Computing & Communications Review*, vol. 5, no. 2, pp. 37–44, 2002.
23. Weizhao Wang, Xiang-Yang Li, Kousha Moaveni-Nejad, Yu Wang, and Wen-Zhan Song, "The spanning ratios of beta-skeletons," in *Canadian Conference on Computational Geomety (CCCG 2003)*, 2003.
24. Xiang-Yang Li, Peng-Jun Wan, and Yu Wang, "Power efficient and sparse spanner for wireless ad hoc networks," in *IEEE Int. Conf. on Computer Communications and Networks (ICCCN01)*, 2001, pp. 564–567.
25. David P. Dobkin, Steven J. Friedman, and Kenneth J. Supowit, "Delaunay graphs are almost as good as complete graphs," *Discrete Computational Geometry*, 1990.
26. J. Mark Keil and Carl A. Gutwin, "Classes of graphs which approximate the complete euclidean graph," *Discrete Computational Geometry*, vol. 7, 1992.
27. Xiang-Yang. Li, Gruia Calinescu, and Peng-Jun Wan, "Distributed construction of planar spanner and routing for ad hoc wireless networks," in *21st IEEE INFOCOM*, 2002, vol. 3.
28. Xiang-Yang Li, Gruia Calinescu, Peng-Jun Wan, and Yu Wang, "Localized delaunay triangulation with application in wireless ad hoc networks," *IEEE Transaction on Parallel and Distributed Processing*, vol. 14, no. 10, pp. 1035–1047, 2003.
29. Jie Gao, Leonidas J. Guibas, John Hershburger, Li Zhang, and An Zhu, "Geometric spanner for routing in mobile networks," in *Proc. of 2nd ACM Symposium on Mobile Ad Hoc Networking and Computing (MobiHoc)*, 2001.
30. Xiang-Yang Li and Ivan Stojmenovic, "Partial delaunay triangulation and degree limited localized bluetooth scatternet formation," in *AdHocNow*, 2002.
31. Gruia Călinescu, "Computing 2-hop neighborhoods in ad hoc wireless networks," in *AdHoc-Now 03*, 2003.
32. Khaled M. Alzoubi, Peng-Jun Wan, and Ophir Frieder, "Message-optimal connected dominating sets in mobile ad hoc networks," in *Proc. of .3rd ACM international symposium on Mobile ad hoc networking & computing.* 2002, pp. 157–164..
33. Yu Wang and Xiang-Yang Li, "Localized construction of bounded degree planar spanner for wireless networks," in *ACM DIALM-POMC Joint Workshop on Foundations of Mobile Computing*, 2003.
34. Tamas Lukovszki, *New Results on Geometric Spanners and Their Applications*, Ph.D. thesis, University of Paderborn, 1999.
35. Xiang-Yang Li, Peng-Jun Wan, Yu Wang, and Ophir Frieder, "Sparse power efficient topology for wireless networks," in *IEEE Hawaii Int. Conf. on System Sciences (HICSS)*, 2002.
36. Roger Wattenhofer, Li Li, Paramvir Bahl, and Yi-Min Wang, "Distributed topology control for wireless multihop ad-hoc networks," in *IEEE INFOCOM'01*, 2001.

37. Li Li, Joseph Y. Halpern, Paramvir Bahl, Yi-Min Wang, and Roger Watten-hofer, "Analysis of a cone-based distributed topology control algorithms for wireless multi-hop networks," in *ACM Symposium on Principle of Distributed Computing (PODC)*, 2001.

38. Matthias Grünewald, Tamas Lukovszki, Christian Schindelhauer, and Klaus Volbert, "Distributed maintenance of resource efficient wireless network topolo-gies," in *Proc. of the 8th European Conference on Parallel Computing (Euro-Par'02)*, 2002.

39. Stefan Rührup, Christian Schindelhauer, Klaus Volbert, and Matthias Grünewald, "Performance of distributed algorithms for topology control in wireless networks," in *Proc. of 17th Intl. Parallel and Distributed Processing Symposium (IPDPS)*, 2003.

40. Yu Wang, Xiang-Yang Li, and Ophir Frieder, "Distributed spanner with bounded degree for wireless networks," *International Journal of Foundations of Computer Science*, vol. 14, no. 2, pp. 183–200, 2003.

41. Harry B. Hunt III, Madhav V. Marathe, Venkatesh Radhakrishnan, S. S. Ravi, Daniel J. Rosenkrantz, and Richard E. Stearns, "NC-approximation schemes for NP- and PSPACE -hard problems for geometric graphs," *Journal of Algorithms*, vol. 26, no. 2, pp. 238–274, 1998.

42. Lujun Jia, Rajmohan Rajaraman, and Christian Scheideler, "On local algorithms for topology control and routing in ad hoc networks," in *Proceedings of the 15th Annual ACM Symposium on Parallel Algorithms and Architectures*, 2003.

43. Christian Schindelhauer, Klaus Volbert, and Martin Ziegler, "Geometric spanners with applications in wireless networks," *Computational Geometry: Theory and Applications*, 2005.

44. Xiang-Yang Li, Ivan Stojmenovic, and Yu Wang, "Partial delaunay triangulation and degree limited localized Bluetooth multihop scatternet formation," *IEEE Trans. on Parallel and Distributed Systems*, vol. 15, no. 4, pp. 350–361, 2004.

45. Prosenjit Bose, Joachim Gudmundsson, and Pat Morin, "Ordered theta graphs," in *Proc. of the Canadian Conference on Computational Geometry (CCCG)*, 2002.

46. Wen-Zhan Song, Yu Wang, Xiang-Yang Li, and Ophir Frieder, "Localized algorithms for energy efficient topology in wireless ad hoc networks," in *5th ACM International Symposium on Mobile Ad Hoc Networking and Computing (MobiHoc 2004)*, Tokyo, Japan, 2004.

47. Peng-Jun Wan, Gruia Calinescu, Xiang-Yang Li, and Ophir Frieder, "Minimum-energy broadcast routing in static ad hoc wireless networks," *ACM Wireless Networks*, 2002, Preliminary version appeared in IEEE INFOCOM 2000.

48. Xiang-Yang Li, Yu Wang, and Wen-Zhan Song, "Applications of k-local MST for topology control and broadcasting in wireless ad hoc networks," *IEEE Trans. on Parallel and Distributed Systems*, vol. 15, no. 12, pp. 1057–1069, 2004.

49. Xiang-Yang Li, "Approximate MST for UDG locally," in *The 9th Annual International Computing and Combinatorics Conference COCOON 2003*, 2003.

50. Xiang-Yang Li, Yu Wang, Peng-Jun Wan, Wen-Zhan Song, and Ophir Frieder, "Localized low weight graph and its applications in wireless ad hoc networks," in *IEEE INFOCOM*, 2004.

51. Gautam Das, Giri Narasimhan, and Jeffrey Salowe, "A new way to weigh malnourished euclidean graphs," in *ACM Symposium of Discrete Algorithms*, 1995.
52. Ning Li, Jennifer C. Hou, and Lui Sha, "Design and analysis of a MST-based topology control algorithm," in *Proc. of IEEE INFOCOM 2003*, 2003.
53. Prosenjit Bose, Joachim Gudmundsson, and Michiel Smid, "Constructing plane spanners of bounded degree and low weight," in *Proceedings of the European Symposium on Algorithms (ESA)*, 2002.
54. Joachim Gudmundsson, Christos Levcopoulos, and Giri Narasimhan, "Improved greedy algorithms for constructing sparse geometric spanners," in *Scandinavian Workshop on Algorithm Theory*, 2000, pp. 314–327.
55. Xiang-Yang Li and Yu Wang, "Efficient construction of low weight bounded degree planar spanner," in *International Journal of Computational Geometry and Applications*, vol. 14, np.1-2, pp.69–84, 2004.
56. Xiang-Yang Li, Wen-Zhan Song, and Wu Wang, "A unified energy efficient topology for unicast and broadcast," in *11th ACM Annual International Conference on Mobile Computing and Networking (MobiCom 2005)*, 2005.
57. Bevan Das and Vaduvur Bharghavan, "Routing in ad-hoc networks using minimum connected dominating sets," in *1997 IEEE International Conference on on Communications (ICC'97)*, 1997, vol. 1, pp. 376–380.
58. Raghupathy Sivakumar, Prasun Sinha, and Vaduvur Bharghavan, "CEDAR: Core extraction distributed ad hoc routing algorithm," *IEEE Journal on Selected Areas in Communications*, vol. 17, no. 8, pp. 1454–1465, 1999.
59. Ivan Stojmenovic, Mahtab Seddigh, and Jovisa Zunic, "Dominating sets and neighbor elimination based broadcasting algorithms in wireless networks," *IEEE Trans. on Parallel and Distributed Systems*, vol. 13, no. 1, pp. 14–25, 2002.
60. Jie Wu and Hailan Li, "A dominating-set-based routing scheme in ad hoc wireless networks," *the special issue on Wireless Networks in the Telecommunication Systems Journal*, vol. 3, pp. 63–84, 2001.
61. V. Chvátal, "A greedy heuristic for the set-covering problem," *Mathematics of Operations Research*, vol. 4, no. 3, pp. 233–235, 1979.
62. Madhav V. Marathe, H. Breu, Harry B. Hunt III, S. S. Ravi, and Daniel J. Rosenkrantz, "Simple heuristics for unit disk graphs," *Networks*, vol. 25, pp. 59–68, 1995.
63. Sudipto Guha and Samir Khuller, "Approximation algorithms for connected dominating sets," in *European Symposium on Algorithms*, 1996, pp. 179–193.
64. Gabriel Robins and Alexander Zelikovsky, "Improved steiner tree approximation in graphs," in *Proc. of ACM/SIAM Symposium on Discrete Algorithms*, 2000.
65. Dorit S. Hochbaum and Wolfgang Maass, "Approximation schemes for covering and packing problems in image processing and vlsi," *Journal of ACM*, vol. 32, pp. 130–136, 1985.
66. Yu Wang and Xiang-Yang Li, "Geometric spanners for wireless ad hoc networks," in *Proc. of 22nd IEEE International Conference on Distributed Computing Systems (ICDCS)*, 2002.
67. Piotr Berman, Matin Furer, and Alexander Zelikovsky, "Applications of matroid parity problem to approximating steiner trees," Tech. Rep. 980021, Computer Science, UCLA, 1998.

68. Xiuzhen Cheng, Xiao Huang, Deying Li, and Ding-Zhu Du, "Polynomial-time approximation scheme for minimum connected dominating set in ad hoc wireless networks," *Networks*, vol. 42, no. 4, pp. 202–208, 2003.
69. Khaled M. Alzoubi, Peng-Jun Wan, and Ophir Frieder, "New distributed algorithm for connected dominating set in wireless ad hoc networks," in *HICSS, Hawaii*, 2002.
70. Alan D. Amis and Ravi Prakash, "Load-balancing clusters in wireless ad hoc networks," in *Proc. of the 3rd IEEE Symposium on Application-Specific Systems and Software Engineering Technology*, 2000.
71. Alan D. Amis, Ravi Prakash, Dung Huynh, and Thai Vuong, "Max-min d-cluster formation in wireless ad hoc networks," in *Proc. of 19th Annual Joint Conference of the IEEE Computer and Communications Societies INFOCOM*, 2000.
72. Imrich Chlamtac and Andras Farago, "A new approach to design and analysis of peer to peer mobile networks," *Wireless Networks*, vol. 5, pp. 149–156, 1999.
73. Chunhung R. Lin and Mario Gerla, "Adaptive clustering for mobile wireless networks," *IEEE Journal of Selected Areas in Communications*, vol. 15, no. 7, pp. 1265–1275, 1997.
74. Ji-Cheng Lin, Shi-Nine Yang, and Maw-Sheng Chern, "An efficient distributed algorithm for minimal connected dominating set problem," in *Proc. of 10th Annual International Phoenix Conference on Computers and Communications*, 1991.
75. Lujun Jia, Rajmohan Rajaraman, and Torsten Suel, "An efficient distributed algorithm for constructing small dominating sets," in *ACM PODC*, 2000.
76. Raghupathy Sivakumar, Bevan Das, and Vaduvur Bharghavan, "The clade vertebrata: spines and routing in ad hoc networks," in *IEEE Symposium on Computers and Communications (ISCC98)*, Athens, Greece, June 1998.
77. Jie Wu and Hailan Li, "Domination and its applications in ad hoc wireless networks with unidirectional links," in *Proc. of the International Conference on Parallel Processing 2000*, 2000, pp. 189–197.
78. Geng Chen, Fabian Garcia, Julio Solano, and Ivan Stojmenovic, "Connectivity based k-hop clustering in wireless networks," in *CD Proc. IEEE Hawaii Int. Conf. System Science*, 2002.
79. Stefano Basagni, "Distributed clustering for ad hoc networks," in *Proceedings of the IEEE International Symposium on Parallel Architectures, Algorithms, and Networks (I-SPAN)*, 1999, pp. 310–315.
80. Peng-Jun Wan, Khaled M. Alzoubi, and Ophir Frieder, "Distributed construction of connected dominating set in wireless ad hoc networks," in *INFOCOM*, 2002.
81. Khaled Alzoubi, Xiang-Yang Li, Yu Wang, Peng-Jun Wan, and Ophir Frieder, "Geometric spanners for wireless ad hoc networks," *IEEE Transactions on Parallel and Distributed Processing*, vol. 14, no. 4, pp. 408–421, 2003..
82. Sudipto Guha and Samir Khuller, "Approximation Algorithms for Connected Dominating Sets," *Algorithmica*, vol. 20, no. 4, pp. 374–387, 1998.
83. Sudipto Guha and Samir Khuller, "Improved methods for approximating node weighted steiner trees and connected dominating sets," *Information and Computation*, vol. 150, no. 1, pp. 57–74, 1999.
84. Damla Turgut. Sajal K. Das, Ramez Elmasri and Begumhan Turgut, "Optimizing clustering algorithm in mobile ad hoc networks using genetic algorithmic approach," in *IEEE GLOBECOM 2002*, 2002.

85. Mainak Chatterjee, Sajal K. Das, and Damla Turgut, "WCA: A weighted clustering algorithm for mobile ad hoc networks," *Journal of Cluster Computing*, vol. 5, no. 2, pp. 193–204, 2002.

86. Christian Bettstetter and Roland Krausser, "Scenario-based stability anlysis of the distributed mobility-adaptive clustering (DMAC) algorithm," in *2nd ACM international symposium on Mobile ad hoc networking & computing*. 2001.

87. Wendi Rabiner Heinzelman, Anantha Chandrakasan, and Hari Balakrishnan, "Energy-efficient communication protocol for wireless microsensor networks," in *Proc. of 33rd IEEE Hawaii International Conference on System Sciences*. 2000.

88. Georgios Smaragdakis, Ibrahim Matta, and Azer Bestavros, "SEP: A stable election protocol for clustered heterogeneous wireless sensor networks," in *2nd International Workshop on Sensor and Actor Network Protocols and Applications (SANPA)*, 2004.

89. Manki Min, Feng Wang, Ding-Zhu Du, and Panos M. Pardalos, "A reliable virtual backbone scheme in mobile ad-hoc networks," in *1st IEEE International Conference on Mobile Ad-hoc and Sensor Systems (MASS)*, 2004.

90. Lichun Bao and J. J. Garcia-Luna-Aceves, "Topology management in ad hoc networks," in *Proceedings of the 4th ACM international symposium on Mobile ad hoc networking & computing*. 2003, pp. 129–140, ACM Press.

91. Yu Wang, WeiZhao Wang, and Xiang-Yang Li, "Efficient distributed low-cost backbone formation for wireless networks," in *6th ACM International Symposium on Mobile Ad Hoc Networking and Computing (MobiHoc)*, 2005.

92. Bevan Das, Raghupathy Sivakumar, and Vaduvur Bharghavan, "Routing in ad hoc networks using a spine," in *IEEE Sixth International Conference on Computer Communications and Networks (ICCCN97)*, 1997.

93. Mathew Penrose, "The longest edge of the random minimal spanning tree," *Annals of Applied Probability*, vol. 7, pp. 340–361, 1997.

94. Mathew Penrose, "On k-connectivity for a geometric random graph," *Random Structures and Algorithms*, vol. 15, pp. 145–164, 1999.

95. Christian Bettstetter, "On the minimum node degree and connectivity of a wireless multihop network," in *3rd ACM International Symposium on Mobile Ad Hoc Networking and Computing (MobiHoc'02)*, June 2002.

96. Xiang-Yang Li, Peng-Jun Wan, Yu Wang, and Chih-Wei Yi, "Fault tolerant deployment and topology control for wireless ad hoc networks," in *4th ACM International Symposium on Mobile Ad Hoc Networking and Computing (MobiHoc)*, 2003.

97. Christos Levcopoulos, Giri Narasimhan, and Michiel Smid , "Improved algorithms for constructing fault tolerant geometric spanners," *Algorithmica*, 2000.

98. MohammadTaghi Hajiaghayi, Nicole Immorlica, and Vahab S. Mirrokni, "Power optimization in fault-tolerant topology control algorithms for wireless multi-hop networks," in *Procd. of 9th ACM international conference on Mobile computing and networking*. 2003.

99. Ram Ramanathan and Regina Hain, "Topology control of multihop wireless networks using transmit power adjustment," in *IEEE INFOCOM (2)*, 2000, pp. 404–413.

100. Martin Burkhart, Pascal von Rickenbach, Roger Wattenhofer, and Aaron Zollinger, "Does topology control reduce interference?," in *Proc. of 5th ACM*

international symposium on Mobile ad hoc networking and computing (Mobi-Hoc). 2004.

101. Miguel Snchez, Pietro Manzoni, and Zygmunt J. Haas, "Determination of critical transmission range in ad-hoc networks," in *Multiaccess, Mobility and Teletraffic for Wireless Communications (MMT'99)*, 1999.

102. Andrea E. F. Clementi, Paolo Penna, and Riccardo Silvestri, "On the power assignment problem in radio networks," *ACM/Kluwer Mobile Networks and Applications (MONET)*, vol. 9, no. 2, pp. 125–140, 2004.

103. Errol L. Lloyd, Rui Liu, Madhav V. Marathe, Ram Ramanathan, and S. S. Ravi, "Algorithmic aspects of topology control problems for ad hoc networks," in *ACM MOBIHOC*, 2002.

104. Xiuzhen Cheng, Bhagirath Narahari, Rahul Simha, Maggie X. Cheng, and Dan Liu, "Strong minimum energy topology in wireless sensor networks: NP-completeness and heuristics," *IEEE Trans. on Mobile Computing*, vol. 2, no. 3, 2003.

105. YYu-Chee Tseng, Yen-Ning Chang, and Bour-Hour Tzeng, "Energy-efficient topology control for wireless ad hoc sensor networks," in *Proc. Int. Conf. Parallel and Distributed Systems (ICPADS)*, 2002.

106. Curt Schurgers. Vlasios Tsiatsis. and Mani B. Srivastava, "STEM: Topology management for energy efficient sensor networks," in *IEEE Aerospace Conference '02*, 2002.

107. Alberto Cerpa and Deborah Estrin, "Ascent: Adaptive self-configuring sensor network topologies," *SIGCOMM Comput. Commun. Rev.*, vol. 32, no. 1, pp. 62–62, 2002.

108. Benjie Chen, Kyle Jamieson, Hari Balakrishnan, and Robert Morris, "Span: an energy-efficient coordination algorithm for topology maintenance in ad hoc wireless networks," *Wireless Network*, vol. 8, no. 5, pp. 481–494, 2002.

109. Jianping Pan, Thomas Hou, Lin Cai, Yi Shi, and Sherman Shen, "Topology control for wireless sensor networks," in *Proc. of 9th annual international conference on Mobile computing and networking (MobiCom).* 2003.

Chapter 6
Boundary Detection for Sensor Networks

Ren-Shiou Liu, Lifeng Sang, and Prasun Sinha

Computer Science and Engineering
Ohio State University, Columbus, OH 43210
{rsliu, sangl, prasun}@cse.ohio-state.edu

1 Introduction

Wireless sensor networks have a variety of applications, such as environment monitoring, structural monitoring, remote exploration, condition-based maintenance, commercial surveillance, and national asset protection. These applications require the network to monitor a certain type of non-local spatiotemporal phenomenon, collaboratively process gathered information, and respond to external events or report results. There are different types of phenomenon that can be observed by a network of sensors. For some phenomena such as fire, gas leak, chemical attack and biological attack, it is critical to track the boundary of the affected area.

An example scenario is illustrated in Figure 1. When a battle field is attacked by chemical or biological weapons, it is desirable to know which areas are covered by the toxic plumes so that effective decisions for evacuation and rescue operations can be made in real time. To do that, UAVs may be directed to the battle field to spread chemical sensors over the air. As soon as sensors land in the field, they self-organize into an ad-hoc network and start sensing, gathering requested information and sending them back to the sink for decision making.

To determine an event region, it suffices to detect the sensor nodes near or right on the boundary of the event. These edge sensor nodes, if not faulty, usually have abrupt changes in readings compared to other sensors not in the region. Thus, the problem of boundary detection for sensor networks is to find the location of these edge sensors. The boundary detection algorithms for sensor networks can be categorized into four classes:

- *Localized edge detection:* Based on a localized algorithm or the data collected from its neighbors, a sensor node determines whether it is positioned on or near a boundary. Designing a localized edge detection algorithm is challenging, but it results in low energy consumption compared to other approaches due to localized communication.

- *Centralized edge determination:* A powerful node or the sink gathers data from all sensor nodes and, through examining these data, edges are accurately determined. Nevertheless, if the sensor field spans across a large geographical area, the cost of collecting data from all sensor nodes would be very high.
- *Hierarchical edge estimation:* To reach a balance between energy consumption and accuracy, several hierarchical edge estimation schemes have been proposed. Sensor nodes are organized into multiple hierarchies, and a parent sensor in a higher level of hierarchy tries to estimate the event boundary based on the data gathered from its child sensor nodes.
- *Distributed region determination:* Distributed algorithms have always been flexible, and thus can be used to detect and track large-scale phenomena autonomously and dynamically.

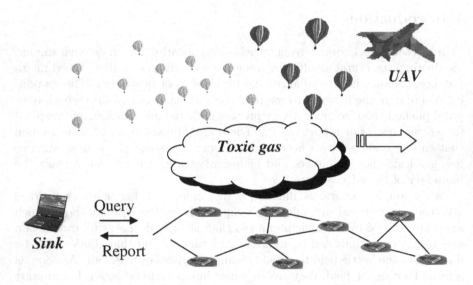

Fig. 1. A sensor network for tracking chemical plumes.

The rest of this chapter is organized as follows. Section 2 presents several classical localized edge detection schemes. Section 3 provides an overview of centralized edge determination and a simple algorithm. Section 4 includes some key algorithms for hierarchical edge estimation. Section 5 provides an overview for distributed region detection algorithms. And finally, Section 6 summarizes this chapter with pointers to some future research directions on boundary detection for sensor networks.

2 Localized Edge Detection

Localized edge detection is a technique by which each sensor node determines either locally or by collecting information from other nodes within its neighborhood whether or not it is an edge sensor. Ideally, a sensor with positive value of event predicate and situated right on the boundary is said to be an edge sensor. However, this is only a description rather than a definition. To define an edge sensor, the notion of *tolerance radius* is introduced. As shown in Figure 2, if a sensor node resides in the event region and there is an edge passing through its tolerance radius, then, it is regarded as an edge sensor. This definition not only provides a definite guideline for discriminating edge sensors from normal sensors, but also offers an in-depth view for possible performance evaluation metrics.

Though the design of a localized edge detection scheme is challenging, it is still a topic of importance for sensor networks. If each node can detect whether it is an edge sensor locally and reliably, the boundary can be easily determined by traversing all the edge sensors of the sensor field of interest and power consumption can, thus, be minimized.

Edge detection has been extensively studied in other fields such as image processing literature and pattern recognition literature. These techniques can be applied to localized edge detection for sensor networks as well. Thus, this section begins with three classical localized edge detection algorithms[1] and then presents the key principles of two edge detection schemes extended from a localized faulty sensor detection algorithm[2].

2.1 Statistical approach

In a sensor network, each node is equipped with a sensing device which can be used to monitor an interesting phenomenon or event. The function which determines whether an event or a phenomenon is detected by a sensor node is denoted as the *event predicate* for that sensor node. Thus, a general statistical approach for a sensor node would be to collect values of event predicates in its neighborhood, perform statistical analysis, and feed the analysis result to a boolean decision function to decide whether it is an edge sensor. The boolean decision function is usually controlled by a threshold value. The larger the threshold, the more likely a node will be claimed as an edge sensor, and the "thicker" will be the detected boundary.

As illustrated in Figure 2, a sensor node S_0 probes the values of event predicates for those sensor nodes whose distances are within a predefined *probing radius*. If the collected values of event predicates form a bi-modal distribution, where the number of 0 and 1 values of event predicates are very close, then an edge is impled. Based on this observation, a simple statistic and a decision making function can be defined as the following:

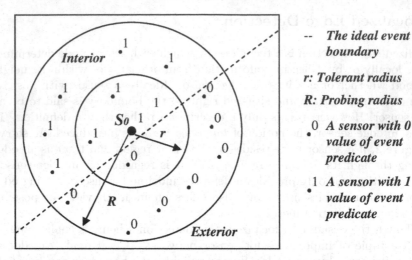

Fig. 2. If the edge is within the distance of a predefined toleracc radius for a sensor node, S_0, which is located in the event region, then, sensor S_0 is claimed to be an edge sensor.

$$S = 1 - \frac{|p_1 - p_0|}{|p_1 + p_0|}, \quad (1)$$

$$F(S) = \begin{cases} 1 \ if \ S \geq t_0, \\ 0 \ if \ S < t_0. \end{cases} \quad (2)$$

In the statistical formula, that is equation (1), p_0 stands for the number of 0 values of event predicates and p_1 represents the number of 1 values of predicates. As p_0 and p_1 get closer, the resulting statistic value S will eventually become larger than the pre-selected threshold t_0 in the decision making function F.

Obviously, the performance of the statistical approach heavily depends on the choice of the threshold t_0 and the probing radius R. The larger the threshold, the higher the precision of edge detection. However, with a large threshold, the missed detection rate will also increase. Similarly, having a large probing area can also improve the performance since the statistical analysis can be more accurate if more values of event predicates can be collected. But the communication overhead for a large probing area will also increase significantly

Thus, an interesting topic here would be the selection of the threshold value t_0 and the size of probing radius R. To reach a satisfactory operation, one can pre-calculate the performance curves and store the selected threshold and probing radius into sensors such that the statistical approach can satisfy the preferred performance criteria.

2.2 Image processing based approach

A number of edge detection schemes have been designed and analyzed in the image processing literature. A typical method is to make use of a high pass filter (e.g., Prewitt, Sobel filters) to detect edges in an image. By convoluting an image of interest with a high pass filter, regions of high spatial gradient that correspond to edges will be emphasized.

Usually, a high pass filter $G(x, y)$ consists of at least a pair of 3x3 convolution masks, one mask for each of the two orthogonal axes. For example, the Prewitt edge detector defines mask G_x to calculate the gradient along the horizontal orientation, and G_y is used to estimate the gradient of the vertical orientation.

$$G_x = \begin{bmatrix} -1 & 0 & 1 \\ -1 & 0 & 1 \\ -1 & 0 & 1 \end{bmatrix}, \tag{3}$$

$$G_y = \begin{bmatrix} 1 & 1 & 1 \\ 0 & 0 & 0 \\ -1 & -1 & -1 \end{bmatrix}. \tag{4}$$

Consider the following 3x3 image window:

$$Filter\ window\ = \begin{bmatrix} v_1 & v_2 & v_3 \\ v_4 & v_5 & v_6 \\ v_7 & v_8 & v_9 \end{bmatrix} \tag{5}$$

where $v_1...v_9$ are grey levels of each pixel in the filter window. By applying the masks to the filter window, we obtain the gradient magnitude along the x and y directions respectively:

$$\sigma_x = -1 * v_1 + 1 * v_3 - 1 * v_4 + 1 * v_6 - 1 * v_7 + 1 * v_9, \tag{6}$$

$$\sigma_y = 1 * v_1 + 1 * v_2 + 1 * v_3 - 1 * v_7 - 1 * v_8 - 1 * v_9. \tag{7}$$

A high value of *Prewitt Gradient*, $\sigma = \sqrt{\sigma_x^2 + \sigma_y^2}$, would indicate the existence of an edge. Similarly, to apply this technique within the context of sensor networks, we treat each node as a pixel, and the values (either 0 or 1) of event predicates as the "grey level" for each node. However, sensor nodes are arbitrarily deployed in a sensor field, thus, there is no spatially defined 3x3 filter window and the computed σ value could be biased due to the uneven deployment as well. To overcome these two problems, a new pair of "convolution masks" (G_x, G_y) and a weighting function $W(x, y)$ which takes sensors' location as argument for each of the perpendicular orientation must be introduced.

154   Ren-Shiou Liu, Lifeng Sang, and Prasun Sinha

Let PA_{s_0} be the set of sensors in the probing area of a sensor S_0 at position (x_s, y_s). Denote the binary value of event predicate for any sensor $s \in PAs_0$ as V_s. σ_x and σ_y for sensor S_0 can be calculated as:

$$\sigma_x = \sum_{\forall s \in PAs_0} W_x(x_s, y_s) G_x(x_s, y_s) V_s, \qquad (8)$$

$$\sigma_y = \sum_{\forall s \in PAs_0} W_y(x_s, y_s) G_y(x_s, y_s) V_s. \qquad (9)$$

By observing equation (6) and (7), we know the basic idea behind the *Prewitt* filters is to find the gradient in the x and y axes by deducting the sum of grey levels of left pixels from the right ones and subtracting the sum of grey levels of upper pixels from the below ones respectively. To simulate this behavior, the new pair of "convolution mask" can be defined as:

$$G_x(x_s, y_s) = \begin{cases} 1 & if\ x_s \geq x_0, \\ -1 & if\ x_s < x_0, \end{cases} \qquad (10)$$

$$G_y(x_s, y_s) = \begin{cases} 1 & if\ y_s \geq y_0, \\ -1 & if\ y_s < y_0. \end{cases} \qquad (11)$$

Thus, the sum of $G_x(x_s, y_s)V_s$ and $G_y(x_s, y_s)V_s$ in equation (8) and (9) represent the gradient of the values of event predicates for sensor S_0 in the x and y directions.

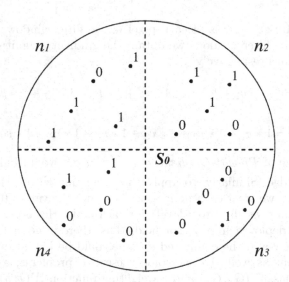

Fig. 3. The four quadrants around sensor S_0, where $n_{1+} = 4, n_{1-} = 1, n_{2+} = 3, n_{2-} = 2, n_{3+} = 1, n_{3-} = 4, n_{4+} = 2, n_{4-} = 3$.

Now, let's discuss the weighting function $G(x, y)$. To take spatial information into consideration, we can divide the region around sensor S_0 into four quadrant areas as shown in Figure 3. Let $(n_{i+}, n_{i-})_{i=1}^{i=4}$ be the number of sensors with 1 and 0 values of event predicates in each quadrant. A simple weighting function is as follows:

$$W_x(x, y) = \begin{cases} \frac{1}{n_{1+} + n_{1-} + n_{4+} + n_{4-}} & if \ x < x_{s_0}, \\ \frac{1}{n_{2+} + n_{2-} + n_{3+} + n_{3-}} & if \ x > x_{s_0}, \end{cases} \tag{12}$$

$$W_y(x, y) = \begin{cases} \frac{1}{n_{1+} + n_{1-} + n_{2+} + n_{2-}} & if \ y > y_{s_0}, \\ \frac{1}{n_{3+} + n_{3-} + n_{4+} + n_{4-}} & if \ y < y_{s_0}. \end{cases} \tag{13}$$

Based on (8), (9), (10), (11), (12), and (13), σ_x and σ_y are given by:

$$\sigma_x = \frac{n_{1+} + n_{4+} - n_{1-} - n_{4-}}{n_{1+} + n_{1+} + n_{4-} + n_{4-}} - \frac{n_{2+} + n_{3+} - n_{2-} - n_{3-}}{n_{2+} + n_{2+} + n_{3-} + n_{3-}}, \tag{14}$$

$$\sigma_y = \frac{n_{1+} + n_{2+} - n_{1-} - n_{2-}}{n_{1+} + n_{1+} + n_{2-} + n_{2-}} - \frac{n_{3+} + n_{4+} - n_{3-} - n_{4-}}{n_{3+} + n_{3+} + n_{4-} + n_{4-}}. \tag{15}$$

Based on (14) and (15), the final $\sigma = \sqrt{\sigma_x^2 + \sigma_y^2}$ can be computed. This σ value represents the gradient of values of event predicates collected from neighborhoods of S_0. If σ is larger than a pre-selected threshold σ_0, then the image processing approach regards S_0 as an edge sensor.

2.3 Classifier-based approach

As the image processing approach comes from the image process literature, the classifier-based approach is based on the pattern recognition literature. Generally, a sensor adopting the classifier-based approach attempts to partition the set of data gathered from its neighborhood into two different classes. If the partition to be assessed by a *partition validity measure* is a successful one, it implies the existence of an edge. Here, a successful partition is defined as a bi-partite data set, such that data with similar attributes lie in the same subset and data with dissimilar attributes lie in different subsets.

The simplest classifier is a linear classifier. If the classifier finds a line $L(a, b, c) \equiv ax + by + c = 0$, such that all sensors with equivalent values of event predicates are on the same side and the distance of that line is within the range of a predefined tolerance radius, the partition is said to be valid and the sensor is regarded as an edge sensor.

Let sensor S_0 be the sensor performing classifier-based edge detection and PAs be the set of sensors in its probing area. A line with the above characteristic must have the highest *classifier score* J_{s_0}:

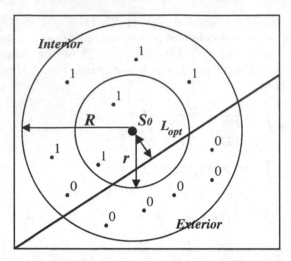

Lopt: Optimal line

r: Tolerant radius

R: Probing radius

0 A sensor with 0 value of event predicate

1 A sensor with 1 value of event predicate

Fig. 4. A simple linear classifier cuts the probing area S_0 into two regions such that sensors with different values of event predicates are at different sides.

$$J_{s_0}(a, b, c) = \left| \sum_{\forall s \in PA_{s_0}} V_s SN(ax_s + by_s + c) \right| \tag{16}$$

where

$$SN(x) = \begin{cases} -1 \; if \; x < 0, \\ 0 \; if \; x = 0, \\ 1 \; if \; x > 0. \end{cases} \tag{17}$$

The proof is straightforward. Based on (16) and (17), for all s above the line, $V_s SN(ax_s + by_s + c) > 0$. If most of the sensors with 1 values of event predicates lie on the same side, say above the line, then J_s will reach a maximum value. However, a partition is regarded as valid if and only if the optimal line $L_{opt}(a, b, c)$ satisfies $\frac{ax_{s_0} + by_{s_0} + c}{\sqrt{(a^2 + b^2)}} \leq r$, which means that the line lies within a predefined tolerance radius.

Generally speaking, as the radius of probing area or sensor density increases, the more accurately the event boundary can be detected. This applies to the statistical approach, image processing approach and the classifier-based approach. However, the classifier-based approach has a far more qualitative characteristic than the others. When the probing area or sensor density increases, the unwanted detection rates for the statistical and image processing approaches also increase, while it's a decrease for the classifier-based approach, which means a thinner edge can be obtained.

2.4 Random bisection approach

The localized edge detection schemes we have discussed so far are based on the 0–1 binary reading (the event predicate) of each sensor. However, this decision making mechanism may have the following drawbacks:

- 0/1 event predicates do not tell any spatial information on deployed sensors.
- 0/1 event predicates are the preprocessed results of the real readings. An edge detection approach based on a second round approximation may not be accurate.
- 0/1 event predicates may offer misleading information due to faulty sensors.

Thus, instead of using the binary reading, the random bisection approach uses the actual reading of an interested factor or phenomenon, such as temperature, light, sound, chemical densities, and so on. Furthermore, the random bisection approach divides a sensor's neighborhood equally into two sectors and extends a faulty sensor detection algorithm to identify edge sensors [2].

Faulty sensor detection

Sensors located in the same region are spatially correlated. A sensor's reading without the support of its neighbors would indicate a faulty sensor. To determine whether a sensor S_i is faulty, its reading is compared with those of its neighbors. Let $N(S_i)$ denote the set of sensors including S_i and its k neighbors $S_{i1}, S_{i2}, ..., S_{ik}$ within the range of a radius R that is centered at S_i. Assume $x_1^{(i)}, x_2^{(i)}, ..., x_k^{(i)}$ represents the measurement at $S_{i1}, S_{i2}, ..., S_{ik}$ respectively. A comparison between x_i and $x_1^{(i)}, x_2^{(i)}, ..., x_k^{(i)}$ can be made by calculating the difference between x_i and the median of $x_1^{(i)}, x_2^{(i)}, ..., x_k^{(i)}$:

$$d_i = x_i - med_i. \tag{18}$$

The reason why the comparison is made with the median instead of the mean is that the value of a mean could easily be biased due to the extreme readings of faulty sensors.

To quantify the extremeness of d_i, let's consider another set of sensors $N^*(S_i)$ which contains S_i and its $n - 1$ neighbors. Based on the notion of equation (18), sensors in $N^*(S_i)$ yield a set of $D = \{d_1, d_2, ..., d_n\}$.

$$\hat{\mu} = \frac{1}{n} \sum_{i=1}^{n} d_i, \tag{19}$$

$$\hat{\sigma} = \sqrt{\frac{1}{n-1} \sum_{i=1}^{n} (d_i - \hat{\mu})^2}. \tag{20}$$

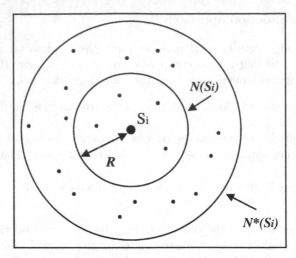

Fig. 5. An example of N^* neighborhood $N^*(S_i)$ of sensor S_i and N neighborhood $N(S_i)$ of sensor S_i inside $N^*(S_i)$. While the N neighborhood is used to compute d_i and the N^* neighborhood is used to quantify the extremeness of d_i, one can simply select $N^*(S_i) = N(S_i)$.

With the mean (19) and standard deviation (20) of the set D, one can standardize D to obtain $Y = \{y_1, y_2, ..., y_n\}$, where:

$$y_1 = \frac{d_1 - \hat{\mu}}{\hat{\sigma}}, ..., y_i = \frac{d_i - \hat{\mu}}{\hat{\sigma}}, ..., y_n = \frac{d_n - \hat{\mu}}{\hat{\sigma}}. \tag{21}$$

Since the standard deviation for a set of statistic values denotes the typical number of steps away from their mean, the standardized set $\{y_1, y_2, ..., y_n\}$ could be used to explain how large the step is compared to the standard deviation for each of d_i. If i) the set of sensor readings $x_1^{(i)}, x_2^{(i)}, ..., x_k^{(i)}$ form a sample of a normal distribution and ii) the number of sensor nodes within S_i's neighborhood is sufficiently large, the set Y will also form a standard normal population $N(0, 1)$. A particularly large value, either positive or negative, in a standard normal distribution will fall into the tail region of the probability density function. A large $|y_i|$ would then imply that the reading of S_i deviates markedly compared to its neighbors, and could be a faulty sensor. Thus, to determine whether a sensor node is faulty, a preselected threshold θ can be introduced, which means if $|y_i| \geq \theta$, then S_i is claimed to be a faulty sensor.

Let's go back to the discussion of the random bisection approach. To determine the event boundary, we have to identify non-faulty sensor nodes whose locations are near or on the boundary and their readings are extreme in their neighborhoods as well. Although the faulty sensor detection algorithm presented above can be of help in the process of identifying sensor nodes with these two characteristics, in some cases, sensor nodes sitting near the boundary cannot be detected efficiently.

Let C_1 denote the set of faulty sensor nodes detected by the faulty sensor detection algorithm. As illustrated in Figure 6, consider a non-faulty sensor node $S_i \in (S-C_1)$ which sits close to the event boundary but outside the event region. Assume sensor nodes are uniformly distributed. Since only a small portion of the disk is covered by the event region, the median of $x_1^{(i)}, x_2^{(i)}, ..., x_k^{(i)}$ will be obtained from a sensor node outside the event region as well. Thus, S_i won't be detected by simply applying the faulty sensor detection algorithm.

In order to solve the problem, the faulty sensor detection algorithm should be modified. Now, if we randomly draw a line through S_i, it will equally divide any closed disk centered at S_i into two half disks. As illustrated in Figure 6, the line randomly chosen intersects the boundary of the disk at points P_1 and P_2, and the boundary of events intersects with the same disk at points A and B. Based on equation (18), one can calculate d_i for each half disk. Again, assume sensors are deployed uniformly, the half disk yielding the largest $|d_i|$, denoted as $NN(S_i)$, would be the one containing P_1, P_2, B and S_i. To make the detection of sensor nodes near the event boundary more effective, the random bisection approach replaces the old d_i for S_i with the d_i resulting from $NN(S_i)$. Then perform calculation in equation (21). If $|y_i| \geq \theta$, the random bisection approach claims S_i as an edge sensor.

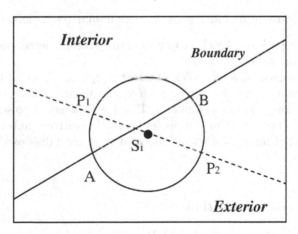

Fig. 6. An illustration of random bisection. The half disk yielding the largest $|d_i|$ is the one containing P_1, P_2, and S_i.

2.5 Random trisection approach

Similar to the random bisection approach, the random trisection approach[2] randomly divides a closed disk centered at S_i into three equal-sized sectors and calculates d_i for a union of any two sectors. Now, $NN(S_i)$ denotes the union yielding the largest $|d_i|$ among the three. Again, the largest d_i will be used instead of the old one to make the final decision.

Let C_2 denote the set of sensors detected by the random bisection or random trisection approach. Recall C_1, the set of faulty sensors claimed by the faulty sensor detection algorithm, may contain some sensors near the event boundary as well. A better edge estimation technique is to find a set of sensors $C_3 \subset C_1 \cup C_2$ excluding those C_1 nodes without a C_2 sensor nearby. Based on the observation that sensor readings are spatially correlated, for a sensor $S_i \in C_1 \cup C_2$, we can draw a closed disk $D(S_i; c)$ with radius c centered at S_i. Since the majority of C_2 sensors sit near the event boundary, if the closed disk $D(S_i; c)$ contains at least one sensor node from C_2, S_i is expected to be an edge sensor.

Thus, to determine C_3 sensors, we have to decide an appropriate radius c first. Since the density of the sensor field heavily effects the accuracy of boundary estimation, it is more desirable to control the number of expected sensor nodes in the closed disk instead of the radius. Assume the total number of sensor nodes in the field is N, and the width of the field is b. The expected number of sensor nodes falling into the closed disk would be $m = \frac{\pi c^2 N}{b^2}$. Given a preselected positive number m, the radius of the disk can be determined as $c = \sqrt{\frac{mb^2}{\pi N}}$.

The procedure of finding C_2 and C_3 is summarized as follows:

1. Construct $\{N\}$ and $\{N*\}$. Apply the faulty sensor detection algorithm to produce the set C_1 ($\theta = \theta_1$).
2. For each sensor $S_i \in (S - C_1)$, obtain the d_i from $NN(S_i)$ to replace the d_i from step 1 while keeping other d values unchanged.
3. Use equation (21) to recompute y_i. If $|y_i| \geq \theta$, assign S_i to set C_2 ($\theta = \theta_2$).
4. Obtain $C_3(m)$, where m is a predetermined positive number representing the expected number of sensor nodes in the closed disk used to detect C_3 sensors.

2.6 The Bayesian algorithm

Unlike other localized methods, the Bayesian algorithm devotes most of its efforts to trying to disambiguate faults from events and relies on other distributed region growing algorithms [10] or centralized methods such as those introduced in Section 3 to estimate the extent of an event region.

The first step in event boundary detection is for each sensor node to determine whether its reading particularly corresponds to any events of interest. Nevertheless, due to the possibility of faulty measurements, there could be unwanted detection or missed detection which makes this problem even more challenging.

However, observation shows that, if sensors are densely deployed in a field, readings at sensors in the same event region are spatially correlated and sensor

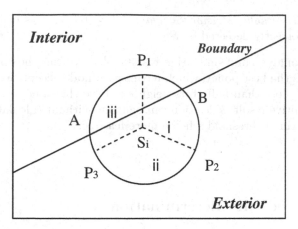

Fig. 7. An illustration of random trisection. The sector yielding the largest $|d_i|$ is the union of i and iii.

errors are likely spatially uncorrelated. By exploiting this notion, the Bayesian algorithm takes a similar approach in the faulty sensor detection described in Section 2.4. Each sensor collects readings of its neighbors and identifies an event or a false alarm locally.

Event disambiguation

The Bayesian algorithm takes a probability reasoning approach to decide whether an event is correctly detected by a sensor node. Assume the probability of an erroneous measurement at a sensor node equals p, then the probability of a correct measurement at the same node is $(1 - p)$. If there are N neighbors around sensor S_i and k of them have the same reading e as S_i does, the probability $P(E)$ that a sensor in the neighborhood of S_i has the same reading e can be modeled as $P(E) = \frac{k}{N}$. By the definition of Bayesian calculation, the probability P_t that S_i detects an event and its reading e is also a correct one can be calculated as:

$$P_t = \frac{P(E) \cdot P(e|E)}{P(E) \cdot P(e|E) + P(\bar{E}) \cdot P(e|\bar{E})} = \frac{\frac{k}{N} \cdot (1 - p)}{\frac{k}{N} \cdot (1 - p) + (1 - \frac{k}{N}) \cdot p}. \tag{22}$$

Based on the result of equation (22), the Bayesian algorithm incorporates the following three different schemes to decide whether an event is correctly detected at S_i:

- *Randomized Decision Scheme:* If P_t is larger than a randomly generated value $u \in (0, 1)$, it is claimed that an event is correctly detected by S_i.
- *Threshold Decision Scheme:* If P_t is larger than a pre-selected threshold $\theta \in (0, 1)$, it is claimed that an event is correctly detected by S_i.

- *Optimal Threshold Decision Scheme:* If $k \geq 0.5N$, it is claimed that an event is correctly detected by S_i.

Both the analysis and simulation results [5] show that the optimal threshold decision is the best policy, which means each node accepts its own reading if and only if more than half of its neighbors have the same reading. Though this is an intuitive result, a decision can be made without calculating P_t which makes the optimal threshold scheme more feasible.

3 Centralized edge determination

Centralized edge determination uses a designated sensor node with sufficient power or the sink to determine event boundaries based on the data collected from the sensor field. Although the cost for the operation of collecting data from all sensor nodes may be very high, sometimes it is still desirable to do so, because boundaries can be detected more accurately and efficiently with a "panorama" of the sensor field of interest. Also, if the total number of sensors is not too many, and all sensor nodes and the sink can hear each other, then energy consumption can be kept at a low level as well.

With a knowledge of the values of event predicates and the positions of all sensor nodes, a number of techniques can be applied in the centralized edge determination approach. Assuming sensor nodes are deployed on a plane, a collection of their values of event predicates can be regarded as a two-dimensional matrix. Edges can be easily detected with the image processing approach and the classifier approach discussed in previous sections.

However, other schemes do exist. In this section, a simple but elegant algorithm based on dual-space transform[6] for centralized edge determination is presented.

3.1 Dual-space approach

The basic idea behind the the dual-space approach is to transform lines and points in the primal space to points and lines in the dual space. A dual space transform has the following useful properties that can be used to assist boundary detection in wireless sensor networks:

- In the primal space, if a point (a, b) is on a line $y = \alpha x + \beta$, then, the corresponding line $\varphi = a\theta + b$ goes through the corresponding point $(-\alpha, \beta)$ in the dual space.
- In the primal space, if a point (a, b) is above a line $y = \alpha x + \beta$, then, the corresponding line $\varphi = a\theta + b$ is above the corresponding point $(-\alpha, \beta)$ in the dual space.

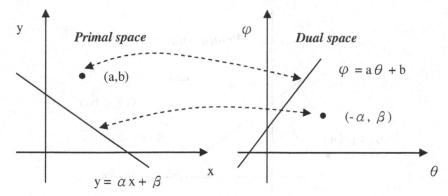

Fig. 8. The mapping between the primal space and the dual space.

- In the primal space, if a line $y = \alpha x + \beta$ performs a continuous motion, the corresponding point $(-\alpha, \beta)$ also performs a continuous motion in the dual space.

Now, consider, in the primal space, a set of sensors $\{S_1, ..., S_4\}$ whose positions are $(a_1, b_1)...(a_4, b_4)$ respectively and a shadow edge represented by a line $L\!: y = \alpha x + \beta$, and sensor S_1 is under the shadow as shown in Figure 9. Using the dual-space transform, each sensor defines a line and a shadow edge defines a point in the dual space, as shown in Figure 10.

According to the first two properties of dual-space transform, since the shadow edge L in the primal space is below sensor S_2, S_3 and is above S_1, its corresponding point l in the dual space will also be below line s_2, s_3 and above line s_1. In other words, in the dual space, point l is bounded by line s_2, s_3 and s_1. Furthermore, if the half plane shadow moves toward the direction of P_4 in the primal space, based on the third property, point l will also move in the dual space and it has to cross one of the boundaries (i.e., s_2 or s_3) before entering another cell, which means the shadow edge must come across either P_2 or P_3 before covering P_4.

This observation is significant to sensor management, because non-frontier sensor nodes like P_4 are unlikely to detect a change in their readings before any of the frontier nodes like P_2 or P_3 does. Thus, they can be turned off or put into deep sleep mode temporarily in order to save power.

For the purpose of tracking the movement of a shadow edge and sensor management, it is essential to solve the problem of finding the frontier nodes. Thanks to dual-space transform, this problem can be also "transformed" to finding the cell where point l resides, and this can be solved easily by linear programming in the dual space:

As illustrated in Figure 9, if the shadow is below its boundary, then any sensor P_i with a **0** reading is above the shadow edge. This implies the following constraint in the dual space:

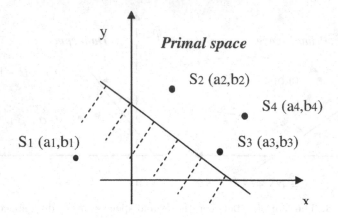

Fig. 9. A set of sensors and a shadow edge.

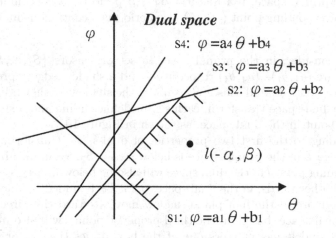

Fig. 10. The dual-space representation of the sensors and the shadow edge in Figure 9.

$$l > p_i.$$

Similarly, any sensor pj with a **1** reading is below the shadow edge and implies another constraint in the dual space:

$$l < p_j.$$

By linear programming, a point at the cell boundary can be found by solving the set of all inequalities. And finally, starting from that point, the cell can be found by walking along the boundaries of the cell which satisfy the set of constraints. Besides the simplicity of finding frontier nodes in the dual space, the movement of the shadow edge can be tracked easily as well. Again, take Figure 9 as an example; if the shadow edge moves toward the direction

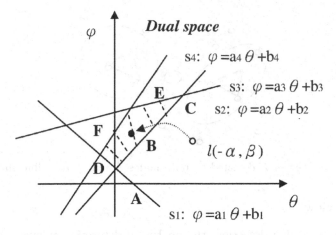

Fig. 11. The trace of the shadow in the dual space.

of P_2 and eventually covers it, as shown in Figure 11, its dual representation l will cross line segment B. It is intuitively clear that the new cell will be $\{B, D, F, E\}$. And it can be obtained by flipping the constraint on line s_2 and walking through the line segments that satisfy the new constraint set.

Though the dual-space is simple and elegant, it has its limitations. Since it is based on the dual-space transform of points and lines, it can not be used to detect or track boundaries with randomly shaped curves. Also, to design a distributed edge detection scheme based on the dual-space transform is another challenge.

4 Distributed Edge Detection

In an application of sensor detection, it is very hard to identify an event simply using the information gathered at one node. Instead, the presence of an event might be better described by a wide range of spatial regions where multiple sensors are deployed. To some extent, boundary estimation is considered a promising solution to the distributed spatial tracking problem.

A sensor node can determine whether it is on the boundary or not based on the information collected from its neighboring nodes. Usually, in a contiguous area, if some nodes observe the same phenomenon, they are considered to be in the same region. But in some other cases, it is not always true. Consider the scenario in Figure 12, where nodes A, B and their neighbors observe the same event E, but they belong to different regions. Thus, we need a distributed computation to distinguish the boundary.

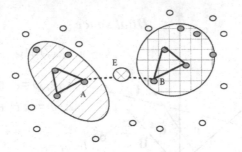

Fig. 12. Same event E detected by both nodes A and B from different regions.

4.1 Overview

In distributed region detection, the goal is to determine a set of distributed point sensors that observe a similar phenomenon in a contiguous area, where the computation is processed in a distributed manner. A 2-dimensional free-form line connecting the sensors that detect similar events can be nearly considered a boundary in a certain region.

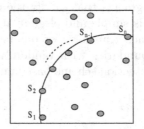

Fig. 13. An example of a boundary approximated by a set of sensor nodes.

Let S_i, S_{i+1} be neighbors on the boundary where they are within the radio range D (i.e., $d(S_i, S_{i+1}) < D$). At any instant of time, S_i and S_{i+1} observe the same phenomena given by the probability distribution of the local measurements, $m(S_i)$ and $m(S_{i+1})$ respectively, as shown in Figure 13. Let B_n be a set of nodes that observe the same events,

$$B_n = \{S_i | 1 \le i \le n, d(S_i, S_{i+1}) < R, m(S_i) = m(S_i + 1)\}. \tag{23}$$

S_1 and S_n are defined to be in the same region if there exists a sequence $m(S_1) = m(S_2) = \cdots = m(S_n)$. If these nodes happen to be on the boundary, then a trace of the position of these nodes can be considered part of the boundary. Note that neighboring nodes on the boundary may be outside the transmission range of each other. In most cases, they are not. So now we need a scheme to figure out the extent of the region where a set of spatially distributed sensors are located.

4.2 Growing Algorithm

Here we will introduce a region growing algorithm which was originally presented in [10]. Suppose the geographic location, (x_S, y_S), is available for node S, which can be determined by distributed localization algorithm [7], and each node has a unique identity I_S (e.g., geographic location). Let us also assign each node a region identifier R_S, which indicates a region the sensor node belongs to. If $R_S = R_{\tilde{S}}$, it means that node S and node $\tilde{S}$ are in the same region. The pseudo code of the algorithms is as follows:

```
/*Region-Growing(S)
  Input: Node S
  Output: Region R_S
*/
Initialize: R_S=I_S
Transmit R_S to all neighbor nodes

while (true)
    R <- set of received region identifiers
    r=min(R)

    if(r<R_S)
        R_S=r
        Transmit R_S to all neighbor nodes
    end if
end while

return R_S
```

The algorithm initializes the region of a node S to contain only S, and then pass this information to all the neighbor nodes within the radio range. At each iteration, the region identifier set R is updated according to the information from S's neighbor nodes. The region of node S, R_S, is assigned to be a minimum set (a set of distinct region identifiers having the same phenomena) from the neighbor's information and its own old region information. If its region set changes, node S sends the new information to its neighbors. The loop terminates when all the nodes in the same region reach the same identifer set.

Figure 14 shows an example [10] illustrating the algorithm, where a square region is to be detected. We assume that the left-top most vertex in the square has the smallest ID (region identifier) and the region growing set starts from here. Initially, the region boundary R only contains the left-top most vertex. After each iteration, the region boundary R moves one hop forward. This phase is termed as the *Growing Phase*. When the size of the boundary R stops

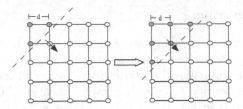

Fig. 14. One move in the Growing Phase.

increasing, the nodes at the other side of the region have the complete boundary information. Then the final boundary set information is passed back. This is called the *Feedback Phase*. At the end of this phase, all the nodes in the square have the same set of region nodes.

- **Running Time:**
  Suppose there are $n \times n$ nodes in the square, then in the worst case, the running time of the growing algorithm is $2n$, since the detected region boundary R first moves forward at the *Growing Phase*, and the final information is passed back to update the local region boundary at previously visited nodes in the *Feedback Phase*.

- **Number of Messages:**
  Let the length of square side be unit 1. The distance between neighboring nodes is $d = 1/n$. Let the radio range be in the range $(1/n, 2/n)$, i.e., sensors would only send messages to its nearest neighbors, and the power required per transmission would be proportional to the area of reception, i.e., kd^2. At the end of the ith iteration, all the sensors within i hops have updated to their final value. So the total transmission power required is [10]:

$$Power = kd^2[\sum_{i=0}^{n-1}(n^2 - \sum_{j=0}^{i}j) + \sum_{i=1}^{n-1}\sum_{j=1}^{i}j] = kd^2n^3 = kn. \quad (24)$$

This means that the total power needed for transmission is proportional to the square root of the number of nodes deployed in the grid.

4.3 Dynamic Boundary Estimation

The distributed boundary estimation described above is based on an assumption that the boundary will not change. But in most cases, the target region may change due to event mobility or faulty sensors. So we need a dynamic boundary estimation technique to enable working sensors to discover such changes.

One such technique is as follows. For each node S, it stores the ID of the neighboring node that transmitted ID of S. Denote this node as $NBD(S)$; thus we have $NBD(root) = root$. At regular intervals, each sensor S compares its region set to the region set of $NBD(S)$. If the region information does not match or the node does not get a response from $NBD(S)$, it resets its region set which only contains its own ID, and passes this information to its neighbors. So the growing region algorithm would run again, and nodes that lie in this region would update their boundary set. Of course, the selection of interval length depends on the balance between accuracy and energy cost.

In [10], the authors deployed six mica2 motes equipped with light sensors on the roof of a building to detect shadow moving. Their simulation results are based on scenarios with 100 nodes randomly distributed on a square space of dimensions 100×100.

We can get a better performance in terms of accuracy of boundary estimation in a distributed manner. However, the message passing overhead could be high, especially in a large area where thousands of sensors are deployed. The hierarchical boundary estimation technique, which is described next, tries to find a reasonable balance between energy cost and accuracy.

5 Hierarchical edge estimation

Other than centralized or distributed boundary estimation, Nowak and Mitra [9] investigate a general class of boundaries in a hierarchical framework, which tries to find a reasonable balance between energy cost and estimation accuracy in terms of performance. As we mentioned before, there are two fundamental problems in boundary detection in sensor networks. (1) Many messages transmitted among active nodes and desired destination would consume the energy so fast that the involved nodes could not work correctly after a short time. (2) The spatial density of deployed nodes and unpredicted noise in the measurements would limit the accuracy of boundary estimation. In real application, it is very hard to quantify the tradeoff between energy cost and estimation accuracy under various conditions and unpredictable situations. However, if we restrict some conditions in certain scenarios, say the distribution of the boundary, we still might get a rough idea about the tradeoff.

5.1 Lipschitz Boundary

Let us take an example from [9] to see how the tradeoff between energy consumption and estimation accuracy could be under certain constraints. Suppose that there are n sensors arranged in a $\sqrt{n} \times \sqrt{n}$ square cell field, and a boundary separates two homogeneous regions, as seen in Figure 15. To make the analysis simple, let us assume the boundary is a Lipschitz function [3], which

Fig. 15. A sensor network in the square cell field.

includes linear boundaries, parametric curves and some boundaries that cannot be described parametrically as well. Based on these assumptions, there will be $O(\sqrt{n})$ nodes lying on the boundary within a resolution of $1/\sqrt{n}$. Also, [3] infers that the mean-square error (MSE) can not decay faster than $O(\sqrt{n})$ given the above conditions.

In order to quantify the total energy that is required to send messages along the boundary, we assume that each node on the boundary just sends one message to inform the desired destination that it detects the boundary. If each message costs a roughly equal unit of energy, the least total energy that is needed would be $O(\sqrt{n})$. According to the description above, we have the following relation between energy cost and boundary estimation [9]:

$$MSE \sim \frac{1}{Energy}. \tag{25}$$

Note that the energy here only contains the basic requirements for transmission. It does not include other necessary energy (e.g., energy needed to identify if a node belongs to the set of boundary nodes). In addition, this formula does not imply that if we provide more energy for a fixed number of nodes, the MSE would be decreased. Actually, both the MSE and energy depend on the number of sensor nodes. This formula just gives us a general idea about how the MSE and energy would behave once the density of nodes increases.

It is easy to find that the transmission cost would grow with the increase of the density of deployed nodes. In [1], the authors discuss possible techniques for boundary detection which rely on the measurements from the neighboring nodes within a probing radius R. It is also mentioned that the accuracy could be improved by increasing the radius R. A distributed scheme requires message transmission among all the nodes within R, so the computation cost would be increased by $O(R^2)$. If a hierarchical framework is used, the transmission between two different clusters would only require messages between the two clusterheads rather than all the messages between each pair (two nodes in the two different clusters). For example, we have two clusters $A = a_0, a_1, \ldots, a_m$ and $B = b_0, b_1, \ldots, b_n$, where a_0 and b_0 are the clusterheads of the corresponding cluster. Simply, in a hierarchical framework, we only need $a_0 \iff b_0$ messages. But in the distributed manner, we would need $a_i \iff b_j, 0 \leq i \leq m, 0 \leq j \leq n$ messages. So the cost of transmission would be decreased by $m \times n$.

5.2 Dyadic Partition Algorithm

In [4], the author introduces a hierarchical structure of "clusterheads" which aggregates information from children nodes (might be also clusterheads if they are in the medium level) and then passes signal estimates to the upper layer in the hierarchy. In each square partition, the children partitions communicate their estimation to a clusterhead. The leaf node in the tree is the sensor node, and all other nodes represent the partitions in the field. In Figure 15, for instance, each square can be considered a partition in the hierarchy.

In general, there are various methods that can be applied to process the collected information at the clusterhead. Consider a simple example where sensor measurements are assumed to be a Gaussion distribution, then in square (i, j), the clusterhead computes an average from collected information to obtain the value as follows,

$$x_{i,j} \sim \mathcal{N}(\mu_{i,j}, \frac{\sigma^2}{m_{i,j}}), \tag{26}$$

where $\mu_{i,j}$ is the mean value, σ^2 is the noise variance, and $m_{i,j}$ is the number of nodes in square (i, j).

In [9], the authors present a hierarchical processing strategy that constructs a non-uniform rectangular partition of the sensor field to adapt to the boundary.

Suppose the sensor domain is a $\sqrt{n} \times \sqrt{n}$ square, and the side length $\sqrt{n}$ is the finest resolution. Theoretically, this can be achieved by a recursively dyadic partition.

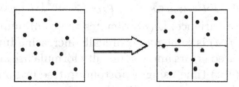

Fig. 16. An illustration of dyadic partition.

First divide a larger square into four sub-squares with equal sizes, as shown in Figure 16, and then repeat this on each partition. So in iteration k, the total number of partition changes from 2^{2k-2} to 2^{2k}. Obviously, the finest resolution needs $\frac{1}{2}log_2 n$ iterations. This process can be represented by a quad-tree structure. And the quad-tree can also be pruned to form a non-uniform rectangular domain as shown in Figure 17.

A consequent question is: how can the pruning process be implemented in the sensor network? Let $\mathcal{P}_n$ denote the set of all possible pruned trees, then for each $p \in \mathcal{P}_n$, p has a corresponding quad-tree structure where each non-leaf node has four children nodes that represent a square region. Consider

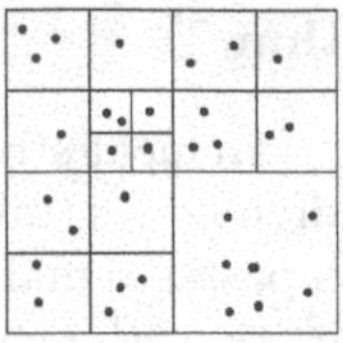

Fig. 17. An illustration of non-uniform rectangular domain.

these squares as clusters, where each cluster has a clusterhead which collects information from the other nodes (here nodes represent sub-partitions) in the region. Consider all potential pruning $p \in \mathcal{P}_n$, each sensor node belongs to a nested hierarchy of side length: $1, 2, 4, \ldots, \sqrt{n}$ (totally $\frac{1}{2} log_2 n$ levels).

Since the raw data $\{x_{i,j}\}$ might be noisy, and transmission of raw data would require a maximum amount of energy for message passing, locally processed data would have a better performance considering accuracy and energy consumption. There could be various methods for the local processing. In [9], for instance, the authors compute the average information from sensors in the square, denoted by $\omega(p)$ for pruning p, so the sum-of-squared errors between average and raw data for pruning p is,

$$\mathcal{E}(\omega, x) = \sum_{i,j=1}^{\sqrt{n}} (\omega(i,j) - x_{i,j})^2. \tag{27}$$

To decrease the effect of unnecessarily high resolution partitions, they also define a complexity penalized estimator as

$$\hat{p}_n = \arg min_{\omega(p):p \in \mathcal{P}_n} \mathcal{E}(\omega(p), x) + 2\sigma^2 f(n)|\omega(p)|. \tag{28}$$

Here σ^2 is a noise variance. $|\omega(p)|$ denotes the total number of squares in the partition p, and $f(n)$ is some monotonically increasing function of n. Since both the sum-of-squared errors and the penalty formula are additive functions, it can be solved in $O(n)$ time using a bottom-up tree pruning algorithm [3].

A remaining problem here is how to choose an appropriate function $f(n)$. Obviously, it depends on the definition of best pruned tree. The authors in [9] set $f(n) = 2/3 \log n$ to reach a nearly optimal performance. They apply the above scheme on a sensor network of size 4^k for $k = 2, 3, \ldots, 8$ in the simulation operated in a environment with three different noise levels ($\sigma^2 = 1, 10, 100$). The results agree very well with their theoretical predictions.

6 Conclusion and future work

The estimation of boundary between regions of distinct behavior in a large physical space is highly desired in many domains (e.g., chemical monitoring).

In this chapter, we presented recent techniques for detecting a boundary in sensor networks. Techniques for boundary detection are classified into four different classes: (1) centralized estimation; (2) localized estimation; (3) distributed estimation; (4) hierarchical estimation.

All of these recent efforts only concerned static sensor fields. The main drawback of a static sensor network is that estimation accuracy relies on the density of sensor deployment. In other words, if the deployment is sparse, we could never expect a nearly precise result. In [8], the authors enumerate the challenges to estimate a boundary using mobile sensing nodes. They also outline a three-dimensional testbed designed for boundary detection in a mobile way. This work is still in progress. Due to advances in battery technologies and sensor hardware, we believe that we can achieve promising accuracy of boundary estimation in the future.

References

1. Krishna K. Chintalapudi and Ramesh Govindan. Localized edge detection in sensor fields. *Ad-hoc Networks Journal*, 2003.
2. Min Ding, Dechang Chen, KaiXing, and Xiuzhen Cheng. Localized fault-tolerant event boundary detection in sensor networks. In *IEEE INFOCOM*, 2005.
3. David L. Donoho. Wedgelets: Nearly minimax estimation of edges. *Ann. Statist.*, 27, 3:859–897, 1999.
4. Deepak Ganesan, Deborah Estrin, and John Heideman. Dimensions: Why do we need a new data handling architecture for sensor networks? In *IEEE/ACM HotNets-I, Princeton, NJ*, Oct. 2002.
5. Bhaskar Krishnamachari and Sitharama Iyengar. Distributed bayesian algorithms for fault-tolerant event region detection in wireless sensor networks. *IEEE Transactions on Computer, Vol. 53, No. 3*, Mar. 2004.
6. Jie Liu, Patrick Cheung, Leonidas Guibas, and Feng Zhao. A dual-space approach to tracking and sensor management in wireless sensor networks. In *International Conference on Mobile Computing and Networking*, pages 131–139, 2002.
7. David Moore, John Leonard, Daniela Rus, and Seth Teller. Robust distributed network localization with noisy range measurements. In *Proceedings of the second ACM Conference on Embedded Networked Sensor Systems*, Nov. 2004.
8. Rober Nowak, Urbashi Mitra, and Rebecca Willett. Estimating inhomogeneous fields using wireless sensor networks. *IEEE Journal on Selected Areas in Communications*, 2004.
9. Robert Nowak and Urbashi Mitra. Boundary estimation in sensor networks: Theory and methods. In *2nd International Workshop on Information Processing in Sensor Networks, Palo Alto, CA*, pages 22–23, Apr. 2003.
10. Anand Panangadan and Gaurav S. Sukhatme. Data segmentation for region detection in a sensor network. *Submitted to International Conference on Distributed Computing in Sensor Systems (DCOSS)*, 2005.
11. Andreas Savvides, Jia Fang, and Dimitrios Lymberopoulos. Using mobile sensing nodes for dynamic boundary estimation. In *Workshop on Applications of Mobile Embedded Systems, held in conjuction with MobiSys, Boston, Massachusetts*, Jun. 6th.

Chapter 7
TPSS: A Time-based Positioning Scheme for Sensor Networks with Short Range Beacons

Fang Liu[1], Xiuzhen Cheng[1], Dong Hua[1], and Dechang Chen[2]

[1] Department of Computer Science
The George Washington University, Washington, DC 20052
{fliu, cheng, gwuhua}@gwu.edu
[2] Department of Preventive Medicine and Biometrics
Uniformed Services University of the Health Sciences, Bethesda, MD 20814
dchen@usuhs.mil

1 Introduction

A wireless sensor network is composed of a large number of small and inexpensive smart sensors for many monitoring, surveillance and control applications. Each sensor makes its own local observation. All active sensors in the network coordinate to provide a global view of the monitored area. It is anticipated that such a network can be used in unattended environments or hostile physical locations. Applications include habitat monitoring [7,25], infrastructure surveillance [40], target tracking in tactical environments [12], etc.

Almost all these applications require sensors to be aware of their physical locations. For example, the physical positions should be reported together with the corresponding observations in wildlife tracking, weather monitoring, location-based authentication, etc [19,24,34]. Location information can also be used to facilitate network functions such as packet routing [9,23] and collaborative signal processing [16], in which the complexity and processing overhead can be substantially reduced. Further, each node can be uniquely identified with its position, thus exempting the difficulty of assigning a unique ID before deployment [36].

However, many challenges exist in designing effective and efficient sensor self-positioning schemes for sensor networks. First, a localization algorithm must scale well to large sensor networks. Further, the location discovery scheme should not aggravate the communication and computation overheads of the network, since low-cost sensors have limited resource budgets such as battery supply, CPU, memory, etc. What's more, the localization scheme should not raise the construction cost of sensor nodes. Finally, the positioning scheme should be robust enough to provide high precision even under noisy environments. In this chapter, we present TPSS, a time-based scheme that meets many of the requirements mentioned above.

TPSS is different from TPS [8] and iTPS [38], even though all three rely on TDoA measurements to calculate a sensor position through trilateration. The beauty of TPSS lies in that there is no requirement for base stations to cover the entire network by powerful long-range beacons. Only short-range beacon nodes with known positions need to be deployed. A beacon node could be a typical sensor mounted with a GPS. Recall that TPS (iTPS) requires three (four) long-range beacon stations with each being able to cover the entire network. TPSS releases this restriction while retaining many nice features of the other two. For example, all these three schemes require no time synchronization among sensors and beacons. In TPSS, each sensor listens passively for signals from the beacons in its neighborhood. A sensor computes the range differences to at least three beacons and then combines them through trilateration to obtain its position estimate. This procedure contains only simple algebraic operations over scalar values, thus incurs low computation overhead. Since a beacon signal is transmitted within a short range only, the communication overhead is low, too. Whenever a sensor resolves its own position, it can work as a beacon and help other nodes on location computation. Simulation results indicate that TPSS is an effective self-positioning scheme for sensor networks with short range beacons.

This chapter is organized as follows. Section 2 summarizes the current research on location discovery. The network model to be studied is described in Section 3. The new positioning scheme, TPSS, is proposed in Section 4. Simulation results are reported in Section 5. And we conclude our chapter in Section 6.

2 An Overview on Current Location Discovery Schemes for Sensor Networks

The popular Global Positioning System(GPS) [39] localization system may not be a practical solution for outdoor sensor networks. It is infeasible to install GPS on each sensor due to cost, form factors, power consumption and antenna requirements. Further, GPS requires direct Light-Of-Sight (LoS) communication, which renders it unfeasible for many outdoor application environments. Therefore in the past several years, extensive research has been directed to designing GPS-less location discovery schemes [1–5, 8, 13–15, 17, 18, 20–22, 26–35, 37]. These positioning algorithms differ in their assumptions on network deployment, device capabilities, node mobility, signal propagation, error requirement, etc. Thus, they can be classified differently. For example, some methods are designed for static sensor networks, where sensors remain stationary after deployment, while others are for dynamic sensor networks where sensors and beacons are mobile [2, 18]. These localization schemes can also be classified as centralized [10, 37], where all computations are performed by a central point (e.g., the base station), or distributed, where sensors estimate their positions independently of each other. Centralized methods have poor scalability and are thus infeasible for large sensor networks. In this section, we will focus on distributed location discovery schemes for stationary sensor networks, which can be further classified as beacon-based and beacon-less depending on whether or not beacons are used, or classified as range-based and range-free according to the type of knowledge used in position estimation.

2.1 Beacon-based and Beacon-less Localization Schemes

Beacon-based Localization

The majority of current location detection systems assume the existence of beacons, whose positions are known through GPS receivers or manual configuration. A typical sensor first measures the distances or angles from itself to several beacons, then obtains position estimation through techniques such as *triangulation, trilateration, multilateration*, etc. Based on the coverage capabilities of beacons, these localization systems can be further classified as systems with long-range beacons or systems with short-range beacons.

Systems with long-range base stations [3,8,28] have a fixed set of powerful beacons, whose transmission range can cover the entire network. Usually these base stations are manually deployed, are time-synchronized, and are equipped with special instruments such as directional antennas. In systems with short-range beacons [20,21,34,35], a small number of sensors with known positions are randomly deployed amongst other ordinary sensors. Some of them rely on transmitting both RF and ultrasound signals at the same time [14,34,35], where the RF is used for time-synchronizing the sender and the receiver.

If a sensor cannot receive signals from enough beacons, none of the previous techniques will work. In this case, network connectivity can be exploited for range estimation [29,30,33,37]. The connectivity information can be broadcasted using global flooding to notify all sensors of the locations of base stations [29,30,33]. A sensor node measures its distance to each beacon in terms of hop counts, then estimates its position based on the average distance per hop which is computed by base stations. Ref. [37] describes a localization scheme based on multidimensional scaling, which requires global connectivity information and centralized computation. These connectivity-based location discovery schemes require either long-range beacons or short-range beacons, but they have poor scalability due to the use of global flooding.

Beacon-less Localization

For a beacon-less localization system, some special nodes must be identified to provide reference for others to compute their positions. Such special sensors can be the perimeter nodes [31], whose distance (hops) to the other nodes can be estimated through flooding. Each non-perimeter node determines its location through an iterative procedure and periodically updates its coordinates as the average of its neighbors' coordinates. A more efficient position estimation algorithm is proposed in [13], which uses *deployment points* to provide reference for location estimation. Sensors are divided into groups. A group of sensors are dropped at the same deployment point. Relying on the prior knowledge about the probability distribution of the sensors' resident positions within each group, a sensor can estimate its location by observing the group memberships of its neighbors. This method requires only one-hop broadcasting, thus involves light communication overhead. However, such a scheme has a strict demand on *a priori* knowledge of the deployment distribution, which is usually not possible in many applications.

2.2 Range-based and Range-free Localization Schemes

Range-based Localization

Range-based localization relies on the availability of point-to-point distance or angle information. The distance/angle can be obtained by measuring Time-of-Arrival (ToA), Time-Difference-of-Arrival (TDOA), Received-Signal-Strength-Indicator (RSSI), and Angle-of-Arrival (AOA), etc. The range-based localization may produce fine-grained resolution, but have strict requirements on signal measurements and time synchronization.

ToA measures the signal arrival times and calculates distances based on transmission times and speeds. GPS [39] is the most popular ToA-based localization system. By precisely synchronizing with a satellite's clock, GPS computes node position based on signal propagation time.

Compared to ToA, TDoA has an advantage as the former's processing delays and non-LOS propagation can introduce larger errors [6]. Ref. [34] proposes a TDoA based scheme (AHLos) that requires base stations to transmit both ultrasound and RF signals simultaneously. The RF signal is used for synchronization purposes. A sensor first measures the difference of the arrival times between the two signals, then determines the range to the base station. Finally, multilateration is applied to combine range estimates and generate location data.

RSSI computes distance based on transmitted and received power levels, and a radio propagation model. RSSI is mainly used with RF signals [1, 17], but the range estimation can be inaccurate due to multipath fading in outdoor environments [34].

AoA-based methods first measure the angle at which a signal arrives at a base station or a sensor, then estimates the position using triangulation. The calculation is quite simple, but AoA techniques require special antenna and may not perform well due to omni-directional multipath reflections. Further, the signals can be difficult to measure accurately if a sensor is surrounded by scattering objects [6]. Ref. [26] proposes a prototype navigation system for autonomous vehicles, which estimates AoA by means of a set of optical sources and a rotating optical sensor. The system is not suitable for outdoor sensor networks due to its cost and complexity. Ref. [28] first transforms TDoA measurements into AoA information, then applies triangulation for location estimates. It requires three base stations with synchronized rotating directional antennae.

Range-free Localization

Range-free localization requires no measurement on distance or angle among nodes. They can be further classified as local techniques and hop-counting techniques [18].

- Local Techniques. A simple centroid algorithm is proposed in [3], in which each sensor estimates its position as the centroid of the locations of the neighboring beacons. The computation error can be reduced by a density adaptive algorithm (HEAP) if beacons are well-positioned [4]. However, this is unfeasible for ad hoc deployment. Later, He *et al.* proposed the APIT method [15], which divides the environment into triangular regions between beacon nodes. Each sensor determines its relative position with the triangles, and estimates its own location as the center of gravity of the intersection of all the triangles that the node may reside in. However, APIT requires long-range beacon stations, which requires expensive high-power transmitters.

- Hop-Counting Techniques. In DV hop [29, 30], base stations flood their positions to all nodes in the network. Sensors compute the minimum distance in hops to several base stations. Base stations compute an average distance per hop to other base stations, which will be flooded to the whole network to facilitate sensors to calculate their positions. Ref. [33] refines location estimates computed by DV-hop by using neighboring sensor positions and distance estimates to help convergence to a better solution. Similarly, Amorphous positioning scheme [27] also uses flooding to inform sensors of their hop-count distances to each beacon. The difference is that Amorphous localization method improves the location estimates through an offline hop-distance computation and neighbor information exchange. The hop-counting method excludes the requirement for densely-distributed beacons. However, the multi-hop flooding involves a large amount of communication overhead, and relies on a network with dense and uniformly-distributed sensors.

2.3 Secure Localization Schemes

Most of the current location discovery schemes assume a benign environment where sensors can get correct reference information from beacons. However, the actual sensor networks may be deployed in hostile environments. Beacons can be compromised, then inject false positioning information into the network. Sensors can be misled and then claim that they are at positions that are far away from their actual locations. In some cases, such false reports may incur disastrous results. For example, in sensor networks designed for military tracking and reconnaissance surveillance, nodes are misled and report themselves in faraway places. The false information may result in a fatal decision-making, when sensors report that they are in a safe region [11]. Hence, it is important to assure that the received beaconing information is true, or the resolved location is correct.

Sastry*et al.* [32] made the first attempt to solve the secure localization problem in wireless sensor networks. A distance bounding protocol, ECHO, is proposed to use both RF and ultrasound signals for secure location verification. However, such a scheme only works for in-region verification, which means that ECHO only verifies whether or not a node is within a region of interest. Besides, ECHO relies on the availability of both RF and ultrasound signals.

Lazos and Poovendran propose a range-independent secure positioning scheme, SeRLoc, in [22]. Using directional antennas, each beacon node transmits different beacon signal at each antenna sector. Thus, if a sensor receives a beacon from a specified antenna sector, the sensor must reside within that sector. Based on the information received about the sector boundary lines and the positions of the beacons, a sensor can identify the overlapping region of all the sectors that it hears and estimate its location as the center of gravity (CoG) of the region. SeRLoc can tolerate the wormhole attack, the sybil attack and compromised sensors. However, SeRLoc does not work well if beacons are compromised.

A novel localization anomaly detection scheme, namely LAD, is proposed by Du *et al.* [11], which works for detecting location estimation anomaly at sensor nodes. LAD assumes *a priori* knowledge of the deployment distribution and the group memberships of node neighbors, and enables sensors to detect localization anomalies. By verifying the inconsistency between the derived locations and the node observations, LAD can determine if an anomaly happens. LAD works effectively against localization anomalies, but requires the availability of the deployment distribution which is hard for many sensor network applications.

Capkun and Hubaux [5] analyze the resistance of positioning techniques to position and distance spoofing attacks, and propose the Verifiable Multilateration mechanism for secure computation and verification of node positions. A secure positioning scheme, SPINE, is also proposed, which can resist distance modification attacks from a large number of attackers.

2.4 TPS, iTPS, and TPSS

TPS [8] and iTPS [38] rely on the transmission of RF signals from beacon stations for location discovery. Such schemes require no time synchronization in the network and minimal extra hardware in sensor construction. No connectivity knowledge is needed, thus they can scale well to large networks. Since sensors just listen passively to beacon signals, no extra communication overhead is introduced. With only local measurements, TPS and iTPS retain the fine-grained computation of range-based schemes, but exclude the necessity of time synchronization among beacon nodes. As the location detection algorithm involves only some simple algebraic operations, the computation overhead is also low.

TPSS retains all the above nice features of TPS and iTPS, but requires no powerful long-range beacons to cover the entire network. With only a few short-range beacons deployed, sensors can compute their positions easily. TPSS can be applied to large-scale sensor networks where the deployment of powerful long-range beacons are too expensive or not practical.

3 Network Model

In this chapter, we consider a sensor network deployed over a two-dimensional monitored area. Actually, our TPSS scheme can be easily extended to higher-dimensional space. In this model, each sensor has limited resources (battery, CPU, etc.), and is equipped with an omni-directional antenna. Some sensors, called *beacons*, have the ability to position themselves. They are deployed together with typical sensors whose positions are to be computed with the TPSS. An example scenario is plotted in Figure 1. The beacon nodes will broadcast beacon signals periodically to assist other sensors with location discovery. Note that the only difference between a beacon and a sensor is whether the location is known. Whenever a sensor gets localized using the TPSS algorithm, it will broadcast its own location and help other sensors for position detection. In other words, it can work as a beacon node.

4 TPSS: A Time-Based Positioning Scheme with Short Range Beacons

In this section, we propose TPSS, a time-based positioning scheme for sensor networks with short range beacons. TPSS consists of three steps. In the first step, a sensor collects all the signals from the neighboring beacons, and groups them according to the sources of the signals. The next two steps work on the signals belonging to the same group: the range differences from beacon nodes to the sensor are computed and then the coordinates are resolved.

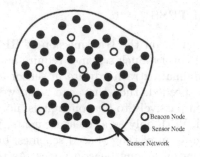

Fig. 1. An Example Sensor Network.

4.1 Step 1: Signal Collection

Assume each beacon node initiates a beacon signal once every T seconds. This signal contains the beacon's location and a TTL (Time To Live) field with an initial value ≥ 3. The format of the message is demonstrated in Figure 2. A beacon node hearing a beacon signal with $TTL > 0$ will broadcast it again after decreasing the TTL value by 1 and after attaching both its own location and the time difference between when the signal is received and when it is re-broadcasted. This is indicated by the *relay* and *delay* fields in the message format shown in Figure 2. Each sensor with unknown location listens passively for the beacon signals and groups them according to the initiators of the messages. If a sensor receives the same signal (originated from the same beacon) at least three times, the location of the sensor can be readily determined by the following two steps.

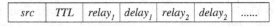

src: location of the node generating the message
TTL: time to live
$relay_i$: location of the i-th node relaying the message
$delay_i$: time bw. when the msg is received and when it is re-broadcasted by the i-th relay

Fig. 2. Format of the Message Transferred.

4.2 Step 2: Range Detection

We only consider groups containing at least three messages originated from the same beacon node. In each group, select three where the involved beacons are *non-colinear*.

We first assume the beacon signal is relayed without loss, that is, the signal from the initiator as well as from all the intermediate relay nodes can successively reach the sensor S. Figure 3 shows one such example. Beacon A starts a message $M=(A,3,-,-)$ which arrives at S and beacon B at time t_1 and t_b, respectively. B modifies M as $M'=(A,2,B,\Delta t_b)$ and re-broadcasts it at time t'_b, where $t'_b = t_b + \Delta t_b$. M' arrives at S and beacon C at time t_2 and t_c, respectively. C modifies M' as $M''=(A,1,B,\Delta t_b,C,\Delta t_c)$ and broadcasts M'' at time t'_c, where $t'_c = t_c + \Delta t_c$. Finally, M'' arrives at S at time t_3. Assume all the nodes transfer the signals at the same speed v. Let d_{sa}, d_{sb}, d_{sc} represent the distances from the sensor S to beacons A, B, C, respectively. Let d_{ab}, d_{ac} denote the distance between beacons A and B, A and C, respectively.

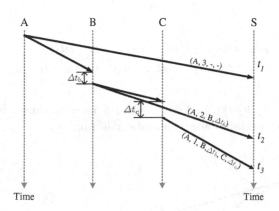

Fig. 3. Range Detection: Signal is Relayed Without Loss.

We have

$$\frac{d_{ab}}{v} + \Delta t_b + \frac{d_{sb}}{v} - \frac{d_{sa}}{v} = t_2 - t_1, \tag{1}$$

$$\frac{d_{bc}}{v} + \Delta t_c + \frac{d_{sc}}{v} - \frac{d_{sb}}{v} = t_3 - t_2, \tag{2}$$

which gives

$$d_{sa} = d_{sb} + k_1, \quad \text{where } k_1 = d_{ab} - v \cdot (t_2 - t_1 - \Delta t_b), \tag{3}$$

$$d_{sc} = d_{sb} + k_2, \quad \text{where } k_2 = -d_{bc} + v \cdot (t_3 - t_2 - \Delta t_c). \tag{4}$$

Equations (3)(4) show that k_1, k_2 can be obtained by measuring t_1, t_2, t_3 with S's local timer, learning the positions of A, B, C and time differences $\Delta t_b, \Delta t_c$ from the beacon signals. We are going to apply trilateration with k_1, k_2 to compute coordinates (x, y) for sensor S in Step 3.

Note that TPSS can still work if some beacon signals get lost during the transmission from the initiator or any intermediate relay nodes. As long as a sensor S receives one signal from three different relay beacons, S's location can be computed with TPSS. For example (Figure 4), M is a beacon signal travelling along beacons 1, 2, 3, 4 and 5. The messages relayed by beacons 1 and 4 are lost or destroyed during the transmission. S receives M only from beacons 2, 3, 5 at time t_0, t_1, t_2, respectively. Let $d_{ij}(d_{sj})$ denote the distance between node $i(s)$ and j, and Δt_i be the time difference information conveyed by beacon node i. We have:

$$\frac{d_{23}}{v} + \Delta t_3 + \frac{d_{s3}}{v} - \frac{d_{s2}}{v} = t_1 - t_0, \tag{5}$$

$$\frac{d_{34}}{v} + \Delta t_4 + \frac{d_{45}}{v} + \Delta t_5 + \frac{d_{s5}}{v} - \frac{d_{s3}}{v} = t_2 - t_1. \tag{6}$$

It follows that,

$$d_{s2} = d_{s3} + k_1, \text{ where } k_1 = d_{23} - v \cdot (t_1 - t_0 - \Delta t_3), \tag{7}$$

$$d_{s5} = d_{s3} + k_2, \text{ where } k_2 = -(d_{34} + d_{45}) + v \cdot (t_2 - t_1 - \Delta t_4 - \Delta t_5). \tag{8}$$

In this case, k_1, k_2 can be known when S receives three messages among all that have been relayed after the same initiator.

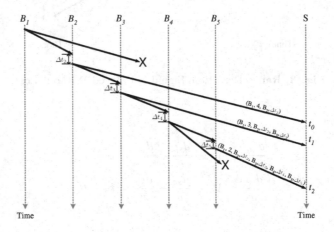

Fig. 4. Range Detection: Signal is Relayed With Loss

Comparing Equations (3)(4) with (7)(8), we can summarize the result of range detection as

$$d_{SA} = d_{SB} + k_1, \tag{9}$$

$$d_{SC} = d_{SB} + k_2, \tag{10}$$

where, A, B, C are the three relay nodes in the same group that convey messages originated from the same source and are sorted according to the sequence in which they relay the signal.

Remarks:
(*i*) All times are estimated locally. For example, the arrival times of the signals $(t_1, t_2,$ etc.) are measured at sensor S's local timer; the time differences at relay nodes $(\Delta t_b, \Delta t_c,$ etc.) are computed based on the beacon's local timer.
(*ii*) For each sensor S, range detection is conducted on each group that contains messages from the same initiator. Corresponding location computation is taken in the next step. Averaging all the results computed for S, the final result is taken as the coordinates of node S.
(*iii*) For each group, there may exist multiple methods to select the three messages. Consider a signal travelling along beacons 1 to 4, and assume all the relayed signals arrive at S finally. We have $d_{s,i} = d_{s,i-1} + k_{i-1}$, where $k_i = v \cdot (t_{i+1} - t_i - \Delta t_{i+1}) - d_{i,i+1}$, $d_{ij}(d_{sj})$ is the distance between node $i(s)$ and j, Δt_i is the time difference at the relay node i, and t_i is the time S receives the message from beacon i, for $i = 2, 3,$ and 4. The three equations can be divided into two overlapping groups. Group I contains $d_{s2} = d_{s1} + k_1$, $d_{s3} = d_{s2} + k_2$; while group II contains $d_{s3} = d_{s2} + k_2$, $d_{s4} = d_{s3} + k_3$. Each group can be used to compute S's coordinates in the next step independently.

4.3 Step 3: Location Computation

From Equations (9)(10), $d_{SA} = d_{SB} + k_1$, $d_{SC} = d_{SB} + k_2$, we get the following three equations with three unknowns x, y and d_{SB} based on trilateration:

$$(x - x_b)^2 + (y - y_b)^2 = d_{sb}^2, \tag{11}$$
$$(x - x_a)^2 + (y - y_a)^2 = (d_{sb} + k_1)^2, \tag{12}$$
$$(x - x_c)^2 + (y - y_c)^2 = (d_{sb} + k_2)^2. \tag{13}$$

As proposed in [8], we can solve these equations in two steps: First, transform the coordinates into a system where A, B, C reside at $(x_1, 0)$, $(0,0)$ and (x_2, y_2), respectively; Second, solve the equations with the efficient method proposed in [8]. Since the positions at the original coordinate system can always be obtained through rotation and translation, the solution provided by [8] can be treated as a general one:

$$x = \frac{-2k_1 d_{sb} - k_1^2 + x_1^2}{2x_1}, \tag{14}$$

$$y = \frac{(2k_1 x_2 - 2k_2 x_1)d_{sb}}{2x_1 y_2} + \frac{k_1^2 x_2 - k_2^2 x_1 + x_2^2 x_1 + y_2^2 x_1 - x_1^2 x_2}{2x_1 y_2}, \tag{15}$$

where d_{sb} is the root of $\alpha d_{sb}^2 + \beta d_{sb} + \gamma = 0$, with

$$\alpha = 4[k_1^2 y_2^2 + (k_1 x_2 - k_2 x_1)^2 - x_1^2 y_2^2], \tag{16}$$
$$\beta = 4[k_1(k_1^2 - x_1^2)y_2^2 + $$
$$\quad (k_1 x_2 - k_2 x_1)(k_1^2 x_2 - k_2^2 x_1 + x_2^2 x_1 + y_2^2 x_1 - x_1^2 x_2)], \tag{17}$$
$$\gamma = (k_1^2 - x_1^2)^2 y_2^2 + (k_1^2 x_2 - k_2^2 x_1 + x_2^2 x_1 + y_2^2 x_1 - x_1^2 x_2)^2. \tag{18}$$

Remarks:
Steps 2 and 3 are repeated once per epoch on all triple messages within each group and all valid groups that can help S estimate its position. The final coordinates (x, y) are obtained by averaging all the results. Once S's position is known, it will become a beacon and help other sensors on location estimation. The iteration of such processes can help more and more sensors get localized, as shown by our simulation results in Section 5.

5 Performance Evaluation

We consider a sensor network deployed over a field of 100 by 100. The transmission range of sensors and beacons is fixed at 10. We assume each sensor can correctly receive from all the beacons within its transmission range. Each beacon initiates a beacon signal once per epoch. A sensor becomes a beacon node after its position is resolved. Since MATLAB provides procedures to randomly deploy sensors and beacons, it is selected to perform all the simulations.

According to Equations (3)(4) and (7)(8), the coordinates (x, y) are obtained from the measurements of t_i's, Δt_i's. The accuracy of t_i's depends on the local timers of the sensor nodes, whose measuring error is affected by the TDoA timer drift, the signal arrival time correlation error, and the reception delays, etc. In the beacon node, Δt_i is computed based on the beacon's local timer and the known system delays, whose inaccuracy is determined by reception and transmission delays, time-stamping inaccuracies, and turn-around delay measurement errors, etc. In our simulation study, we only consider inaccuracy of the TDoA measurement at the sensors (t_i's), since Δt_i's play the same role. Such inaccuracy is modeled as a normal distribution in the simulation.

We will evaluate the effectiveness of TPSS. First, we want to study the percentage of sensors whose locations can be resolved while varying the number of initial beacons. We consider a network with 300 nodes. Figure 5 reports the results for the first nine epochs. We can tell that the percentage of resolved nodes increases as the number of the initial beacons increases. This also holds true as the number of epochs increases. Another observation is that the more the initial beacons are deployed, the less epochs TPSS will require to achieve a high percentage of the resolved nodes in the network. Second, we test the impact of network density on the localization process. Figure 6 illustrates the percentage of resolved sensors when the number of initial beacons varies under different network density. The number of epochs is set to 10. It shows that as the network density increases, more and more sensors get localized. This is reasonable. Given a fixed number of beacons deployed in a fixed-sized network, the more sensors within the network, the more nodes can be covered by a three-beacon group. Therefore an increase of the number of sensors will not require the number of beacons to be increased as well, as long as the existent

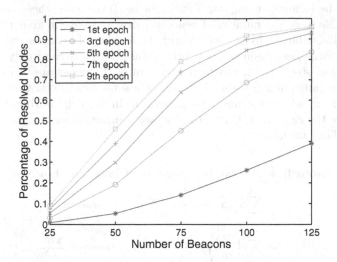

Fig. 5. Percentage of resolved nodes vs. the number of the initial beacons: the first 9 epochs.

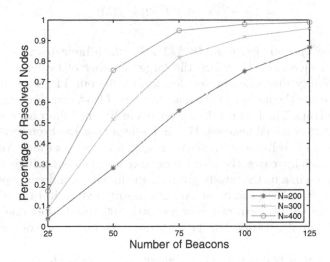

Fig. 6. Percentage of resolved nodes vs. the number of the initial beacons: with different network density.

beacons can cover most of the network. All the results are the average over 100 runs.

We obtain two observations from Figure 5 and 6. First, the more beacons deployed, the more sensors get localized. Second, once more and more sensors resolve their positions, more and more sensors get localized. Thus we can expect that with only a small number of short-range beacons deployed, many sensors can be localized using our TPSS scheme. Intuitively, these two results are reasonable since the number of beacons increases. We can give a brief statistical analysis about why the increase of the number of beacons can result in a better performance. Assume a network contains N nodes randomly deployed over an area of size L by L, in which q percent of the nodes are beacons. The transmission range of a node is R. Whether a sensor can determine its position depends on whether it has enough beacons in the neighborhood. We will not consider the case when three beacons are colinear, since the possibility is quite low. Thus we have:

$$P(S \text{ is resolved}) \approx P(S \text{ can be reached by at least three beacons})$$

$$= \sum_{d=3}^{Nq} P(S \text{ can be reached by } d \text{ beacons})$$

$$= \sum_{d=3}^{Nq} \binom{Nq}{d} p^d (1-p)^{Nq-d}, \text{ where } p = \frac{\pi R^2}{L^2}$$

$$\rightarrow \sum_{d=3}^{Nq} \frac{\lambda^d}{d!} \cdot e^{-\lambda}, \text{ as } N \rightarrow \infty, \text{ where } \lambda = Nqp, p = \frac{\pi R^2}{L^2}$$

$$= 1 - e^{-\lambda}(1 + \lambda + \lambda^2/2) = f(\lambda).$$

Since $\lambda = Npq > 0$, $f'(\lambda) = \lambda^2 e^{-\lambda}/2 > 0$, which indicates that $f(\lambda)$ will increase as λ increases. Therefore the larger number of beacons (Nq), the higher probability that a sensor gets localized using our TPSS scheme.

Next we study the impact of the inaccuracy of TDoA measurements on the localization errors. The first result is reported in Figure 7 for a network of 400 nodes with 20% of initial beacons. For each sensor that has been resolved, the estimated location is linked with the corresponding real position. We observe that as the epoch increases, the position error tends to increase. This trend can also be observed in a further study given on the impact of different epochs and measurement errors on position errors. The result is given in Figure 8, which shows the computation errors (averaged over 100 tests) after one or three epochs for different network density with the same initial beacon percentage 25%.

The increase of positioning errors along with epochs shows the effect of cumulative errors. Recall that once a sensor gets localized, it will use its computed position to help other sensors on position estimation. Considering the unavoidable measuring errors, such a process makes it possible to "pass" computation errors from resolved sensors to the others, though it does help in reducing the number of beacons necessary for location discovery. As more and more sensors get localized, more and more computation errors are introduced, that is, the inaccuracy gets cumulated. However, Figures 7–8 show that such an error cumulation is quite slow in TPSS. For most of the resolved sensors, the localization error is still tolerable compared with the transmission range.

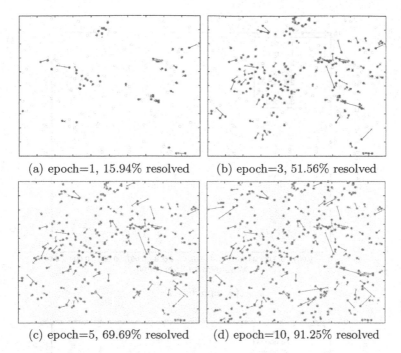

(a) epoch=1, 15.94% resolved   (b) epoch=3, 51.56% resolved

(c) epoch=5, 69.69% resolved   (d) epoch=10, 91.25% resolved

Fig. 7. Illustration of TPSS in terms of variant epochs and resolved percentage. The measuring errors are assumed normally distributed w.r.t. N(0, 0.05). In each figure, "o" represents a beacon, "x" represents the estimated location of a sensor which is linked to the real position (denoted by *), and "." represents a node whose location is not resolved yet.

Another observation from Figure 8 is that the computation errors increase along with the TDoA measurement errors. This trend shows the impact of measurement errors in local timers at sensors, which can be easily understood from Equations (3)(4) and (7)(8). Thus the larger the TDoA measuring error, the larger the position error.

6 Conclusion

In this chapter, we present TPSS, a time-based localization scheme which uses only short-range beacons. While retaining most of the benefits that TPS, iTPS have, TPSS relaxes the strict requirement that the beacon stations should be able to reach all the sensor nodes in the network. Simulation results show that TPSS is a simple, effective and practical location discovery scheme that can be used in sensor networks.

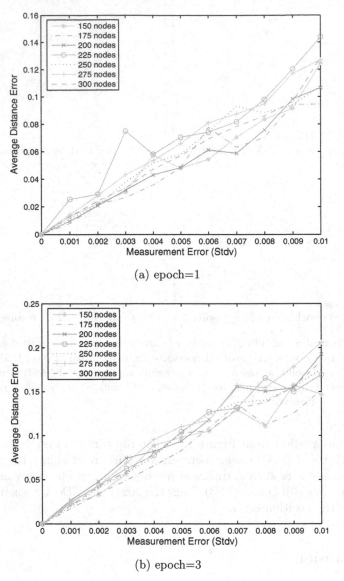

(a) epoch=1

(b) epoch=3

Fig. 8. Illustration of Position Errors in terms of Different Epochs and Measurement Errors: with Different Network Density.

References

1. Paramvir Bahl, Venkata N. Padmanabhan, RADAR: an In-Building RFBased RFBased User Location and Tracking System, *IEEE INFOCOM 2000*, Vol. 2, pp. 775–784.
2. P. Bergamo, G. Mazzini, Localization in Sensor Networks with Fading and Mobility, *IEEE PIMRC*, September 2002.
3. Nirupama Bulusu, John Heidemann, Deborah Estrin, GPS-less Low Cost Outdoor Localization for Very Small Devices, *IEEE Personal Communications* 7(5), Oct. 2000, pp. 28-34.
4. Nirupama Bulusu, John Heidemann, Deborah Estrin, Density adaptive algorithms for beacon placement, *IEEE ICDCS 2001*, April 2001.
5. Srdjan Capkun, Jean-Pierre Hubaux, Secure positioning of wireless devices with application to sensor networks, *IEEE INFOCOM*, March 2005, Miami, FL, USA.
6. J. J. Caffery, Jr and G. L. Stüber, Subscriber Location in CDMA Cellular Networks, *IEEE Transactions on Vehicular Technology*, Vol. 47, No. 2, (1998), pp. 406–416.
7. Alberto Cerpa, Jeremy Elson, Deborah Estrin, Lewis Girod, Michael Hamilton, Jerry. Zhao, Habitat monitoring: application driver for wireless communications technology, *Proc. ACM SIGCOMM Workshop on Data Communications in Latin America and the Caribbean*, 2001.
8. Xiuzhen Cheng, Andrew Thaeler, Guoliang Xue, Dechang Chen, TPS: A time-based positioning scheme for outdoor wireless sensor networks, *IEEE INFOCOM*, 2004.
9. Swades De, Chunming Qiao, Hongyi Wu, Meshed multipath routing: an efficient strategy in wireless sensor networks, *Computer Networks, Special Issue on Wireless Sensor Networks*, 2003.
10. Lance Doherty, Kristofer Pister, Laurent. E. Ghaoui, Convex Position Estimation in Wireless Sensor Networks, *IEEE INFOCOM 2001*, April 2001.
11. Wenliang Du, Lei Fang, Peng Ning. LAD: Localization Anomaly Detection for Wireless Sensor Networks, *Proc. The 19th International Parallel and Distributed Processing Symposium (IPDPS)*, April 4-8, 2005, Denver, Colorado, USA.
12. Qing Fang, Feng Zhao, Leonidas Guibas, Lightweight sensing and communication protocols for target enumeration and aggregation, *ACM MOBIHOC*, 2003, pp. 165–176.
13. Lei Fang, Wenliang Du, Peng Ning, A Beacon-Less Location Discovery Scheme for Wireless Sensor Networks, *IEEE INFOCOM*, 2005, Miami, FL, USA.
14. Lewis Girod, Deborah Estrin, Robust range estimation using acoustic and multimodal sensing, *International Conference on Intelligent Robots and Systems*, Oct. 2001.
15. Tian He, Chengdu Huang, Brian M. Blum, John A. Stankovic, Tarek Abdelzaher, Range-Free Localization Schemes in Large Scale Sensor Networks, *Proc. of Mobile Computing and Networking (MobiCom 2003)*, San Diego, CA, Sep 2003, pp. 81–95.
16. John Heidemann, Nirupama Bulusu, Using geospatial information in sensor networks, *ACM MOBICOM*, 2000.
17. Jeffrey Hightower, Roy Want, Gaetano Borriello, SpotON: an Indoor 3d Location Sensing Technology Based on RF Signal Strength, *UW CSE 2000-02-02, Univ. Washington, Seattle*, 2000.

18. Lingxuan Hu, David Evans, Localization for Mobile Sensor Networks, *ACM MOBICOM*, 2004.
19. Chalermek Intanagonwiwat, Ramesh Govindan, Deborah Estrin, Directed diffision: a scalable and robust communication paradigm for sensor networks, *ACM MOBICOM*, 2000, pp. 56–67.
20. F. Koushanfar, S. Slijepcevic, M. Potkonjak, A. Sangiovanni-Vincentelli, Location discovery in ad-hoc wireless sensor networks, in X. Cheng, X. Huang and D.-Z. Du (Eds.) *Ad Hoc Wireless Networking*, (Kluwer Academic Publisher, 2003), pp. 137–173.
21. Koen Langendoen, Niels Reijers, Distributed localization in wireless sensor networks: a quantitative comparison, *The International Journal of Computer and Telecommunications Networking*, 43(4), Special issue on Wireless sensor networks (November 2003) pp. 499–518.
22. Loukas Lazos, Radha Poovendran, Serloc: Secure range-independent localization for wireless sensor networks, *ACM workshop on Wireless security (ACM WiSe 2004)*, Philadelphia, PA, October 1 2004.
23. Jinyang Li, John Jannotti, Douglas S. J. De Couto, David R. Karger, Robert Morris, A scalable location service for geographic ad hoc routing, *ACM MOBICOM*, 2000.
24. Samuel Madden, Michael J. Franklin, Joseph M. Hellerstein, Wei Hong, TAG: a tiny aggregation service for ad-hoc sensor networks, *OSDI*, 2002.
25. Alan Mainwaring, Josep Polastre, Robert Szewczyk, David Culler, Wireless sensor networks for habitat monitoring, *ACM Workshop on Sensor Netowrks and Applications*, 2002.
26. C.D. McGillem, T.S. Rappaport, A Beacon Navigation Method for Autonomous Vehicles, *IEEE Transactions on Vehicular Technology*, Vol. 38, No. 3, 1989, pp. 132–139.
27. Radhika Nagpal, Howard Shrobe, Jonathan Bachrach, Organizing a Global Coordinate System from Local Information on an Ad Hoc Sensor Network, *Proc. of the Second International Workshop on Information Processing in Sensor Networks (IPSN'03)*, April 2003.
28. Asis Nasipuri, Kai Li, A directionality based location discovery scheme for wireless sensor networks, *ACM WSNA'02*, 2002, pp. 105–111.
29. Dragos Niculescu, and Badri Nath, Ad hoc positioning system (APS), *IEEE GlobeCom*, 2001.
30. Dragos Niculescu, Badri Nath, DV Based Positioning in Ad hoc Networks, *Kluwer Journal of Telecommunication Systems*, 2003.
31. Ananth Rao, Sylvia Ratnasamy, Christos Papadimitriou, Scott Shenker, Ion Stoica, Geographic routing without location information, *Proc. of ACM MOBICOM 2003*, September 2003, pp. 96–108.
32. Naveen Sastry, Umesh Shankar, David Wagner, Secure verification of location claims, *ACM Workshop on Wireless Security (WiSe 2003)*, 2003.
33. Chris Savarese, Jan Rabaey, Koen Langendoen, Robust positioning algorithms for distributed ad-hoc wireless sensor networks, *USENIX technical annual conference*, Monterey, CA, 2002, pp. 317–328.
34. Andreas Savvides, ChihChieh Han, Mani B. Srivastava, Dynamic fine-grained localization in ad-hoc networks of sensors, *ACM MOBICOM*, 2001, pp. 166–179.
35. Andreas Savvides, Heemin Park, Mani B. Srivastava, The bits and flops of the N-hop multilateration primitive for node localization problems, *ACM WSNA'02*, Atlanta, GA, 2002, pp. 112–121.

36. Curt Schurgers, Gautam Kulkarni, Mani B. Srivastava, Distributed on-demand address assignment in wireless sensor networks, *IEEE Transactions on Parallel and Distributed Systems*, 13(10) (2002) pp. 1056–1065.

37. Yi Shang, Wheeler Ruml, Yng. Zhang, Markus Fromherz, Localization from mere connectivity, *ACM MOBIHOC*, 2003.

38. Andrew Thaeler, Min Ding, Xiuzhen Cheng, iTPS: An Improved Location Discovery Scheme for Sensor Networks with Long Range Beacons, *Journal of Parallel and Distributed Computing*, Special Issue on Theoretical and Algorithmic Aspects of Sensor, Ad Hoc Wireless, and Peer-to-Peer Networks, 2004.

39. B. H. Wellenhof, H. Lichtenegger, J. Collins, *Global Positioning System: Theory and Practice*, Springer Verlag, 4th ed., 1997.

40. Wei Ye, John Heidemann, Deborah Estrin, An energy-efficient MAC protocol for wireless sensor networks, *IEEE INFOCOM*, 2002.

Chapter 8
Wakeup Strategies in Wireless Sensor Networks

Curt Schurgers

Electrical and Computer Engineering Department
University of California, San Diego, CA 92093
curts@ece.ucsd.edu

1 Introduction: The Wakeup Principle

1.1 The Need for Sleep

Low-power operation has been recognized as being one of the crucial design requirements in sensor networks [1]. Often these networks will be deployed in environments where no external source of electrical power is available, such as in outdoor environmental monitoring applications or battlefield scenarios. Even in indoor scenarios, such as machine or structural health monitoring, it is often prohibitive to attach power cables to each sensor node, especially if the network spans tens or even hundreds of devices. In addition, many sensor network applications require the devices to be unobtrusive, possibly even implantable, or deployable without extensive infrastructure support. Because of all of these reasons, sensor nodes should operate as self-contained entities, powered by sources such as batteries, fuel cells or scavenged energy. Since all of these energy sources are fundamentally limited by the small device form factor, energy-efficient design is imperative to ensure a sufficiently long operational lifetime of the network.

The challenge of energy-efficient operation has to be tackled on all levels of the network design, from hardware devices and algorithms to protocols and applications. Although sensing and data processing could be significant as well, depending on the specifics of the application, the communication portion of a system is often a very significant contributor to the overall energy consumption. It has been observed, for example, that in typical sensor node devices, it takes about the same amount of energy to communicate one bit of information as to execute a few hundred instructions on the embedded processor [1]. It is therefore important that the network communications, a crucial enabler of the networked behavior as an autonomous distributed sensor system, are designed to be as energy efficient as possible.

195

In order to do this, the characteristics of typical radios used in sensor networks, need to be investigated. Figure 1 shows the power consumption of three representative and often-used radio platforms: the RFM TR1000 (used in MICA [2] and Medusa MK-II nodes [3]), the Chipcon CC1000 (used in MICA2 nodes [2]) and the Chipcon CC2420 (used in MICAz [2], Telos [4] and XYZ nodes [5]). These power numbers were obtained from product data sheets and reported measurement values [3] [5] [6]. Four different operational modes can be distinguished: Tx (transmit), Rx (receive), idle (the radio is on, but nothing is received or transmitted) and sleep (the radio is turned off).

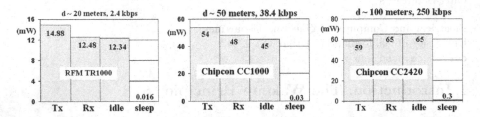

Fig. 1. Radio power consumption numbers.

An important observation is that for these typical radios, which have relatively short transmission range compared to other systems such as cellular phones, the transmit, receive and idle power are comparable. In other words, whenever the radio is on, the power consumption does not vary much and the only way to reduce it significantly is to turn the radio off. In sensor networks, the node spends a large fraction of time in a state where it is not actively participating in data communication. If it would keep its radio on throughout, it would spend a majority of its lifetime in the idle listening mode. In typical scenarios, the energy associated with this idle listening could overwhelmingly dominate the overall communication energy consumption. Cases where nodes spend more than 90% or more of their time in idle listening have been reported [7] [8] [9]. Substantial node lifetime improvements can be obtained by transitioning the radio into the much more power efficient sleep state instead. This realization has driven most of the research in energy-efficient protocol for sensor networks, such as for medium access control (MAC) [10] or topology management.

1.2 Wakeup and Medium Access

In sensor networks, many applications are characterized by very sporadic traffic and therefore contain substantial periods of radio inactivity. In general, the data communication rate is low compared to the available bandwidth. To ensure energy-efficient operation, sensor nodes should therefore switch between a state in which they communicate, the length of which is an active communication epoch T_{active}, and the radio sleep state. The average amount of information transferred during such communication epochs, L (in bits), can be expressed as a function of the average time between such epochs T_{period} (in seconds) and the required communication data rate R_{data} (in bits/second) of a node:

$$\frac{L}{T_{period}} \geq R_{data}. \tag{1}$$

In principle, this equation deals with time averages. One particular instantiation, assuming a periodic arrangement, is shown in Figure 2.

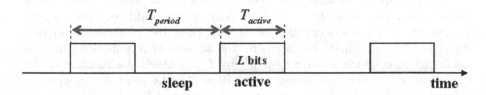

Fig. 2. Abstract representation of a basic transmission scheme.

Numerous medium access control (MAC) protocols have been proposed for sensor networks which in addition to managing access to the wireless medium, try to minimize the energy spent [10]. Combined with reducing collisions, overhearing and overhead, this is achieved by minimizing the time spent idle listening. Ideally, this means that expression (1) holds with equality. Even then, L and T_{period} could still be varied over a large range, as long as their ratio remains the same. For example, this could mean that data is not transmitted right away, but is buffered instead and transmitted in larger, yet less frequent, communication epochs. The benefit of this strategy is reducing the overhead of radio startup [11].

The required communication rate R_{data} of a node is not a constant, however. In many applications, there are long periods with only very sporadic traffic, interspersed by an occasional burst of high activity. Consider, for example, a network to monitor forest fires that should remain active for years. During most of its lifetime, the network will be quasi-dormant, with only infrequent network management packets being sent, such as to check on the status of the network every hour. Since the network is static, attributes such as self-localization or routing tables likely do not need to be updated more frequently either. However, once a fire is detected, this triggers nodes to send data, possibly engaging in local collaboration, all of which result in a period of high traffic activity. A possible scenario is depicted in Figure 3.

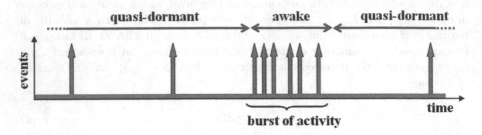

Fig. 3. A typical activity profile.

In this chapter, the focus is on those quasi-dormant periods during which there is only very sporadic network activity, which could constitute a vast portion of the total system lifetime. In this case, the communication rate R_{data} is extremely small. Furthermore, the amount of information during a communication epoch is lower bounded by L_{min}, which is a function of the minimum packet size. According to equation (1), the most energy-efficient solution would require the average inter-epoch interval T_{period} to become very large:

$$\frac{L}{T_{period}} = R_{data} \Rightarrow \tag{2}$$

$$\lim_{R_{data} \to 0} (T_{period}) = \lim_{R_{data} \to 0} (\frac{L}{R_{data}}) = \lim_{R_{data} \to 0} (\frac{L_{min}}{R_{data}}) = \infty. \tag{3}$$

A very large value of T_{period} essentially means that a node does not attempt to communicate for a very long time and keeps its radio off. However, in most practical applications there is a bound on how long a node can sleep at a time. Another node should be able to contact it, for example to forward some critical data within a particular maximum time span. This time span is essentially a delay bound for data to move between nodes, and is directly related to the responsiveness of the network. In the forest fire detection example, an end-to-end delay bound limits the maximum time between the detection of an event and when this information has been forwarded to the user. Delay bounds of individual node-pairs can be related to such an end-to-end delay bound.

Wakeup deals with this network state in which the traffic is so sporadic that the node would sleep for prohibitively long time periods if only traffic activity would be taken into account. Instead, a provision has to be made that a node can be contacted within a certain time period, called the wakeup delay D_{wakeup}, which is bounded by a certain maximum value:

$$D_{wakeup} \leq D_{max}. \tag{4}$$

This maximum wakeup delay D_{max} could be different for each node, and might be optimized based on an overall network lifetime maximization [35]. Once a node has become active, it can participate in data communication. Consequent channel access is governed by the MAC protocol. Several MAC protocols that were designed for sensor networks are able to adapt to the traffic load [10], essentially approximating equation (1). As was shown in Figure 3, the MAC protocol operates during bursts of traffic activity. In principle, during periods of very low traffic activity, the regular MAC protocol could be used as well, adjusting its parameters to such low expected rates.

However, as explained earlier through equation (3), if the traffic is very sparse the protocol settings can no longer be governed by the traffic rate. Instead the wakeup latency becomes the determining factor, as given in equation (4). This state of very sparse traffic activity is called the quasi-dormant state or the "region of wakeup" in Figure 3. In this state, the node might have to perform some checks at certain intervals to make sure it can be contacted within the delay bound, but the traffic rate is so low that in most intervals the node will not have to wake up. This is simply another way of saying that the behavior is mainly governed by equation (4) rather than equation (3).

Although in principle, a MAC protocol could be used in this quasi-dormant state, it is often more efficient to utilize a dedicated wakeup protocol. The reason is that in this state, only a protocol is needed to contact a sleeping node and tell it to transition to a more awake state. However, a MAC protocol typically also incorporates a lot of extra functionality that is not needed in this case, such as supporting a certain throughput and ensuring fairness. After a node becomes awake, it needs to select the MAC protocol and its parameters to actually participate in communication [12]. The MAC protocol could learn the traffic behavior or even use advanced knowledge of the application to optimally tune its behavior. These aspects are issues related to MAC layer design and fall outside the scope of this chapter.

1.3 The Energy-Delay Tradeoff

Most wakeup protocols allow the designer to trade off the wakeup delay D_{wakeup} versus the power consumption in the quasi-dormant state. This behavior can be understood by considering again Figure 2. If the wakeup protocol involves a periodic active-sleep pattern, as is the case in most synchronous and asynchronous schemes (See sections 4 and 5), the worst-case wakeup delay can be approximated as:

$$D_{wakeup} \approx T_{period} - T_{active}. \tag{5}$$

This delay can be normalized with respect to the length of the active period, which should be chosen as small as possible:

$$D_{norm} = \frac{D_{wakeup}}{T_{active}} \approx \frac{T_{period}}{T_{active}} - 1. \tag{6}$$

The energy consumption, on the other hand, depends on the fraction of time the node is in the active versus the sleep state. It is instructive to assume that the power in the idle, transmit and receive mode are approximately equal, and that the power in the sleep mode is negligible. In addition, the control and energy overhead of the switching itself has been neglected, as is commonly done. However, some work has investigated the effect of the switching overhead as well [19] [11].

The above assumptions are typically reasonable first-cut approximations, as can be seen in Figure 1. In this case, the average energy consumption, normalized versus a scenario where a node never transitions to the sleep mode, is given by:

$$E_{norm} \approx \frac{T_{period}}{T_{active}}. \tag{7}$$

By combining equations (6) and (7), the normalized energy consumption in the quasi-dormant state can be expressed as a function of the normalized worst case wakeup delay:

$$E_{norm} \approx \frac{1}{D_{norm} + 1}. \tag{8}$$

This equation expresses the fundamental tradeoff between energy and delay that is present in the majority of proposed wakeup solutions. Figure 4 illustrates the nature of this tradeoff. By allowing a small delay, large energy savings can be obtained initially. The exact behavior and shape of the tradeoff curve depend on the specifics of protocol [13]. Instead of analyzing various protocols in detail, this fundamental tradeoff provides a solid and easy method for a rough comparison between them. Essentially, the tradeoff behavior of equation (8) underlies most of them, and the main difference between them is the minimum value of T_{active}, which maps the normalized wakeup delay to the absolute one (which is the actual constraint). Solutions with a smaller T_{active} are generally preferable, although other factors also come into play, as will be detailed further in the later sections of this chapter.

2 Classification

A substantial number of alternatives to implement the wakeup functionality have been proposed for sensor networks. They all deal with the fundamental question that was discussed in the previous section: *What is the required functionality such that sleeping nodes can be contacted with a bounded delay in the case of very low traffic demand while minimizing the energy consumption?*

Some solutions have been cast specifically as a wakeup protocol, working in this low traffic regime of the network. Others have been proposed as more generic MAC protocols, which gracefully move into conditions of very low traffic and where they therefore can be considered as operating as wakeup

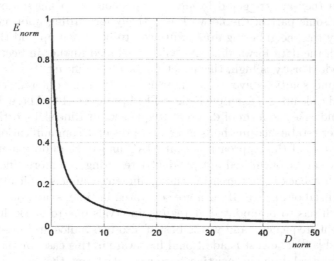

Fig. 4. Normalized energy - delay tradeoff.

protocols. In this chapter, both these types are discussed jointly. However, two important ways of classifying the different approaches are introduced first in the next two subsections.

2.1 In-band versus Out-of-band

A first way to classify wakeup schemes is as either in-band or out-of-band. In this case, the division refers to wakeup operating in the same band as the regular MAC protocol or not. Often, not all nodes are always in a dormant state at the same time. If one node is awake, it is running a MAC protocol, while its dormant neighbor could rely on a wakeup protocol instead. Whether both operate in the same logical channel (in-band) or utilize different channels (out-of-band) critically affects their mutual interference.

When the wakeup protocol is in-band, it will interact with the MAC protocols since both are using the same channel. To avoid negatively impacting the ongoing packet transmission, the wakeup protocol could be augmented with some basic medium access provisions beyond the simple need to be able to contact a sleeping device. An obvious example of this solution would be to use the regular MAC protocol also in the dormant state. However, the drawback is that these extra medium access provisions do not come for free and reduce the energy efficiency when only very sparse traffic is present.

Another approach is to have the wakeup protocol ignore the presence of other traffic and have the MAC protocol absorb the resulting interference effects. Since node wakeup is by definition a rare event, this solution might be acceptable. However, in sensor networks, event occurrences are often correlated when they are triggered by physical phenomena being sensed. As a result, when some part of the network is actively forwarding information, it is more likely that neighboring areas will need to be woken up and therefore interfere with the data forwarding. As will be detailed further in Section 5.2, when the node density is high, this effect might be significant.

Out-of-band solutions avoid this interference by using different channels for MAC and wakeup. An example is the STEM protocol [13]. These different channels could take the form of different frequencies or time slots, orthogonal codes or other established methods of creating disjoint communication channels. The benefit of this approach is that MAC and wakeup do not interfere and therefore can be optimized independently resulting in a more efficient solution. The drawback is that creating these different channels typically comes with an overhead of its own. If both are separated in time, synchronization is needed, which has to be updated at regular intervals due to clock drifts [8]. Using different frequency band works best if also two radios are present, one for each band [13]. The cost is additional hardware in this case, or the inability to use these solutions on existing hardware platforms that only posses a single radio.

2.2 Paging, Synchronous and Asynchronous Wakeup

An orthogonal classification of possible wakeup solutions divides them into on-demand paging, synchronous schemes and asynchronous ones. Other related, although slightly different, nomenclatures have been proposed as well [14].

In on-demand paging, a physically separate device is used for the wakeup, where this other device has a much lower standby power then the main radio. This is analogous to using a traditional pager to contact someone who is otherwise unreachable. In terms of the terminology used in Section 1.2, this solution can be viewed as one where $T_{period} = \infty$ or $T_{active} = 0$, and the contribution of the paging device has to be added to the energy consumption in Section 1.3. Various alternatives of on-demand paging have been proposed, which differ mainly in the technology used and the resulting design choices [15] [16] [17] [18] [19]. A common challenge of this solution is that the paging device does not always have the same transmission range as the main data radio. This often limits the applicability of this technique in multi-hop networks, but it may offer a valuable solution if infrastructure support is available. On-demand paging is discussed in detail in Section 3 of this chapter.

An alternative to having a low-power paging device is duty cycling a regular radio, essentially using the setup that was shown in Figure 2 earlier. When a radio is in the sleep mode most of the time and only occasionally checks to see if someone wants to communicate with it, this can effectively emulate an average low power behavior. This principle has formed the basis for both the other two classes of schemes: synchronous and asynchronous. The difference between these two is whether neighboring nodes maintain some form of time synchronization or not. This categorization has a parallel in MAC protocols where designs are schedule-based or contention-based.

In general, synchronous wakeup schemes allow easier in-band integration with MAC since this can be done in the time domain. The drawback is that maintaining synchronicity under various levels of clock drift causes synchronization overhead, which somewhat reduces the energy-efficiency of the wakeup scheme. On the other hand, asynchronous solutions, although avoiding synchronization overhead, cannot use the time dimension to limit interaction with the MAC protocol. They therefore need other solutions to make them out-of-band, if this is the design goal. Synchronous and asynchronous wakeup protocols will be discussed in Sections 4 and 5 of this chapter, respectively.

3 On-demand Paging

3.1 Principle

In on-demand paging, the main radio is completely turned off when the node is in the dormant state. The wakeup functionality is offloaded to a separate device, which typically has substantially lower power consumption. This separate paging device can therefore always be kept active, and messages sent to it can be used to instruct the node to turn on the main radio.

This basic idea was proposed for PicoRadio [15] [16]. Specialized hardware is used to serve as a wakeup page receiver. Since this functionality is substantially less complex than the full radio receiver design, this specialized piece of hardware consumes only very limited idle power. In principle, the wakeup page could use the same resources as the regular data channel, and therefore be categorized as in-band. By using a different frequency, an out-of-band scheme is created. Overall, using a dedicated device to handle the wakeup is the most flexible and energy efficient solution, but might be difficult or costly to produce.

A less sophisticated solution is utilizing another radio technology to serve as the wakeup communication channel. This is the principle behind wake-on-wireless [17]. In this project, hand-held devices, in this case iPAQs, are proposed as versatile platforms to support wireless interactive voice applications such as IP telephony. To enable a sufficiently long lifetime, their standby power has to be reduced, which is accomplished by turning their IEEE 802.11-based wireless radio off when there is no ongoing communication. The handheld is equipped with a second, simpler and more energy efficient radio to serve as a wakeup device. A similar approach was proposed using the Bluetooth modules that are already integrated in a lot of hand-held devices [18]. In most sensor networks, however, the main radio is already relatively simple, since data rates are typically low. As a result, it is hard to find another radio technology that would have a substantially lower idle power than the main radio itself.

Devices such as RFID (radio frequency identification) tags could be used for wakeup as well [19]. In this case, the RFID reader sends an interrogation signal to the tags that also provides them with power. However, this RFID reader consumes considerable power. Such a solution therefore works well for an infrastructure-type network, where the base station can host the reader and has abundant energy resources. In distributed infrastructure-less networks, such as most sensor networks, this solution is not a viable one.

3.2 Range Disparity

In addition to the issues discussed in the previous section, a common problem of all these on-demand paging schemes is range disparity. It has been observed that if different technologies are used for the main data radio and the separate paging device, which is inherently needed to make sure the idle power consumption is lower, the transmit ranging is not exactly the same [15] [17] [18]. Depending on the actual technologies used, these differences may be small or large.

The case where the communication ranges are only slightly different is shown in the left-hand side of Figure 5. Here, R_D and R_P denote the range of the data and paging radio respectively. When $R_D < R_P$, a sleeping device can always be reached with a page. The problem occurs in the case that $R_D > R_P$, which is shown in the figure. In this case, node A should not be allowed to turn off its main radio completely, since it cannot be reached with a page. A possible solution is to send an explicit "go to sleep" message to A via the paging device, such that the node only turns off its radio if it is indeed within paging range [18]. If node mobility is present, these pages have to be repeated periodically to also account for the situation where a node, such as B, is initially within paging range but then moves out of it while sleeping [18].

On the other hand, if the communication ranges of the data radio and the paging radio are vastly different, using this approach by itself would severely limit the possible benefits of low-power paging. One solution would be to duplicate the paging infrastructure, as shown on the right hand side of Figure 5 [17]. This again has to be combined with the periodic paging updates discussed earlier. To be applicable to less infrastructure-oriented networks, a type of paging backbone would need to be established, possibly with nodes specifically dedicated for this functionality. One could envision a heterogeneous sensor network, where specialized nodes are designed and deployed solely to create a wakeup infrastructure. Since these nodes only require limited functionality, they could be substantially cheaper and therefore could be deployed in a higher density.

Due to the distributed nature of sensor networks, dealing with range disparity is a non-trivial problem. If it is dealt with appropriately, on-demand paging is an extremely powerful technique to enable low-power consumption in the dormant state [15]. Synchronous and asynchronous wakeup essentially

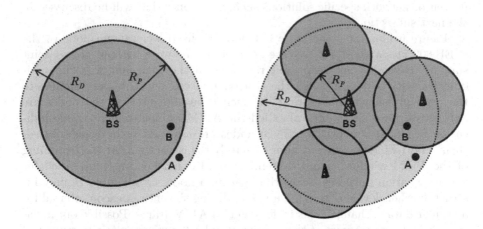

Fig. 5. Solutions to range disparity.

aim at mimicking the behavior of a low-power paging channel by duty cycling a regular radio. It is also possible to apply such duty cycling on top of the on-demand paging, to combine the gains of both approaches and enable ultra-low energy consumption [13].

4 Synchronous Wakeup

The principle of synchronous wakeup is allowing nodes to duty cycle their radio in a coordinated, i.e. synchronous, fashion. The benefit of such coordination is that wakeup and MAC are naturally separated in time as they can be assigned to distinct time intervals. As such, it is often easy to design synchronous schemes to be out-of-band.

Before discussing schemes that were proposed specifically for sensor networks, the power saving options of two existing standards proposed by the IEEE will be briefly described first in the next subsection. These standards not only introduce some of the common design choices that appear in other synchronous solutions as well, but also relate to some of the asynchronous schemes that will be treated in Section 5.

4.1 Standards

The IEEE 802.11 standard specifies both the physical and medium access control sublayers for local area networks [20]. As such, it is not directly geared towards sensor networks. However, its use has been proposed for more general ad hoc networks, and the basic design principles are important background for sensor network-specific solutions such as the ones that will be discussed in the next subsection.

Figure 6 illustrates the basic behavior of the power saving mode of the IEEE 802.11 standard, for the case of an ad hoc network without access point support. Nodes do not keep their radio on all the time, but wake up periodically, with a period called the beacon interval, which is very similar to the principle shown in Figure 2. In such a beacon interval, the nodes are only awake for a short interval called the ATIM (announcement traffic indication message) window [20]. Since nodes are assumed to be synchronized, their ATIM windows start at approximately the same time. At the beginning of the ATIM window, nodes contend to send out a beacon frame, used for synchronization purposes. After the beacon, a node, for example B, may instruct another device C to remain active during the entire beacon interval for a regular data exchange. This is done via an ATIM frame. Possible optimizations, which are not part of the current standard, are dynamic adjustment of the ATIM window size to the channel contention level, and allowing nodes to return to the sleep state after finishing their data transfer [21].

This power saving protocol critically relies on maintaining synchronization between nodes. In dense multi-hop ad hoc networks, where not all nodes can hear each other, the desired level of synchronization is hard to achieve [22]. This has led to synchronous variants of this standard, which will be discussed in Section 5.1.

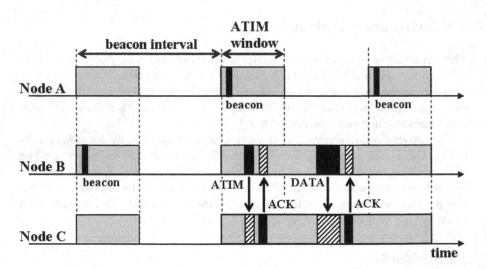

Fig. 6. IEEE 802.11 power saving mode without access point support.

Another relevant standard is IEEE 802.15.4, which targets low-rate wireless personal area networks [23]. Two different types of devices are considered here: FFDs (full function devices), which can act as coordinators, and RFDs (reduced function devices), which can only be regular network devices and not take on coordinator functionalities. Network devices are allowed to sleep and decide independently when to wake up and poll for data from their coordinator. This allows for very power efficient operation for these network devices, but they can only act as leaf nodes in a network topology. Two different modes are defined in the standard: beacon enabled and non-beacon enabled. The beacon enabled mode allows coordinator devices to save energy through duty cycling, as shown in Figure 7. At the start of a beacon interval, coordinators send out beacons that advertise to their associated leaf nodes whether traffic is pending for them. Upon hearing these beacons, the leaf node can request data from its coordinator. The network device is not required to wake up each beacon interval, and it can elect to skip listening to some of the beacons to further lower its energy consumption. By imposing synchronized operation in this beacon enabled mode, coordinators can also save power by restricting communication to an active period (superframe duration) that is only a fraction of the beacon interval.

At present, the inter-coordinator aspects of this mode are not covered in the standard. Especially, synchronization between coordinators could lead to issues similar to those discussed for IEEE 802.11, where synchronization is hard to maintain for multi-hop ad hoc networks. The current power saving provisions in the IEEE 802.15.4 standard are therefore mainly geared towards specific network topologies. In star-like topologies, network devices are leaf nodes and can be extremely low power. In multi-hop ad hoc networks, also known as mesh networks, the backbone nodes need to be coordinators and could be less energy constrained.

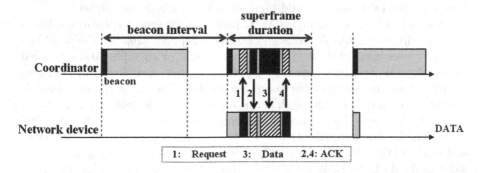

Fig. 7. IEEE 802.15.4 beacon enabled mode.

4.2 Sensor Network Proposals

Several synchronized MAC protocols have been proposed specifically for sensor networks. When the traffic rate is low, they essentially behave as a wakeup protocol. However, their operation is not specifically optimized for the low throughput conditions that characterize the quasi-dormant state, and they typically contain more than the strictly needed functionality in this case.

One early proposal was the S-MAC protocol [8]. The design philosophy behind it is to improve the energy efficiency of the carrier sense multiple access (CSMA) mechanism in a contention-based MAC such as IEEE 802.11. Nodes are synchronized within a virtual cluster and operate in a duty cycled fashion which is similar to the basic scheme of Figure 2 and also the power saving mode of Figure 6. Each period starts with a time to exchange synchronization packets, as shown in Figure 8. This is followed by an active duration, which occupies a fraction of the period. The CSMA collision avoidance handshake (RTS/CTS) is executed in this active duration, and nodes remain awake if they need to exchange data. The length of the active duration is fixed, and the duty cycle period can be chosen based on the expected traffic demands. An enhancement to S-MAC, called T-MAC, introduces an adaptive duty cycle [7]. In this case, the active duration is controlled by a timeout mechanism, while the duty cycle period is fixed. Both S-MAC and T-MAC have the disadvantage that they concentrate the traffic to a fraction of the available time, which results in inefficiencies at high traffic load. In the wakeup regime, at low traffic load, they also are suboptimal. The energy efficiency of both is given by the ratio of the active duration and the duty cycle period. Ideally under low traffic load, the active duration should be the minimum possible to allow nodes to be contacted, while the duty cycle is limited by the wakeup delay, as explained in Section 1.3 and illustrated in Figure 8 as well. However, S-MAC has a fixed active duration, which is tailored to the expected traffic load, while T-MAC has a fixed duty cycle that is not necessarily determined by the maximum wakeup delay (although it could be designed this way in principle).

Another class of synchronous MAC protocols for sensor networks is based on time division multiple access (TDMA) [24] [25] [26]. In the TRAMA protocol, time is divided into random access slots for signaling and scheduled access slots for transmissions [26]. By vacating reserved slots and assigning priorities to nodes for grabbing these vacated slots, fluctuating traffic demands can be accommodated. Although this solution is very flexible and adaptive, it suffers from increased implementation complexity as compared to S-MAC [10].

A TDMA-based protocol that explicitly includes provisions for device wakeup is TDMA-W [25]. The basic operation is illustrated in Figure 9. Consider node A. If there is no traffic, A is asleep and only wakes up in its "wakeup" slot. Another node, B, that wants to communicate with A contacts it by sending a request in that wakeup slot. Upon receiving this request, A listens to the "send" slot of B which is used to communicate the data. Each node is assigned a send slot such that there are no collisions between data

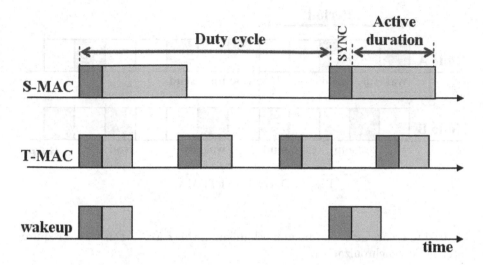

Fig. 8. Comparison between S-MAC, T-MAC and wakeup.

packets. In the wakeup regime, where there is very little traffic, a node essentially only wakes up in its assigned wakeup slot. In principle, the time between wakeup slots could be as large as allowed by the wakeup delay to minimize the power consumption [25]. However, the actual data transmission might incur an extra delay waiting for the send slot. Although no provisions are incorporated in TDMA-W, the number of send slots could also be made adaptive similar to what is done in TRAMA to accommodate fluctuating traffic demands. With appropriately chosen period, TDMA-W behaves as a true synchronous wakeup protocol. Its asynchronous counterpart, STEM [13], will be discussed in Section 5.1. The extra overhead of a synchronous solution is the need to maintain synchronization. Once data has to be transferred and a MAC protocol is needed, TDMA is a logical choice as it is both energy efficient and can leverage the fact that synchronization between nodes is already maintained.

5 Asynchronous Wakeup

Asynchronous wakeup solutions do not suffer from the overhead of maintaining synchronization, and could therefore result in lower power consumption as compared to synchronous algorithms. However, since nodes are not aware of each others' schedule, the cost of contacting a sleeping node might be higher. In addition, care has to be taken that wakeup does not aversely affect the medium access protocol or vice-versa, given the fact that time division cannot

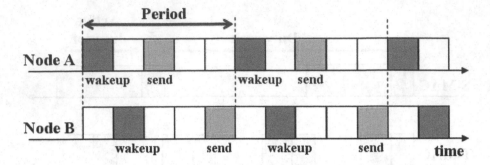

Fig. 9. Operation of TDMA-W.

be used to create an out-of-band mechanism in this case, as this would require inter-node synchronization.

5.1 Design Alternatives

A variety of protocols have been proposed that can be classified as asynchronous wakeup solutions. It is possible to cast these into a unified framework consisting of three basic design alternatives: rendezvous-based, sender-based and receiver-based asynchronous wakeup. In this subsection, these three alternatives are discussed from a high-level point of view to highlight their fundamental behavior and mutual differences. Specific instantiations of these alternatives also differ in how wakeup is integrated into the MAC protocol, the discussion of which is the subject of Section 5.2.

Rendezvous-based wakeup evolved as an asynchronous version of the IEEE 802.11 power saving mode, which was discussed in Section 4.1 [22]. It was observed that for relatively dense multi-hop ad hoc networks, such as most sensor networks, the synchronization required in IEEE 802.11 power saving mode is hard to maintain. Instead, the times a node sends its beacon and listens to the channel should be chosen carefully in such a way that nodes can hear each others' beacons within a certain bounded period of time, even if they are completely non-synchronized. This is illustrated in Figure 10. Within each period, a node has a set of listen slots, at the beginning of which it may send a beacon to contact another node. The vertical arrow in the figure denotes the start of a wakeup event, i.e., node B has a packet destined for sleeping node A. The slots are chosen such that A can hear a beacon from B at least once within one period, for any offset between the node schedules. A number of variations have been proposed, which differ in the way the listen slots are selected [14] [22] [27]. The goal is to minimize the listen time within each period while still guaranteeing the minimum overlap to hear at least one beacon irrespective of the mutual schedule offset.

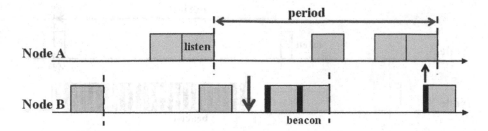

Fig. 10. Rendezvous-based asynchronous wakeup.

Sender-based asynchronous wakeup shifts the wakeup burden to the sender, i.e., the node that wants to contact a sleeping neighbor. Figure 11 illustrates the basic principle. A sleeping node, e.g., node A, periodically listens to the channel for a short duration. If node B wants to contact A, it continuously sends beacon messages until it receives a response from A, which can at most take one period [13] [28]. The node that periodically wakes up therefore has to listen long enough such that it can surely hear one beacon. The benefit of using beacons is that it is possible to selectively wake up a specific node. This solution is adopted in STEM-B [13].

An alternative solution replaces the succession of beacons by a continuous tone. Once a node A detects this tone, it wakes up, but unless it has a separate channel available, it cannot respond to B. Node B therefore has to continue the tone until A has surely heard it, i.e., for the duration of one period. Also, nodes are not addressed individually with a tone, and all neighbors of B therefore wake up. On the other hand, the listen duration to detect a tone can be significantly shorter than that of a beacon [13], such that the sleeping node only has to wake up for a very short amount of time [29]. This tone-based approach is used in STEM-T [13]. It also forms the basis of pre-amble sampling [30] [31] [32]. In preamble sampling, a packet is proceeded by a long preamble, fulfilling the role of the wakeup tone. The receiver periodically wakes up to sample the channel and detect the presence of this preamble.

Sender-based asynchronous wakeup can also be viewed as a non-synchronized alternative to TDMA-W, which is discussed in Section 4.2 and illustrated in Figure 9. In both cases, sleeping nodes wake up periodically to check for a beacon or tone. In the synchronous case, the sender knows the listen slot of the receiver and therefore can limit the contacting overhead, however at the cost of maintaining synchronization. Whether the reduction of contacting overhead on the part of the sender outweighs the synchronization overhead depends on the expected frequency of wakeup events.

Receiver-based asynchronous wakeup is essentially the mirror image of sender-based, where the wakeup burden is now with the receiver. Figure 12 shows the principle, which underlies the Etiquette protocol [33]. A sleeping

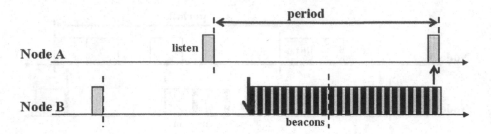

Fig. 11. Sender-based asynchronous wakeup.

node A now periodically sends announcements and listens for a reply. A node B that wants to wake up A listens until it hears such an announcement and then sends a reply back. The maximum time is again equal to the period (although some variations have been proposed [33]). In Etiquette, after a sleeping node has been contacted, it arranges a future time to schedule the data transmission, which essentially corresponds to a particular choice of MAC protocol. In its basic form, the wakeup portion of the protocol can be viewed as a receiver-based solution.

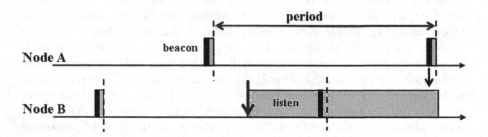

Fig. 12. Receiver-based asynchronous wakeup.

It is possible to directly compare the characteristics of rendezvous-based, sender-based and receiver-based asynchronous wakeup by investigating Figures 10, 11 and 12, which all result in approximately the same maximum wakeup delay, namely one period. In rendezvous-based wakeup, the contacting or sender node, in this case B, has less of an overhead compared to the other two schemes. However, the sleeping node A, has to be awake for a larger fraction of the period and therefore has higher average power consumption, as follows from equation (7) in Section 1.3. If wakeup events are rare, as is often the case in sensor networks, the more efficient sleep state of sender- and receiver-based solutions result in an overall lower power design than the rendezvous-based one. Note that once packets arrive more frequently, the network is basically no longer in the quasi-dormant state, but moves into a more awake state where it needs medium access, as was explained in Section 1.2. Section 5.2 will further detail the interaction between MAC and asynchronous wakeup.

The power efficiency of sender- versus receiver-based alternatives depends on the fraction of time a sleeping node has to be awake either to listen for or send information. Both essentially correspond pretty closely to the basic scheme that was shown in Figure 4 of Section 1.3 and are well-analyzed by the analysis there. In principle, a sender-based solution with a wakeup tone results in the shortest active time, and therefore the lowest power consumption. However, in the case of a wakeup event, all neighboring nodes to the sender will wake up. Whether the overall average power consumption is still better depends on the frequency of such wakeup events and the density of the network. If the active fraction is the same for a sender- and receiver-based solution, their main difference lies in the probability of beacon/announcement collisions. In the case of receiver-based wakeup, where sleeping nodes periodically send out the announcements, this probability is a function of the network density and the period. In sender-based wakeup, the period and the local frequency of wakeup events are the main contributors. In both cases, such collisions could either result in a longer than expected wakeup delay or lead to energy inefficiencies, depending on the specifics of the actual protocol.

5.2 Interaction with MAC

Although they allow for a very low power sleep mode, asynchronous schemes typically have a sizable overhead associated with the wakeup event. It has been realized that due to this overhead, it is inefficient to use these schemes when wakeup events are relatively frequent [12]. This basically means that asynchronous wakeup protocols are not well suited as pure MAC protocols. Instead, knowledge of expected packet arrivals can be used to schedule designated wakeup times in the future [12] [14] [30] [33], which essentially corresponds to starting a local TDMA schedule. In principle, other MAC solutions could be used as well.

In addition, a successful wakeup event can be used as a synchronization point for nodes to learn each other clocks. This could potentially allow a reduction of wakeup overhead since the wakeup becomes more synchronized. This synchronization between nodes will eventually degrade due to clock drifts, slowly moving the wakeup regime from synchronous to asynchronous. Whether synchronicity should be maintained, or it is more efficient to allow the system to gradually revert to an asynchronous wakeup solution, depends on the specifics of the application.

Another issue is detecting the start of a new quasi-dormant period, where it is beneficial to turn the MAC protocol off and only resort to a wakeup protocol. This could be based on a soft timer that fires when no activity is detected within a certain time period, or be based on application layer information. A source node could, for example, indicate that a packet is the last one of an active communication stream, which is analogous to a termination message in circuit switching systems.

In addition to the transitions between wakeup and MAC, the problem of coexistence between these two is important. It is possible that one pair of nodes is actively communicating information and utilizing a particular MAC protocol, while other nodes in the vicinity are quasi-dormant and need to be woken up to establish another communication path. Unlike paging solutions which are naturally out-of-band, or synchronous wakeup where time division multiplexing is a logical choice to create an out-of-band solution, the issue is more complex in asynchronous wakeup. When wakeup and MAC use the same logical channel (same frequency band, spreading code, etc.), they have to contend for the same medium. One option is to give wakeup precedence over regular medium access, for example in a sender-based asynchronous wakeup scheme [30]. However, while a wakeup event is ongoing, other nodes in the neighborhood cannot send their data. Since this could take as long as one period, which can be very long, data forwarding might suffer substantially. This could be important depending on the frequency of such wakeup events and on whether it is more likely that a wakeup is needed in an already active part of the network. If, on the other hand, data has priority over wakeup, no delay bound can be guaranteed as the wakeup event could be queued behind ongoing data transmissions [28]. To completely avoid such interference and arrive at an out-of-band wakeup solution, different channels have to be used, for example implemented as different frequency bands. If in addition, this frequency separation is implemented by providing a separate radio for data transmission (governed by the MAC) and wakeup, one node can be engaged in traffic forwarding and at the same time participate in wakeup [13]. This complete decoupling of the two functionalities also has the benefit that wakeup could potentially use another type of radio, which allows combining the benefits of asynchronous wakeup with those of paging. However, the range disparity problem would also be inherited in this case.

6 Conclusions

Three distinct classes of wakeup solutions (paging, synchronous and asynchronous wakeup) were discussed, where each class has its own benefits and drawbacks. In the current state of research, there is no clear best algorithm, and it is expected that there will be no single solution that best fits all possible scenarios. What algorithm is chosen for a particular system will depend on such factors as the frequency of wakeup events, the node density and practical constraints such as the availability of a two-radio sensor node platform or of low-power paging technology. In addition, these factors might be dynamic and non-uniform in space, which may require an adaptive solution.

In principle if no paging channel is available, a sender-based asynchronous solution with a wakeup tone has the least amount of overhead for a sleeping node. Therefore it is expected to result in the lowest average energy consumption for a given wakeup delay constraint, if wakeup events are very infrequent. However, this conclusion only considers a single link. In multi-hop networks, the total end-to-end setup latency of a path should be considered rather than that of one hop alone. Staggering the wakeup of consecutive links has been proposed to reduce this latency [8] [29], and is potentially more effective in synchronized scenarios. In addition, tight integration with routing [34] or topology management [13] can further lower the average power consumption. Finally, the wakeup delay of each link in the network does not need to be equal. Since some nodes are more energy-critical than others, it would be beneficial to have them in a deeper sleep state, while ensuring the network-wide end-to-end latency is still bounded. Since wakeup delay can be traded off with energy consumption, distributing the wakeup delay intelligently over the network could potentially improve the overall network lifetime. These issues and other network-wide interactions between wakeup schemes and other higher layer protocols, are the subject of ongoing research efforts.

References

1. Vijay Raghunathan, Curt Schurgers, Sung Park, Mani B. Srivastava, Energy-Aware Wireless Microsensor Networks, *IEEE Signal Processing Magazine*, Vol.19, No.2 (2002) pp. 40–50.
2. Crossbow, *MICA motes*, http://www.xbow.com/Products/, last accessed March 2005.
3. Andreas Savvides, ChihChieh Han, Mani B. Srivastava, Dynamic fine-grained localization in ad-hoc networks of sensors, *MobiCom 2001*, Rome, Italy, (2001) pp.166–179.
4. Moteiv, *Telos node*, http://www.moteiv.com/products-reva.php, last accessed March 2005.
5. Dimitrios Lymberopoulos, Andreas Savvides, XYZ: A motion-enabled, power aware sensor node platform for distributed sensor network applications, *IPSN'05*, Los Angeles, CA (2005).
6. G. Anastasi, M. Conti, A. Falchi, E. Gregori, A. Passarella, Performance Measurements of Mote Sensor Networks, *MSWiM 2004*, Venice, Italy (2004).
7. Tijs van Dam, Koen Langendoen, An Adaptive Energy-Efficient MAC Protocol for Wireless Sensor Networks, *ACM Sensys*, Los Angeles, CA (2003).
8. Wei Ye, John Heidemann, Deborah Estrin, Medium Access Control with Coordinated Adaptive Sleeping for Wireless Sensor Networks, *IEEE/ACM Transactions on Networking*, Vol. 12, No. 3 (2004) pp. 493–506.
9. Robert Szewczyk, Joseph Polastre, Alan Mainwaring, David Culler, Lessons from a Sensor Network Expedition, *Proc. EWSN'04*, Berlin, Germany, (2004).
10. Koen Langendoen, Gertjan Halkes, Energy-efficient medium access control, *Book chapter in the Embedded Systems Handbook*, R. Zurawski (editor), CRC press, to appear.

11. Rex Min, Anantha Chandrakasan, A framework for energy-scalable communication in high-density wireless networks, *ISPED'02*, Monterey, CA (2002) pp. 36–40.
12. Matthew J. Miller, Nitin H. Vaidya, Minimizing Energy Consumption in Sensor Networks Using A Wakeup Radio, *WCNC 2004*, Atlanta, CA (2004).
13. Curt Schurgers, Vlasios Tsiatsis, Saurabh Ganeriwal, Mani Srivastava, Optimizing Sensor Networks in the Energy-Latency-Density Design Space, *IEEE Transactions on Mobile Computing*, Vol.1, No.1 (2002) pp. 70–80.
14. Rong Zheng, Jennifer C. Hou, Lui Sha, Asynchronous Wakeup for Ad Hoc Networks, *Mobihoc'03*, Annapolis, MD, (2003).
15. Chunlong Guo, Lizhi C. Zhong, Jan M. Rabaey, Low-power distributed MAC for ad hoc sensor radio networks, *Globecom'01*, San Antonio, TX (2001).
16. J. Rabaey, J. Ammer, J.L. da Silva, D. Patel, PicoRadio: Ad-hoc wireless networking of ubiquitous low-energy sensor/monitor nodes, *IEEE Computer Society Workshop on VLSI 2000*, Orlando, FL (2000) pp. 9–12.
17. E. Shih, P. Bahl, M.J. Sinclair, Wake on Wireless: an event driven energy saving strategy for battery operated devices, *Mobicom'02*, Atlanta, GA (2002).
18. Yuvraj Agarwal, Curt Schurgers, Rajesh Gupta, Dynamic Power Management using On Demand Paging for Networked Embedded Systems, *ASP-DAC'05*, Shanghai, China (2005).
19. Carla F. Chiasserini, Ramesh R. Rao, A distributed power management policy for wireless ad hoc networks, *WCNC'00*, Chicago, IL (2000).
20. IEEE 802.11, 1999 Edition (ISO/IEC 8802-11: 1999),*Local and Metropolitan Area Networks*.
21. Eun-Sun Jung, Nitin H. Vaidya, An energy efficient MAC protocol for wireless LANs, *Infocom'02*, New York, NY (2002).
22. Yu-Chee Tseng, Chih-Shun Hsu, Ten-Yueng Hsieh, Power-saving protocols for IEEE 802.11-based multi-hop ad hoc networks, *Journalof Computer and Telecommunications Networking*, Vol.43, No.3 (2003) pp.317–337.
23. IEEE 802.15.4, Part 15.4: *Wireless Medium Access Control (MAC) and Physical Layer (PHY) Specifications for Low-Rate Wireless Personal Area Networks (LR-WPANs)*.
24. Katayoun Sohrabi, Jay Gao, Vishal Ailawadhi, Gregory J. Pottie, Protocols for Self-Organization of a Wireless Sensor Network, *IEEE Personal Communications Mag.*, Vol.7, No.5 (2000) pp.16–27.
25. Z. Chen, A. Khokhar, Self organization and energy efficient TDMA MAC protocol by wake up for wireless sensor networks, *SECON'04*, Santa Clara, CA (2004).
26. Venkatesh Rajendran, Katia Obraczka, J.J. Garcia-Luna-Aceves, Energy-efficient, collision-free medium access control for wireless sensor networks, *SenSys'03*, Los Angeles, CA (2003) pp.182–192.
27. Michael J. McGlynn, Steven A. Borbash, Birthday protocols for low energy deployment and flexible neighbor discovery in ad hoc wireless networks, *MobiHoc'01*, Long Beach, CA (2001) pp. 137–145.
28. A. Salkintzis, C. Chamzas, An in-band power-saving protocol for mobile data networks, *IEEE Transactions on Communications*, Vol. 46 (1998) pp.1194–1205.
29. Xue Yang, Nitin H. Vaidya, A wakeup scheme for sensor networks: achieving balance between energy saving and end-to-end delay, *Real-Time and Embedded Technology and Applications Symposium*, Toronto, Canada (2004) pp.19–26.

30. A. El-Hoiydi, J.-D. Decotignie, WiseMAC: An Ultra Low Power MAC Protocol for Multi-hop Wireless Sensor Networks, *ALGOSENSORS'04*, Lecture Notes in Computer Science, LNCS 3121, Springer-Verlag (2004) pp.18–31, 2004.

31. Jonathan M. Reason, Jan M. Rabaey, A Study of Energy Consumption and Reliability in a Multi-Hop Sensor Network, *ACM SIGMOBILE Mobile Computing and Communications Review*, Vol. 8, No. 1 (2004) pp. 84–97, Jan 2004.

32. Joseph Polastre, Jaso. Hill, David Culler, Versatile Low Power Media Access for Wireless Sensor Networks, *SenSys'04*, Baltimore, MD (2004).

33. Samir Goel, Tomasz Imielinski, Etiquette Protocol for Ultra Low Power Operation in Sensor Networks, *Technical Report DCS-TR-552*, CS Dept., Rutgers University (2004).

34. Michele Zorzi, Ramesh R. Rao, Geographic Random Forwarding (GeRaF) for Ad Hoc and Sensor Networks: Multihop Performance, *Transactions on Mobile Computing*, Vol. 2, No. 4 (2003).

35. Maryam Owrang, Diba Mirza, Curt Schurgers, Delay-bounded Adaptive Power Saving for Ad hoc and Sensor Networks, *Vehicular Technology Conference (VTC05 Fall)*, Dallas, TX (2005).

Chapter 9
Time-Synchronization Challenges and Techniques

Weilian Su

Department of Electrical and Computer Engineering
Naval Postgraduate School
Monterey, CA 93943
weilian@nps.edu

1 Introduction

The advancement of *Micro Electro-Mechanical Systems* technology, wireless communications, and digital electronics has enabled the development of low-cost, low-power, multifunctional sensor nodes that are small in size and communicate untethered in short distances. The sensor nodes may be used in military, environmental, and commercial applications [1]. Each of these applications may require a different level of clock precision among the sensor nodes. For example, the clock precision required for security time-stamping and target tracking may be different. In addition, sensor nodes with a common view of time may fuse and display voice and video data in a meaningful way. Also, they may be able to use *Time Division Multiple Access* (TDMA) to access the channel and turn off the radio whenever possible to save energy. Thus, time synchronization is needed for different types of services that require coordination and precision. If services do not require time, then time synchronization may be an overhead for the sensor networks.

Since some applications and protocols need time synchronization, this chapter explores the design challenges, factors influencing time precision, and the state-of-the-art in time synchronization for wireless sensor networks. The purpose of any time synchronization technique is to maintain a similar time within a certain tolerance throughout the lifetime of the network or among a specific set of nodes in the network. To achieve the purpose, the time synchronization protocol has to take into account the energy as well as the low-end nature of the sensor nodes in a multi-hop environment. Hence, this requirement makes a challenging problem to solve.

In addition, the sensor nodes may be left unattended for a long period of time, e.g., in a cave or on an ocean floor. When messages are exchanged using short distance multi-hop broadcast, the software and medium access time and the variation of the access time may contribute the most in time fluctuations and differences in the path delays. Also, the time difference between sensor nodes may be significant over time due to the drifting effect of the local clocks.

In this chapter, the background of time synchronization is provided, and it is intended to enable new developments/enhancements of current timing techniques. First, some sensor network nodes are described in Section 2. Second, the factors affecting the quality of the synchronized time are discussed in Section 3. Afterwards, the design challenges are described in Section 4. In addition, the fundamentals of time synchronization for sensor networks are explained in Section 5. Lastly, the state-of-the-art of time synchronization protocols for sensor networks is reviewed in Section 7.

2 Sensor Network Nodes

There are few sensor network nodes in which sensor networks may be built for testing/research. These nodes are listed below:

- MICA Mote [13]: It has a 4 MHz clock and runs on the 915 MHz band. Newer generation of mote runs on 2.4 GHz band. In addition, the mote runs on TinyOS operating system.
- XYZ Sensor Node [12]: It has a ML67 series ARM /THUMB microcontroller from OKI Semiconductor and a CC2420 Zigbee compliant radio from Chipcon. In addition, the platform is open-source.
- Scatterweb Node [17]: It operates in the 868 MHz to 915 MHz band and utilizes frequency hopping. It also has bluetooth and WLAN capabilities.
- Intel Mote [9]: It has an integrated wireless microcontroller consisting of an ARM7 core, a Bluetooth radio, RAM and FLASH memory as well as various I/O options. In addition, it runs on TinyOS operating system.

Each of these nodes uses different technology. Thus, the timing precision of each will be different. In addition, each of these nodes will have to address the factors affecting time synchronization. The factors affecting the quality of synchronized time are described in the following section.

3 Influencing Factors

A time synchronization protocol has to address some of the inherent factors that influence the quality of the synchronized time. In addition, small and low-end sensor nodes may exhibit device behaviors that may be much worse than the large systems such as *personal computers* (*PCs*). As a result, time synchronization with these sensor nodes presents a different set of problems. Some of the factors influencing the quality of the synchronized time in large

Table 1. Factors influencing the quality of the synchronized time.

Factor	Description
(1) Temperature	-Since sensor nodes are deployed in various places, the temperature variation throughout the day may cause the clock to speed up or slow down. For a typical PC, the clock drifts a few *parts per million* (*ppm*) during the day [15]. For low end sensor nodes, the drifting may be even worse.
(2) Phase noise	-Some of the causes of phase noise are due to access fluctuation at the hardware interface, response variation of the operating system to interrupts, and jitter in the network delay. The jitter in the network delay may be due to medium access and queueing delays.
(3) Frequency noise	-The frequency noise is due to the unstability of the clock crystal [2]. A low-end crystal may experience large frequency fluctuation, because the frequency spectrum of the crystal has large sidebands on adjacent frequencies. The drift rate ρ values for quartz oscillators are between 10^{-4} and 10^{-6} [5].
(4) Asymmetric delay	-Since sensor nodes communicate with each other through the wireless medium, the delay of the path from one node to another may be different than the return path. As a result, an asymmetric delay may cause an offset to the clock that can not be detected by a variance type method [10]. If the asymmetric delay is static, the time offset between any two nodes is also static. The asymmetric delay is bounded by one-half the round trip time between the two nodes [10].
(5) Clock glitches	-Clock glitches are sudden jumps in time. This may be caused by hardware or software anomalies such as frequency and time steps.

systems also apply to sensor networks [10]; these factors are *temperature, phase noise, frequency noise, asymmetric delays,* and *clock glitches,* and they are described in Table 1.

Since sensor nodes are randomly deployed and their broadcast ranges are small, communications between the sensor nodes may rely on multi-level hierarchical architecture. Also, other influencing factors may shape the design of the time synchronization protocol. For example, larger asymmetric delays may cause more constant offset. In addition, the links between the sensor nodes may not be reliable. As a result, the influencing factors may have to be addressed differently. In the following section, the challenges in designing a time synchronization protocol are discussed.

4 Design Challenges

In the future, many low-end sensor nodes will be deployed to minimize the cost of the sensor networks. These nodes may work collaboratively together to provide time synchronization for the whole sensor network. The precision of the synchronized clocks depends on the needs of the applications. For example, a sensor network requiring TDMA service may require microseconds difference among the neighbor nodes while a data gathering application for sensor networks requires only milliseconds of precision.

As sensor networks are application driven, the design challenges of a time synchronization protocol are also dictated by the application. These challenges are to provide an overall guideline and requirement when considering the features of a time synchronization protocol for sensor networks; they are *robust, energy aware, server-less, light-weight,* and *tunable service.*

- *Robust:* Sensor nodes may fail, and the failures should not have significant effect on the time synchronization error. If sensor nodes depend on a specific master to synchronize their clocks, a failure or anomaly of the master's clock may create a cascade effect that nodes in the network may become unsynchronized. So, a time synchronization protocol has to handle the unexpected or periodic failures of the sensor nodes. If failures do occur, the errors caused by these failures should not be propagated throughout the network.

- *Energy aware:* Since each node is power/energy limited, the use of resources should be evenly spread and controlled. A time synchronization protocol should use the minimum number of messages to synchronize the nodes in the earliest time. In addition, the load for time synchronization should be shared, so some nodes in the network do not fail earlier than others. If some parts of the network fail earlier than others, the partitioned networks may drift apart from each other and become unsynchronized.

- *Server-less:* A precise time server may not be available. Even if the time servers are available, they may fail when placed in the sensor field. As a result, sensor nodes should be able to synchronize to a common time without the precise time servers. This server-less feature also helps to address the robustness challenge as stated earlier. Also, if precise time servers are used by the server-less architecture, the quality of the synchronized clocks as well as the time to synchronize the clocks of the network should be much better.

- *Light-weight:* The complexity of the time synchronization protocol has to be low in order to be programmed into the sensor nodes. Besides being energy limited, the sensor nodes are memory and CPU limited as well.

The synchronization protocol may be programmed into a FPGA or designed into an ASIC. By having the time synchronization protocol tightly integrated with the hardware, the delay and variation of the processing may be smaller. With the increase of precision, the cost of a sensor node is higher.

- *Tunable service:* Some services such as medium access may require time synchronization to be always ON while others only need it when there is an event. Since time synchronization can consume a lot of energy, a tunable time synchronization service is applicable for some applications. Nevertheless, there are needs for both type of synchronization protocols.

The above challenges provide a guideline for developing various types of time synchronization protocols that are applicable to the sensor networks. A time synchronization protocol may have a mixture of these design features. In addition, some applications in the sensor networks may not require the time synchronization protocol to meet all these requirements. For example, a data gathering application may require the tunable service and light-weight features more than the server-less capability. The tunable service and light-weight features allow the application to gather precise data when the users require it. In addition, the nodes that are not part of this data gathering process may not have to be synchronized. Also, the precision of the time does not need to be high, because the users may only need milliseconds precision to satisfy their needs.

As these design challenges are important for guiding the development of a time synchronization protocol, the reader still needs to acquire the fundamentals of time synchronization. These fundamentals are discussed in Section 5.

5 Time Synchronization Fundamentals

As the factors described in Section 3 influence the error budget of the synchronized clocks, the purpose of a time synchronization protocol is to minimize the effects of these factors. Before developing a solution to address these factors, some basics of time synchronization for sensor networks need to be discussed. These basics are to provide the fundamentals for designing a time synchronization protocol.

If a better clock crystal is used, the drift rate ρ may be much smaller. Usually, the hardware clock time $H(t)$ at real-time t is within a linear envelope of the real-time as illustrated in Figure 1. Since the clock drifts away from real-time, the time difference between two events measured with the same hardware clock may have a maximum error of $\rho(b - a)$ [5], where a and b are the time of occurrence of first and second events, respectively. For modern computers, the clock granularity may be negligible since the operating frequency is in the MHz or GHz range, but it may contribute a significant portion to the error

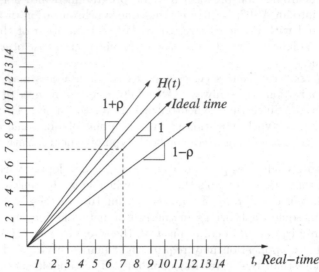

Fig. 1. Drifting of hardware clock time.

budget if the clock of a sensor node is really coarse, running at KHz range instead of MHz. In certain applications, a sensor node may have a volume of cm^3 [16], so a fast oscillator may not be possible or suitable.

Regardless of the clock granularity, the hardware clock time $H(t)$ is usually translated into a virtual clock time by adding an adjustment constant to it. Normally, it is the virtual clock time that we read from a computer. Hence, a time synchronization protocol may adjust the virtual clock time and/or discipline the hardware clock to compensate for the time difference between the clocks of the nodes. Either approach has to deal with the factors influencing time synchronization as described earlier.

When an application issues a request to obtain the time, the time is returned after a certain delay. This software access delay may fluctuate according to the loading of the system. This type of fluctuation is nondeterministic and may be less if real time operation system and hardware architecture are used. For low-end sensor nodes, the software access time may be in the order of few hundred microseconds. For example, a Mica mote is running at 4 MHz [13] having clock granularity of $0.25\mu s$. If the node is 80% loaded and it takes 100 cycles to obtain the time, the software access time is around $125\mu s$.

In addition to the software access time, the medium access time also contributes to the nondeterministic delay that a message experiences. If *carrier-sense multiple access* (CSMA) is used, the back-off window size as well as the traffic load affect the medium access time [3, 4, 19]. Once the sensor node obtains the channel, the transmission and propagation times are pretty de-

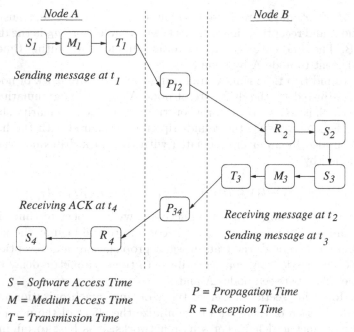

Fig. 2. Round-trip time.

terministic, and they can be estimated by the packet size, transmission rate, and speed-of-light.

In summary, the delays experienced when sending a message at real-time t_1 and receiving an acknowledgement (ACK) at real-time t_4 are shown in Figure 2. The message from node A incurs the software access, medium access, transmission, and propagation times. These times are represented by S_1, M_1, T_1, and P_{12}. Once the message is received by node B at t_2, it will incur extra delays through receiving and processing. After the message is processed, an ACK is sent to node A at t_3. The total delay at node B is the summation of R_2, S_2, $(1 \pm \rho_B)(t_3 - t_2)$, S_3, M_3, and T_3. After node B sends the ACK, the ACK propagates through the wireless medium and arrives at node A. After the reception, node A processes the ACK. The path delays for sending and receiving the ACK from node B to A are P_{34}, R_4, and S_4. The round-trip time in real-time t for sending a message and receiving an ACK is calculated by

$$
\begin{aligned}
t_4 - t_1 = {} & S_1 + M_1 + T_1 + P_{12} + R_2 + S_2 \\
& + (1 \pm \rho_B)(t_3 - t_2) + S_3 + M_3 \\
& + T_3 + P_{34} + R_4 + S_4,
\end{aligned} \tag{1}
$$

where S, M, T, P, and R are the software access, medium access, transmission, propagation, and reception times, respectively. In addition, ρ_B is the drift rate at node B. The difference $(t_3 - t_2)$ is to account for the waiting time before an ACK is sent to node A by node B.

If the round-trip time is measured using the hardware clock of node A, it has to be adjusted by the drift rate of node A ρ_A. If the granularity of the hardware clock is coarse, the error δ contributed by the granularity should be accounted for. As a result, the round-trip time measured with the hardware clock is bounded by an error associated with the clock drift and granularity as determined by

$$(1 - \rho_A)(t_4 - t_1) \leq H(t_4) - H(t_1) < (1 + \rho_A)(t_4 - t_1) + \delta \qquad (2)$$

The bound for the round-trip time fluctuates with respect to time since the software and medium access fluctuate according to the load at the node and in the channel. Although the transmission, propagation, and reception times may be deterministic, they may contribute to the asymmetric delay that can cause time offset between nodes A and B.

In the following section, different types of time synchronization protocols are described. Each of them tries to minimize the effect of the nondeterministic and asymmetric delays. For sensor networks, it is best to minimize the propagation delay variation. For example, the delays and jitters between two nodes may be different in the forward and return paths. In addition, the jitters may vary significantly due to frequent node failures, since the messages are relayed hop-by-hop between the two nodes. The synchronization protocols in the following section focus on synchronizing nodes hop-by-hop, so the propagation time and variation do not play too much effect on the error of the synchronized clocks. Although the sensor nodes are densely deployed and they can take advantage of the close distance, the medium and software access times may contribute the most in the nondeterministic of the path delay during a one-hop synchronization. The way to provide time synchronization for sensor networks may be different for different applications. The current timing techniques that are available for different applications are described in the following section.

6 State-of-the-Art Time Synchronization Protocols

Since time synchronization is to synchronize the time within the sensor networks, the timing techniques are methods/protocols that achieve this. There are three types of timing techniques as shown in Table 2, and each of these types has to address the factors and design challenges affecting time synchronization as mentioned in Sections 3 and 4, respectively. In addition, the timing techniques have to address the time representation differences between the sensor networks and the Internet, e.g., universal coordinated time. For

Table 2. Three types of timing techniques.

Type	Description
(1) Relies on fixed time servers to synchronize the network	-The nodes are synchronized to time servers that are readily available. These time servers are expected to be robust and highly precise.
(2) Translates time throughout from the network	-The time is translated hop-by-hop for the source to the sink. In essence, it is a time translation service.
(3) Self-organizes to synchronize the network	-The protocol does not depend on specialized time servers. It automatically organizes and determines the master nodes as the temporary time-servers.

example, the time representation in sensor networks may be just an aggregate sum of the time difference between sensor nodes. Thus, it has to be translated into the universal coordinated time. In the following, examples of these types of timing techniques are described, namely the *Network Time Protocol* (NTP) [14], *Timing-sync Protocol for Sensor Networks* (TPSN) [7], *Reference-Broadcast Synchronization* (RBS) [6], *Time-Diffusion Synchronization Protocol* (TDP) [18] and *asynchronous rate-based diffusion algorithm* [11].

In Internet, the NTP is used to discipline the frequency of each node's oscillator. The accuracy of the NTP synchronization is in the order of milliseconds [8]. It may be useful to use NTP to discipline the oscillators of the sensor nodes, but the connection to the time servers may not be possible because of frequent sensor node failures. In addition, disciplining all the sensor nodes in the sensor field may be a problem due to interference from the environment and large variation of delay between different parts of the sensor field. The interference can temporarily disjoint the sensor field into multiple smaller fields causing undisciplined clocks among these smaller fields. The NTP protocol may be considered as the timing technique of type (1). In addition, it has to be refined in order to address the design challenges presented by the sensor networks.

As of now, the NTP is very computational intensive and requires a precise time server to synchronize the nodes in the network. In addition, it does not take into account the energy consumption required for time synchronization. As a result, the NTP does not satisfy the energy aware, server-less, and lightweight design challenges of the sensor networks. Although the NTP can be robust, it may suffer large propagation delay when sending timing messages to the time servers. In addition, the nodes are synchronized in a hierarchical manner, and some time servers in the middle of the hierarchy may fail causing unsynchronized nodes in the network. Once these nodes fail, it is hard to reconfigure the network since the hierarchy is manually configured.

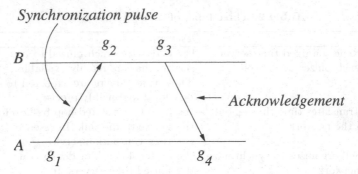

Fig. 3. Two-way message handshake.

Another time synchronization technique that adopts some concepts from NTP is TPSN. The TPSN requires the root node to synchronize all or part of the nodes in the sensor field. The root node synchronizes the nodes in a hierarchical way. Before synchronization, the root node constructs the hierarchy by broadcasting a *level_discovery* packet. The first level of the hierarchy is level 0, which is where the root node resides. The nodes receiving the *level_discovery* packet from the root node are the nodes belonging to level 1. The nodes in level 1 broadcast their *level_discovery* packet after receiving from level 0, and neighbor nodes receiving the *level_discovery* packet for the first time are the level 2 nodes. This process continues until each node in the sensor field has a level number.

The root node sends a *time_sync* packet to initialize the time synchronization process. Afterwards, the nodes in level 1 synchronize to level 0 by performing the two-way handshake as shown in Figure 3. This type of handshake is used by the NTP to synchronize the clocks of distributed computer systems. At the end of the handshake at time g_4, node A obtains the times g_1, g_2, and g_3 from the acknowledgement packet. The times g_2 and g_3 are obtained from the clock of sensor node B while g_1 and g_4 are from the node A. After processing the acknowledgment packet, the node A readjusts its clock by the clock drift value Δ, where $\Delta = \frac{(g_2-g_1)-(g_4-g_3)}{2}$. At the same time, the level 2 nodes overhear this message handshake and wait for a random time before synchronizing with level 1 nodes. This synchronization process continues until all the nodes in the network are synchronized. Since TPSN enables time synchronization from one root node, it is the timing technique of type (1).

The TPSN is based on a sender-receiver synchronization model, where the receiver synchronizes with the time of the sender according to the two-way message handshake as shown in Figure 3. It is trying to provide a light-weight and tunable time synchronization service. On the other hand, it requires a time server and does not address the robust and energy aware design goal. Since the design of TPSN is based on a hierarchical methodology similar to NTP,

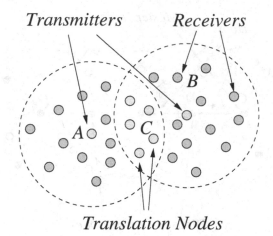

Fig. 4. Illustration of the RBS.

nodes within the hierarchy may fail and cause nodes to be unsynchronized. In addition, node movements may render the hierarchy useless, because nodes may move out of their levels. Hence, nodes at level i can not synchronize with nodes at level $i - 1$. Thus, synchronization may fail throughout the network.

As for the timing technique of type (2), the RBS provides an instantaneous time synchronization among a set of receivers that are within the reference broadcast of the transmitter. The transmitter broadcasts m reference packets. Each of the receivers that are within the broadcast range records the time-of-arrival of the reference packets. Afterwards, the receivers communicate with each other to determine the offsets. To provide multi-hop synchronization, it is proposed to use nodes that are receiving two or more reference broadcasts from different transmitters as translation nodes. These translation nodes are used to translate the time between different broadcast domains.

As shown in Figure 4, nodes A, B, and C are the transmitter, receiver, and translation nodes, respectively. The transmitter nodes broadcast their timing messages, and the receiver nodes receive these messages. Afterwards, the receiver nodes synchronize with each other. The sensor nodes that are within the broadcast regions of both transmitter nodes A are the translation nodes. When an event occurs, a message describing the event with a time-stamp is translated by the translation nodes when the message is routed back to the sink. Although this time synchronization service is tunable and light-weight, there may not be translation nodes on the route path over which the message is relayed. As a result, services may not be available on some routes. In addition, this protocol is not suitable for medium access scheme such as TDMA since the clocks of all the nodes in the network are not adjusted to a common time.

Another emerging timing technique is the TDP. The TDP is used to maintain the time throughout the network within a certain tolerance. The tolerance

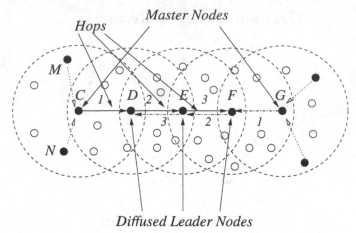

Fig. 5. TDP concept.

level can be adjusted based on the purpose of the sensor networks. The TDP automatically self-configures by electing master nodes to synchronize the sensor network. In addition, the election process is sensitive to energy requirement as well as the quality of the clocks. The sensor network may be deployed in unattended areas, and the TDP still synchronizes the unattended network to a common time. It is considered as the timing technique of type (3).

The TDP concept is illustrated in Figure 5. The elected master nodes are nodes C and G. First, the master nodes send a message to their neighbors to measure the round-trip times. Once the neighbors receive the message, they self-determine if they should become diffuse leader nodes. The ones elected to become diffuse leader nodes reply to the master nodes and start sending a message to measure the round-trip to their neighbors. As shown in Figure 5, nodes M, N, and D are the diffused leader nodes of node C. Once the replies are received by the master nodes, the round-trip time and the standard deviation of the round-trip time are calculated. The one-way delay from the master nodes to the neighbor nodes is half of the measured round-trip time. After the calculation, the master nodes send a time-stamped message containing the standard deviation to the neighbor nodes. The time in the time-stamped message is adjusted with the one-way delay. Once the diffuse leader nodes receive the time-stamped message, they broadcast the time-stamped message after adjusting the time, which is in the message, with their measured one-way delay and inserting their standard deviation of the round-trip time. This diffusion process continues for n times, where n is the number of hops from the master nodes. From Figure 5, the time is diffused three hops from the master nodes C and G. The nodes D, E, and F are the diffused leader nodes that diffuse the time-stamped messages originated from the master nodes.

For the nodes that have received more than one time-stamped messages originated from different master nodes, they use the standard deviations carried in the time-stamped messages as weighted ratio of their time contribution to the new time. In essence, the nodes weight the times diffused by the master nodes to obtain a new time for them. This process is to provide a smooth time variation between the nodes in the network. The smooth transition is important for some applications such as target tracking and speed estimating.

The master nodes are autonomously elected, so the network is robust to failures. Although some of the nodes may die, there are still other nodes in the network that can self-determine to become master nodes. This feature also enables the network to become server-less if necessary and to reach an equilibrium time. In addition, the master and diffusion leader nodes are self-determined based on their own energy level. Also, the TDP is light-weight, but it may not be as tunable as the RBS.

Li and Rus propose an asynchronous rate-based diffusion algorithm [11], which aims to converge the time in the sensor network to the average time of the network. The asynchronous rate-based diffusion algorithm is given in Table 3. A sensor node obtains the clock readings from its neighboring nodes and computes the average of these readings. Once the average is computed, it is sent back to the neighboring nodes for update.

Table 3. Asynchronous Diffusion Algorithm

Step	Description
(1)	For each node N with uniform probability
(2)	Obtain clock readings from neighbor nodes
(3)	Compute the average of the clock readings
(4)	Send the average reading back to neighbors, which then update the clock

This approach is considered as the timing technique of type (3) since no precise time server is needed. Although the asynchronous diffusion algorithm will converge to an average value, the amount of overhead is large since each node needs to perform the algorithm. Also, the convergence varies with the size of the sensor networks and range of the transmission radius.

In summary, these timing techniques may be used for different types of applications; each of them has its own benefits. All of these techniques try to address the factors influencing time synchronization while designed according to the challenges as described in Section 4. Depending on the types of services required by the applications or the hardware limitation of the sensor nodes, some of these timing techniques may be applied.

7 Conclusions

The factors influencing time synchronization and design challenges are described in Sections 3 and 4, respectively. They are to provide guidelines for developing time synchronization protocols. The requirements of sensor networks are different from traditional distributed computer systems. As a result, new types of timing techniques are required to address the specific needs of the applications. These techniques are described in Section 6. Since the range of applications in the sensor networks is wide, new timing techniques are encouraged for different types of applications. This is to provide optimized schemes tailored for unique environments and purposes.

References

1. I. F. Akyildiz, W. Su, Y. Sankarasubramaniam, and E. Cayirci, Wireless Sensor Networks: A Survey, *Computer Networks (Elsevier) Journal* (March 2002) pp. 393–422.
2. David W. Allan, Time and Frequency (Time-Domain) Characterization, Estimation, and Prediction of Precision Clocks and Oscillators, *IEEE Trans. on Ultrasonics, Ferroelectrics, and Frequency Control* Vol.34 No.6 (1987) pp. 647–654.
3. Giuseppe Bianchi, Performance Analysis of the IEEE 802.11 Distributed Coordination Function, *IEEE Journal on Selected Areas in Communications* Vol.18 No.3 (2000) pp. 535–547.
4. B. P. Crow, I. Widjaja, J. G. Kim and P. Sakai, Investigation of the IEEE 802.11 Medium Access Control (MAC) Sublayer Functions, *IEEE INFOCOM'97,* (Kobe, Japan, 1997) pp. 126–133.
5. Flaviu Cristian and Christof Fetzer, Probabilistic Internal Clock Synchronization, *Proceedings of the Thirteenth Symposium on Reliable Distributed Systems,* (Dana Point, CA, 1994) pp. 22–31.
6. Jeremy Elson, Lewis Girod, and Deborah Estrin, Fine-Grained Network Time Synchronization using Reference Broadcasts, *Proceedings of the Fifth Symposium on Operating Systems Design and Implementation (OSDI 2002),* (Boston, MA, 2002).
7. Saurabh Ganeriwal, Ram Kumar, and Mani B. Srivastava, Timing-Sync Protocol for Sensor Networks, *ACM SenSys 2003,* (Los Angeles, CA, 2003).
8. IEEE 1588, Standard for a Precision Clock Synchronization Protocol for Networked Measurement and Control Systems, (2002).
9. Intel Motes, http://www.intel.com.
10. Judah Levine, Time Synchronization Over the Internet Using an Adaptive Frequency-Locked Loop, *IEEE Transaction on Ultrasonics, Ferroelectrics, and Frequency Control* Vol.46 No.4 (1999) pp. 888–896.
11. Qun Li and Daniela Rus, Global Clock Synchronization in Sensor Networks, *IEEE INFOCOM 2004,* Vol.1 (Hong Kong, China, 2004) pp. 564–574.
12. Dimitrios Lymberopoulos and Andreas Savvides, XYZ: A Motion-Enabled, Power Aware Sensor Node Platform for Distributed Sensor Network Applications, *Proceedings of IPSN 05,* (Los Angeles, CA, 2005).
13. MICA Motes and Sensors, http://www.xbow.com.
14. David L. Mills, Internet Time Synchronization: The Network Time Protocol, *Global States and Time in Distributed Systems,* (IEEE Computer Society Press, 1994).
15. David L. Mills, Adaptive Hybrid Clock Discipline Algorithm for the Network Time Protocol, *IEEE/ACM Trans. on Networking* Vol.6 No.5 (1998) pp. 505–514.

16. G.J. Pottie and W.J. Kaiser, Wireless Integrated Network Sensors, *Communications of the ACM*Vol.43 No.5 (2000) pp. 551–558.
17. Scatterweb Nodes, `http://www.scatterweb.net`.
18. Weilian Su and Ian F. Akyildiz, Time-diffusion synchronization protocol for sensor networks, *IEEE/ACM Transactions on Networking*Vol.13 No.2 (2005) pp. 384–397.
19. Y. C. Tay and K. C. Chua, A Capacity Analysis for the IEEE 802.11 MAC Protocol, *ACM Wireless Networks Journal* Vol.7 (2001) pp. 159–171.

Chapter 10
Location Service, Information Dissemination and Object Tracking in Wireless Sensor Networks by Using Quorum Methods

Dan-Dan Liu[1] and Xiao-Hua Jia[21]

[1] Computer School
Wuhan University, Wuhan, China 430072
liudd2004@hotmail.com
[2] Department of Computer Science
City University of HongKong, HongKong
jia@cs.cityu.edu.hk

1 Introduction

1.1 Quorum System

Quorum methods were originally used in consistency control for data replicas in distributed database systems. Replication of data is the key technology for high availability and fault tolerance in a distributed system. Upon receiving a request to perform an operation on a particular datum, the server is responsible for cooperating with other servers in the group that have copies of the data. Different replication schemes involve different numbers of servers for the successful accomplishment of an operation. For example, in the traditional read-any/write-all scheme, a writing request must be finished by all servers in the system, so that a read operation can be performed by any single server. However, this scheme is not reliable because failure any one of the servers will cause failure of the write operation, and finally failure of data accessing. The quorum consensus method aims at reducing the number of servers taking part in a data operation. A quorum is a subgroup of servers whose size gives it the right to make decisions. For example, if having a majority is the criterion, a quorum must consist of at least $n/2$ servers cooperating to carry out operations, where n is the total number of servers in the system.

The quorum method was used early on in [1]. Gifford in his paper developed a file replication scheme in which a number of 'votes' is assigned to each physical copy at a replica manager of a single logical file. In each transaction, a read quorum of R votes must be collected to proceed with a read operation, and a write quorum of W votes must be collected to perform a write operation. The R and W are set as:

W > half the total votes,

R+W > total number of votes for the group.

This ensures that there is at least one common copy involved in an operation between any pair of a read quorum and a write quorum or two write quorums. There is always a subset of the representatives of a file whose votes total to W that are current. Thus, any read quorum is guaranteed to get a current copy, which is determined by the version numbers.

The quorum method has also been used in preventing transactions in different partitions of networks from producing inconsistent results [2]. It requires that an update operation on a logical object should be completed successfully within a quorum. Without enough members to form a quorum, operations will not be performed thus avoiding conflicting results.

The reliability and performance characteristics of the quorum method can be controlled by appropriately adjusting the R and W. In the general situation, comparative to the file replication scheme in [1], each physical copy at a single server can be regarded as being assigned the same votes, say 1. Thus, W and R determine the number of nodes composing each quorum. There is a tradeoff between overhead consumption in write operations and read operations. The characteristics of writes improve as W decreases, and similarly for reads by decreasing R. The choice of R and W will depend on an application's read-to-write ratio, the cost of reading and writing, and the desired reliability and performance.

In [3], the number of nodes within a quorum has possibly been reduced to approximately $\sqrt{n}$. That is, n servers in the system can be partitioned conceptually into $\sqrt{n}$ rows and $\sqrt{n}$ columns. Each column and row serves as a quorum; all of the quorums form a quorum system. There is always a server located in the intersection of each pair of row and column. The overhead of the system is controlled at $O(\sqrt{n})$. Compared with the $O(n)$ servers involved for accessing data in traditional read-any/write-all or read-all/write-one replica schemes, to $O(n/2)$ in those having majority criterion schemes, and to $O(\sqrt{n})$, the quorum method has significantly reduced traffic in the system which can be translated into significant energy savings.

1.2 Problems in Wireless Sensor Networks

In recent years, the Wireless Sensor Network (WSN) [4] has received significant interest from the research community. A sensor network usually consists of hundreds or thousands of tiny and inexpensive sensor nodes, which are deployed on the ground, in the air, in vehicles, on bodies, under water and inside buildings without any sensing infrastructure a priori, providing functions of data sensing, information processing and communication. Because of its spatial coverage and multiplicity in sensing aspect and modality, a sensor network can be used for many military and civil applications, such as environment or habitat monitoring, target surveillance and object tracking, traffic monitoring and traffic control, and so on [5].

A WSN can be treated as a distributed database system. In such a system each sensor node operates autonomously with no central node of control. It can be a data source (producing data) as well as a data sink (consuming data). Each node will update sensed data to the networks in an efficient way (write operation) so that interested querying nodes are able to get the current copy of the new data (read operation) as soon as possible. Each of these operations is based on the node's local information.

Several challenges are in front of us for the design and implementation of such a distributed information system for resource constrained WSNs. First, the system is limited by the energy capacity of WSNs. Sensors are powered by batteries and it may not be possible to recharge or replace them in many applications. The system operations must be energy efficient. Second, the system is limited by the bandwidth capacity of sensor nodes. The interactions (i.e., communications) among the sensors must be kept minimal. Third, sensor nodes do not have global topology information and they, sometimes, even do not have global identifiers. Each sensor node only knows its own and its neighbors' positions, and its operations must be based on its local information.

There are three important problems in such a distributed WSN, namely location service, information dissemination and object tracking.

A. Location Service

Location service is a general obstacle for distributed networks. Without a central node of control, updated location information about nodes should be timely obtained before data can be exchanged among nodes correctly. However, due to the limitation of their power and hardware capability, sensors will be exhausted if they maintain tables for the location of all the others. Moreover, if mobility is available, sensors are even harder to trace than other nodes. Thus, location both in time and space has been identified as a key technology for the successful deployment and operation of context-aware sensor network services.

B. Information Dissemination

The main goal for WSNs is to provide distributed information services on sensed data efficiently. When a node senses data, it will process the data and advertise the data to others that are interested in it. If other users need to access certain data, they make a query to the network, and whoever is holding the data will pass it to them. However, the challenge is that the querying node generally has no idea which sensor owns such data, and the sensing node doesn't know which sensor will be interested in new data either. Thus, many current researches focus on disseminating sensed information through the network in a distributed and efficient way, which can guarantee the current one to be captured quickly.

C. Object Tracking

Object tracking in a military battlefield situation is one of the most important applications of WSNs. A sensor node deployed in a battlefield can detect vehicles or soldiers intruding into its sensing scope. It will generate a reliable report, containing the location or ID of the intruder, and advertise to the network through established routes and nodes. Individuals who need the current location of certain vehicles or troops later can send a request to the network and get proper information from sensor nodes inside the network. It has strict requirements on energy consumption, since sensors are impossible to recharge or replace during a battle.

Because of its flexibility, interrelated to energy efficiency as introduced above, the quorum method can be considered as a good means to deal with these three important problems in wireless sensor networks. The rest of this chapter is organized as follows: we overview the location service problem and different protocols to solve it from the view of the quorum method in Section 2; Section 3 discusses the information dissemination problem and focuses on the employment of quorum-based method protocols combined with negotiation. Its performance is shown through mathematical analysis and simulation comparison. One of the major applications of wireless sensor networks—object tracking is discussed in Section 4. If we combine the frequency of object detection and request with the consideration of different quorum size, minor modification of the quorum-based method can receive even better results. Conclusion about this chapter is made in Section 5.

2 Location Service

There are two classes of protocols that deal with the routings among nodes, topology-based and position-based [6]. Since nodes may easily die out by running out of energy or moving out of their original place, the topology of sensor networks is changed frequently. Therefore position-based routing is introduced to eliminate these deficiencies. The first issue to address in the position-based routing is location service. A location tracking mechanism is essential for updating and retrieving location information about nodes to establish connections before data is routed. Nevertheless, because of the limitation of power and hardware capability, sensors will be exhausted if they maintain tables for the locations of all the other nodes. Moreover, if mobility is available, sensors are even harder to trace than others. Thus how to facilitate location service in a distributed way is not a trivial task.

Location service includes two major tasks. First is the location update or location registration, where nodes periodically disseminate their up-to-date position information. Second is the destination search. The current location of a node can be obtained from some servers when communication to that node is initiated. There exist many interesting issues in the management of location information for these nodes which is similar to many mobile networks [7], [8]:

1) Frequency of location updates. There are basically three alternatives, namely time-based, movement-based and distance-based strategies to determine update intervals [9].

2) Information organization. There are several distributed strategies for hierarchical organization of location information proposed in [10], [11].

3) Information update and retrieval. There can be multiple location servers in the networks. It is the tradeoff between performance of the write/read quorum and the system overhead.

4) Load balance of servers. In distributed database architecture, some location servers may be overloaded with location updates and query requests while other servers are relatively idle. We should distribute those servers, balance the load, and make full use of those available resources to prolong the life of networks.

So far, there have been several protocols proposed to solve this location service problem. They can be typically divided into two main categories: proactive and reactive approaches. They both take ideas from the quorum method.

2.1 Proactive Protocols

In many proactive protocols, one node has to maintain locations of all the other nodes. They periodically propagate up-to-date location information throughout the network. The method is like the write-all/read-one scheme in a distributed database system. Updates take place in all nodes, and whichever node receives a command can start data retrieval immediately. However, this will cause high overheads affecting bandwidth utilization, throughput as well as power usage [12]. It has low scalability. For a large scale wireless sensor network, or a network composed of nodes with high mobility, large number of updating interchanges among nodes will consume considerable energy and even cause many flooding problems.

For example, within the Distance Routing Effect Algorithm for Mobility (DREAM) framework [13], each node maintains a position database that stores position information about other nodes that are parts of the network. Locations of nodes will be disseminated throughout the network periodically. More specific metrics are given to control the frequency of the update to balance the trade-off between overhead in full updating and accurate information acquisition.

2.2 Reactive Protocols

In reactive (on demand) protocols, a path discovery mechanism is initiated only when a source node tries to find a route to a destination node that is moving around. The path information is maintained as long as it is needed by the source. Generally, reactive protocols consume fewer overheads than proactive protocols. When there is no significant movement, there is neither a need to periodically send advertisements, nor to receive them. However, the delay caused by searching a new route is inevitable.

The Location Aided Routing proposal [14], for example, proposes the use of position information to enhance the route discovery phase of reactive routing approaches. A source broadcasts a route request message to all its neighbors, searching for the destination. Neighbors that are within the request zone will forward them further. After the destination node, which should be within the zone, receives such a query, it will send back a route reply message as well as its current location. Such protocol works as the read-some/write-one scheme. Nodes don't need to update their location to others immediately after the movements. They reply only when requests are received.

2.3 Rendezvous-Based Protocols

Recently, many protocols have been proposed in a novel fashion, called rendezvous based protocols. The basic idea in this kind of protocols is that all nodes in the network agree with a mapping. When nodes are going to send out location updates, they choose a subset of available nodes. When nodes need to find some other nodes, they send out location queries to a potentially different subset of nodes. Different protocols should be designd to make sure that the intersection of two subsets is not empty. These rendezvous nodes act as location servers where location updates are stored and location queries are looked up. From the terms of the quorum method, it ensures that a read quorum can get the current copy of latest location data. Note that the traditional scheme requires to satisfy the inequality of $R+W>n$ (n is the total number of nodes), while the rendezvous based method never needs all nodes cooperating for each data accessing.

Two different approaches to performing the mapping, hashing-based and quorum-based, have been proposed [15].

A. Hashing-Based Protocols

In hashing-based protocols, each node chooses its location server via a hashing function, either in the node identifier space or in the location space. All location servers form a quorum. The size of quorum is closely related to hierarchical division and location servers' selection. Recall that either in the traditional read-one/write-all scheme, or one with a majority criterion, the size R of the read quorum and size W of the write quorum should abide by $R+W> n$ (n is the total number of nodes), no matter what adjustment is made between them. More efficiently, in this kind of method, updates only take place on location servers, a subset of N nodes inside the network, which are selected through mapping with a well-known hashing function. Later, location is retrieved from the same group of location servers. The availability of this method lies in the common knowledge for producing a quorum intersection.

Hashing-based protocols can be further divided into hierarchical hashing and flat hashing. In the hierarchical hashing-based protocols (for example [16], [17]), networks are divided into several hierarchical grids. One or more nodes in each level are designated as location servers for each node, so that location updates and queries only need to traverse up or down the hierarchy to find them. Because the height of the hierarchy is $O(log\ n)$, effectively each node's location is disseminated to $O(log\ n)$ location servers.

Another kind of hashing is flat hashing (for example [18], [19], [20]). In such protocols, each node calculates for itself a home region, which may consist of one or more nodes within a fixed area in the network, through a uniform and well-known hash function. This home region, acting as location server, will store the location update and reply to corresponding queries for that node. The number of location servers for each node is independent of the total number of nodes n, but the energy consumption on these $O(1)$ servers is comparatively high, which may cause some other problems such as a bottleneck in a network.

B. Quorum-Based Protocols

For the same purpose, to reduce the number of nodes involved in forming a read quorum and write quorum as in the hashing-based method, the quorum-based method also never needs all nodes to collaborate in each data accessing. The number involved in each quorum is significantly reduced to $O(\sqrt{n})$, where n is the total number of nodes residing in the network. Moreover, there is no preliminary information about the hash function in each node. Authors in [21] have discussed several methods for generating quorum systems.

In [22], the author applied a similar idea, as in [3] with some modification, to form a simple and efficient quorum system to wireless networks. Recall that in [3], n servers in the system are evenly partitioned into $\sqrt{n}$ rows and $\sqrt{n}$ columns, so that intersections occur between rows and columns. However, there are no strict rows or columns inside real networks. Nevertheless, with some modification, the protocol works well as follows: nodes exchange location information with immediate neighbors whenever a link associated with the nodes is broken or created. After the number of such link changes reaches a certain threshold value, the node broadcasts a location update packet to its neighbors. Then the packet is retransmitted along the north-south direction of this node (forming a column) by the northernmost and southernmost neighbor of each iteration until it reaches the end of this 'column'. A destination search packet from the source is forwarded in a similar fashion. It is first broadcasted to the easternmost and westernmost neighbors of the source, and retransmitted along its east-west direction (forming a row) until it reaches the end. The location update and destination search process can form a cross shape inside the network (Figure 1).

Figure 1 (a) is the best situation that quorum method is used in a regular grid system. Obviously, a row and a column are bound to intersect. Figure 1 (b) shows the situation that the quorum method is applied to common wireless sensor networks. Sensors along the north-south direction and the east-west direction form the column and row respectively. Intuitively, queries can be answered by at least one rendezvous.

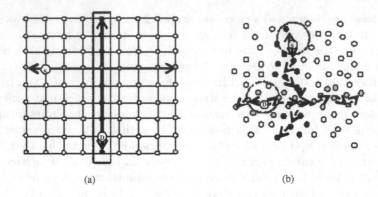

(a)   (b)

Fig. 1. Illustration of the quorum-based location management.

In a comparatively sparse network, rows and columns will be more likely formed in a diagonal or zigzag way, not vertically or horizontally as desired. Thus the probability of intersection will decrease as the density decreases. To increase the reliability of quorum intersection, each 'column' and 'row' can be expanded to a thicker quorum. Face routing on the perimeter of the network can be added as well, which will be discussed specifically in the following subsection, to make sure the intersection between read and write quorums exists. Figure 2 (all data are acquired from [22]) shows the success rate and flooding rate (number of transmissions divided by n) for quorum-based schemes for $n=100$ nodes in the network, respectively. The thickness of each column (p) and row (s) is varied from 1 to 2. The average number of neighbors of each node (k) is varied from 4 to 12. As we can see, a quorum-based scheme can achieve high success rate with low energy cost. It is an energy efficient method to deal with the transaction of data accessing.

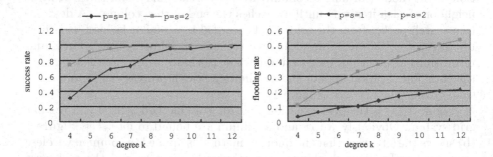

Fig. 2. Performance of the quorum method.

The quorum method has another advantage when all networks move dynamically together in a given direction, such as a rescue team or army. Because the correlation among nodes within each quorum is almost stable, less traffic is needed to maintain neighbor information than other methods.

3 Information Dissemination

WSNs aim at disseminating information to querying nodes as soon as possible. Since WSNs are designed in a distributed fashion, sensors have to make decisions based on its local information. They have no idea about which node will ask to consume produced information in the future. Obviously, if all recently sensed data are broadcasted throughout the whole network, all consumers are sure to get one copy. However, this will cause energy waste. Alternately, more efficient quorums should be selected to cut down overhead while maintaining high quality performance of both updates and requests.

Generally, the sensing scopes by different nodes are more likely to overlap due to the unattended nature of sensor infrastructure, and the sensed information is much larger in volume. There is no need to refresh each piece of integral produced information to others every time. This is different from location service. Therefore negotiation can be combined with. By negotiation, integral data are updated in the source (sensed sensor) only. A meta description about the data regarded as advertisement is disseminated to its write quorum. Later, when destination search is transmitted within a read quorum, the rendezvous can help match the request with recorded advertisements. With the location provided in advertisement, request packets can correctly reach the source. Finally, the complete information can be obtained from the source. Negotiation helps reduce the traffic in disseminating redundant or duplicate data.

3.1 Traditional Protocols

There are many previous protocols to solve this information dissemination problem. The simplest one is by flooding. Such a straightforward protocol is stateless and it disseminates information quickly in a network. However, it incurs heavy cost and a message implosion problem.

To overcome the deficiencies of the classic flooding, Heinzelman et al [23] proposed a family of adaptive protocols for information dissemination in WSNs, called Sensor Protocols for Information via Negotiation (SPIN). They introduced an important mechanism of negotiation. Meta-data that describes the observed data are broadcast to neighbors through advertisement (ADV). Negotiation helps ensure that only useful information is transmitted so as to save energy.

SPIN is an event-driven method, which pushes new data to the network regardless of whether the data will be consumed. Another important data-centric routing, called directed diffusion [24], was proposed to diffuse data queries in an on-demand fashion. An interest message is broadcasted by a sink node through its neighbors when it needs to access data. The sink node then starts to report back after receiving such an interest message.

The common disadvantage of these three typical protocols is that each node is required to play a role in every transaction of data accessing, joining either the write quorum or the read quorum. Lots of problems exist due to the large amount of traffic among nodes.

Gossiping [25] is an alternative to the classic flooding that avoids the imploding problem and achieves energy efficiency through randomization [26], [27]. However, it disseminates information slowly and cannot even guarantee the eventual delivery of the data to querying nodes.

3.2 Quorum-Based Method

In [28], the authors discuss a distributed processing system of WSNs that provides distributed information services on sensed data efficiently. In such a system each sensor node operates autonomously with no central node of control in the network. Each node can be a data source (producing data) as well as a data sink (consuming data). In such an environment, the system is robust and fault tolerant. It can continue to function properly in the presence of failures of individual sensor nodes.

A. Quorum-Based Method Description

Specifically, the quorum method is used in conjunction with a negotiation mechanism that was first introduced in SPIN.

Transmission of ADV message -When a node s has sensed new data, it broadcasts an ADV to its neighbors in northward and southward directions. As for the northward direction, the neighbor with the largest y-coordinate will broadcast the message further to its neighbors. The ADV is propagated northward hop-by-hop until it reaches the node at the north boundary of the network. At the same time, the same operation is taken to propagate the ADV in the southward direction. Figure 3 illustrates the transmission of ADV/REQ, where s is the source node, t the querying node and u the rendezvous node.

Transmission of REQ message -When a node intends to acquire the data that it is interested in, it broadcasts a REQ to its neighbors. Similarly to ADV propagation, the REQ is propagated in both eastward and westward directions until it reaches the west and east boundaries. Figure 3(a) also illustrates the propagation of the REQ. The most important fact is that when the row and column intersect, some nodes (in the case of Figure 3(a), node u and two other nodes in the small square) must have received both ADV and REQ, which are rendezvous nodes.

Transmission of DATA message -The first rendezvous, in which a pair of ADV and REQ matches, continues to send the REQ to the source node along the route where the matched ADV was transmitted. Upon receiving the REQ, the source node transmits DATA message to the querying node along the same route as the REQ. This can avoid extra routing for DATA messages, which could save significant routing overhead in sensor networks. An alternative method used after ADV and REQ are matched is geometric routing, such as Greedy Perimeter Stateless Routing (GPSR) [29], Geometric Adaptive Face Routing (GOAFR) [30], or Greedy-Face-Greedy (GFG) [31]. Such geometric routing will help build the shortest path between source node and querying node.

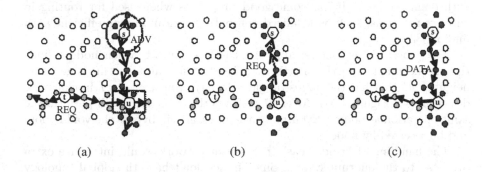

(a)   (b)   (c)

Fig. 3. Illustration of the quorum-based information dissemination.

Note that there is no need of ordering ADV and REQ for the matched data. Arrived messages will be stored for future matching until expiration time is reached.

In this scheme, the quorum system is constructed in a similar way as it is applied to location service. The difference is that the negotiation message, ADV, is forwarded to the write quorum, while new data only updates in the sensing node. ADV contains description information, which is much shorter than complete data. Thus write and read operations take much less consumption than the previous quorum method without negotiation. They achieve further energy efficiency.

B. Recovery Scheme

However, forming quorums only by row and column is not sufficient for their intersection. There are a couple of technical problems that should be addressed.

Now, suppose that a node v receives an ADV from node w that should be forwarded northward, but all its neighbors have smaller y-coordinates than itself. In this case Figure 4(a), the ADV reaches a local maximum with respect to the direction to the north (i.e., a node without any better neighbors). This situation will occur when the deployment of sensor nodes has some "void areas" (i.e., the small areas that do not have any sensor nodes).

This failure of further forwarding is due to the inherence of greedy algorithms. Greedy algorithms work in phases. In each phase, a decision is made that appears to be the best, without regard for future consequences. There are three basic greedy algorithms, known as: DIR [13], [14], [30], GEDIR [34], [35] and MFR [36].

In order to direct the message to leave out of the local maximum v, the protocol should execute a recovery scheme. So it applies the right-hand rule of face routing [30] on the Gabriel graph [32]. The Gabriel graph is a long-known planar graph that contains edges between nodes u and v if and only if no other nodes are located within the circle centered in the middle of edge (u,v) and with diameter $\|uv\|$. It has some good properties when used for routing in wireless networks, such as localized computing and an energy efficient path finding [33].

The process is as follows: applying the face routing, when node v finds that no neighbor is further north than itself, it forwards the message to its neighbor $v1$ that has the largest angle α formed from wv to $vv1$ in clockwise direction (see Figure 4(a)). After $v1$ receives the message, it will perform the same operation as node v. Eventually, the message will bypass the void region, and be received by node u.

The handling of "void areas" in a sensor network would introduce extra overhead to the quorum system. Since nodes don't have the global topology of the entire network, the message received by the nodes truly located on the boundary of the network will be propagated along the boundary until it traverses back to either node v as shown in Figure 4(b), or meets some node at its traversed route as shown in Figure 4(c). In either case, the message travels a lot of unnecessary distance. However, this overhead is inevitable if the case of "void areas" has to be handled.

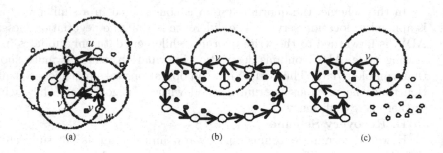

(a)   (b)   (c)

Fig. 4. Protocol Implementation.

C. Performance Analysis of Quorum System

Authors in [28] also studied the efficiency of the quorum method through some mathematical analysis in two special network topologies, the $(m \times m)$-grid and $(m \times m)$-hexagonal grid. Both topologies are very popular in wireless communications, where many ad hoc networks or randomly deployed sensor

networks can be approximated by grid or hexagonal topologies. Two performance metrics are evaluated: 1) The number of nodes that are required to
forward an ADV/REQ, denoted by f_Q; 2) The hop counts of the route between the source node and querying node, denoted by h_Q. The hop counts
indicate the distance data would travel. Each node in the network is supposed
to have the same independent possibility to disseminate and inquire about
the information.

i. Numbers of Forwarding Nodes

We first consider the case where the network graph is an $(m \times m)$-grid, and
for easy presentation, let m=2k+1.

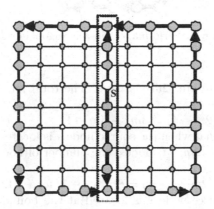

Fig. 5. Performances in a grid.

Theorem 3.1 *The expected value of f_Q is $E[f_Q] < 5m$.*

Proof. The message is transmitted to both north and south directions in parallel and stops after traversing along the boundary under non-duplicated face
routing (Figure 5). It is easy to find that when the source node s is located
inside the grid, the number of nodes required to forward the message is

$f_Q = (2k - 2) + 2(2k - 1) + 2(2k + 1) = 10k - 2$.

When the source node s is located at the boundary of the grid, the number
required is

$f_Q = 2(2k - 1) + 2(2k + 1) - 1 = 8k - 1$.

Therefore, we have

$E[f_Q] = \frac{(2k-1)^2}{m^2}(10k - 2) + \frac{8k}{m^2}(8k - 1) < 5m$.

The proof is then finished.

We now consider the case where the network graph is an $(m \times m)$ hexagonal
grid.

Theorem 3.2 *The expected value of f_Q is $E[f_Q] < 68m/9$.*

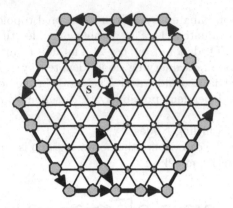

Fig. 6. Performances in a hexagonal grid.

Proof. Note that there are $(2m-1)$ rows. The total number of nodes in the network is (Figure 6):

$$\sum_{i=2}^{m}(2m-i) + (2m-1) = 3m^2 - 3m + 1.$$

It is easy to find that when the source node s is located inside the grid and at the column having $(2m-i)$ nodes, the number of nodes that are required to forward the message is

$$f_Q = 6(m-1) + (2m-i-1) = 8m - i - 7, \text{ for } i = 1, 2, \ldots, m;$$

and when the source node s is located at the boundary of the grid, the number required is $f_Q = 6m - 7$. Thus we have

$$E[f_Q] = \tfrac{1}{3m^2-3m+1}[6(m-1)(6m-7)$$
$$+2\sum_{i=1}^{m-1}(2m-i-2)(8m-i-7) - (2m-3)(8m-8)] < 68m/9.$$

The proof is then finished.

From the above theorems, we can see that the quorum-based protocol needs only $O(\sqrt{n})$ nodes to forward messages in grids, where n is the total number of nodes inside the network. They achieve significant energy savings when compared with the classic flooding, which requires $O(n)$ nodes.

ii. Hop Counts of Generated Paths

Similarly, let's first consider the case where the network graph is the $(m \times m)$-grid (Figure 5), and for the easy presentation, let m=2k+1.

Theorem 3.3 *The expected value of h_Q is $E[h_Q] < 4m/3$.*

Proof. Clearly, there are a total of $m^2(m^2-1)/2$ possible pairs of source and querying nodes. Note that given any, the quorum-based protocol produces a shortest path between them. Let $f(m)$ be the sum of hop counts of the shortest paths between all node pairs in an $(m \times m)$-grid. By solving a set of six linear equations, we can obtain

$$f(m) = (2m^5 - 16m^4 + 94m^3 - 620m^2 + 1404m - 864)/3.$$

Therefore, we have $E[h_Q] = 2f(m)/m^2(m^2-1) < 4m/3$.

The proof is then finished.

Now consider the case where the network graph is an $(m \times m)$ hexagonal grid (Figure 6). Using the same analysis method of **Theorem 3**, we can prove the following theorem.

Theorem 3.4 *The expected value of h_Q is $E[h_Q] < 41m/45$.*

Proof. Clearly, there are a total of $3m(m-1)(3m^2 - 3m + 1)/2$ possible pairs of source and querying nodes. f(m) is defined as above. We then can obtain
$f(m) = m(82m^4 - 205m^3 + 200m^2 - 95m - 18)/20$.
Therefore we have $E[h_Q] < 41m/45$.
The proof is then finished.

3.3 Other Quorum Methods

Aydin and Shen [37] proposed a match-making method in ad hoc and WSNs for producers and consumers to forward their ADV/SUB without flooding (SUB for data SUBscription, which is similar to REQ). The quorum system is constructed in a different way. Each ADV and SUB spreads along four main sections (east, west, north and south) as defined by a threshold angle. The size of each quorum is related to the density of networks and the threshold angle. In fact, this match-making method only performs well when the network is dense enough or source and destination nodes are close to each other.

Figure 7 (from [28]) compares the success rate and forwarding rate (number of forwarding nodes divided by n) for quorum-based and match-making methods for n=100 nodes in the network, respectively. The transmission radius of node varies from 13 to 40. According to the comparison, the quorum based scheme can achieve a much higher success rate and requires about 30 percent of its nodes to forward messages. It is an energy efficient method to deal with data accessing transactions. Although the match-making protocol requires fewer nodes to forward packets, it is at the sacrifice of a much lower success rate.

4 Object Tracking

Object tracking is one of the most important applications of WSNs in our society, especially for military usage. Assume existence of a battlefield, within which some tanks and soldiers are patrolling around. Thousands of sensor nodes are deployed in an unattended fashion. They should collect information about intruders and sound alarms to the military in good time. On one hand, once sensor nodes detect a new object moving into its surveillant scope, they should generate robust and reliable sensing reports, and forward the report quickly and efficiently to the multiple data sinks (moving soldiers or static command centers) that have interest in it [38]. Alternately, the data report

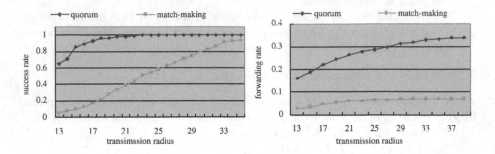

Fig. 7. Quorum method vs Match-making method.

can be saved locally waiting for queries from other nodes [39]. On the other hand, soldiers need the up-to-date location information of other tanks or soldiers from time to time. They should send their request to the appropriate sensors that can provide desired information or initiate detection as soon as possible. Note that moving objects are free to traverse around within a large area. Such a tracking requires non-local collaboration among sensors. It can reduce the bandwidth consumption thus preserve the energy efficiency, and alleviate the risk of individual node/link failures. In addition, adding negotiation before integral data transmission helps reduce redundant and duplicate data dissemination. Therefore, object tracking combines the problems existing in location service and information dissemination and can be dealt with by similar methods.

4.1 Traditional Protocols

If we apply traditional methods to object tracking, some similar deficiencies appear as in location service and information dissemination. For example under SPIN [23] or Directed Diffusion [24], all nodes in the network (i.e. n) are required to participate in data accessing. This is very costly especially when the frequency of event occurrence and interest is not equivalent. In addition, both of them use some sort of flooding which suffers many drawbacks in wireless networks, such as excessive message redundancy, contention, collision [40], and unreliability [41].

To reduce the energy cost in disseminating queries through all nodes, like Directed Diffusion, authors in [42] introduce a hierarchical data querying method. Each registration points, leaders of data source and sensor nodes meeting multi-resolution needs construct a hierarchy of three levels. New detections are updated locally, while advertisements are registered to registration points. Any requests only need to traverse down the hierarchy to find answers. Simulation shows it outperforms the directed diffusion by achieving higher delivery rate with lower energy cost.

More recently, many researches concentrate on dynamic sensor collaboration and aggregation with constrained energy. Data are aggregated to a certain leader or root, on which full update operation is carried out. Zhao et al. [43], [44], [45] apply information driven approaches to deal with this issue. A sensor node/leader is selected to detect the object, and the object moves, the responsibility of tracking will be handed off to another node/leader according to some criterion measuring information gain. Cerpa et al. [46] suggested collaborating those multiple sensor nodes surrounding the object so that the data provided could be more complete, reliable and accurate. Zhang et al. in [47] proposed a dynamic convoy tree-based collaboration (DCTC) framework for object tracking. Sensor nodes surrounding the moving object will construct an initial convoy tree. The root will be the final recipient of reports from each node and will process them using certain algorithms [48], [49] to generate a consolidated sensing report that will be saved locally, waiting for query, or sent to the sinks. An improvement on selecting a new root to replace the old one as an object moves far away is introduced in [50].

4.2 Quorum-Based Method

A. Method Description

To further improve the performance of write and read operation, we can also apply a quorum-based method to track moving objects. The basic idea is that when any sensor node has detected e.g., a new tank, it updates this event locally, and advertises this information by propagating an ADV in both north and south directions until reaching the north and south boundaries of the network, to form a write quorum; and when any soldier needs to access some information (this node is called a querying node), it sends out certain REQ in both east and west directions. Nodes on this east-west direction are collected as a read quorum. The REQ is bound to meet corresponding ADV at a rendezvous node if the DATA was advertised before. This rendezvous node will provide the matched description about DATA, and forward the REQ to the sensing node along the route that was traversed by ADV before. After correctly arriving at the sensing node, the integral data of the event will be read and forwarded to the soldier along the reverse route that the REQ traversed. On the whole, the network has been divided conceptually into different rows and columns. By using this quorum system, the message cost for new data dissemination is greatly reduced to $O(\sqrt{n})$.

Consider the situation, three tanks move into the sensing region of node A, B, and C, respectively (see Figure 8). Each of these nodes broadcast the advertisement on detecting tanks in north-south directions (formed by black nodes), which form three columns with certain thickness. Thus every node in each column takes a record of the advertisement. Later on, when a soldier needs to take control of the overall situation on the battlefield, he sends out a request entering the sensor network at node S. This request will be transmitted in the east-west direction (formed by gray nodes). For example, he may simply ask: "Where is the tank, whose ID is 5?" Obviously, there are three different groups of rendezvous nodes that havevreceived both request and new advertisement, respectively. They will take a comparison and only the one that has the matched ADV will respond and continue to forward the REQ towards the sensing source. In another case the soldier may ask: "How many tanks are there in the battlefield at the time 4:00 pm?" As a result, none of the single rendezvous nodes can reply with a complete answer. Collaboration among the groups is needed. Rendezvous nodes can combine receiving replies with its own data, and proceed with aggregation before sending out further replies . This will help reduce bandwidth consumption. Alternately, raw data are directly forwarded to the soldier to minimize delay.

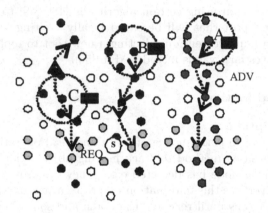

Fig. 8. Illustration of the quorum-based object tracking.

Similarly, if one tank moves from place A to place C via place B (Figure 8), the quorum based method still works well. For example, the soldier requires: "Report back the location of the tank every 30 seconds." Sensor nodes will disseminate information detection whenever a new tank moves into its range. But rendezvous nodes in the row will take an aggregation, and only reply with the location of the tank every 30 seconds. Alternately, a mechanism adjusting the frequency of new location information dissemination is added, so that the number of columns is limited.

B. Frequency Consideration

Recall that due to the "void areas" mentioned in Subsection 3.2.2, face routing should be added to guarantee that any update information could arrive at an extreme point of the network. However, the negative affect is that nodes on the perimeter of a network will also execute face routing due to its lack of global information. Specifically, a write quorum should collect nodes on a "column" as well as on a face of local maxima to perform updates, so that read quorum collecting nodes on a "row" as well as on the face are sure to get current data.

However, the frequency of new events detected by sensors and that of data really needed by a soldier is not equivalent most of the time. The new event sensed by a node is distributed in a large domain, while sometimes soldiers are really interested in the data within some specific area. As a result, collecting nodes in such a symmetrical way for both write and read quorums will cost considerable system overhead, although only advertisement instead of complete DATA is updated through write quorums by negotiation. The way to reduce this consumption is let only one of the quorums execute face routing while the other one will stop forwarding packets when they arrive at local maxima. This mechanism should combine with the frequency of new event advertisement and soldier requests. The more frequent an operation, the fewer nodes the corresponding quorum must collect.

Thus, the quorum-based method can be enhanced by adding a minor modification as follow: if sensors are assigned to disseminate whenever new information is detected, then ADV will be only propagated to the end of each "column". It will stop if no further neighbor in the given direction can be found. On the other hand, REQ have to finish the whole quorum. It is first forwarded along the east and west directions, then bypasses the void area if any, and finally stops after traversing the outer boundary of the network. On the contrary, if request is more frequent than detection, we should let the traversal of REQ be shorter than that of ADV.

Note that there is a tradeoff between system overhead and data delivery rate. Decreasing nodes in constructing either quorum will reduce the possibility of successful intersection. Thickness of each "column", "row", and "boundary" can be increased to reduce delay and increase reliability. In addition, sensor nodes often detach from the original quorum it resided in without warning due to mobility or depletion of energy. If those nodes that were supposed to be in the intersected places are unavailable, the required information will not be accessible. Therefore, a mechanism is needed to transfer the information database to other nodes remaining in or moving into the same places, which substitutes as the new database. Thus nodes in the quorums can transmit a database with information being picked up by all neighboring nodes when necessary.

4.3 Other Quorum-Based Protocols

In a recent work, Liu et al [51] proposed a comb-needle query support model, which forms different quorum systems (Figure 9). Each sensor node advertises its DATA message to form a vertical needle with length $2l$ (write quorum). A querying node disseminates its REQ to form a vertical comb with gap s between the teeth (read quorum). When $s \leq 2l$, the REQ message is bound to meet the DATA message. The advantage is that parameters s and l can be adjusted depending on frequencies of events and queries in the system, dynamically. However, in an irregular network, the REQ messages can hardly follow a comb shape, and the comb may miss the needle (i.e., the success rate of an REQ finding its matched data is poor). This problem will be even more severe in the presence of "void areas" in the network.

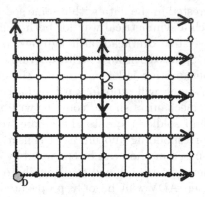

Fig. 9. Comb-needle model.

5 Conclusion

In this chapter, we tried to present an overview of the quorum method applied to three main problems in wireless networks. They are: location service, information dissemination and object tracking. Location service is the general obstacle for distributed networks, since the current location of a destination node should be known before any data can be delivered correctly. The main goal of wireless sensor networks is to provide required and latest data sensed at a source node to any other nodes that are interested in the data. Therefore, the central issue that needs to be addressed is to develop energy efficient protocols to disseminate information. Object tracking in a military battlefield situation is one of the most important applications of sensor networks. It is a combination of the other two problems and can be dealt with by similar methods.

The challenge of these problems is that there is no central control node. Source nodes can only disseminate data to the networks from their local information, and querying nodes have to forward requests to nodes that can provide them with desired data or initiate detection as soon as possible. Quorum methods are designed to facilitate these operations. A subset of nodes is collected to form a write quorum, in which update operations take place.

A potential different subset of nodes is collected to form a read quorum, so that retrieval processes are executed. The availability of this quorum method lies in that each quorum proceed with enough nodes to make sure intersection between write and read quorums exists.

Traditional protocols solving these problems prepare each node to participate in data accessing, either in forming write quorums or read quorums. The system overhead is $O(n)$. Later on, networks can be divided into several hierarchies. One or more nodes in each level are selected to be members of each quorum. Thus the size of quorum becomes proportional to the height of the hierarchy. Another significant improvement in reducing system overhead is that by conceptually and evenly dividing the networks into rows and columns, the size of quorums has decreased to $O(\sqrt{n})$. Moreover, negotiation and frequency control can be combined in constructing quorum systems. Negotiation helps avoid redundant data dissemination. Selecting nodes to form quorums according to the frequency of operation occurrence improves the performance of quorums even more.

Quorum methodology is one sort of efficient way to deal with transaction of data accessing. A wireless sensor network can be treated as a database system. The performance of WSN can be improved by appropriately adjusting the parameters of the quorum method. As technology has developed and knowledge has accumulated, WSN has been applied to many applications for human beings. More challenging work is coming.

References

1. Gifford, D.K.(1979). Weighted voting for replicated data, *in Proceedings 7th Symposium on Operating Systems Principles, ACM*, pp.150–62.
2. G. Coulouris, J. Dollimore, T. Kindberg, Distributed systems: concepts and design, *3rd edition*, ISBN 0-201-61918-0.
3. M. Maekawa, A $n^{1/2}$ algorithm for mutual exclusion in decentralized systems, *ACM Transactions in Computer Systems*, 14-159, May 1985.
4. D. Culler, D. Estrin, and M. Srivastava, Overview of sensor networks, *Computer*, Vol. 37, No. 8, 2004, pp. 41–49.
5. K. Martinez, J. K. Hart, and R. Ong, Sensor network applications, *Computer*, Vol. 37, No. 8, 2004, pp. 50–56.
6. M. Mauve, J. Widmer, and H. Hartenstein, A survey on position-based routing in mobile ad hoc networks, *IEEE Network*, vol.15, no.6, 2001.
7. R. Prakash, Z. Haas, M. Singhal, Load-balanced location management for cellular mobile systems using quorums and dynamic hashing, *ACM/Baltzer Wireless Networks (WINET) Journal*, Volume 7, Number 5, Pages 497-512, September 2001.
8. G. Krishnamurthi, M. Azizoglu and A. K. Somani, Optimal location management algorithms for mobile networks, *Proc. 4th Annual ACM/IEEE Int. Conf. on Mobile Computing and Networking MOBICOM'98*, 223-232,1998.
9. A. Bar-Noy and I. Kessler and M. Sidi, Mobile users: to update or not to update? *in Proceedings of IEEE INFOCOM (1994)*, pp. 570–576.

10. B. Awerbuch and D. Peleg, Online tracking of mobile users, *Journal of the Association for Computing Machinery 42(5)*, (September 1995) 1021-1058.

11. J. Z. Wang, A fully distributed location registration strategy for universal personal communication systems, *IEEE Journal on Selected Areas in Communications 11*, (August 1993) 850-860.

12. S.Sesay, Z. Yang and J. H, A survey on mobile ad hoc wireless network, *Information Technology Journal 3(2)*, :168-175, 2004 ISSN 1682-6027.

13. S. Basagni, I. Chlamtac, V. R. Syrotiuk, and B. A. Woodward, A distance routing effect algorithm for mobility (DREAM), *MOBICOM 98*, Dallas Texas USA.

14. Y.-B. Ko and N. H. Vaidya, Location-aided routing (LAR) in mobile ad hoc networks, *ACM/Baltzer WINET J.*, vol. 6, no. 4, 2000, pp. 307–21.

15. S. M. Das, H. Pucha and Y. C. Hu, Performance comparison of scalable location services for geographic ad hoc routing, *IEEE INFOCOM*, 2005.

16. J. Li, J. Jannotti D. S. J. D. Couto, D. R. Karger, and R. Morris, A scalable location service for geographic ad hoc routing, *in Proc. of ACM MobiCom*, August 2000.

17. Y. Xue, B. Li, and K. Nahrstedt, A scalable location management scheme in mobile ad hoc networks, *in Proc. of IEEE LCN*, November 2001.

18. I. Stojmenovic, Home region based location updates and destination search schemes in ad hoc wireless networks, SITE, University of Ottawa, *Tech. Rep. TR-99-10*, September 1999.

19. S. Giordano and M. Hami, Mobility management: the virtual home region, *EPFL, Tech. Rep. SSC/037*, October 1999.

20. S. -C. M. Woo and S. Singh, Scalable routing protocol for ad hoc networks, *Wireless Networks*, vol.7, no. 5, pp. 513–529, 2001.

21. Z. J. Haas and B. Liang, Ad hoc mobility management with uniform quorum systems, *IEEE/ACM Transactions on Netwoking*, vol.7, no.2, pp.228–240, April 1999.

22. I. Stojmenovic, A scalable quorum based location update scheme for routing in ad hoc wireless networks, SITE, University of Ottawa, *Tech. Rep. TR-99-09*, September1999.

23. W. R. Heinzelman, J. Kulit, and H. Balakrishnan, Adaptive protocols for information dissemination in wireless sensor networks, *The 5th ACM/IEEE Annual International Conference on Mobile Computing and Networking (MOBICOM)*, Seattle, WA, Aug 1999.

24. C. Intanagonwiwat, R. Govindan, and D. Estrin, Directed diffusion: a scalable and robust communication paradigm for sensor networks, *The 6th Annual ACM/IEEE International Conference on Mobile Computing and Networking (MOBICOM)*, Boston, MA, Aug 2000.

25. S. M. Hedetniemi, S. T. Hedetniemi, and A. L. Liestman, A survey of gossiping and broadcasting in communication networks, *Networks*, Vol. 18, No. 4, pp. 319–349, 1988.

26. B. S. Chlebus, Randomized communication in radio networks, *Handbook of Randomized Computing*, Vol.1-2, pp. 401–456, Kluwer Academic Publishers, Dordrecht, 2001.

27. L. Orecchia, A. Panconesi, C. Petrioli, and A. Vitaletti, Localized techniques for broadcasting in wireless sensor networks, *ACM DIALM-PODC Workshop at MOBICOM*, Philadelphia, PA, 2004.

28. D. Liu, X. Hu, and X. Jia, Energy efficient information dissemination protocols by negotiation for wireless sensor networks, *submitted to Computer Communications*.

29. B. Karp and H. T. Hung, GPSR: greedy perimeter stateless routing for wireless networks, *The 6th Annual ACM/IEEE International Conference on Mobile Computing and Networking (MOBICOM)*, Boston, MA, Aug 2000.

30. E. Kranakis, H. Singh, and J. Urrutia, Compass routing on geometric networks, *The 11th Canadian Conference on Computational Geometry (CCCG)*, Vancouver, Canada, Aug 1999.

31. P. Bose, P. Morin, I. Stojmenovic, and J. Urrutia, Routing With guaranteed delivery in ad hoc wireless networks, *Wireless Networks*, Vol. 7, pp. 609–616, 2001.

32. K. Gabriel and R. Sokal, A new statistical approach to geographic variation analysis, *Systematic Zoology*, Vol. 18, pp. 259–278, 1969.

33. F. Kuhn, R. Wattenhofer, Y. Zhang, and A. Zollinger, Geometric ad-hoc routing: of theory and practice, *The 22nd ACM International Symposium on the Principles of Distributed Computing (PODC)*, Boston, MA, July 2003.

34. G.G. Finn, Routing and addressing problems in large metropolitan-scale internetworks, *ISI Research Report ISU/RR-87-180*, March 1987.

35. I. Stojmenovic and X. Lin, Loop-free hybrid single-path/flooding routing algorithms with guaranteed delivery for wireless networks, *IEEE Transactions on Parallel and Distributed Systems*, Vol. 12, No. 10, October 2001, 1023-1032.

36. H. Takagi and L. Kleinrock, Optimal transmission ranges for randomly distributed packet radio terminals, *IEEE Trans. on Communications*, 32, 3, 1984, 246-257.

37. K. Martinez I. Aydin and C. C. Shen, Facilitating match-making service in ad hoc and sensor networks using pseudo quorum, *The 11th IEEE International Conference Computer Communication Networks (ICCCN)*, Miami, Florida, Oct 2002.

38. F. Ye, H. Luo, J. Cheng, S. Lu, and L. Zhang, A two-tier data dissemination model for large-scale wireless sensor networks, *ACM MOBICOM'02*, pp. 148–159, September 2002.

39. S. Ratnasamy, B. Karp, S. Shenker, D. Estrin, R. Govindan, L. Yin and F. Yu, Data-centric storage in sensornets with GHT, a geographic hash table, *Mobile Networks and Applications*, Vol. 8, 2003, pp.427–442.

40. S. Y. Ni, Y. C. Tseng, Y. S. Chen and J. P. Sheu, The broadcast storm problem in a mobile ad hoc network, *5th annual International Conference on Mobile Computing and Networking (MobiCom'99)*, Seattle, Washington, Aug. 15-20 1999.

41. P. Sinha, R. Sivakumar and V. Bharghavan, Enhancing ad hoc routing with dynamic virtual infrastructures, *IEEE INFOCOM 2001*, pp. 1763–1772.

42. J. Chen, Y. Guan, and U. Pooch, An efficient data dissemination method in wireless sensor networks, *IEEE INFOCOM 2004*.

43. J. Liu, J. Liu, L. Reich, P. Cheung, and F. Zhao, Distributed group management for track initiation and maintenance in target localization applications, *2nd Workshop on Information Processing in Sensor Networks (IPSN)*, April 2003.

44. F. Zhao, J. Shin and J. Reich, Information-driven dynamic sensor collaboration for tracking applications, *IEEE Signal Processing Magazine*, pp.68–77, March 2002.

45. M. Chu, H. Haussecker and F. Zhao, Scalable information-driven sensor querying and routing for ad hoc heterogeneous sensor networks, *International Journal of High Performance Computing Applications*, 2002.
46. A. Cerpa, J. Elson, M. Hamilton, and J. Zhao, Habitat monitoring: application driver for wireless communications technology, *First ACM SIGCOMM Workshop on Data Communications in Latin America and the Caribbean*, April 2001.
47. W. Zhang, and G. Cao, DCTC: dynamic convoy tree-based collaboration for target tracking in sensor networks, *IEEE Transactions on Wireless Communication*, http://www.cse.psu.edu/ gcao..
48. B. Brooks, C. Griffin and D. Friedlander, Self-organized distributed sensor network entity tracking, *International Journal of High Performance Computing Applications*, Special Issue on Sensor Networks, 2002.
49. D. Li, K. Wong, Y. Hu and A. Sayeed, Detection, classification and tracking of targets in distributed sensor networks, *IEEE, Signal Processing Magazine*, pp. 17–29, March 2002.
50. W. Zhang, and G. Cao, Optimizing tree reconfiguration for mobile target tracking in sensor networks, *IEEE INFOCOM*, March, 2004.
51. X. Liu, Q. Huang, and Y Zhang, Combs, needles, haystacks: balancing push and pull for discovery in large-scale sensor networks, *The 2nd ACM Conference on Embedded Networked Sensor Systems*, (SenSys), Baltimore, Maryland, Nov 2004.

Chapter 11
Maximizing the Lifetime of an Always-On Wireless Sensor Network Application: A Case Study

Santosh Kumar[1], Anish Arora[2], and Ten H. Lai[2]

[1] Department of Computer Science
The University of Memphis, Memphis, TN 38152
santosh.kumar@memphis.edu
[2] Department of Computer Science and Engineering
The Ohio State University, Columbus, OH 43210
{anish, lai}@cse.ohio-state.edu

1 Introduction

Most applications of wireless sensor networks (WSNs) [2, 4, 10, 19, 21, 23, 24] require long term (several months or even years of) unattended operation from their networks. But, significant challenges still remain in achieving long-term unattended operation from large-scale wireless sensor networks. Critical among those are the problems of power management. An important distinction between wireless sensor networks and most existing systems is the tremendous gap between the energy available to a sensor node and that required for its long-term unattended operation. A typical sensor node such as ones from the Mica family [8, 9] can last 3–5 days on a pair of AA batteries in its fully active mode. In real life applications, though, we would like a sensor network (comprised of these motes) to last at least a few months. The story is not very different with other platforms. The question then is: How can we fill this huge energy gap? The approaches and techniques applied to fill this energy gap are collectively referred to as *Power Management* in wireless sensor networks.

Always-On and Always-off Applications of WSN: Applications of WSNs are broadly divided into two categories — *always-on* and *always-off*. In an always-on application, it is necessary to monitor the environment continuously because the events of interest can occur at any time. In most of these applications, it is also required to notify a base station of an event as soon as it is observed so that retaliatory actions (or preventive measures) can be taken quickly. Examples of such applications are intrusion detection [2], where intruders can breach a protected region any time, shooter localization [23], where shooting by a sniper can occur anytime, and radiation detection [4],

259

where terrorists can explode a simple radiological dispersion device at any time.

In an always-off application, it is not necessary to monitor the environment continuously; periodic monitoring is enough because the environment does not change very abruptly. Examples of such applications are habitat monitoring [21], where the environment of a bird nest does not change abruptly, and the monitoring of subgalacial bed formation [19], where the glaciers do not change their position or temperature abruptly.

Classification of Power Management Approaches: An application faces the problem of power management if the active life of the sensor nodes comprising a WSN is less than the desired life of the network. In such a case, we need to find ways to extend the lifetime of the network. We divide the approaches for doing so in two major categories:

- *Fine-Grained Power Management:* This approach extends the active lifetime of individual sensor nodes by exploiting redundancy already existing in the network. For example, in an always-off application it is not necessary to sample the environment continuously. So, all the sensor nodes can be put to sleep, to wake up only periodically for sampling the environment. As another example, in an always-on application, selected components of sensor nodes (such as the radio) can be put to sleep to be woken up either on demand or periodically, while still meeting the monitoring and notification requirements of the application. Fine-grained power management schemes do not require deploying any more sensor nodes than are absolutely necessary to meet the monitoring requirements of an application.
- *Coarse-grained Power Management:* In this approach, more sensor nodes are assumed to be deployed than are necessary to meet the monitoring and notification requirements of an application. The redundancy in the number of sensor nodes is then exploited to increase the network lifetime. Time is divided into intervals and in each interval, only that many sensor nodes are active as are necessary to provide the desired level of monitoring. The redundant nodes are put into deep sleep by putting all their components (the processor, the radio, and all the sensors) to sleep. The nodes that remain active are sometimes called *sentries* [15].

These two approaches are complementary in the sense that we can first use fine-grained power management schemes to extend the active lifetime of individual sensor nodes by the maximum extent possible. If this extended active lifetime of the sensor nodes still falls short of the desired lifetime of the network, coarse-grained power management schemes can be used to extend the network lifetime further. Another alternative to using coarse-grained power management schemes (which will require deploying redundant sensor nodes) is to deploy redundant batteries per node or to use more expensive but higher capacity batteries. Which alternative to use (deploying redundant sensor nodes or deploying redundant batteries) will require a careful cost-benefit analysis specific to the application and sensor platforms in consideration, and is out of scope for this chapter. But, using fine-grained power management schemes to extend the lifetime of a WSN is basic. It does not require incurring any additional expenditure (due to deploying redundant batteries or deploying redundant nodes). It comes for free.

Applying Fine-grained Power Management Schemes: In several always-off applications, it was possible to extend the network lifetime by more than 10 times by using fine-grained power management schemes alone [19, 21]. In the habitat monitoring application [21], sensor nodes were allowed to sleep for 20 minutes, at the end of which they woke up for 70 seconds, collected data, transmitted it to a gateway, and then went back to sleep. By doing so, it was possible to extend the lifetime of a sensor node from five days to 67 days, a factor of more than 13 times.

It is obvious that the strategy of putting all the sensor nodes to sleep and have them all wake up periodically to sample the environment will not work for always-on applications because of a need to continuously monitor the environment. It has been widely believed that significant lifetime extensions (a factor of 10 or more) for always-on applications can only be achieved by using coarse-grained power management schemes [1, 5, 6, 12, 13, 17, 26, 27] that require deploying more sensor nodes than are absolutely necessary to meet the monitoring and notification requirements of the application. To the best of our knowledge, there have been no studies of how much lifetime extension can be achieved for always-on sensor networks by using fine-grained power management schemes alone.

In this chapter, we address the following question: *How long can an always-on sensor network last if only a minimal number of sensor nodes are deployed so that all the deployed nodes are required to be always active to provide the desired level of monitoring?* We show that an always-on sensor network can also achieve comparable lifetime extensions as an always-off sensor network by using only fine-grained power management schemes. We describe several fine-grained power management schemes (e.g., hierarchical sensing, low power listening [20]), where selected components of a sensor node are put to sleep while still meeting the continuous monitoring and instantaneous notification requirements (notifying a base station of an event as soon as it occurs) of an always-on application. We show by using derivations and concrete numbers the extent of lifetime extensions that can be achieved with these fine-grained power management schemes.

As a case study, we analyze the lifetime of ExScal [2] — a wireless sensor network deployed to detect and classify intruders of different kinds[3]. Our analysis reveals that using low power listening [20] can extend the ExScal lifetime from three days to eight days (Section 4.4). Using hierarchical sensing

---

[3] The ExScal network (consisting of close to 1000 wireless sensor nodes) was deployed on the ground in December 2004 to demonstrate the proof of concept. Incidentally, this was the largest wireless sensor network deployed on the ground till year 2004.

further extends it to 36 days (Section 4.5). If it were possible to eliminate the periodic control messages, the ExScal network could be made to last 48 days, which represents a lifetime extension by 16 times (Section 4.6). Using other schemes such as in-network data aggregation and reduced reprogramming can increase the lifetime of ExScal further and none of these schemes require deploying any more sensor nodes in the network than are absolutely necessary to provide the desired level of monitoring.

After reading this chapter, the readers will be able to assess the suitability of various fine-grained power management approaches for always-on applications of wireless sensor networks. More importantly, our measured data and lifetime analysis will help readers formulate better (i.e., more accurate) models in their research on power management. For example, the assumption that a mote from the Mica family (a popular sensor platform) [7, 14] lasts 3–5 days on a pair of AA batteries if deployed in an always-on sensor network should be changed to 30–50 days. Also, the claim that in-network data aggregation can extend the network lifetime by more than 50% becomes questionable because our analysis reveals that in-network data aggregation can extend the lifetime of ExScal by at most 8.91%.

Organization of the Chapter. In Section 2, we discuss several fine-grained power management schemes that can be used to extend the lifetime of a wireless sensor network deployed for an always-on application. In Section 3, we provide an overview of the ExScal application, the sensor platform used in ExScal, and major factors that affect the network lifetime of ExScal. In Section 4, we analyze the lifetime of ExScal, illustrating the lifetime extensions achievable by using various fine-grained power management schemes. Section 5 concludes the paper.

2 Fine-grained Power Management Schemes

In this section, we discuss some fine-grained power management techniques that can be applied to extend the lifetime of a WSN deployed for an always-on application. All of these schemes exploit some redundancy already existing in the network to extend network lifetime without affecting the quality of service offered by the network.

2.1 Low Power Listening (LPL)

In an always-on application such as ExScal, most of the time there is no communication in the network. However, the radio can not be turned off on all sensor nodes, because as soon as an event occurs, the event notification message should be quickly propagated to a base station using radios on other sensor nodes that sit in the path of the sensor detecting an event and the base station. Therefore, ideally, we would like to have a radio that can wake up from the sleep mode by hearing a transmission from a neighbor so that it can be put to sleep when there is no communication in its neighborhood. Such a radio, called radio-triggered wakeup radio, was proposed in [11]. However, it is not yet available on current sensor platforms.

Low Power Listening (LPL) proposed in [20] is an approximation to the radio-triggered wakeup. It allows a sensor node to put its radio (and the processor) to sleep mode for a certain interval and wake it up periodically to sample the channel. If the radio detects preamble bytes, it stays awake and extracts the entire packet. Otherwise, it returns to sleep. This feature was implemented on the sensor platform used in ExScal.

One downside of using the low power listening feature is that the sender has to send a preamble at least as long as the sleep period of the radio. So, there is a trade-off in choosing the sleep period, as was pointed out in [20]. We will analyze the effect of this trade-off in Section 4. Despite this trade-off, the low power listening feature can significantly extend the lifetime of WSNs deployed for always-on applications because communication is rare (less than 10 packets every minute) in most of them. *In Section 4.4, we show that by using LPL we can extend the lifetime of ExScal by 2.6 times.*

2.2 Hierarchical Sensing

The concept of hierarchical sensing was originally introduced in [9] under the name of energy-quality hierarchy. Here, we provide a more general definition of the concept and identify its defining characteristics so that it can be used in other always-on applications.

In most always-on applications, the environment needs to be monitored continuously. However, keeping all the sensors and the processor continuously active consumes significant energy. For example, in ExScal, if all the sensors and the processor were left continuously active, a sensor node would have lasted less than five days, even if the radio was always turned off. If a sensor can sense the environment without the processor being active, then we can significantly extend the network lifetime by putting the processor to sleep until an event is detected. Further lifetime extensions are possible if the following holds for an always-on application:

- The sensing platform used is intended to detect multiple types of events. (In ExScal, the network is required to detect persons on foot and vehicles.)
- All event types are accompanied by a common simple event. (In ExScal, every intruder is a moving object so that the simple event is the movement.)
- A subset of sensors (called wakeup sensors) can detect the simple event. (In ExScal, PIR sensor detects all moving objects.)

A sensor (or a set of sensors) qualifies as a *wakeup sensor*, if it has the following features:

1. It does not need the processor to be active to perform an event detection. Sampling of the environment, signal processing of the sampled data, and

thresholding (for detecting an abrupt change in the environment due to an event) can be done in the sensor hardware without involving the processor.
2. It has the hardware circuitry to raise an interrupt that can wake up a sleeping processor.
3. It can detect the common simple event. (This feature is necessary because otherwise some events can be missed by the network.)
4. It has the longest sensing range of all the sensors mounted on a sensor node. (Again, this feature is necessary because otherwise some events can be missed by the network.)

A sensor platform is said to have the *Hierarchical Sensing* feature if it has at least one wakeup sensor. If a platform has the hierarchical sensing feature, it can just keep the wakeup sensor active continuously and put the processor and all the other sensors to sleep. In case an event is detected by the wakeup sensor, it will wake up the processor, which will further process the sensor data to determine if a real event has occurred, and if so, it will wake up all the sleeping sensors to detect other properties of the event using different sensing modalities. For example, in ExScal, the wakeup sensor can detect the presence of an intruder and the sleeping sensors can help classify the type of the intruder.

For the hierarchical sensor scheme to work, the choice of wakeup sensor is critical. The wakeup sensor should not wake up the processor very frequently due to false alarms. The best wakeup sensor is the one that draws a small current. For the sleeping sensors, it is important to have a low startup time so that when they are woken up, they do not miss an event. *In Section 4.5, we show that by using hierarchical sensing (with PIR sensor as the wakeup sensor) together with LPL we can extend the lifetime of ExScal by 12 times.*

2.3 Other Fine-grained Power Management Schemes

There are several other fine-grained power management schemes that can be used in an always-on application to extend the network lifetime. Some of these are:

1. **Reducing Periodic Messages:** Reducing periodic control messages can result in significant lifetime extensions. *The lifetime of ExScal can be increased by 31.6% if there were no periodic messages.*
2. **In-Network Data Aggregation:** Aggregating the event detection messages as it flows towards the base station can also extend network lifetime. *In ExScal, using data aggregation can result in a lifetime extension of upto 8.91%.*
3. **Reduced Control Operations:** Reducing the number of control operations such as wireless reprogramming results in further lifetime extensions.
4. **Reduced Actuations:** Actuations such as blinking LEDs and sounding buzzers can consume significant energy. *For example, keeping even one LED continuously active will reduce ExScal's lifetime by more than half.*

We provide the details of calculation on how to analyze the effect of the above schemes on the lifetime of a WSN in Section 4.

Finally, we discuss two more fine-grained power management techniques without analyzing their effects on the lifetime of ExScal.

- **Duty Cycling the Wakeup Sensor:** In some sensors such as the acoustic, it is possible to reduce the energy consumption of this sensor by letting the sensor sleep in between its samplings. In ExScal, an acoustic sensor collected samples at the rate of 4 kHz for 30 ms, after every 300 ms. Since the startup time of the acoustic sensor is less than 1 ms, it can be put to sleep in between its samplings to save energy. After it collects one set of samples, it can be put to sleep for the next 269 ms, at the end of which it will wake up, collect another set of samples for 30 ms and go back to sleep. If its sampling frequency is reduced (so that it sleeps for more than 269 ms in every cycle), in order to conserve even more energy, its sensing range may get reduced. It may still be possible to meet the monitoring requirements of the application with this reduced sensing range. A careful analysis needs to be performed before reducing the sensing range of a sensor in order to ensure that the application requirements with respect to coverage can still be met with the reduced sensing range. If the acoustic sensor was used as a wakeup sensor, significant energy savings could have been achieved with this duty cycling. Unfortunately, duty cycling could not be used to reduce the energy consumption of the PIR sensor (which was the wakeup sensor in ExScal that remained continuously active) because of its high startup time (more than 1 second).

- **Reducing the Transmitter Power Level:** With the radio used in XSM and in motes from the Mica family, the energy consumed in transmission depends on the power level used. Using a lower power level means lower energy consumption at the expense of a reduced transmission range. Using a lower transmission range also means lower interference in the network. On the other hand, using a lower transmission range can result in more hops in a multi-hop network. The reliability of transmitting a packet across multiple hops decreases as the number of hops increases in the path of the packet. Therefore, a careful analysis should be performed before reducing the transmission range to ensure that the connectivity and packet reliability requirements of the application are still met with a reduced transmission range.

There may be more fine-grained approaches to extend the lifetime of a WSN than what we have discussed in this chapter. An application developer should explore all these options before deciding to deploy redundant sensor nodes or redundant batteries in order to get a desired lifetime from the network.

3 The ExScal Application and the XSM Platform

In this section, we provide an overview of the ExScal application [2], an overview of the sensor platform used in ExScal (called XSM) and the major requirements (or features) of ExScal that have a significant impact on its lifetime.

The goal in the ExScal application was to deploy a wireless sensor network over a large region to monitor intrusion activities. The network was required to detect different types of intruders breaching the perimeter of the protected region, classify them into some predetermined categories (e.g., person, soldier, car, tank), and track their trajectories of intrusion. The network was also required to notify the nearest base station of an intrusion event in less than two seconds.

The key issues in ExScal were to minimize the cost of coverage, minimize the power consumption to maximize the network lifetime, provide accurate (i.e., low false alarm rate) and timely (i.e., less than two seconds from the occurrence of the event) detection of intrusion events in the face of unavoidable hardware and software failures, and do all of this with low human involvement.

Minimizing the cost of coverage required minimizing the number of sensor nodes needed (which for our purpose means not deploying any more sensor nodes than are absolutely necessary to meet the monitoring and notification requirements of the application). This, in turn, required deploying nodes in an optimal topology[4]. We refer the readers to [16] for details on the layout of sensor nodes that was used in ExScal. Minimizing the cost of coverage also required finding off-the-shelf sensors with the largest sensing ranges and using radios that provided the largest communication range with the lowest energy consumption, while keeping the cost low.

Accurate and timely detection of intruders was critical to ExScal. Accuracy had priority over timeliness. What good is a network that gives false detections quickly? Therefore, the network was required to have a low false alarm rate. If the detection message does not reach the base station quickly, an intruder may compromise the asset being protected by the sensor network. Therefore, low latency of event notification was also critical to ExScal. ExScal was required to achieve both low false alarm rate and low latency of detection in the face of unavoidable failures (both hardware and software). We refer the readers to [3] for a list of hardware, software, deployment, localization, and other failures encountered in the ExScal demonstration.

Finally, low human involvement is a key to the operation of a large scale sensor network. Imagine the effort and time needed if one thousand sensor nodes deployed over a 1 km long region have to be touched individually by a human for some reason (e.g., to turn them on and off). Therefore, a large

---

[4] The appropriate notion of coverage for intrusion detection application is *barrier coverage* [18], where sensors form a barrier for intruders. For a precise definition of the concept of barrier coverage and several interesting results, including the optimal topology to achieve k-barrier coverage, we refer the readers to [18].

scale sensor network such as the ExScal needed to provide easy operation, require minimal or no touching of individual sensor nodes, and allow monitoring of network health and reconfiguration of network parameters from a remote central location.

A new sensor platform, called an Extreme Scale Mote (XSM) [9], was developed for ExScal. It was a refinement of Mica2 [7]. The details of this platform with regard to its power management capabilities appear in Section 3.1. The operating system used on this platform was TinyOS. Several middleware services such as routing, time synchronization, and localization were custom developed for ExScal. The signal chains that were used by the XSMs to locally process the sensor data were also custom developed. Finally, the application software to detect and classify intruders were also developed in-house.

To demonstrate the concept, approximately 1000 XSMs were deployed in a 1,200 m × 288 m rectangular region [16] and intruders such as persons and Sport Utility Vehicles (SUVs) were shown to be detected and classified by the sensor network. At the end of year 2004, this was the largest wireless sensor network in the world deployed on the ground. Figure 1 shows the XSMs deployed for ExScal demonstration.

Fig. 1. XSMs (white dots forming a grid) deployed on the ground (a 1,200 m × 288 m rectangular region) for ExScal demonstration. Figure 2 zooms on a single XSM.

Each XSM ran on a pair of AA batteries. If the XSMs were left continuously active, the ExScal network would have lasted only three days (see Section 4.3 for details of the calculation). However, when a wireless sensor network is deployed on the ground for real-life application (rather than to demonstrate the concept), such a network would be required to last for months, if not years. This motivated us to investigate the various power management schemes that can be used to extend the lifetime of the ExScal network from three days to several months, without deploying redundant sensor nodes or redundant batteries per node (keeping in mind the cost minimization objective of ExScal).

3.1 The XSM Platform

The XSM (Extreme Scale Mote) [9] is a sensor platform developed for the ExScal project. It was a refinement of the Mica 2 platform [7]. Its design was optimized for use in intrusion detection applications. Figure 2 shows an XSM deployed on the ground in its usual enclosure. The XSM had three types of sensor — a 2-axis Magnetometer to detect ferrous materials, a Passive Infrared (PIR) to detect motion, and an Acoustic sensor to detect objects making sounds (e.g., vehicles). Figure 3 shows the circuit board of an XSM. The sensing ranges for these sensors for various types of objects appear in Table 1.

Fig. 2. An XSM (Extreme Scale Mote) deployed on the ground in its usual enclosure during the ExScal demonstration.

The current consumption of the major components of XSM appear in Table 2. We use mA (milliamperes) for the unit of current consumption. The amount of energy consumed by a component will depend on the amount of time that it is used.

Fig. 3. Inside an XSM.

Table 1. Sensing ranges (in meters) of the three sensors used in the ExScal project.

Sensor	Sensed Object	Sensing Range
Magnetometer	SUV	7 m
PIR	SUV	30 m
	Person	12 m
Acoustic	SUV	30 m

3.2 Factors Affecting ExScal's Lifetime

The major factors affecting the network lifetime of ExScal are as follows:

1. **Continuous Monitoring:** The region should be continuously monitored so that intruders can be detected instantly. This may require keeping at least one sensor continuously active, consuming significant energy.
2. **Event Notification Requirement:** Intrusion detection events should be communicated to a base station quickly. In the ExScal application, the requirement was to receive event detection notification at the nearest base station within 2 seconds. In order to communicate event-notification messages quickly over a multi-hop wireless sensor network, several, if not all, sensors need to keep their radio in the receive mode either continuously or frequently enough so that they can route an urgent event-detection message towards the base station. This again consumes significant energy.
3. **Periodic Control Messages:** Two middleware services, namely *routing* and *time synchronization*, required every XSM to transmit periodic messages. As we will see in Section 4.6, sending periodic control messages consumes significant energy.

Table 2. Current consumption of major components in the XSM platform.

Component	State	Current (in mA)
Processor	active	8
	sleep	0.01
Radio	active	8
	transmit	16
	sleep	0.001
PIR	active	0.292
	sleep	0.001
Acoustic	active	0.575
	sleep	0.001
Magnetometer	active	6.48
	sleep	0.001
One LED	active	2.2
	sleep	0.001
Flash	Read	6.2
	Write	18.4
	Sleep	0.002
Buzzer	active	15
	sleep	0.001

4. **One-Time Control Operations:** There were several one-time activities performed in the ExScal application. The major ones among them were wireless reprogramming and localization. These operations required the sensor nodes to be active for a long duration (on the order of tens of minutes), send a large number of messages (in reprogramming), and perform actuation activities (e.g., sounding buzzers). All of these consume significant energy.

5. **Frequency of Events:** Every event requires the sensors near the event to not only stay awake for a few seconds to detect the event but also to transmit messages in a multi-hop sensor network, and potentially route other XSM's messages. Staying awake with the processor and all the sensors active consumes significant energy and the total energy consumed this way depends on the frequency of the events.

Each of the above factors dictate which fine-grained power management schemes can be used in ExScal and which ones are not usable. For example, LPL can be used in ExScal but the periodic sleeping time of the radio should be low enough (less than 400 ms) to satisfy the two second event notification latency.

4 Lifetime Analysis of ExScal

In this section, we analyze the lifetime of ExScal. We first discuss some key assumptions needed in the lifetime analysis, then we derive the parameters needed in the lifetime analysis. Next, we use these parameters to derive the network lifetime in the fully active mode, when using the LPL feature, and when using the hierarchical sensing feature. Finally, we analyze the effects of other fine-grained power management schemes such as varying the frequency of periodic control messages, performing in-network data aggregation, tuning the number of wireless reprogrammings, and controlling the amount of actuations performed in the network, on the lifetime of ExScal.

We define the lifetime of a WSN to be the time period during which the network continuously satisfies the application requirement. The application requirement can be stated in various forms. One simple way to express the requirement of an always-on application is in terms of the degree of coverage and the notification latency. For example, in ExScal, all intruders were required to be detected by the network at least five times in their trajectory through the network (in order to perform detection with a high probability) and the event notification was required to reach the closest base station in at most two seconds. We derive a lower bound on the lifetime of ExScal. The purpose of doing so is to allow some buffer so that even if some factors are missed in the analysis (which almost always are), the network has a high likelihood of lasting at least as long as predicted by the analysis.

4.1 Key Assumptions Needed in Lifetime Analysis

In analyzing the lifetime of any WSN, some key assumptions need to be made based on the expected use of the network. We make the following assumptions for ExScal, with the goal of deriving a conservative estimate of its lifetime:

1. The lifetime of the network is determined by the heaviest-loaded XSM. This is an XSM close to the base station. This is conservative because ExScal network will continue to meet its requirements even if all XSMs within one hop of a base station fail.
2. Every hour, six intrusion events occur in the vicinity of the heaviest-loaded XSM[5]. With equal probability, the event can be the intrusion of a person or that of an SUV. Further, the intruders are assumed to follow the least-covered path through the network. With this last assumption, the number of sensors detecting an intruder in the ExScal network is given by the values in Table 3.
3. Every time an event occurs, the heaviest-loaded XSM keeps its processor as well as all three of its sensors active for an average of 10 seconds. This is because, on average, a slow moving target (a person on foot) will spend an average of 10 seconds in the sensing range of a sensor.
4. One-eighth of the event detection messages generated in the vicinity of the heaviest-loaded XSM are routed by the heaviest-loaded XSM[6].

---

[5] This event rate is higher than what ExScal was required to handle.
[6] This is because grid routing [25] is used in ExScal, which balances the routing load on multiple routes and because of the topology used in ExScal [16].

5. The average number of times a data packet is transmitted for reliable delivery across a single hop is $1/0.7 = 1.43$. This is because the per-hop reliability of data packets was 0.7 in ExScal[7]. If we assume the probability of losing a packet is independent and identically distributed, the expected number of times a packet needs to be transmitted for successful delivery is $1/p$ (expectation of geometric distribution [22]), where p is the probability of success in each transmission[8].

6. Periodic control messages such as routing and time synchronization updates are never retransmitted.

7. We assume a fixed packet length of 36 bytes, which is the maximum length of a packet in B-MAC [20] (the MAC protocol used in ExScal), and that it takes 20 ms to transmit a packet. In practice, event detection messages are very short, and therefore the packet length will be smaller and so will the transmission time.

The assumptions for any other always-on application will mostly be along the lines of the above assumptions with some changes specific to that application.

Table 3. Number of sensors detecting an intruder type in the ExScal application.

Intruder	# of PIRs	# of Acoustic	# of Magnetometers
SUV	30	30	5
Person	10	None	None

4.2 Parameters for Lifetime Analysis

In this section, we define the parameters used in analyzing the lifetime of an always-on WSN and derive their values in the ExScal application.

The notation for the parameters used in lifetime analysis appears in Table 4. In the following, we derive the values or expressions for those parameters whose values are not straightforward to calculate or whose values are variable (in the context of the ExScal application).

t_{slp}^{lpl}: Sleep period of the radio in the LPL mode. It can take a value of 0.01, 0.02, 0.05, 0.1, 0.2, 0.4, 0.8, or 1.6 seconds [20]. We do not use sleep periods of 0.8 seconds and 1.6 seconds in our analysis because the notification latency requirement of 2 seconds can not be satisfied with these sleep periods.

[7] The per-hop reliability was close to 1 in the absence of interference but was 0.7 in the presence of interference (as is the case in an operating sensor network).

[8] The value of 1.43 is an approximation. The actual value will be lower than 1.43 because the maximum times a packet was transmitted was 3, whereas in geometric distribution the maximum number of trials is assumed to be infinite (trials are made until there is a success).

Table 4. Notations for parameters used in the lifetime analysis and their values in ExScal. The values of the parameters that are variable are derived in Section 4.2.

Identifier	Meaning	Value
$e_{battery}$	Usable capacity of the batteries	1800 mA-hr
i_{act}^{proc}	Current drawn by the processor in active mode	8 mA
i_{act}^{rad}	Current drawn by the radio in active mode	8 mA
i_{tx}^{rad}	Current drawn by the radio in transmit mode	16 mA
t_{tx}^{pkt}	Time to transmit a packet	0.02 s
t_{slp}^{lpl}	Sleep period of the radio in the LPL mode	variable
i_{lpl}	Amortized current drawn by an XSM in the LPL mode	variable
m_{pr}	# control messages transmitted every hour	240
m_e	# event-detection messages generated by the heaviest-loaded XSM every hour	variable
m_{pp}	# event-detection messages routed by the heaviest-loaded XSM every hour	variable
i_{act}^{msg}	Current drawn in transmitting 1 packet when the radio is in active mode (no LPL)	variable
i_{lpl}^{msg}	Current drawn in transmitting 1 packet when the radio is in LPL mode	variable
i_{awk}^{event}	Amortized current drawn in staying awake due to events	variable
i_{sensor}	Current drawn by continuously active sensors	variable
f_{repr}	# reprogramming is performed wirelessly	6
e_{repr}	Energy spent in 1 wireless reprogramming	18.22 mA-hr
$e_{localization}$	Energy spent in 1 localization	4 mA-hr

i_{lpl}: Amortized current drawn by an XSM in the LPL mode. Its value depends on the following four factors:

1. t_{slp}^{lpl} - The sleep period used for the radio (listed above).
2. i_{slp}^{lpl} - The average current consumed by an XSM when the processor and radio are sleeping (excluding the current consumed by any active sensor). By measurement on an XSM, we found that i_{slp}^{lpl} =0.1974 mA[9].

---

[9] This is a significantly higher value than expected in sleep mode. We expected it to be close to 0.035 mA. The higher value of 0.1974 mA is because in the LPL mode, the XSM wakes up every 27.6 ms. Every time it wakes up, it follows the following pattern: it consumes 0.035 mA during the 27.6 ms that the XSM is sleeping, it consumes 0.4 mA for the next 0.8 ms, 0.75 mA for the next 2.25 ms, and 6.35 mA for the next 0.5 ms, after which the 27.6 ms of sleep period follows. With careful configuration and some hardware improvements, the value of i_{slp}^{lpl} may be brought down to 0.035 mA, which will significantly increase an XSM's lifetime.

3. i_{sample}^{lpl} - The average current consumed by an XSM in sampling the channel every time the radio wakes up. By measurement on an XSM, we found that $i_{sample}^{lpl} = 9.6571$ mA[10].

4. t_{sample}^{lpl} - Time taken to sample the channel every time the radio wakes up to sample the channel. By measurement on an XSM, we found that $t_{sample}^{lpl} = 0.014$ seconds.

Using the above values, we obtain

$$i_{lpl} = \frac{i_{slp}^{lpl} * t_{slp}^{lpl} + i_{sample}^{lpl} * t_{sample}^{lpl}}{t_{slp}^{lpl} + t_{sample}^{lpl}}$$

$$= \frac{0.1974 * t_{slp}^{lpl} + (9.6571 * 0.014)}{t_{slp}^{lpl} + 0.014}. \tag{1}$$

m_{pr}: Number of control messages transmitted every hour. With the configuration used in the ExScal application, every XSM sends three routing messages and one time synchronization message every minute, for a total of 240 messages every hour. Therefore, in ExScal, $m_{pr} = 240$.

m_e: Number of event-detection messages generated by the heaviest-loaded XSM every hour. Two messages are generated for every sensor for every event. It means an XSM detecting an event sends two messages per sensor per event, for a total of six messages. With our assumption of six events per hour and a per-hop retransmission factor of 1.43 per event-detection message, $m_e = 52$.

m_{pp}: Number of event-detection messages routed by the heaviest-loaded XSM every hour. The heaviest-loaded XSM is the one close to the base station. Every event generates two messages per sensor from every XSM that detects this event. The number of XSMs that detect an intruder type appears in Table 3. These numbers depend on the topology of the sensor network deployed [16] and the assumption that intruders always cross through the network via least-covered paths. Assuming both the intruder types are equally likely to occur, every event results in the generation of $2 * ((30 + 30 + 5) + (10 + 0 + 0))/2 = 75$ messages (using the values from Table 3). The routing used in the ExScal application [25] balances the routing load on eight XSMs that are within one hop of the base station. Therefore, the most energy constrained XSM routes an average of 10 messages for every event. Assuming a retransmission factor of 1.43, it will transmit an average of 15 messages for every event. Since six events are assumed to occur every hour, 90 event detection messages are routed by the most energy constrained XSM every hour. Therefore, in ExScal, $m_{pp} = 90$.

i_{act}^{msg}: Current drawn in transmitting one packet when the radio is in active mode (no LPL). Its value is given by the following expression:

---

[10] Similar values for i_{sample}^{lpl} were reported in [9].

$$i_{act}^{msg} = \frac{(m_{pr} + m_e + m_{pp}) * t_{tx}^{pkt} * (i_{tx}^{rad} - i_{act}^{rad})}{3600}$$

$$= \frac{(240 + 52 + 90) * 0.02 * (16 - 8)}{3600}$$

$$= 0.02\text{mA}. \tag{2}$$

i_{lpl}^{msg}: Current drawn in transmitting one packet when the radio is in LPL mode. Its value depends on the sleep period, t_{slp}^{lpl} used by the radio. More specifically,

$$i_{lpl}^{msg} =$$

$$\frac{(m_{pr} + m_e + m_{pp}) * (t_{tx}^{pkt} + t_{slp}^{lpl}) * (i_{act}^{proc} + i_{tx}^{rad})}{3600}$$

$$= \frac{(240 + 52 + 90) * (0.02 + t_{slp}^{lpl}) * (8 + 16)}{3600}. \tag{3}$$

i_{awk}^{event}: Amortized current drawn in staying awake due to events. Its value depends on two factors:

1. t_{awk} - Time (in seconds) that the heaviest-loaded XSM is awake every hour due to events. We assume that an XSM close to the base station stays awake for 10 s after the occurrence of an event. This may be for routing all event detection messages. With the assumption of six events every hour, $t_{awk} = 60$ seconds in ExScal.
2. $i_{sensors}^{slp}$ - The current consumed in the active mode by all the non-wakeup sensors. From Table 2, we obtain, $i_{senors}^{slp} = 0.595 + 6.48 = 7.075$ mA.

With the above values and the fact that the processor is also awake when the XSM is awake due to events, we obtain,

$$i_{awk}^{event} = \frac{t^{awk} * (i_{act}^{proc} + i_{sensors}^{slp})}{3600}$$

$$= \frac{60 * (8 + 7.075)}{3600} = 0.2618\text{mA}. \tag{4}$$

i_{sensor}: Current drawn by continuously active sensors. Its value depends on which sensors are kept continuously active. The current consumption for the sensors used on the XSM appear in Table 2.

e_{repr}: Energy spent in one wireless reprogramming. One reprogramming of 55 kByte program (the size of ExScal program) requires every XSM to stay awake for approximately 45 minutes. Assuming the XSMs are not in the LPL mode during reprogramming, just staying awake for 45 minutes consumes 18 mA-hr of energy[11]. The reprogramming of 55 kByte requires

---

[11] Keeping XSMs in the LPL mode during reprogramming will cause a higher energy consumption because the XSMs will need to send long preambles, consuming

the most constrained XSM to send out 1,942 packets, where each packet has 29 bytes of data. Assuming a retransmission factor of 1.43, approximately 2,771 packets are sent by the most energy constrained XSM. One packet transmission takes 20 ms and consumes an extra current of 8 mA. Therefore, the additional energy spent in transmission of 2771 packets is 0.12 mA-hr (8*2771*0.02/3600.). Writing 55 kByte to flash takes less than four seconds. Each second, it consumes 18.4 mA of current. So, total energy consumed in flash writing is less than 0.02 mA-hr. Adding up the energy consumed in staying awake for 45 minutes (18 mA-hr), in transmissions (0.12 mA-hr), and in flash writing (0.02 mA-hr), we get a total of approximately 18.14 mA-hr of energy consumed in 1 reprogramming. Therefore, in ExScal, $e_{repr} = 18.14$ mA-hr.

$e_{localization}$: Energy spent in one localization. As seen in the calculation done above for reprogramming, the energy consumed in staying awake is the dominant part of energy consumption. In ExScal, the XSMs were awake for 10 minutes during localization, consuming 4 mA-hr. Therefore, $e_{localization} = 4$mA-hr.

4.3 Lifetime in the Fully Active Mode

If a sensor node is always in the active mode, its lifetime, ℓ_{hr} (in hours) will be given by:

$$\ell_{hr} = \frac{e_{battery} - f_{repr} * e_{repr} - e_{localization}}{i_{act}^{proc} + i_{act}^{rad} + i_{act}^{msg} + i^{sensor}}. \tag{5}$$

Substituting the following values

$$i_{act}^{msg} = 0.02\text{mA}, \quad \text{(from (2))}$$
$$i^{sensor} = 0.292 + 0.575 + 6.48 = 7.347\text{mA}, \quad \text{(from Table 2)}$$

and those from Table 4, we obtain $\ell_{hr} = 72.2$ hours (or three days) for the lifetime of ExScal.

4.4 Lifetime When Using Low Power Listening (LPL)

If we use the low power listening mode (see Section 2.1), then the network lifetime, ℓ_{hr} (in hours) is given by

$$\ell_{hr} = \frac{e_{battery} - f_{repr} * e_{repr} - e_{localization}}{i_{lpl} + i_{lpl}^{msg} + i_{sensor} + i_{awk}^{event}}. \tag{6}$$

Substituting

---

significant energy. Also, it will take much longer than 45 minutes to reprogram the network if the XSMs are in the LPL mode, because of reduced channel capacity in the LPL mode.

$$i_{lpl} = \frac{(0.1974 * t_{slp}^{lpl}) + (9.6571 * 0.014)}{t_{slp}^{lpl} + 0.014}, \quad \text{(from (1))}$$

$$i_{lpl}^{msg} = \frac{(382) * (0.02 + t_{slp}^{lpl}) * (8 + 16)}{3600}, \quad \text{(from (3))}$$

$$i^{sensor} = 0.292 + 0.575 + 6.48 = 7.347, \quad \text{(from Table 2)}$$

$$i_{awk}^{event} = 0.2618 \text{mA}, \quad \text{(from (4))}$$

and those from Table 4, we obtain a graph of the ℓ_{hr} as a function of t_{slp}^{lpl} shown in Figure 4 for the lifetime of ExScal. The lifetime curve is concave because there is trade-off in choosing the wakeup period for the radio in the LPL mode. The higher the wakeup interval, the lower the energy consumption when an XSM is sleeping, but the higher the energy consumed in sending a longer preamble. The optimal value of lifetime occurs at 187.99 hours or 7.83 days. This represents an increase by a factor of 2.6 over that in the fully active mode.

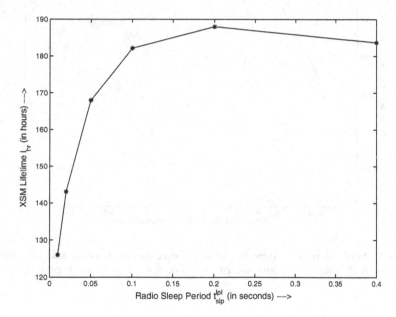

Fig. 4. ExScal network lifetime in the low power listening mode as a function of radio sleep period, t_{slp}^{lpl}.

4.5 Lifetime When Using Hierarchical Sensing With LPL

When using a hierarchical sensor with the LPL mode, the network lifetime is still given by (6), except that now the value of i_{sensor} becomes lower because some other sensors are put to sleep.

In ExScal, the PIR sensor qualifies as a wakeup sensor. Fortunately, this is also the lowest energy consuming sensor, drawing 20 times less current than a magnetometer. Figure 5 shows ℓ_{hr} for ExScal as a function of t_{slp}^{lpl}. Here ℓ_{hr} is given by (6) with $i_{sensor} = 0.292$ mA. We observe that the maximum lifetime achievable increases to 878.85 hours (or 36.62 days). This represents an increase by a factor of 4.67 over that achieved by just using the LPL mode and a factor of 12 over that achieved in the fully active mode.

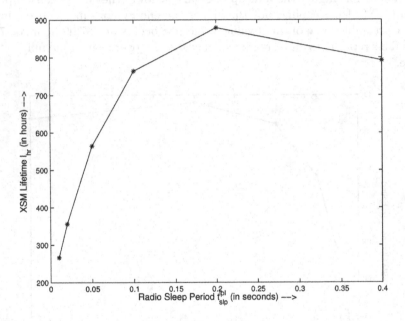

Fig. 5. ExScal network lifetime in the low power listening mode and hierarchical sensing with PIR as the wakeup sensor, as a function of radio sleep period, t_{slp}^{lpl}.

4.6 Effect of Periodic Control Messages on the Lifetime

In this section, we analyze the effect of varying the frequency of periodic control messages on the network lifetime. To study the effect of periodic messages on the lifetime, we vary the value of m_{pr}. The effect of varying m_{pr} on the lifetime in the fully active mode is straightforward (derive a new value for i_{act}^{msg} in (5)). Analyzing the effect of varying m_{pr} when the network is using the LPL mode is, however, nontrivial, because the optimal lifetime now occurs at different values of t_{slp}^{lpl} depending on the range of values of m_{pr}.

The optimal value of ℓ_{hr} (given by (6)) occurs at $t_{slp}^{lpl} = 0.4$ seconds when $m_{pr} \leq 82$, at $t_{slp}^{lpl} = 0.2$ seconds when $83 \leq m_{pr} \leq 672$, and at $t_{slp}^{lpl} = 0.1$ seconds when $673 \leq m_{pr} \leq 2580$. We plot the optimal values of lifetime when m_{pr} is varied from 0 to 2580 to analyze the effect of periodic messages on the lifetime of ExScal in Figure 6 when hierarchical sensing and LPL both are used. We notice that if there were no periodic messages, ExScal's life increases to 1157.1 hours (or 48.2 days). This represents an improvement of 31.67%.

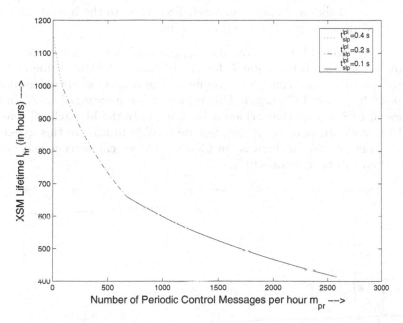

Fig. 6. Optimal ExScal network lifetime in the low power listening mode and hierarchical sensing when the number of periodic control messages (m_{pr}) is varied from 0 to 2580 messages per hour.

4.7 Effect of In-Network Data Aggregation on the Lifetime

In this section, we analyze the effect of in-network data aggregation on the lifetime of a WSN. The lifetime of a WSN with data aggregation is still given by (5) and (6), but with new values for m_e and m_{pp}. The amount of data aggregation that can be performed in a WSN depends on the application traffic generated and on the topology as well as the routing protocol used. We can perform the following data aggregation in ExScal, assuming the most optimistic scenario:

1. We can combine the detection message for all three sensors at an XSM into one message. This will result in reducing m_e by a factor of 1/3 to 17.
2. We can perform aggregation of detection messages flowing upward in a routing tree. Assuming that both intruder types are equally likely to occur, an average of $(30+10)/2 = 20$ XSMs detect an event (from Table 3). Since the routing load is distributed on 8 XSMs, each XSM forwards the detection messages from at most three other XSMs, all of whose data can be combined into one packet. Since each XSM generates two messages for every event, separated in time, an XSM close to the base station will need to forward two packets per event. Assuming a retransmission factor of 1.43, and six events per hour, each XSM close to the base station will forward 18 messages. Therefore, $m_{pp} = 18$.

Substituting $m_e = 17$, $m_{pp} = 18$, and $i_{sensor} = 0.292$ mA in (6), we obtain a graph of ℓ_{hr}, shown in Figure 7, for the lifetime of ExScal, if hierarchical sensing and LPL mode continue to be used. The maximum life achievable is now 954.6 hours (or 39.78 days). This represents an increase of 8.91% in the lifetime of ExScal over that achieved by using only the hierarchical sensing and LPL mode. In practice, it may not be feasible to achieve this extent of data aggregation. So, the increase in lifetime that we can achieve using data aggregation will be at most 8.91%.

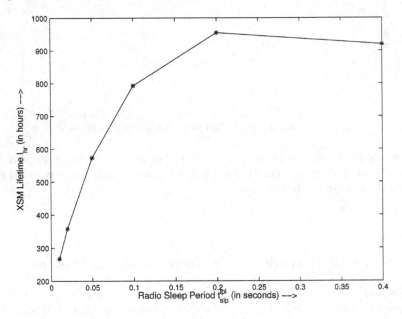

Fig. 7. ExScal network lifetime in the low power listening mode with PIR as the wakeup sensor and in-network data aggregation, as a function of radio sleep period, t_{slp}^{lpl}.

4.8 Effect of Wireless Reprogramming and Actuation on the Lifetime

In this section, we analyze the effects of performing frequent wireless reprogramming, blinking LEDs, and sounding buzzers on the lifetime of ExScal.

One wireless reprogramming consumes 18.14 mA-hr of energy. From (6), we get that if f_{repr} is reduced from 6 to 5, the lifetime of ExScal will increase from 871.81 hours to 881.2 hours, an increase of approximately 10 hours.

Today's sensors have limited actuation abilities (e.g., blinking LEDs or sounding a buzzer). In the future, sensor nodes are expected to have more actuation abilities. Actuations are often a major source of energy drain. To analyze the effect of actuations on the lifetime, we can use (5) and (6) with a new term in the denominator to represent the average current draw per hour.

For example, an LED draws a current of 2.2 mA on an XSM(see Table 2). If one LED is kept active continuously, then the lifetime of ExScal will decrease from 871.81 hours to 412.4 hours (i.e., reduce it by more than half). (Substitute $i_{sensor} = 0.292$ mA in (6) and use a new term with a value of 2.2 in the denominator.) If an LED blinks instead of being continuously active, we can use the following approach. Let f denote the fraction of a second that the LED is on. Then, it can be assumed that the LED in consideration draws 2.2 mA $\times f$ amount of current continuously. The remaining analysis will be similar as in the case when an LED is active continuously.

Similarly, to analyze the effect of sounding a buzzer for 1 minute every hour on the lifetime of ExScal, substitute $i_{sensor} = 0.292$ mA in (6) and use a new term with a value of $15/60 = 0.3642$ mA in the denominator (because the buzzer draws 15 mA of current on an XSM). By doing so, we find that an XSM's life will decrease from 871.81 hours to 780.38 hours (a decrease of more than 90 hours of life) as a result of sounding the buzzer for one minute every hour by the actuator.

5 Conclusion

In this chapter, we discussed several fine-grained power management techniques that can be used to extend the lifetime of an event-based (always-on) application of wireless sensor network without requiring any additional sensor nodes than is absolutely necessary to meet the application's monitoring requirements. We showed using concrete numbers that the lifetime of ExScal — an application of wireless sensor network for intrusion detection and classification, can be extended by more than 16 times by using low power listening and hierarchical listening alone, both of which are existing features of the XSM platform. Contrary to popular belief, we showed that it is possible to achieve comparable network lifetime extensions for event-based (always-on) applications as for data gathering (always-off) applications, without deploying any more sensor nodes than are absolutely necessary to meet the application's monitoring requirements.

282

282   Santosh Kumar, Anish Arora, and Ten H. Lai

Acknowledgments

We would like to thank Sandip Bapat, Hui Cao, and Hongwei Zhang from
the Ohio State University for their valuable feedback on an earlier draft of
this chapter. We would also like to thank Emre Ertin from the Ohio State
University and Prabal K. Dutta from University of California, Berkeley for
sharing with us their knowledge of hierarchical sensing and power management
features of the XSM.

References

1. Z. Abrams, A. Goel, and S. Plotkin, Set k-Cover Algorithms for Energy Efficient Monitoring in Wireless Sensor Networks, *In Proceedings of the Third International Conference on Information Processing in Sensor Networks (IPSN)*, Berkeley, CA, 2004.
2. A. Arora, R. Ramnath, E. Ertin, P. Sinha, S. Bapat, V. Naik, V. Kulathumani, H. Zhang, H. Cao, M. Sridhara, S. Kumar, N. Seddon, C. Anderson, T. Herman, N. Trivedi, C. Zhang, M. Gouda, Y.-R. Choi, M. Nesterenko, R. Shah, S. Kulkarni, M. Aramugam, L. Wang, D. Culler, P. Dutta, C. Sharp, G. Tolle, M. Grimmer, B. Ferriera, K. Parker, "ExScal: Elements of an Extreme Scale Wireless Sensor Network," *In Proceedings of the Eleventh IEEE International Conference on Real-Time Computing Systems and Applications (IEEE RTCSA)*, Hongkong, 2005.
3. S. Bapat, V. Kulathumani and A. Arora, Analyzing the Yield of ExScal, A Large-Scale Wireless Sensor Network Experiment, *IEEE ICNP*, Boston, 2005.
4. S.M. Brennan, A.M. Mielke, D.C. Torney, and A.B. McCabe, Radiation Detection with Distributed Sensor Networks, *IEEE Computer*, Vol.37, No.8, August 2004, pp. 57-59.
5. M. Cardei, M. Thai and W. Wu, Energy-Efficient Target Coverage in Wireless Sensor Networks, *IEEE Infocom*, Miami, FL, 2005.
6. H. Chen, H. Wu and N.F. Tzeng, Grid-Based Approach for Working Node Selection in Wireless Sensor Networks, *IEEE International Conference on Communications (ICC)*, Paris, FR, 2004.
7. *Mica2 Series Motes*, http://www.xbow.com, 2004.
8. M. Horton, D. Culler, K. Pister and J. Hill, R. Szewczyk, and A. Woo, The Commercialization of Microsensor Motes, *Sensors Magazine*, Vol.19 No.4, April 2002, pp. 40-48.
9. P. Dutta, M. Grimmer, A. Arora, S. Bibyk, and D. Culler, Design of a Wireless Sensor Network Platform for Detecting Rare, Random, and Ephemeral Events, *In Proceedings of the Fourth International Conference on Information Processing in Sensor Networks (IPSN)*, Los Angeles, CA, 2005.
10. J. Elson and D. Estrin, Sensor Networks: A Bridge to the Physical World, in C.S. Raghavendra, K.M. Sivalingam and T. Znati (eds.) *Wireless Sensor Networks*, Boston, Kluwer Academic Publisher, 2004, pp. 3-20.
11. L. Gu and J.A. Stankovic, Radio Triggered Wake-Up Capability for Sensor Networks, *In Proceedings of Real Time Applications Symposium*, May 2004.
12. H. Gupta, S.R. Das, and Q. Gu, Connected Sensor Cover: Self-Organization of Sensor Networks for Efficient Query Execution, *In Proceedings of the Fourth*

International Symposium on Mobile Ad Hoc Networking and Computing (ACM MobiHoc), Annapolis, MD, 2003, pp. 189-200.

13. T. He, S. Krishnamurthy, J.A. Stankovic, T. Abdelzaher, L. Luo, R. Stoleru, T. Yan, and L. Hu, Energy-Efficient Surveillance System Using Wireless Sensor Networks, *In proceedings of the Second International Conference on Mobile Systems, Applications, and Services (ACM Mobisys)*, Boston, MA, 2004, pp. 270-283.

14. J. Hill and D. Culler, Mica: A Wireless Platform for Deeply Embedded Networks, *IEEE Micro*, Vol.22 No.6, 2002, pp. 12-24.

15. J. Hui, Z. Ren, and B. H Krogh, Sentry-Based Power Management in Wireless Sensor Networks, *In Proceedings of the Second International Conference on Information Processing in Sensor Networks (IPSN)*, Palo Alto, CA, 2003.

16. S. Kumar and A. Arora, Topology and Naming for ExScal Clean Point Demonstration, *ExScal Note Series ExScal-OSU-EN03-2004-12-05*, December 2004.

17. S. Kumar, T.H. Lai, and J. Balogh, On k-Coverage in a Mostly Sleeping Sensor Network, *In proceedings of the Tenth International Conference on Mobile Computing and Networking (ACM MobiCom)*, Philadelphia, PA, 2004, pp. 144-158.

18. S. Kumar, T.H. Lai, and A. Arora, "Barrier Coverage with Wireless Sensors," *In Proceedings of the Eleventh Annual International Conference on Mobile Computing and Networking (ACM MobiCom)*, Cologne, Germany, 2005.

19. K. Martinez, J.K. Hart, and R. Ong, Environmental Sensor Networks *IEEE Computer*, Vol.37, No.8, August 2004, pp. 50-56.

20. J. Polastre, J. Hill, and D. Culler, Versatile Low Power Media Access for Wireless Sensor Networks, *In proceedings of the Second ACM Conference on Embedded Networked Sensor Systems (ACM SenSys)*, Baltimore, MD, 2004.

21. J. Polastre, R. Szewczyk, A. Mainwaring, D. Culler, and J. Anderson, Analysis of Wireless Sensor Networks for Habitat Monitoring, in C.S. Raghavendra, K.M. Sivalingam and T. Znati (eds.) *Wireless Sensor Networks*, Boston, Kluwer Academic Publisher, 2004, pp. 399 423.

22. S.M. Ross, *Introduction to Probability Models*, Academic Press, 2001.

23. G. Simon, M. Maroti, A. Ledeczi, G. Balogh, B. Kusy, A. Nadas, G. Pap, J. Sallai and K. Frampton, Sensor Network-Based Countersniper System, *In proceedings of the Second ACM Conference on Embedded Networked Sensor Systems (ACM SenSys)*, Baltimore, MD, 2004.

24. N. Xu, S. Rangwala, K.K. Chintalapudi, D. Ganesan, A. Broad, R. Govindan, and D. Estrin, A Wireless Sensor Network for Structural Monitoring, *In proceedings of the Second ACM Conference on Embedded Networked Sensor Systems (ACM SenSys)*, Baltimore, MD, 2004.

25. Y. Choi, M.G. Gouda, H. Zhang and A. Arora, Routing on a Logical Grid in Sensor Networks, *UTCS Technical Report TR-04-09*, 2004.

26. H. Zhang and J. Hou, Maintaining Sensing Coverage and Connectivity in Large Sensor Networks, *In Proceedings of the NSF International Workshop on Theoretical and Algorithmic Aspects of Sensor, Ad Hoc Wirelsss, and Peer-to-Peer Networks*, 2004.

27. Z. Zhou, S.R. Das, and H. Gupta, Connected k-Coverage problem in Sensor Networks, *In Proceedings of International Conference on Computer Communications and Networks (ICCCN)*, Chicago, IL, 2004.

SECTION III
DATA MANAGEMENT

Chapter 12
Data Management in Sensor Networks

Jinbao Li[1], Zhipeng Cai[2], and Jianzhong Li[1]

[1] School of Computer Science & Technology
Harbin Institute of Technology, Harbin, China, 150001
{lijinbao, lizj}@hit.edu.cn
[2] Department of Computing Science
University of Alberta, Edmonton, Alberta, Canada, T6G 2E8
zhipeng@cs.ualberta.ca

The purpose of data management in sensor networks is to separate the logical view (name, access, operation) from the physical view of the data. Users and applications need not be concerned about the details of sensor networks, but the logical structures of queries. From the data management point of view, the data management system of a sensor network can be seen as a distributed database system, but it is different from traditional ones. The data management system of a sensor network organizes and manages perceptible information from the inspected area and answers queries from users or applications. This chapter discusses the methods and techniques of data management in sensor networks, including the difference between data management systems in sensor networks and in traditional distributed database systems, the architecture of a data management system in a sensor network, the data model and the query language, the storing and indexing techniques of sensor data, the operating algorithms, the query processing techniques and two examples of data management systems in sensor networks: TinyDB and Cougar.

1 Difference Between Data Management Systems In Sensor Networks and In Distributed Database Systems

In some applications, by querying and analyzing the perceptible data from sensors, the targets or areas can be monitored effectively. For example, we can collect data from disasters, monitor and control the traffic in a traffic management system, spy for military purposes, monitor special objects, etc. In these applications, data are divided into two types. One is static data, such as data describing characteristics of sensors. The other is dynamic data, such as perceptible data from sensors. The data set of the perceptible data is similar with the one in a large distributed database, which needs to be

287

maintained by a software system. This kind of software system is called a Data Management System of a sensor network. Different from traditional data management methods, it does not integrate perceptible data from all the sensors to a central node, but processes data within a sensor network (in-network) [23, 8]. This reduces the power consumed and extends the lifetime of a sensor network [1, 19].

The differences between data management systems of sensor networks and the distributed database systems are remarkable. The first difference is the network environment. In traditional distributed database systems, data management and query processing are just applications of the network systems, and the details of the networks should not be of concern. While in a sensor network, the details of the networks must be of concern, since sensors may be disabled at any moment, the network layer provides weak services, each node in a sensor network has very limited storage space, computing ability and battery power and query processing of the perceptive data is highly related with the network environment.

The second difference is that, the data produced by a sensor is an infinite data stream. The data management system of a sensor network manages a large number of distributed data streams. Infinite data streams cannot be managed by traditional database systems. The data management system of a sensor network requires new query processing and analyzing techniques, which use limited storage space, computing ability and the power to complete the query and the analysis of a large number of distributed infinite data streams.

The third difference is that, the perceptible data from sensors are not accurate. The error can be described by some continuous probability distribution functions, such as Gauss distribution. At present, the errors in sensor networks are described by discrete probability distribution functions. The data management system of a sensor network should have the ability to process the errors of the perceptible data and try to provide credible data.

The forth difference is that, the power of a sensor is very limited. The data management system of a sensor network needs to reduce the waste of power to extend the network lifetime. The communication cost is greater than the computing cost, so the purpose of a sensor network is to reduce transmission load. Each sensor processes the data produced by itself locally to reduce the amount of data transmitted. For example, the sensors for measuring traffic compute the number of cars passed by and record the pressures. Each sensor transforms the pressure to flux, then sends out the number of cars passed by. Those numbers are aggregated for transmission. Thus, the transmission cost is greatly reduced. Queries in sensor networks will change depending on different times, positions and the requirements of users. For example, commuters concerned about traffic will concentrate on some streets in peak hours, and not care about other streets. Thus, the control of sampling rate and delivery rate of sensors is a good method to reduce the communication cost.

The fifth difference is that, there are two kinds of queries in the data management system of a sensor network. The first kind is a long-running query. It continuously observes the status of the monitored area during the period the user specified. Traditional database systems do not have the ability to process long-running queries. The second kind of query is an ad hoc or snapshot query, which is for querying the current status of the monitored area. Given the limited resources in sensor networks, the data management system should balance the accuracy of the query results and the resources wasted during the query. For example, N sensors are deployed in an area to measure temperature. To compute the average temperature accurately, the data from all the N sensors should be obtained and aggregated, which will cost a lot of power. Random sampling techniques can be adopted in this case. By satisfying user-requested-accuracy, only the data from M sensors $(M < N)$ should be used. Thus, the cost is reduced dramatically. A traditional database does not support such a technique.

The sixth difference is that, query processing techniques in a traditional database system are not suitable for sensor networks. The reasons are as follows:

- The query optimization technique in a traditional data-base system is based on a fixed cost model and statistical information. There is no reliable statistical information about data in sensor networks, and it is very difficult to forecast the action of data streams from sensors. The query plan in sensor networks must minimize the power consumption and be suitable for the actions of data streams.
- A traditional database system locks the data and unlocks them when errors occur. This is unsuitable for sensor networks since the actions of data streams are uncertain and the query may last for a long time.
- A traditional database system operates on an existing and fixed database. Answers for queries are fixed. In sensor networks, the objects operated on are infinite and uncertain data streams. Answers for queries are approximate.
- Query processing in sensor networks focuses on query response time. The goal of sensor networks is to monitor the status of the factual world, such as traffic accidents, fire accidents and etc. Thus, real-time query processing is needed and the query results should be returned to users in a timely manner.

The seventh difference is that, the amount of data from sensors is very large and not all of the data can be stored. At the same time, limited by the bandwidth, the processing ability and power of each sensor, the centralized storage scheme and the calculation are not suitable for sensor networks and not good for fault-tolerance. To improve the performance and the fault-tolerance ability, the data management system of sensor networks needs power efficient in-network distributed data processing algorithms to implement efficient query processing and data management.

2 Architecture of Data Management System in Sensor Networks

Four system models will be introduced in this section. They are: centralized model, semi-distributed model, distributed model, and hierarchical model.

2.1 Centralized Model

In a centralized model, query processing and access to sensor networks are separated. The centralized approach proceeds in two steps. First, data is extracted from the sensor network in a predefined way and is stored in a database located on a central server. Subsequently, query processing takes place on the centralized database. This approach is simple. However, the central server is the performance bottleneck and single point of failure. In addition, all sensors are required to send data to the central server, which incurs large communication cost.

2.2 Semi-distributed Model

Sensors nowadays have improved computation and storage capabilities. Therefore, certain computations can be performed on the raw data at each sensor node. Most recent research focuses on the semi-distributed model. We present two representative systems for this model.

(1) Fjord

Fjord, part of Telegraph (a developing project at UC Berkeley) [13], is an adaptive dataflow system. Fjord has two major components: adaptive query processing engine and sensor proxy. Fjord processes queries based on a dataflow computation model. In Fjord, data streams are pushed to the query processing engine instead of being pulled as in traditional database systems. At the same time, non-sensor data is pulled by the query processing engine. Therefore, Fjord is a query processing engine combining push and pull mechanisms. In addition, Fjord integrates Eddy to adaptively change the execution plans according to computing environments on a tuple-per-tuple basis. The second major component of Fjord is sensor proxy, an interface between a single sensor and query processor as shown in Figure 1. A sensor node only needs to deliver data to its sensor proxy. Then the sensor proxy delivers the data to the query processor. Thus, the sensor proxy shields the sensor from having to deliver data to hundreds of interested end-users. In addition, the sensor proxy directs sensors to perform certain local computations to aggregate samples in a predefined way. Moreover, the sensor proxy actively monitors sensors, evaluates user needs and current power conditions, and appropriately programs and controls sensors' sampling rate and delivery rate to achieve acceptable

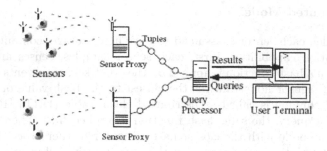

Fig. 1. Architecture of Fjord [13].

sensor battery lifetime and performance.

(2) Cougar

Cougar is a sensor database project developed at Cornell University [7, 4]. The basic idea of this project is to push as much computation as possible into the sensor network to reduce the communication between sensor nodes and front-end server(s). In this model, the query workload determines the data that should be extracted from sensors. The approach is thus flexible and efficient since only relevant data are extracted from the sensor network. Different from Fjord, sensors in Cougar not only performs local computation over its own sampling data, it also communicates with nearby sensors to perform certain aggregations, labelled as "in-network aggregation" in Figure 2.

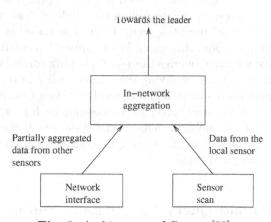

Fig. 2. Architecture of Cougar [22].

2.3 Distributed Model

In this model, each sensor is assumed to have high storage, computation and communication capabilities. First, each sensor samples, senses and detects events. Then a hash function is applied on the event key, and events are stored at a "home" sensor node which is the closest to the hash value of the event key. This technique is called a Distributed Hash Table (DHT) [16, 17, 18]. To process a query, the same hash function is applied first. Then the query is sent to the node with the closest hash value for further processing. From the above description, we can see that this model pushes all computation and communication to sensor nodes.

The problem with this model is that sensors are assumed to have almost the same communication and computation capabilities as normal computers. In addition, DHT is only suitable for key queries, which incurs large communication cost.

2.4 Hierarchical model

Based on the above survey on existing works on sensor data management in pervasive computing, [9] proposes a new hierarchical system model, which is shown in Figure 3. This model includes two layers: sensor network layer and proxy network layer. This model combines in-network programming, adaptive query processing and efficient content-based search techniques. In the lower level, sensor network layer, sensor nodes have certain computation and storage capabilities. Sensors have three functions: receiving commands from proxy, performing local computation and delivering data to proxy. Sensor nodes receive control commands including sampling rate, delivery rate and operations that need to be performed from the proxy layer. The nodes at proxy network layer have high computation, storage and communication capabilities. Proxies have five functions: receiving queries from users, issuing control commands and other information to sensors, receiving data from sensors, processing queries, and delivering query results to users. After receiving data from sensors, instead of relaying all data to a central server for processing, each proxy processes the query in a decentralized way and delivers the results to the users. From the above introduction, we can see that computation and communication loads are distributed among all proxies.

3 Data Model and Query Language in Sensor Networks

3.1 Data Model

There are a lot of research works on the data model in sensor networks. These research works mainly focus on limited extensions of the traditional relational model, object relational model and time serial model. Some research

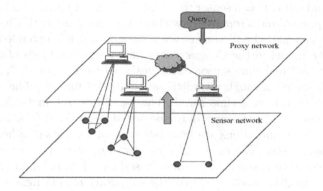

Fig. 3. Hierarchical model [9].

works regard sensor data as relations in multiple nodes and regard a sensor network as a distributed database. Some other research works regard a whole sensor network as a distributed database system composed of some distributed data streams. Other research works use a time serial and probability model to represent the time features and the uncertainty of sensor data. TinyDB developed by UC Berkely [15, 10, 21] and the COUGAR system developed by Cornell [3, 4] are two examples to introduce the data model in sensor networks.

The data model in TinyDB simply extends the traditional relational data model. It defines the sensed data as a single, infinitely long logical table. The table has two kinds of attributes. One is perceptive data attributes, such as pressure, temperature, etc. The other kind of attributes describes the features of the sensed data, the features and status of sensors such as sensorID, the data type of the sensed data (light, voice, pressure, temperature, humidity) and the measurement units of sensed data. This table conceptually contains one row for each reading generated by any sensor, and hence the table can be thought of streaming infinitely over time. Table 1 is an example of the relational table for TinyDB. The operation set in an unlimited relational table is the extension from a traditional relational algebraic to an unlimited relational table.

Table 1. An example of a relational table for TinyDB.

Sensor ID	Query Cycle	Time	Humidity	Light	Tempe-rature	Horizontal Acceleration	Vertical Acceleration	Horizontal magnetometer	Vertical magnetometer	Voice	Tone	Original voice	Original Tone
1	1	03.5.1	562	598	235	421	855	74	154	425	0.2	524	0.6
2	1	03.5.1	457	237	524	635	589	52	321	652	0.5	256	0.4
3	1	03.5.1	586	256	458	365	652	29	456	256	0.3	652	0.6
1	2	03.5.2	562	235	462	652	425	35	458	152	0.5	456	0.2
2	2	03.5.2	459	263	652	354	562	45	485	263	148	368	0.2
3	2	03.5.2	587	266	454	365	652	29	456	256	0.3	652	0.6

A sensor network is looked at as a large distributed database system in the Cougar system developed by Cornell University. Each sensor corresponds to a node in a distributed database system and stores part of the data. Cougar does not send data at each sensor to a central node for storage and processing. It tries to process data separately within the sensor network. Resources are saved efficiently and the lifetime of the sensor network is extended.

The data model in the Cougar system supports two kinds of data types: stored data and real-time sensor data produced by sensors [2, 7, 22]. Stored data are presented through a traditional relational model, while sensor data are described through a time serial. The operation set in Cougar includes relational algebraic operations and time serial operations. The inputs of relational algebraic operations are base relations or outputs of other relational algebraic operations. The inputs of time serial operations are base serial or outputs of other time serial operations. Based on relational data and the time serial data, the data model supports three operations: (1) Relational projection, which translates a time serial to a relation. (2) Product, which takes a relation and a time serial as input, and a new time serial is the output. (3) Aggregation, which takes a time serial as the input and produces a relation as the output.

A query in Cougar consists of a query on stored data and query on sensor data. That is, a query on relational data and a query on time serial data. A continuous query is defined as a permanent view which remains unchangeable in a given period. During the continuous query in Cougar, the queried relation and the time serial can be updated. Update on relational data includes inserting into, deleting from and updating on tuples in the table. Update on time serial means inserting a new tuple into the time serial.

3.2 Query Language

There are a lot of characteristics of sensor data in sensor networks, such as real time, periodicity, uncertainty etc. Till now, query schemes proposed include snapshot query, continuous query, event-based query, life-cycle based query and accuracy-based query. For sensor networks, it is very important to design a general, simple, efficient, extendable, expressible query language based on query schemes and characteristics of sensor data.

Query Language in TinyDB

TinyDB's query language is based on SQL, and we will refer to it as TinySQL. Query Language in TinySQL supports selection, projection, determining sampling rate, group aggregation, user defined aggregation, event trigger, lifetime query, setting storing point and simple join [15].

The Grammar of TinySQL query language is as follows:

SELECT select-list
[FROM sensors]
WHERE predicate

[GROUP BY gb-list]
[HAVING predicate]
[TRIGGER ACTION command-name[(param)]]
[EPOCH DURATION time]

where, *select − list* is the attribute list of the unlimited virtual relational table, which can include an aggregation function. *predicate* is the query condition. *gb − list* is an attributes list. *command − name* is a trigger operation. *param* is the parameters of trigger. *time* is the value of time. *TRIGGERACTION* is the subordinate clause which defines the trigger. It determines the operations executed when *WHERE* clause is satisfied. *EPOCH DURATION* defines the query cycle. The meaning of the other clauses is the same as SQL. Following is an example of a TinyDB query.

SELECT room_no, AVERAGE(light), AVERAGE(volume)
FROM sensors
GROUP BY room_no
HAVING AVERAGE(light) > l AND AVERAGE(volume) > v
EPOCH DURATION 5min

The meaning of the query is detecting rooms per five minutes in which the average light exceeds threshold 1 and the average temperature exceeds threshold v, and returning the room ID and its average light and temperature.

Currently, the functions of TinyDB are very limited. Some functions supported by SQL are not supported by TinyDB.

- The WHERE and HAVING clauses only contain simple conjunctions over arithmetic comparison operators, string matching comparisons (SQL's LIKE and SIMILAR constructs). There is no support for the Boolean operators OR and NOT.
- There is currently no support for sub-SELECTs (subqueries).
- There is currently no support for column renaming (SQL's AS construct) in the *gb − list*.
- Arithmetic expressions are currently limited to the form *column op constant*, where *op* is one of $\{+, -, *, /\}$.

TinyDB includes a facility for simple triggers. Currently, triggers can be executed only in response to some local sensor readings that satisfy the conditions specified in the WHERE clause of the query. Whenever a query result satisfies the WHERE clause of a query, the trigger action is executed. As an example of what triggers can be used for, consider an application where the user wants to sound an alarm whenever the temperature monitored by a sensor goes above some threshold. This can be accomplished via the simple trigger query:

SELECT temp
FROM sensors
WHERE temp > thresh
TRIGGER ACTION SetSnd(512)
EPOCH DURATION 512

The *SetSnd* command sounds the alarm, and the value 512 specifies a sound duration of $512ms$.

The following example is the query on the unlimited virtual relation shown in Table 1. The results are shown in Table 2.

Select nodeID, light
FROM sensors
WHERE light > 200

Node ID	Light
1	598
1	235
2	237
2	263
3	256
3	266
......	......

Table 2. Query result.

Query Language in Cougar

Cougar also provides a SQL-like query language. In most sensor network applications, it is important to detect the environment periodically. Thus, the query language in Cougar supports continuous periodical query. The grammar of query language in Cougar is as follows.

SELECT select-list
FROM [Sensordata S]
[WHERE predicate]
[GROUP BY attributes]
[HAVING predicate]
DURATION time-interval
EVERY time-span

where, DURATION specifies the lifetime of the query. EVERY determines the execution cycle, that is, executes the query per *time − span* minutes. The other clauses are the same as in TinyDB. It can be seen from the query language that Cougar does not support trigger operation. An example is given below.

SELECT AVG(R.concentration)
FROM ChemicalSensor R
WHERE R.loc IN region
HAVING AVG(R.concentration)>0.6
DURATION (now, now+3600)
EVERY 10

The query is to detect whether the density of some chemical gas in a given area exceeds the limit. The lifetime of the query is 3600 minutes from the moment the query is submitted. The detecting is done per 10 minutes to see if the density exceeds 0.6.

4 Storage and Index Techniques in Sensor Networks

For sensor networks, one of the most challenging problems is to name data. Researchers have developed many data centric routing algorithms and communication protocols [16, 17, 18, 8, 5]. Besides these algorithms and protocols, sensor networks also need flexible data centric storage methods. For data centric storage systems, every data generated by each sensor is stored at some sensor(s) in the network according to its name. In the same way, it is easy to find the corresponding data in the sensor network. This section talks about the data centric storage and index techniques for sensor networks.

4.1 Data Centric Naming

There are many data naming approaches, and the naming scheme sometimes depends on the applications. For example, some systems use hierarchical naming. In such systems, data generated by a camera sensor may be named:

US/Universities/USC/CS/cameral

The name is divided into five hierarchies. The first four hierarchies are used to specify the location of the sensor while the last hierarchy is used to specify the type of the data. On the other hand, some systems use an attribute-value naming scheme. In such systems, the data generated by the camera sensor in the previous example would be named:

type = camera
value = image.jpg
location = "CS Dept, Univ. of Southern California"

These naming schemes implicitly define a set of ways in which the data may be accessed. The hierarchical naming scheme used by the above camera sensor implicitly defines the following accessing methods:

1. Accessing the camera sensor data within all US universities;
2. Accessing the camera sensor data within a given US university;
3. Accessing the camera sensor data in the computer science department of a given US university.

4.2 The Performance of Data-centric Storage Systems

Data names are used when storing and receiving data in data centric storage. It uses a mapping between a sensor and the name of a data to store the data. Figure 4 describes such a data centric storage algorithm [16, 18]. Assume sensor nodes A and B want to insert a data named *bird-sighting* and this data is hashed to node C, so the data is routed to node C by the routing protocol. Similarly, a query also uses the name of the data to acquire the location where the data is stored and the query is sent to that sensor.

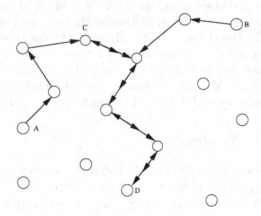

Fig. 4. Data centric storage algorithm [16].

Besides data centric storage, we consider two alternatives: an External Storage scheme in which all events are stored at a node outside the network; and a Local Storage scheme where each event is stored at the node at which it is generated.

For external storage, the cost of accessing events is zero, since all events are available at one node. However, the cost of transporting data to this external node is non-trivial; there is an energy cost in sending events to this node, and significant energy is spent at nodes near the external node in receiving all these events (these nodes become hot-spots). If events are accessed far more frequently than they are generated, external storage might be an acceptable alternative (assuming the event generation rate does not form the bottleneck). At the other end of the spectrum, local storage incurs zero communication cost in storing the data, but incurs a large communication cost, a network flood, in accessing the data. Local storage may therefore be feasible when events are accessed less frequently than they are generated. Data-centric storage lies somewhere in between, since it incurs a non-zero cost both in storing events and retrieving them.

Consider a network of n nodes, in which the cost of sending messages to all nodes (e.g., a flood) is $O(n)$ and the cost of sending a message to a designated node is $O(\sqrt{n})$. Let us denote by D_e the total number of the detected events, Q the number of the queries, and D_q the number of the events which are returned as answers for the Q queries. Furthermore, we assume that the data stored can either be a list of events of a given type, or a summary of such events. Table 3 shows the network-wide communication cost, as well as the hot-spot energy usage for the three schemes. This analysis shows that the data-centric storage scheme becomes more preferable as the size of the network increases, or when many more events are generated than can be usefully queried. This performance advantage increases when summaries are returned as answers. Thus, the data-centric storage scheme is an attractive alternative as sensor networks scale.

Table 3. [16].

Storage method	Total energy consmption	Hot-spot energy consmption
External	$D_e \sqrt{N}$	D_e
Local	$Q_n + D_q \sqrt{n}$	$Q + D_q$
Data-centric	$Q\sqrt{n} + D_e\sqrt{n} + D_q\sqrt{n}$	$Q + D_q$

4.3 Mechanisms for Data-centric Storage

Our discussion has introduced data-centric storage as a concept, without describing the specifics of a particular instance of a data-centric storage system. In this section, we describe a system called a Geographic Hash Table (GHT) [16, 17] and focus on its mechanistic underpinnings. We introduce GHT, a geography-based routing protocol GPSR, its usage in GHT, the robustness of GHT and its structured replication technique.

Geographic Hash Tables

We have said that the essence of a data-centric storage system is captured at its interface, which supports a *put*() operation that stores data by name within the network, and a *get*() operation that retrieves data by name. In the following discussion, *keys* are used to represent a whole named data or part of it.

Geographic Hash Tables (GHTs) is an implementation of this interface for sensor networks. In a GHT, event names are randomly hashed to a geographic location (i.e., an x, y coordinate). This mapping is multi-to-one. Then, a *put*() operation stores an event at the node which is the closest to the hashed location, and a *get*() operation retrieves one or more events from that node.

Implicitly, a GHT specifies a set of queries that it allows. The simplest kind of query it allows is an enumeration query, a list of all events matching a key k. It can also trivially support any statistic (e.g., count, sum, average) defined on that enumeration. Applications can determine which parts of an event name are used to compute the geographic hash value. This choice can crucially affect the performance of the overall system, as well as the set of supported queries, of course. For example, an application can hash events by sensor type so that all temperature sensor readings are stored at one node. Alternatively, an application may choose to hash sensor values to different locations so that temperature readings with a value of $10°C$ can be stored at a different node than, say readings of $20°C$.

GPSR: an Overview

GPSR is a geographic routing protocol that was originally designed for mobile ad-hoc networks. Given the coordinates of a node, GPSR routes a packet to that node using location information only. To do this, GPSR contains two different algorithms: *greedy forwarding* and *perimeter forwarding*.

Greedy forwarding is conceptually simple. Assume each node in a network knows its own location, and that of its neighbors. When a node receives a message destined to location D, it sends the message to another neighbor C which is closer to D than itself. Such a neighbor might not always exist; in this case, GPSR invokes perimeter routing at that node. We now describe perimeter routing. When a packet finds itself at a node which has no neighbors closer to the destination than itself, we say that the packet has encountered a *void*. Figure 5 depicts a situation where a packet destined for node D arrives at a node A. No neighbor of A is closer to D than A itself, indicating the existence of a void. Voids can result from irregular deployment of nodes, as well as from radio-opaque obstacles. A natural technique to route around a void is the right-hand rule (Figure 5). According to this rule, a traversal walks around the perimeter of the void. However, it can be shown that using the right-hand rule on the graph formed by mere connectivity between nodes may not work in many cases. To circumvent this, GPSR computes a planar subgraph of this graph in a distributed manner, and applies the right-hand rule to this subgraph. When this traversal reaches a node that is closer to D than A, greedy forwarding resumes.

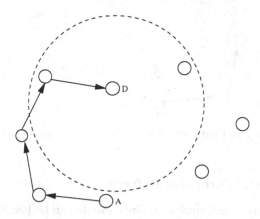

Fig. 5. Get around void space using right-hand rule [16].

From our discussions so far, two facts are obvious. First, GPSR provides the functionality to deliver a packet to a node at a specified location. Second, GHT requires the ability to store an event at the node closest to a specified location (called the home node for an event). (More precisely, GHT maps an event's name to a geographic location, and one way of implementing a GHT would be to store the event at the node closest to that location). Thus, there is a subtle difference between what GPSR provides and what GHTs require. In particular, GPSR would drop a packet if there exists no node at the destination location specified in the packet header, while GHT will store the data at the nearest node to the destination. We will discuss how GHT uses GPRS.

Assume that GHT hashes an event to a destination location d, and, without loss of generality, that no node exists at that location (Figure 6). When GPSR routes the packet containing the event, it will enter perimeter mode at the home node (by definition, the home node will have no neighbor closer to the destination than itself). Furthermore, the packet will remain in perimeter mode and return to the home node in that mode (again, by definition, no other node on the perimeter can be closer to the destination than the home node). GHT uses this property to detect and store events at the home node. When a packet returns in perimeter mode to the node that originated the perimeter traversal, the corresponding event is stored at that node.

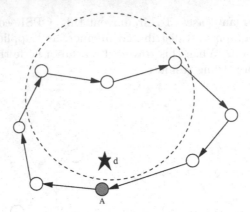

Fig. 6. Find host node using perimeter mode [16].

GHT Robustness: Perimeter Refresh

However, this alone is not sufficient, since events can be lost if the home node fails. Furthermore, if new nodes are deployed, the definition of a home node may change. To solve these problems, robustness of sensor networks is needed.

GHTs use a simple perimeter-refresh protocol to maintain the associations with a set of given sensor nodes. The set of sensors are called home node associations. Periodically, for a given event, a home node will send a message destined to the corresponding location periodically. This refresh message will traverse the perimeter around the specified location. As this message traverses the perimeter, each node on the perimeter stores a local copy of the event. Each node also associates a timer with the event. This timer is reset whenever a subsequent refresh is received. If the timer expires, nodes use this as an indication of the home node failure, and initiate a refresh message themselves. In this manner, home node failures are detected, and the correct new home node is discovered.

As the refresh message traverses the perimeter, it may encounter a new node that is closer to the specified location. By GPSR's forwarding rules, this node will initiate a new perimeter traversal that will pass through the previous home node. The previous home node will detect this condition and remove its association as a home node for that event. When the perimeter traversal returns to the new home node, the association between the event and that node will have been completed. In this manner, GHTs are able to detect and adjust for the arrival of new nodes into the system.

GHT Scaling: Structured Replication

If many events are hashed to the same location, the home node can become a hot-spot which will affect the performance and the network lifetime.

To avoid this, structured replication hierarchically decomposes the geographical region enclosing the sensor network in a manner shown in Figure 7. In structured replication, the rectangular or square boundary encompassing the sensor network is split into 2D equally sized sub-regions, where D is the depth of the replication. Consider an event whose home node is x; x is called the root node for the event. Clearly x is located in one of the sub-regions defined by the spatial decomposition. In each of the remaining sub-regions, one can then compute the location of a mirror of x; this mirror has the same coordinates in its sub-region as x has in its own.

This spatial decomposition can be used to define a hierarchy of mirrors, as shown in Figure 7. The $level - 1$ mirrors of the root are those that would have been selected if d had been 1; these $level - 1$ mirrors are the children of the root in this hierarchy. A similar recursive definition can be applied to levels greater than 1. Notice that different events will have different hierarchies since the spatial decomposition is defined for a given event name.

A node that generates an event would, instead of storing the event at the root (or home) node, store it at the nearest mirror. This mirror is computed using simple geometric operations, knowing d and the boundary of the sensor network (the rectangle encompassing the sensor network). Thus, the root node is no longer a hot-spot since events are distributed across the network. However, queries for a particular event now have to be directed to all the mirrors. The mirror hierarchy is used for this in a straightforward way: the query is sent directly to the root, which then forwards the query to its children, and so on, until it arrives at all the mirrors. Replies make their way up the hierarchy in the reverse direction, and may get aggregation along the way.

Note that, structured replication does not replicate data at multiple nodes; rather, in some sense, the home node for an event is now replicated in several sub-regions to alleviate hot-spots. This is how the name comes.

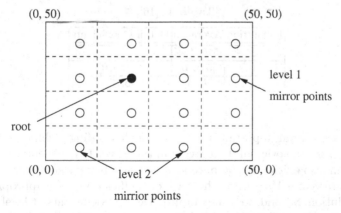

Fig. 7. Structure Duplication [16].

4.4 Hierarchical Search Structures

A system can be useful in sensor networks where users do not know *a priori* what to look for, but can use low-overhead queries to drill-down to phenomena of interests, such as regions where the temperature is/was unusually high. Consider a system that allows users to efficiently search for such patterns by, for example, asking a sequence of questions such as "What was the average temperature in area X an hour ago?" and then "What was the average temperature in sub-area A of area X in the last 10 minutes of that hour?". An important leverage point for the design of such systems is that the answers to such questions can be *approximate*.

The DIMENSIONS system [16, 6] is a data-centric storage system designed to handle such queries. It builds upon prior work that describes approximate querying of large datasets using wavelet coefficients of the data. While an extended treatment of wavelets is beyond the scope of this book, we briefly introduce wavelet encoding of data sets to give the readers an intuitive understanding of what is possible with the DIMENSIONS system. Consider a vector $V = [5, 6, 4, 4]$. The simplest wavelet transform of this vector takes elements pairwise and computes averages recursively. Table 4 shows this process, where each level of averaging constitutes a different resolution. Clearly, each step of the averaging loses some information; the lost information is captured by the detail coefficients shown in this table. Each detail coefficient is the difference between the computed average and the second of the pair of numbers from which that average was computed. For example, vector V has two pairs of elements: $(5, 6)$ and $(4, 4)$. The averages are $5.5 = ((5 + 6)/2)$ and $4 = ((4 + 4)/2)$. The detail coefficients are $- 0.5$ and 0. The overall average, together with an ordered (starting from the lowest resolution) list of the detail coefficients, constitutes the wavelet coefficients of V.

Table 4. [16].

Resolution	Averages	Detail Coefficients
2	$[5, 6, 4, 4]$	–
1	$[5.5, 4]$	$[-0.5, 0]$
0	$[4.75]$	$[0.75]$

There are several important properties of this coding technique. First, we can reconstruct the original data given all the wavelet coefficients. As a corollary, we can also efficiently compute averages of arbitrary subsequences of the original data vector V by using the wavelet coefficients at the appropriate levels of resolution. Second, we can compute wavelet coefficients at level i merely from the wavelet coefficients at level $i + 1$. Finally, if the detail coefficients are small, they can be neglected with some loss of accuracy in computed averages. In this sense, wavelet coding is *multi-resolution*.

Wavelet encoding can be used to support spatial-temporal queries. Consider a sensor network where each sensor node periodically generates temperature samples. Viewed across the entire network, the collection of temperature samples can be represented by a 2D array of temperature values indexed by location and time. If all these values could be collected in a central location, then it is clear that one could compute wavelet coefficients on the data to efficiently answer spatial-temporal queries described above. However, the design of the DIMENSIONS system makes the observation that these wavelet coefficients can be computed and stored far more efficiently in a distributed fashion. This capability rests on the two properties: resolution in the spatial dimension corresponds to differently sized regions of the sensor field, and that lower resolution wavelet coefficients can be computed from higher-resolution coefficients. DIMENSIONS constructs a storage hierarchy using data-centric storage concepts, and stores successively lower resolution coefficients in the higher levels of the hierarchy. Given a number of levels of resolution d, the system effectively divides the geographic region occupied by the sensors into d levels recursively. The 0-level has only one region, that is, the area covered by the sensor network. The i-level has 2^i sub-regions. The d-level has 2^d sub-regions. The size of each sub-region in i-level is four times the size of a sub-region in $i + 1$-level. To construct the 1-level from the 0-level in the hierarchical structure, the system first hashes the names of the datasets corresponding to 0-level to a location in sub-region of 0-level. The home node corresponding to this location is the root of the hierarchy, called the *apex*. Then the sub-region in a 0-level are divided into four equal sized quadrants, which constitute the 1-level in the hierarchical structure. One node is selected in each quadrant of the sensor network's geographic region as a cluster head. All the cluster heads are sub-nodes of the apex in 0-level. To construct the 2-level from the 1-level, each cluster head in 1-level is regarded as the apex of that sub-region. Then each sub-region in a 1-level are divided into four equal sized quadrants, which constitute the 2-level in the hierarchical structure. One node is selected in each sub-region in 2-level as a cluster head. All the cluster heads in 2-level are sub-nodes of the apex in 1-level. This process continues recursively until d levels are all constructed in the hierarchical structure. Figure 8 shows the construction of the hierarchical structure.

4.5 Distributed Indices on a Single Key

Besides spatial-temporal aggregates and exact match queries, sensor network applications will need range queries of the form: 'List all the events for which the temperature values were between $50°C$ and $60°C$'. Equally useful are geographically constrained range queries: 'List all the events that occurred in region A of the sensor network for which the temperature values were between $50°C$ and $60°C$'.

The Distributed Index for Features in Sensor networks (DIFS) [16] system takes a slightly different approach that increases the efficiency of range queries.

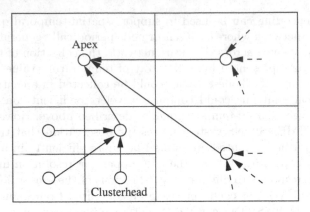

Fig. 8. The DIMENSIONS hierarchy [16].

Similar with DIMENSIONS, DIFS uses only one key attribute of the sensor data. Geographic hashing and spatial decomposition are used to construct the multi-rooted hierarchical structure, which is a one-dimension index. This index has two features. First, it builds a geographically-aligned multi-rooted hierarchy designed to avoid the root as a bottleneck in DIMENSIONS. Second, it efficiently propagates information summarizing the hierarchy that can be used to prune traversal at higher levels of the hierarchy.

We take temperature as an example to introduce how one dimension index is built in DIFS. Suppose the range of temperature is between $1°C$ and $100°C$. The construction process of the index is best described with reference to Figure 9. As with DIMENSIONS, DIFS divides the geographical area encompassed by the sensor network equally, which constructs the d-level hierarchical tree. The difference from DIMENSIONS is that the tree has multiple roots instead of one. Now, suppose that an event with a temperature value 26 is generated at some node within the network. It is stored in a logical leaf node of the DIFS hierarchy as follows. (1) Hash a unique name for the index (say 'temperature') together with a textual representation of the range of values ('0 : 100' in our example). (2) The logical leaf node of the DIFS is obtained by the hashing in step (1). (3) The event is stored at this logical leaf node. Thus, each local leaf is responsible for storing all the events detected in its sub-region.

Each local leaf node has b parents, where b is a tunable system parameter. Each leaf node computes a histogram of the event values it has; it then splits up the histogram into b equal parts, and passes these parts to its b parents. Thus, in Figure 9 where b is 2, the leaf node would pass up the histogram for temperature values between 0 and 49 to one parent, and the histogram for values 50 to 99 to another parent. Through hashing the name of the index together with the appropriate range, the leaf node locates its parents. In this way, each parent node is responsible for $1/b$ of the value range, but serves four times the geographic area covered by the child. Higher-levels of the hierarchy

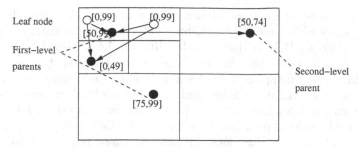

Fig. 9. DIFs multiple roots structure [16].

are built up recursively until the whole b hierarchies are constructed. The top-level of this hierarchy can contain many roots, each of which is responsible for a small part of the value range, but which covers the entire geographic region.

Given a range query for events within a temperature range say [50, 60], the originating node first picks the set of root nodes whose individual ranges cover the query range, and starts traversal. At each node, the histograms obtained from the children can be used to determine if the matching events exist, thereby pruning the descent that contains only unrelated events. For geographically constrained range queries (e.g., all events within the temperature range [50, 60] and in region A), the querying node can pick some intermediate nodes in the hierarchy (those that cover part of the query range and the querying region A) and initiate traversal from there.

4.6 Distributed Multi-dimensional Indices

We mentioned earlier that DIFS allows range queries over two keys or attributes where one of the attributes is geographical location and the other is a range of values. This kind of query is called a two-dimensional range query. In this section we consider an index that permits range queries over multi-dimensional data. A multi-dimensional range query has some constraints on multi-attributes. As an example of the need for such queries, consider scientists analyzing the growth of marine micro-organisms. They might be interested in events that occurred within the temperature range from $50°C$ to $60°C$ and the light range from 10 to 20. The query may be expressed as 'List all events that have temperatures between $50°C$ and $60°C$, and light levels between 10 and 20'. In this example, the scientists are interested in the effects of geographical region, temperature and light on the growth of marine micro-organisms.

In traditional database systems, such range queries are supported using pre-computed multiple-dimensional indices. Such indices trade-off some initial pre-computation cost to achieve a significantly more efficient querying capability. We discuss the design of a distributed index structure called Distributed Index for Multidimensional data (DIM) [24, 16] for supporting multi-dimensional queries in sensor networks.

The key to resolve multiple-dimensional range queries efficiently is data locality: events with comparable attribute values are stored nearby. The basic insight underlying DIM is that data locality can be obtained by a *locality-preserving geographic* hash function. The geographic hash function finds a locality-preserving mapping from the multi-dimensional space to a 2-d geographic space. This mapping is inspired by $k-d$ trees [2]. Moreover, each node in the network self-organizes to claim part of the attribute space for itself (we say that each node owns a zone), so the events falling into that space are routed to and stored at that node. Intuitively, a zone is a sub-division of the geographic extent of a sensor field (Figure 10).

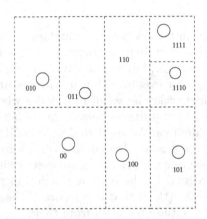

Fig. 10. Zone of sensor network [24].

A zone is defined by the following constructive procedure. Consider a rectangle R on the x–y plane. Intuitively, R is the bounding rectangle that contains all the sensors within the network. We call a sub-rectangle Z of R a zone, if Z is obtained by dividing R k times, $k \geq 0$, using a procedure that satisfies the following property:

1. After the i-th division, $0 \geq i \geq k$, R is partitioned into $2i$ equal sized rectangles;
2. If i is an odd number, the i-th division is parallel to the y-axis; otherwise the division is parallel to the x-axis.

Following is the procedure by which a zone is constructed. The bounding rectangle R is first sub-divided into two zones at level 0 by a vertical line that splits R into two equal pieces, each of these sub-zones can be split into two zones at level 1 by a horizontal line, and so on. For each zone Z, there is a non-negative integer k that indicates the level of zone Z, i.e., $level(Z) = k$. As a result of this division process, each zone is assigned a bit string, called its zone code that reflects its position in the splitting process. The splitting process can itself be represented as a binary tree, called the *zone tree*.

In DIM, each network node is mapped to a unique zone. If the sensor network is deployed in a grid-like fashion, then it is easy to see that there exists a k such that each node maps into a distinct level-k zone. In general, however, the node placements within a sensor field are likely to be less regular than the grid. For a given k, some zones may be empty and other zones might have more than one node situated within them. In DIM, nodes can have differently-sized zones (as Figure 10 illustrates), and each node automatically discovers its zone codes. The zone tree corresponding to Figure 10 is shown in Figure 11.

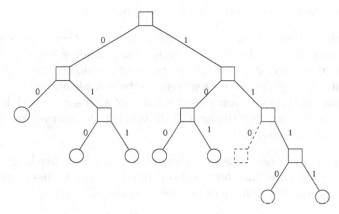

Fig. 11. Zone tree of sensor network [24].

Let us discuss how events are hashed to zones. Consider a DIM that aims to support m distinct attributes. Let us denote these attributes $A_l, ..., A_m$. For ease of exposition, assume that the depth of every zone in the network is k, m is a sub-multiple of k, and that this value of k is known to every node. Furthermore, assume that all attribute values have been normalized to be between 0 and 1. The DIM hashing scheme assigns a k bit zone code to an event as follows. For $0 \le i \le m$, if $A_i < 0.5$, the i-th bit of the zone code is assigned 0, else 1. For $m+1 \le i \le 2m$, if $A_{i-m} < 0.25$ or $0.5 \le A_{i-m} < 0.75$, the i-th bit of the zone is assigned 0, else 1. This procedure repeats until all k bits have been assigned. As an example, consider event $< 0.3, 0.8 >$. For this event, the 5-bit zone code is 01110.

At least conceptually, the rest of the DIM system is relatively easy to describe. To insert an event e, DIM computes the zone code of e. GPSR is then used to route e to zone Z whose zone code has the longest matching prefix of the e's zone code. Since e's zone code can be mapped to a geographic location, the target zone will be somewhere 'near' that location. Finally, notice a two-dimensional range query 'list all the events in $[0.3 - 0.5, 0.4 - 0.8]$'. The range of the query $[0.3 - 0.5, 0.4 - 0.8]$ intersects with a set of zones and the query can be resolved by routing the request to the nodes that own those zones.

5 Query Processing in Sensor Networks

We can observe some physical phenomena in the natural environment by querying and analyzing data from wireless sensor networks, e.g., monitoring the level of rainfall in a certain region, obtaining the status of a disaster area, supervising the vehicles in a big city, etc. Most queries about the data in sensor networks can be classified into three types [2, 3]:

- **Historical query**: it queries the historical data gathered from a wireless sensor network, e.g., 'list the average level of rainfall in region A for 1999.'
- **Snapshot query**: it retrieves the status of a sensor network at a given moment, e.g., 'return the current temperature of all sensors.'
- **Continuous query**: it concerns the status of a sensor network for a given time interval, e.g., 'For the next 36 hours, list the average rainfall every 30 minutes in region A.'

Queries in sensor networks can be expressed by a SQL-like languagewhich has been introduced in the above section. Here, we will discuss several up-to-date query processing techniques in sensor networks.

5.1 Centralized and Distributed Query Processing

There are two kinds of techniques to process queries in sensor networks, centralized query processing and distributed query processing. Both of these techniques have their advantages and disadvantages, and can be applied in different circumstances.

Centralized query processing

Centralized query processing contains two steps. First, it periodically retrieves data from the sensor network and stores the data at a centralized database. Second, it processes the queries on the centralized database. These two steps can be executed at the same time.

A centralized approach is suitable for historical query processing, but this method has many limitations. If the period of storing data to the centralized database server is too long or the sampling frequency of sensors is too low, the database server cannot retrieve all the data, which is necessary for query processing, from the sensor network. For example, if the period of storing data to the centralized database is 30 minutes, the query 'retrieve every minute the rainfall in BeiJing' cannot be processed accurately. In order to answer the query by the centralized method, the database server needs to frequently retrieve data from all the sensors. Since this method will rapidly exhaust the energy of the sensors and produce a lot of redundant data, it cannot be applied in practice. Actually, it is unnecessary to retrieve data from the entire sensor network just for processing a query. In the above example, instead of retrieving data from all the sensors, the database server only needs to increase the sampling rate of the sensors in BeiJing. Generally, a sensor node is equipped with processor and memory. Hence, a sensor network can perform distributed computation and storage over all the sensor nodes. This efficiently reduces the data transmission cost and the energy consumption of the sensors, also it improves the performance of the sensor network. Actually, centralized query processing can only be applied in the condition that sensors have sufficient power supply and low sampling rate.

Distributed query processing

Considering the drawbacks of centralized query processing, researchers at Cornell propose some distributed query processing techniques [2, 3]. In their methods, a query determines which data should be retrieved from the sensor network and the aggregations in the query are processed in-network. Different queries need different data and only those data related to the queries will be retrieved. The rest of this section compares the difference between centralized and distributed query processing through an example and illustrates the advantage of the distributed approach.

Given the sample query 'for every 30 seconds, return the average temperature of the sensors whose readings are higher than $30°C$', we will illustrate how to process it by the two query processing techniques, which is demonstrated in Figure 12. In the figure, the smaller rectangles represent the data acquired from the sensor nodes and the ellipses denote aggregate operations which compute an average value. The database is a centralized one. The sensors in this example are temperature sensors.

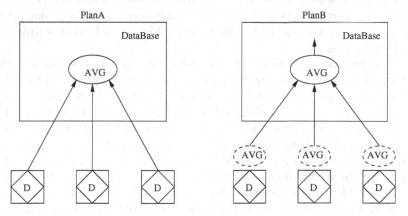

Fig. 12. Comparison of two query processing techniques.

PlanA in Figure 12 shows the centralized query processing technique. Every sensor returns the current temperature at a user defined sampling rate. When the sampling data arrives at the database server, the values which are lower than $30°C$ are filtered out, and the arithmetic mean of the remained data is calculated. Apparently, the query only concerns sensors that have readings greater than $30°C$, whereas those values lower than the threshold are useless. However, since all the sensors must return their values according to planA, it wastes the limited energy, increases the load of the sensor network, produces unnecessary transmissions and causes congestion in the network.

PlanB is the distributed query processing technique. During query processing, the *select* and *aggregate* operations are performed on the sensor nodes separately. In PlanB, only qualified data are involved in aggregation and only partial aggregations are sent to the central database to derive the final results. Consequently, this reduces the communication traffic in sensor networks and saves bandwidth resource.

5.2 Aggregation Processing in Queries

Aggregation is a common operation for queries. How to process aggregation is one of the key issues in query processing in sensor networks. This section introduces some primary aggregation processing techniques (aggregation techniques in short).

Centralized and distributed aggregation [10, 12]

In a centralized aggregation, a client host first gathers readings from all the sensors and then computes the aggregate result. Figure 13(a) illustrates this scheme. In the distributed approach, aggregation is achieved by the collaboration of many sensor nodes. While routing the data, sensor nodes compute the whole or partial aggregate value of the data they transfer. Finally, those aggregate results are sent to the client host. Figure 13(b) demonstrates the distributed approach.

Figure 14 gives an example of processing aggregation in sensor networks. All the sensor nodes form a tree, which is called a routing tree. In the figure, the dash lines represent connections between the sensor nodes; the solid lines denote the edges of the routing tree which are used to transfer data from the leaf nodes to the upper nodes while computing the aggregation. In the centralized method, every sensor node must send its readings to the client host. Suppose the depth of a sensor node is n, and it needs $n - 1$ communications to transmit the data produced by the sensor node to the root of the routing tree. Figure 14(a) illustrates the centralized aggregate approach. Each node is labelled by its distance from the root of the routing tree. It requires 16 messages to send the aggregate result to the client host using the centralized method.

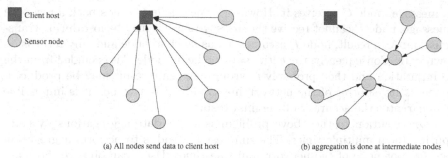

(a) All nodes send data to client host   (b) aggregation is done at intermediate nodes

Fig. 13. Centralized and distributed aggregate.

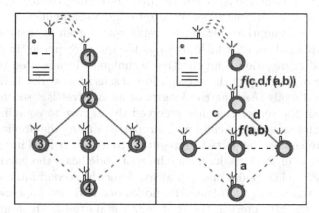

Fig. 14. Examples of two aggregate approaches [12].

Figure 14(b) presents the distributed aggregate scheme. In this approach, the leaf nodes of the routing tree only need to send the data to their parent nodes. Intermediate nodes first accumulate their data with the readings of their children according to an aggregation function f. Then the partial aggregate result is propagated along the routing tree. While the partial aggregate result is being transmitted, it is updated with any required extra data until it reaches the root node. The amount of the data transmitted in this solution depends on the aggregation function, e.g., in order to compute an average function, every intermediate node needs to know the sum and the number of the nodes in its subtree. In Figure 14(b), it requires five messages to compute the average function before the root sends the result to the client host.

Pipelined aggregation [10, 12]

During processing aggregation in sensor networks, because of communication failure or movement of sensor nodes, it is difficult to ensure accuracy of the results. Suppose node P only has one child node C. After node P broadcasts a message, node C receives it. However, when node C sends back a response message, node P cannot receive the message since it may be lost during transmission. As a result, node P assumes it has no child node and only returns its own data. Consequently, the entire subtree below node P is excluded from the computation and then probably a wrong aggregate result may be produced. In fact, any subtree of the network may fail in this way, i.e., it is impossible to guarantee the accuracy of the final result.

One solution to the above problem is to validate aggregations by computing them multiple times. The simplest method is to perform aggregation at the root node of the network multiple times. Users can observe those aggregates and make a reasonable decision about which is the true value. The problem of this technique is that it requires re-sending the aggregate request along the network multiple times, causing a large communication cost and a large energy consumption cost. Users must wait for an aggregation interval for each additional result, which prolongs the query response time.

Pipelined aggregation is an effective technique which is used to overcome the problem of accuracy of the aggregation in sensor networks. It divides time into many intervals. Assume the length of an interval is i seconds. During each interval, the sensor that has received the aggregate combines its local readings with the values its child nodes reported during the previous interval, and then propagates the partial aggregation to its upper level in the network. Accordingly, after the first duration, the root node hears the partial aggregation sent by its child nodes one hop away. After the second interval, the root gets the partial aggregation from the nodes one and two hops away, and so forth. After the kth interval, the root gets the partial aggregation from the child nodes less than $k - 1$ hops away. When the nodes that do not receive the aggregate request receive the partial results from other nodes, they will send the partial results to the nodes that are on the upper level.

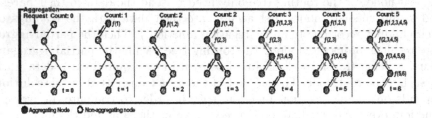

Fig. 15. Pipelined aggregate [12].

Not only does this tend to include the nodes that would have been excluded from a single pass aggregate, but the pipelined aggregate technique also has two interesting properties. First, after aggregates have been reported by the leaf nodes, new aggregates will arrive every i seconds. The value of i is very small. It is about the time it takes for a sensor to produce and transmit a value. Second, assume the total time for an aggregation request to reach the leaf nodes and return to the root is about t. Then, the root node starts to get the first approximate aggregation after interval t and then it receives additional aggregations every i seconds. According to the above properties, the pipelined aggregation can provide users an aggregate stream. Since the stream can reveal the change of the sensor data or the sensor network, generally, it is more significant than a single aggregate value. Figure 15 illustrates a pipelined aggregate in a small sensor network.

The most significant drawback of a pipelined aggregate is that a number of extra messages are transmitted in order to get the first aggregation of all the sensors. Figure 15 is an example. It requires 22 messages for the first result, since every aggregating node needs to transmit a message in each time interval. The non-pipelined approach only needs to propagate 10 messages, five down and five up along the network. In this example, after 12 initial messages overhead, it only needs five messages to produce each additional aggregate at the rate of one update per time interval. The pipelined aggregation can still be optimized to reduce the transmitting overhead. One option is that each node does not transmit any data until the aggregate of its subtree is changed, and intermediate nodes assume aggregates of their child nodes remain unchanged unless they receive different values. This method efficiently reduces the amount of messages sent by nodes.

Channel sharing during aggregation [12]

While discussing pipelined aggregate, the fact that sensor nodes use a shared channel to communicate with each other is ignored. Messages are broadcasted and all sensor nodes within the range can receive them. Taking the advantage of a shared channel, some techniques can reduce the traffic and increase the accuracy of aggregation in the face of transmission failures.

If a sensor node missed the initial aggregate request, it can still use the shared channel to monitor the communication of the nodes nearby and participate in the aggregate if the nodes near it propagate their aggregates.

This not only increases the number of sensor nodes engaged in aggregation, the shared channel technique also reduces transmitted messages. Once a sensor node finds that others propagate aggregate messages, it can join the procedure without any extra information. In Figure 15, those messages denoted by black arrows are not obliged to transmit. Consequently, the transmitted messages are reduced from 22 to 17. Listening techniques can also be used to reduce the number of the transmitted messages.

Hypnosis testing during aggregation [12]

Although pipelined aggregation can conserve the bandwidth and improve the accuracy of results, it still requires all sensor nodes to participate in the aggregate computation. Hypnosis testing can be applied to reduce the number of the nodes involved in aggregating. By monitoring the transmission of nearby nodes, this technique permits only the nodes that can greatly affect the final aggregation to propagate messages.

For example, suppose the aggregate function is MAX or MIN and every sensor node can hear the values transmitted by others. If local reading cannot affect the final result, i.e. it is lower (for MAX) or greater (for MIN) than the broadcasted value, a sensor will not send out its data. Despite the fact that hypnosis testing can be applied to process aggregate functions MAX and MIN directly, some aggregate functions, such as SUM and $COUNT$, cannot use this technique.

This section introduces some aggregate techniques in sensor networks. Pipelined aggregation can increase throughput of the network, and cope with transmission failures. Taking the advantages of a shared channel can reduce the number of transmitted messages and improve the accuracy of aggregate. Using hypnosis testing can also reduce total traffic in the sensor networks.

While processing aggregate function $AVERAGE$ with hypnosis testing, a user defined error range is required. If the aggregate error does not exceed the threshold after discarding some readings, those data do not need to be transmitted.

5.3 Continuous Query Processing

Query processing in sensor networks is a kind of distributed query processing. It involves one global query processor and some local query processors at each sensor node. We begin with the local query processors. In this section, we discuss continues query processing which is suitable for local query processors.

Infinite real-time data streams are produced in wireless sensor networks, which are the query objects of users. Continuous query is commonly used by users. After a continuous query is proposed, the global query processor decomposes the query into a set of sub-queries and sends them to the corresponding sensors to process. Sub-queries are also continuous queries. They scan, filter (select) and integrate the corresponding infinite real-time data streams and produce continuous partial results to return to the global query processor. The global query processor processes the results further and returns the final result to users. Local query processing is the key of continuous query. The same as global continuous query processing, the execution of continuous sub-queries will take a long time. During this period, the sensor nodes, the characteristics of the data they produce, and the workload of the sensor nodes are all changed. So it is very important to make the local processor adapt to the change of the environment.

A Continuously Adaptive Continuous Queries over Streams (CACQ) can be used in a local query processor in sensor networks. It will be introduced in two aspects: single continuous query and multiple continuous query. Suppose no *join* operator exists in a query.

Single Query
    The query is decomposed into a set of operators that constitute the processing that must be applied to every tuple flowing into the system. Since we are not considering *join* at the moment, the only operators that can exist are *scan* operators, which fetch tuples, and *select* operators, which filter those tuples based on a user-specified Boolean predicate. For now, we assume that the queries contain only conjunctions (ANDs) of predicates.
    At the core of the system is a single eddy that routes tuples to operators for processing. Each operator has an input queue of tuples waiting to be processed by it. Operators dequeue tuples, process them, and return them to the eddy for further routing. The eddy maintains a pool of tuples that are waiting to be placed on the input queue of some operator. When the pool is empty, the eddy can schedule a *scan* operator to cause more tuples to be fetched or produced.

Multiple Queries
    The goal of the multiple-query solution in the absence of *join* is to use a single eddy to route tuples among all of the continuous queries currently in the system. In our solution, tuples are never copied: two different queries with two different predicates over the same relation should operate over exactly the same tuples. This is important for two reasons: tuples occupy storage that must be conserved, and copying takes valuable processor cycles. A key part of the multiple query solution without *join* is the grouped filter that allows us to share work between multiple selections over the attribute of a relation.

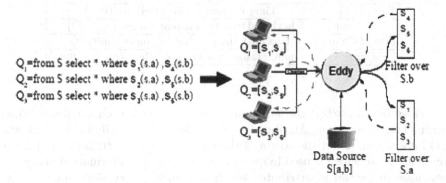

Q_1=from S select * where S_1(s.a) ,S_4(s.b)
Q_2=from S select * where S_2(s.a) ,S_5(s.b)
Q_3=from S select * where S_3(s.a) ,S_6(s.b)

Q_1=[S_1,S_4]
Q_2=[S_2,S_5]
Q_3=[S_3,S_6]

Eddy

Data Source
S[a,b]

Filter over
S.b

Filter over
S.a

S_4
S_5
S_6

S_1
S_2
S_3

Fig. 16. The Architecture of Continuous Query processing [11].

Figure 16 shows the basic architecture. Users submit queries Q_1, Q_2 and Q_3, consisting of selection predicates S_1 through S_6, over two fields, a and b of source S. All the queries are submitted to a single eddy, with just one filter operator (and its associated grouped filter) for field a, and one for field b. The eddy tracks when the tuples are ready to be output to each query, and sends the tuples back to the appropriate end-users as required.

5.4 Query Processing of TinyDB

Metadata Management

Each node in TinyDB maintains a catalog of metadata that describes its local attributes, events, and user-defined functions. This metadata is periodically copied to the root of the network for use by the optimizer. Metadata is registered with the system via static linking done at compile time using the TinyOS C-like programming language. Events and attributes pertaining to various operating systems and TinyDB components are made available to queries by declaring them in an interface file and providing a small handler function. For example, in order to expose network topology to the query processor, the TinyOS Network component defines the attribute parent of type integer and registers a handler that returns the ID of the node's parent in the current routing tree.

Event metadata consists of a name, a signature, and a frequency estimate that is used in query optimization. User-defined predicates also have a name and a signature, along with a selectivity estimate which is provided by the author of the function.

Table 5. Metadata fields kept with each attribute.

Metadata	Description
Power	Cost to sample this attribute (in J)
Sample Time	Time to sample this attribute (in s)
Constant	Is this attribute constant-valued (e.g., ID)
Rate of Change	How fast the attribute changes (units/s)
Range	Dynamic range of attribute values (pair of units)

Table 5 summarizes the metadata associated with each attribute, along with a brief description. Attribute metadata is used primarily in two contexts: (1) information about the cost and the time to fetch an attribute, and range of an attribute which is used in query optimization, (2) information about the semantic properties of attributes which is used in query dissemination and result processing. Notice that the power consumption and time to sample can differ across sensors by several orders of magnitude.

The catalog also contains metadata about TinyDB's extensible aggregate system. The catalog includes names of aggregates and pointers to their code.

Each aggregate consists of three functions, that initialize, merge, and update the final value of partial aggregate records as they flow through the system. The one that defines the extensible aggregate functions must provide information about functional properties. In TinyDB, two properties must be satisfied: that the aggregate is monotonic and whether it is exemplary or summary. *COUNT* is a monotonic aggregate as its value can only become larger as more values are aggregated. *MIN* is an exemplary aggregate, as it returns a single value from the set of aggregate values, while *AVERAGE* is a summary aggregate because it computes some result over the entire set of values.

TinyDB also stores metadata information about the costs of processing and delivering data, which is used in query-lifetime estimation. The costs of these phases in TinyDB, which are shown in Figure 17, range from $2mA$ while sleeping, to over $20mA$ while transmitting and processing.

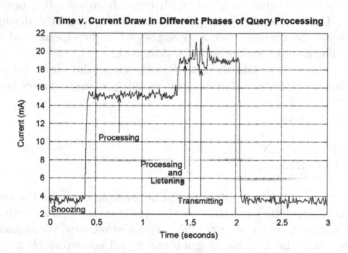

Fig. 17. Costs of Different Phases of Query Processing [6] [14].

Ordering of Sampling And Predicates

Sampling is often an expensive operation in terms of power. However, a sample from a sensor s must be taken to evaluate any predicate over the attribute $sensors.s$. If a predicate discards a tuple in the sensors table, then subsequent predicates need not examine the tuple — and hence the corresponding cost of sampling can be avoided. Thus these predicates are 'expensive', and need to be ordered carefully. The predicate ordering problem here is somewhat different than in the earlier literature because (a) an attribute may be referenced in multiple predicates, and (b) expensive predicates are only on a single table, $sensors$.

To model this issue, we treat the sampling of a sensor t as a separate 'job' τ to be scheduled along with the predicates. Hence a set of predicates $P = \{p_1, p_2...p_m\}$ is rewritten as a set of operations $S = \{s_1, ..., s_n\}$, where $P \subset S$, and $S - P = \{\tau_1, \tau_2, ..., \tau_{n-m}\}$ contains one sampling operator for each distinct attribute referenced in P. The selectivity of sampling operators is always 1. The selectivity of selection operators is derived by assuming that attributes have a uniform distribution over their range (which is available in the catalog). Relaxing this assumption by, for example, storing histograms or time-dependent functions per-attribute remains an area of future work. The cost of an operator (predicate or sample) can be determined by consulting the metadata, as described in the previous section.

We also introduce a partial order on S, where τ_i must precede p_j if p_j references the attribute sampled by τ_i. The combination of sampling operators and the dependency of predicates on samples determines the costs of sampling operators and the sharing of sampling operators across predicates. The partial order induced on S forms a graph with edges from sampling operators to predicates. This is a simple series-parallel graph. An optimal ordering of jobs with series-parallel constraints is a topic treated in the Operational Research literature that inspired earlier optimization work.

The basic idea is to add them to S with appropriate selectivities, costs, and ordering constraints. As an example of this process, consider the query:

SELECT $accel$, mag
FROM $sensors$
WHERE $accel > c_1$ AND $mag > c_2$
SAMPLE INTERVAL $1s$

The order of magnitude difference in per-sample costs for the accelerometer and magnetometer suggests that the power costs of plans with different orders of sampling and selection will vary substantially. We consider three possible plans: in the first, the magnetometer and accelerometer are sampled before either selection is applied. In the second, the magnetometer is sampled and the selection over its reading (which we call Smag) is applied before the accelerometer is sampled or filtered. In the third plan, the accelerometer is sampled first and its selection (Saccel) is applied before the magnetometer is sampled.

We compared the costs of these three plans, and, as expected, found that the first was always more expensive than the other two. More interestingly, the second can be an order of magnitude more expensive than the third, when Saccel is much more selective than Smag. Conversely, when Smag is highly selective, it can be cheaper to sample the magnetometer first.

Similarly, we note that there are certain kinds of aggregate functions where the same kind of interleaving of sampling and processing can also lead to a performance savings. Consider the query:

SELECT MAX(*light*)
FROM *sensors*
WHERE *mag* > *x*
SAMPLE INTERVAL 8*s*

In this query, the maximum of eight seconds worth of *light* readings will be computed, but only *light* readings from sensors whose magnetometers read greater than *x* will be considered. Interestingly, it turns out that, unless the *x* predicate is very selective, it will be cheaper to evaluate this query by checking to see if each new light reading is greater than the previous reading and then applying the selection predicate over *mag*, rather than first sampling *mag*.

Event Query Batching to Conserve Power

As a second example of the benefit of power-aware optimization, we consider the optimization of the query:

ON EVENT *e*(*nodeid*)
SELECT a_1
FROM *sensors* AS *s*
WHERE *s.nodeid* = *e.nodein*
SAMPLE INTERVAL *d* FOR *k*

This query will cause an instance of the internal query (SELECT ...) to be started every time the event *e* occurs. The internal query samples results at every *d* seconds for a duration of *k* seconds, at which point it stops running. Note that, by the semantics formulated above, it is possible for multiple instances of the internal query to be running at the same time. If enough such queries are running simultaneously, the benefit of event-based queries (e.g. not having to poll for results) will be outweighed by the fact that each instance of the query consumes significant energy sampling and delivering (independent) results. To alleviate the burden of running multiple copies of the same identical query, we employ a multi-query optimization technique based on rewriting. To do this, we convert external events (of type *e*) into a stream of events, and rewrite the entire set of independent internal queries as a sliding window join between events and sensors, with a window size of *k* seconds on the event stream, and no window on the sensor stream. For example:

SELECT a_1
FROM *sensors* AS *s*
WHERE *s.nodeid* = *e.nodein*
SAMPLE INTERVAL *d* FOR *k*

The advantage of this approach is that only one query runs at a time no matter how frequently the events of type *e* are triggered. This offers a large potential savings in sampling and transmission cost.

6 Sensor Network Data Management System

A sensor network data management system is a system for extracting, storing and managing sensor data. It mainly concerns query optimization and processing of sensor data. In this section, we present two examples of a sensor network data management system: TinyDB of UC Berkeley and COUGAR of Cornell. The data model and the query language of the two systems have been discussed in Section 3, and only internal architectures and implementation techniques are described here.

6.1 Sensor Network Data Management System - TinyDB

Introduction to TinyDB

TinyDB, which was developed by UC Berkeley, is a sensor network data management system. TinyDB provides a simple, SQL-like interface to query sensor data much as you would pose queries against a traditional database. It is not necessary to know the details of the network, which makes the network transparent to users. Given a query specifying your data interests, TinyDB collects that data from motes in the environment, filters it, aggregates it together, and routes it out to a PC. Some of the features of TinyDB include:

1. **Metadata Management**: TinyDB provides a metadata catalog to describe the attributes of a sensor network including the kinds of the sensor readings, the parameters of the software and hardware etc. It also provides a lot of commands to manage metadata.
2. **High Level Queries**: TinyDB uses a SQL-like declarative query language that allows users to describe the data they want, without requiring users to say how to obtain it. This makes it easier for users to write applications, and helps guarantee that the applications continue to run efficiently as the sensor network changes.
3. **Network Topology**: TinyDB manages the underlying radio network by tracking neighbors, maintaining routing tables, and ensuring that every mote in the network can efficiently and (relatively) reliably deliver its data to users.
4. **Multiple Queries**: TinyDB allows multiple queries to be run on the same set of motes at the same time. Queries can have different sample rates and access different sensor types, and TinyDB efficiently balances work among queries when possible, which increases the speed and efficiency of query processing.
5. **Incremental Deployment**: To expand a TinyDB sensor network, users simply download the standard TinyDB code to new motes, and TinyDB does the rest. No programming or configuration of the new motes is required beyond installing TinyDB.

The Architecture of TinyDB

TinyDB consists of three major parts: Client, TinyDB Server and Sensor networks (Figure 18). The client connects with a base station node via serial port, and sensor nodes connect with each other via wireless networks. Java-based TinyDB Client API should be installed on Client, which is convenient for users. Each node in the sensor network must be installed with the Sensor Network Software (TinyQP). TinyDB Server accepts queries from client, parses and decomposes them, then sends these queries to the related nodes in the network. Of course, TinyDB server also receives query results and returns them to clients.

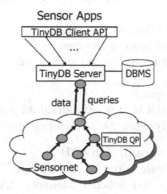

Fig. 18. The Architecture of TinyDB [21].

The TinyDB system can be broadly classified into two subsystems: Sensor Network Software and Client Interface. Sensor Network Software is the heart of TinyDB, it runs on each mote in the network, and consists of several major pieces:

1. **Sensor Catalog and Schema Manager**: The catalog is responsible for tracking the set of attributes, or types of readings (e.g., light, sound, voltage) and properties (e.g., network parent, node ID) available on each sensor. In general, this catalog is not identical for each sensor: networks may consist of heterogeneous collections of devices, and may be able to report different properties.
2. **Query Processor**: The main component of TinyDB is a small query processor. The query processor uses the catalog to fetch the values of local attributes, receives sensor readings from neighboring nodes over the radio, combines and aggregates these values together, filters out undesired data, and outputs values to parents.
3. **Memory Manager**: TinyDB extends TinyOS with a small, handle-based dynamic memory manager.

4. **Network Topology Manager**: TinyDB manages the connectivity of motes in the network, to efficiently route data and query sub-results through the network.

There are two kinds of User Interface in TinyDB. The first is an SQL-like query language, called TinySQL. TinySQL can be used by a client, which has been described in detail in Section 3. The second is Java-based Client Interface, which supports client programming. TinyDB Java-based Client Interface consists of a set of Java classes and applications. Major classes include:

1. A network interface class that allows applications to inject queries and listen for results.
2. Classes to build and transmit queries.
3. A class to receive and parse query results.
4. A class to extract information about the attributes and capabilities of devices.
5. A GUI to construct queries.
6. A graph and table GUI to display individual sensor results.
7. A GUI to visualize dynamic network topologies.

Sensor Network Software of TinyDB

Sensor Network Software is the heart of TinyDB. It consists of four components: Sensor Catalog and Schema Manager, Query Processor, Memory Manager, Network Topology Manager.

(1) Sensor Catalog and Schema Manager

Sensor Catalog and Schema Manager manages the scheme of sensors in TinyDB. We have introduced in Section 3 that TinyDB describes sensors as a virtual 'database table'. Schema is a formal description to the sensor table. It also contains system commands and sub-routings used to query and update the table. This table can contain any types of attributes. It can also contain handles to a set of commands that can be run within the query executor, much like "methods" in the Object-Relational extensions to SQL.

Sensor Catalog and Schema Manager consists of six major components: Attr, Command, TinyDBAttr, TinyDBCommand, Tuple and QueryResult.

The Attr and Command components contain the code to manage the schema of the mote. The Attr component implements interfaces for getting and setting the values of attributes. The Command module includes the codes to implement all the commands in the schema and provides the schema to invoke the commands.

TinyDBAttr is the hub for all the built-in attributes of TinyDB. It wires all the components that implement the built-in attributes together. This component must be updated if you add a new component that implements new attributes for TinyDB.

TinyDBCommand is the hub for all the built-in commands of TinyDB. It wires all the components that implement the built-in commands together.

This component must be updated if a new component that implements new commands for TinyDB is added.

Tuple provides fairly straightforward utilities to manage the Tuple data structure.

QueryResult converts between Tuples, QueryResults, and byte-strings. A Tuple is a vector of values; a QueryResult holds a tuple and some metadata, including the query ID, an index of the result set, etc.

(2) Query Processor

Query Processor implements query processing of TinyDB and it consists of three major components: TupleRouter, SelOperator and AggOperator.

TupleRouter component, which is at the heart of the TinyDB system, provides the main query processing functionality on a mote. It is called a tuple 'router' because it routes tuples among a variety of local query processing components. Note that other components take charge of network routing, not this component! The TupleRouter component runs on a single sensor node and contains three main functions: handling of new query messages, result computation and propagation, subtree result message handling.

- *Handling of New Query Messages.* When a new query comes, TupleRouter records the query message such as globally unique ID, attributes to retrieve, a single selection predicate or aggregation function to apply, etc. Then the TupleRouter allocates space to hold a single, 'in-flight' tuple for that query, which is called tuple space. At last, TupleRouter starts the mote's clock to fire at the appropriate data-delivery rate for all of the current queries in the system.

- *Result computation and propagation.* Whenever a clock event occurs in TupleRouter, the router must perform four actions: deliver tuples that were completed on the previous clock event, decrement the counters for all queries, fetch data for each query firing this epoch and fill the data in the tuple space, route filled-in tuples to query operators and process them in the pipeline. For example, fetched data are first routed to selections to filter, then the filtered data are aggregated by the aggregate operator (if it exists).

- *Subtree result message handling.* When a result arrives from a neighbor, this result needs to be integrated into the aggregate values being computed locally. If the result corresponds to an aggregate query, that result or the received data is forwarded up along the routing tree towards the root.

(3) Memory Manager

TinyDB Memory Manager allocates memory and stores data compactly (to save storage space). It can move memory around in the frame without changing all the external references.

(4) Network Topology Manager

The Network Topology Manager handles all the mote-to-mote and mote-to-base-station communication for TinyDB, that is routing query and data messages. Most of the code in this component manages the network topology. The network topology is maintained as a routing tree, with Mote #0 at the root. As a rule, query messages flood down the tree in a straightforward fashion. Data messages flow back up the tree, participating in more complex query processing algorithms. Mote #0 passes result data to the end user or applications.

By default, a simple tree-maintenance algorithm is used. This algorithm has each mote keep track of a list of other motes from which it receives messages (neighbors). Among these neighbors, it chooses the best one as its parent in the tree.

TinyOS components, that can be used in TinyDB

Finally, we will introduce several TinyOS components that are used in TinyDB. More detail can be seen in TinyOS.

- Clock: provides a system clock, and clock interrupts.
- GenericComm: a generic communication layer, supporting radio and serial communications.
- Leds: control of the LED indicators on the motes.
- Main: a shell to initialize subordinate modules, and start them up.
- Pot: get and set the level of the potentiometer (transmission-power controller) on the radio.
- RandomLFSR: a psuedo-random number generator.
- Reset: reset a mote.
- Timer: a service for setting (multiple) timers to generate subsequent interrupts according to a given rate.

6.2 Cougar System

The COUGAR System is a sensor network data management system, developed by Cornell University. The COUGAR System is a platform for testing query processing techniques over sensor networks.

The Cougar system consists of three components: the QueryProxy, FrontEnd, and GUI (Figure 19). GUI is a graphical user interface, through which users can send queries to sensor networks. FrontEnd is a powerful query proxy. It connects with PCs outside the sensor network and runs on some selected nodes. It acts both as a gateway between the sensor network and the outside world and as a gateway between the GUI and the QueryProxies. The QueryProxy, which is the core of Coguar, runs on each sensor node in the network to parse and execute queries. It is a small software for query processing in a sensor network. GUI is implemented by Java and runs on any platform that supports Java and Swing. The QueryProxy and FrontEnd are

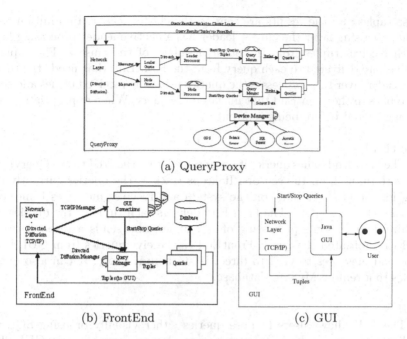

(a) QueryProxy

(b) FrontEnd   (c) GUI

Fig. 19. The Architecture of COUGAR [7, 4].

built using C++ and run under Linux on either x86 or Sensoria WINS NG node hardware.

Communications within the sensor network are transmitted using Directed Diffusion and are formatted as XML. The GUI and FrontEnd communicate over TCP/IP sockets. Let us briefly introduce QueryProxy, FrontEnd and GUI.

QueryProxy

The QueryProxy consists of three parts: the device manager, the node layer, and the leader layer. Cougar divides the nodes in the sensor network into several clusters. Each cluster contains several nodes but only one leader. The sensor nodes are capable of acting as leaders or normal query processing/signal processing nodes. When the network is set up, clusters are formed and leaders are elected from the nodes in the clusters. The QueryProxy system has a hierarchical structure, with the FrontEnd communicating with nodes that act as cluster leaders, and with cluster leaders communicating with the FrontEnd and with the other sensor nodes in their clusters. The device manager takes readings from the sensors. The node layer manages the execution of queries on the sensor node and the interaction with the sensors via the device manager. When a query is to be processed, the node layer requests the required tuples from the device manager. Then, the query is processed using those tuples and the results are sent to the cluster leader. In addition to its node processing layer the cluster leader has an active leader processing layer, which receives tuples from the other members of the cluster. The tuples it receives are delivered to each query from the FrontEnd that needs the tuples. The leader layer then processes the queries using the received tuples and sends the replies to the FrontEnd that initiated the query. When appropriate, tuples are aggregated before being sent out.

FrontEnd

The FrontEnd issues queries it has received from the GUI to the QueryProxy software running on the sensors. It keeps track of the queries currently running for the GUIs running on the system and receives messages from nodes that are cluster leaders. The FrontEnd delivers each tuple to the queries that require it, does some processing of the tuples, and sends a response to the GUI that initiated the query. FrontEnd can receive queries from GUI. It can also send messages to GUI to direct it start up a query. It can also output tuples to a remote MySQL database.

GUI

The GUI allows users to pose queries either visually or using SQL and to display query results in tabular format. A map component in GUI allows users to visualize the topology of the sensors in the network. Users can collect nodes into clusters, which automatically elect a leader. The map is also used to specify a region that the query should run over (Figure 20(a)). Results from queries are displayed in a simple table for easy viewing (Figure 20(b)).

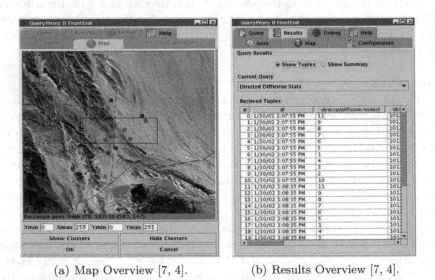

(a) Map Overview [7, 4].   (b) Results Overview [7, 4].

Fig. 20. The Architecture of COUGAR [7, 4].

References

1. Ian F. Akyildiz, Weilian Su, Yogesh Sankarasubramaniam and Erdal Cayirci, A Survey on Sensor Networks, IEEE Communications Magazine, 40(8):102–114, 2002.
2. Philippe Bonnet and Johannes Gehrke, Querying the Physical World, IEEE Personal Communication, October 2000.
3. Philippe Bonnet, Johannes E. Gehrke and Praveen Seshadri, Towards Sensor Database Systems, In Proceedings of the Second International Conference on Mobile Data Management, Hong Kong, January 2001.
4. The Cougar Sensor Database Project, http://www.cs.cornell.edu/database/cougar/, Cornell University.
5. Directed Diffusion, http://www.isi.edu/scadds/projects/diffusion.html, UCLA.
6. Deepak Ganesan, Deborah Estrin and John Heidemann, Dimensions: why do we need a new data handling architecture for sensor networks, ACM SIGCOMM Computer Communication Review, 33(1), January 2003.
7. Johannes Gehrke, COUGAR design and implementation, http://www.cs.cornell.edu/database/cougar/.
8. Bhaskar Krishnamachari, Impact of Data Aggregation in Wireless Sensor Networks, In International Workshop of Distributed Event Based Systems (DEBS), Vienna, Austria, July 2002.
9. Mei Li and Yuexin Liu, Sensor Data Management in Pervasive Computing, Pennsylvania State University Project Report.
10. Samuel Madden, Joe Hellerstein and Wei Hong, TinyDB: In-Network Query Processing in TinyOS, Intel Research, RB-TR-02-014, Oct. 1, 2002.
11. Samuel R. Madden, Michael J. Franklin, The stream: An architechture for queries over streaming sensor data, Proceedings of the ICDE Conference. Los Alamitos: IEEE Computer Press, pp.555 666, 2002.
12. Samuel R. Madden, Robert Szewczyk, Michael J. Franklin and David Culler, Supporting Aggregate Queries Over Ad-Hoc Wireless Sensor Networks, Workshop on Mobile Computing and Systems Applications, 2002.
13. Samuel R. Madden and Michael J. Franklin, Fjording the Stream: An Architecture for Queries over Streaming Sensor Data, ICDE Conference, 2002.
14. Samuel R. Madden, Michael J. Franklin, Joseph M. Hellerstein and Wei Hong, The design of an acquisitional query processor for sensor networks, Proceedings of the SIGMOD Conference. New York: ACM Press, pp.491–502, 2003.
15. Samuel Madden, The Design and Evaluation of a Query Processing Architecture for Sensor Networks, Ph.D. Thesis. UC Berkeley. Fall, 2003.
16. C. S. Raghavendra, K. M.Sivalingam, T. Zhati(Eds.), Wireless Sensor Networks, Kluwer Academic Publishers, pp.185-252, 2004.
17. Sylvia Ratnasamy and Brad Karp, GHT: A Geographic Hash Table for Data-Centric Storage, The First ACM International Workshop on Wireless Sensor Networks and Applications (WSNA 2002), Atlanta, GA, September, 2002.
18. Sylvia Ratnasamy and Deborah Estrin, Data-Centric Storage in Sensornets, Submitted to SIGCOMM 2002.
19. Praveen Rentala, Ravi Musunuri, Shashidhar Gandham, Udit Saxena, Survey on sensor networks, Technical Report, UTDCS-33-02, University of Texas at Dallas, 2002.
20. TinyOS, http://webs.cs.berkeley.edu/tos, UC Berkeley.

21. TinyDB, http://telegraph.cs.berkeley.edu/tinydb/, UC Berkeley.
22. Yong Yao and Johannes Gehrke, The cougar approach to in-network query processing in sensor networks, SIGMOD Record, 31(3):9 18, 2002.
23. Yong Yao and Johannes Gehrke, Query Processing for Sensor Networks, Proceedings of 1st Biennial Conference on Innovative Data Systems Research (CIDR 2003), Asilomar, CA, Jan 2003.
24. XinLi Young, Jin Kim, Ramesh Govindan and Wei Hong, Multi-dimensional Range Queries in Sensor Networks, SenSys03.

Chapter 13
Data Aggregation in Wireless Sensor Networks

Kai-Wei Fan, Sha Liu, and Prasun Sinha

Computer Science and Engineering Department
The Ohio State University, Columbus, OH 43210
{fank, liusha, prasun}@cse.ohio-state.edu

1 Introduction

With advance in technology, sensor networks composed of small and cost effective sensing devices equipped with wireless radio transceiver for environment monitoring have become feasible. The key advantage of using these small devices to monitor the environment is that it does not require infrastructure such as electric mains for power supply and wired lines for Internet connections to collect data, nor need human interaction while deploying. These sensor nodes can monitor the environment by collecting information from their surroundings, and work cooperatively to send the data to a base station, or sink, for analysis.

However, currently there are two limitations on these sensor nodes. First, the power supply is limited. Without electric infrastructure, the nodes are powered by batteries. Once the batteries run out of energy, the nodes die. Battery replacement is not economic, and sometimes infeasible. The sensor nodes will be very cheap once they are mass production products. Deploying new sensor nodes will be more economic than human power. Sometimes the sensor network may be deployed in a hostile or unreachable environment, such as a battle field or chemical waste disposal, and therefore it is not possible for a human to replace a depleted battery.

Second, the bandwidth of the radio transceiver is limited. Unlike the current 802.11 wireless LAN which can reach up to 54Mbps, current radio transceivers of these sensor nodes can only reach to a few hundreds Kbps, and some only have 30 $\sim$ 40 Kbps. Therefore the amount of data that can be transmitted within the sensor network is limited.

To reduce energy consumption and traffic load of a sensor network, the amount of the data transmitted in the network must be reduced. Consider the dynamics of a sensor network. It collects data from its surrounding environment. This data is usually highly correlated within the sensor's area, thus the data collected by sensor nodes close to each other is usually closely related. Temperature readings, for example, are usually the same from each of a cluster of sensors. If every node transmits its sensed data to the sink, these multiple packets will contain duplicate readings. Also, for applications that ask only for averages, sums or total counts from sensor nodes, transmissions form individual sensors in the cluster only consume more energy and reduce the bandwidth. .

Data Aggregation is a mechanism to reduce the size of packet transmissions. Instead of sending all data to the sink, data aggregation processes the data in-network, and only sends processed data to the sink. For example when the sensing task is to collect the average temperature, data aggregation allows nodes to combine multiple readings into one report containing the average temperature T collected from N sensor nodes. When two packets, each of them containing (T_1, N_1) and (T_2, N_2) respectively, are aggregated, they can be combined into one packet with (T, N) where $T = (T_1 \times N_1 + T_2 \times N_2)/(N_1 + N_2)$ and $N = N_1 + N_2$. *Aggregation* also can be applied when the sensing task is to collect the MAX or MIN value of the sensor readings. This can effectively reduce the traffic load, and therefore reduce energy consumption.

There are many aggregation approaches. One is opportunistic aggregation. Packets are aggregated opportunistically in the network when multiple packets are met at the same node while being forwarded to the sink. Other approaches are clustering or constructing aggregation trees. Nodes in the network form multiple clusters, and nodes send their sensing data to their clusterheads or tree root. Packets are aggregated at these clusterheads or roots and then sent to the sink. In this chapter, we introduce some aggregation approaches in this current research field.

2 Directed Diffusion

Directed Diffusion [1] is a data centric routing and aggregating protocol for robust and energy efficient communication in sensor networks. In Directed Diffusion, data is a named attribute-value pair. The sink injects an *interest* which describes its data for a particular event to the sensors in the network. The dissemination of the interest sets up *gradients*, which form multiple paths from sensor nodes to the sink. When sensors sense the events that match the interest, they send the sensing data along multiple paths to the sink. These data are aggregated opportunistically at the intermediate nodes. The network reinforces one or more paths on which higher data rate, or higher quality of data, can be propagated to the sink.

The processes of directed diffusion are illustrated in Figure 2. The sink first broadcasts the *interest* describing its interest for data to the network. The *interest* is a set of name-value pairs. For example, if the sink is interested in receiving the data of events for vehicle movement, the interest may look like:

type: vehicle-movement
interval: 1s
duration: 10s
rect: [100, 100, 200, 400]

The *interval* specifies the data report rate when a sensor senses the event, and the *duration* specifies the expiration time for this interest. The *rect* specifies the rectangular location of the interested area. The attribute naming scheme must be selected before designing the directed diffusion scheme for the network. When the *interest* is propagated through the network, the *gradients* are constructed. Every sensor that receives the *interest* creates a *gradient* that points to the sensor from which the interest is received. The *gradient* specifies the next node to forward packets to the sink, and also the interval and duration to report/forward packets that match the interest. This process is illustrated in Figure 2(a) and 2(b).

After the *gradients* are constructed, sensors can send packets to the sink along the *gradients* if they sense the events that the sink is interested in, as shown in Figure 2(c). The data generated by the sensor is still attribute-value pairs, and may look like:

type: vehicle-movement
instance: SUV
location: [150, 180]
timestamp: [13:22:24]

which specifies the instance of the type, the node location, and the time the report is generated.

The data are forwarded to the sink along the gradient paths that are constructed during interest dissemination. When a node receives a packet, it checks to see if it also contains a packet with similar reported data (such as the data with the same type, located within an area) and a close timestamp. The data in such packets are supposed to be for the same event and are aggregated. Thus packets are aggregated opportunistically on their way to the sink.

When the sink receives the packets, it can decide to reinforce one or more paths to transmit data at a higher data rate by sending a new interest with a shorter interval back to the source along those paths, as shown in Figure 2(d). The decision of which path to reinforce depends on the applications. The sink can choose those paths with shorter delay, or paths from which more packets are received. Nodes receiving the new interest update their *gradients* such that they can forward packets to the sink at higher data rates, as shown in Figure 2(e).

Each interest has a *duration* field specifying how long the interest will be effective. The *gradient* also contains this field to decide when the nodes should stop reporting the events. Therefore the sink has to send *interest* to the reinforced paths to update the *gradients* to maintain the paths. Un-reinforced paths will stop forwarding packets to the sink after the *gradient* expires, as shown in Figure 2(f). This reduces unnecessary duplicated packet transmissions. To further reduce unnecessary transmissions, the sink can send negative-reinforcement messages to stop some paths from forwarding packets.

Directed Diffusion can achieve robust communication by forwarding packets on multiple paths that are selected by the reinforcement mechanism and are preferred by the sink. When sensors sense an event, the event is reported to the sink as long as there is at least one feasible path from the source to the sink. This makes directed diffusion highly reliable in error-prone sensor network communication. When the event is received by the sink, the sink can decide only to receive reports from a

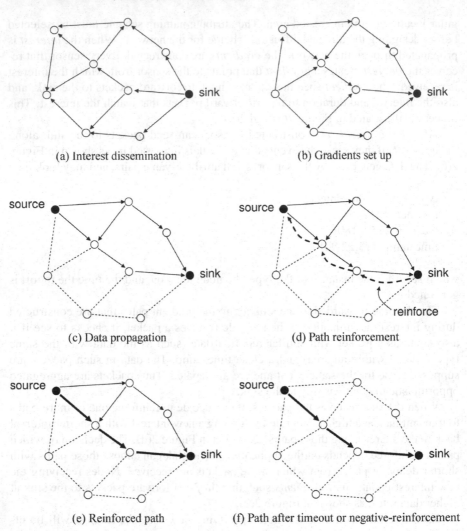

(a) Interest dissemination

(b) Gradients set up

(c) Data propagation

(d) Path reinforcement

(e) Reinforced path

(f) Path after timeout or negative-reinforcement

Fig. 1. Steps in Directed Diffusion.

single path or a few paths with higher quality of data, which reduces the network traffic load by avoiding packets being flooded throughout the network. Therefore directed diffusion is suited for highly dynamic sensor networks that require reliable and also energy efficient communication.

3 Low-Energy Adaptive Clustering Hierarchy

Low-Energy Adaptive Clustering Hierarchy (LEACH) [2, 3] is a distributed clus-tering protocol that utilizes randomized rotation of local clusterheads to evenly dis-tribute energy consumption among sensors in the network. The basic idea is that nodes elect themselves as clusterheads according to some probability. Nodes that are not clusterheads join the cluster of the closest clusterhead, as shown in Figure 2. After the clusters are formed, nodes send their packets to their clusterheads, the clusterhead aggregates their packets and sends the aggregated data to the sink di-rectly. The clusterhead selection process is performed once every round, and nodes that have been selected as clusterheads will not become clusterheads again in the following rounds before all nodes in the network have been selected as clusterheads. This protocol ensures that every sensor node in the network has the same probabil-ity to be selected as a clusterhead, thus evenly distributing energy load to all nodes. Therefore it can increase the network life time compared with conventional routing protocols.

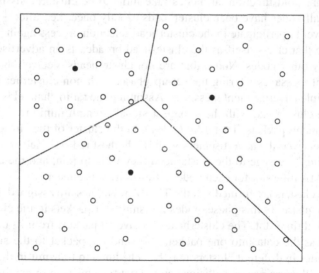

Fig. 2. Cluster formation for 60 nodes network with 5% nodes as clusterheads, which creates three clusters in the network. Nodes within one cluster only communicate with their cluster-head.

In LEACH, nodes have the capability to adjust their transmission power such that they can use low transmission power to communicate with their neighbors, and use high transmission power to send packets directly to the sink. If all nodes send packets to the sink directly, nodes will die out very soon, especially for those nodes that are far away from the sink. If nodes use the minimum transmission energy (MTE) routing protocol [4] to forward packets to their closest neighbor, nodes closer to the sink will handle more traffic than nodes farther away from the sink, and therefore will deplete their energy quicker. LEACH eliminates these problems by selecting some nodes, which are the clusterheads, to send packets to the sink directly, and let other nodes only send packets to the clusterheads. However, if the clusterheads are fixed, they will consume more energy than other nodes and die quickly because they have to participate in all communications. Therefore LEACH randomly selects different nodes as clusterheads in each round to avoid this problem.

The operation of LEACH is divided into rounds, where each round contains a set-up phase and a steady-phase. In the set-up phase, each node decides whether or not to become a clusterhead by choosing a random number between 0 and 1. If the number is less than a threshold, than the node becomes a clusterhead. Node n calculates the threshold as follows:

$$T(n) = \begin{cases} \frac{P}{1-P\times(r \bmod \frac{1}{P})} & if \ n \in G, \\ 0 & otherwise, \end{cases}$$

where P is the percentage of nodes that are clusterheads, r is the current round, and G is the set of nodes that have not been selected as clusterheads in the last $\frac{1}{P}$ rounds. Using this threshold function, all nodes take turns to be clusterheads in a random order. After all nodes have been clusterheads exactly once, i.e., after $\frac{1}{p}$ rounds, all nodes start over to participate in the clusterhead selection process again.

The node that elects itself as the clusterhead broadcasts an advertisement message to notify other nodes. Nodes that are not clusterheads receive the clusterhead advertisement messages. During the set-up phase, each non-clusterhead node may receive multiple advertisement messages. Assuming the radio channel is symmetric, choosing the clusterhead with the strongest signal strength minimizes the required energy to transmit packets. Therefore nodes join the cluster of the clusterhead from which they received the advertisement with the highest radio signal strength. Nodes send a "joining" message to the clusterhead they want to join, and the clusterheads assign a TDMA time slot for each node to transmit in its cluster.

After the clusters are formed and the TDMA schedules are assigned, the network enters steady-phase. In this phase, nodes transmit their packets to the clusterhead in their scheduled time slot. The clusterheads receive all packets from its cluster members, compress the data into one packet, and send the packet to the sink directly. However, nodes in different clusters may be scheduled to transmit in the same time slot, which will cause packet collisions and affect transmission in neighboring clusters. To reduce interference, each cluster chooses one CDMA code that is different from other clusters to communicate within the cluster. The CDMA codes are broadcast when the clusterheads broadcast their advertisement messages.

PEGASIS [5] extends LEACH by organizing nodes to form a chain, and forwarding and aggregating packets along the chain to reduce the number of transmissions to save more energy. Both LEACH and PEGASIS use randomized rotation to select nodes that communicate directly with the sink to reduce energy consumption and distribute it among the sensor nodes in the network. For more detail about PEGASIS please refer to [5].

4 Tiny Aggregation

Tiny Aggregation (TAG) [6] is an aggregation service for low-power and distributed wireless ad hoc networks, such as sensor networks. It provides a SQL-like interface to query and aggregate the interested attributes from the network. TAG distributes the aggregation queries into the network from a base station, and sensors route requested attributes of matched data back to the base station through a routing tree rooted at the base station. Packets are aggregated while they flow up to the base station along the tree. Because of the in-network aggregation and discarding of irrelevant data, TAG reduces the number of transmissions, thus achieving energy efficient data gathering.

TAG consists of two phases: a distribution phase and a collection phase. In the distribution phase, aggregate queries are propagated throughout the network. In the collection phase, aggregate values are gathered from the network. The aggregate queries are SQL-like syntax language. For example, if we want to collect data about indoor temperature in a building, we may issue a query such as:

SELECT AVG(temperature), room FROM sensors
   WHERE floor = 2
   GROUP BY room
   HAVING AVG(temperature) > 80
   EPOCH DURATION 60s

This query collects average temperature and room number of each room located on the second floor, with average temperature greater than 80 degrees. It is very similar to database SQL query language, with the exception of EPOCH DURATION. In database query, the returned value is a set of matched attributes. However, the result of a TAG query is a stream of values, such as the continuous environment monitoring results. EPOCH DURATION defines the collected data reporting interval, which is the amount of time between two consecutive samplings. This time interval is called an epoch. Sensors executing the query transmit the data that matches the SQL query condition to the base station at each time interval defined by the EPOCH DURATION.

In the collection phase, sensors report the sensed data back to the base station along the routing tree created by the underlying routing protocol. Instead of aggregating packets at the base station, TAG aggregates packets in-network whenever possible to reduce the number of transmissions. In order to reduce the number of transmissions as much as possible, nodes should wait until they have received all packets from their children before they transmit. As nodes send their sensed data once in each epoch, TAG has to separate the transmission time slot for nodes at different levels of the tree, i.e., for nodes that have a different number of hops to the base station, such that the transmission time slots are scheduled from the tree leaves to the base station, as shown in Figure 3.

If we assume that the tree depth is d, we can divide an epoch time into (EPOCH DURATION)/d intervals such that nodes at i_{th} level transmit during i_{th} interval. While nodes are not receiving or transmitting, they can turn off their radio and sensing devices to reduce the idle power consumption. However, if the tree depth is high, or the network sampling rate is high, the length of an interval may not be long enough

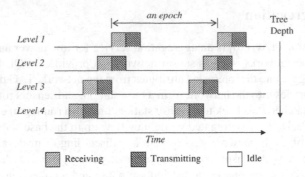

Fig. 3. Receiving and transmitting schedule for nodes at different depths of the tree.

for transmitting a packet. In this case, the packet may be delayed by one or more epochs.

While the data packets are routed up to the root of the tree, the intermediate nodes keep aggregating the data. For the example described above, two packets can be aggregated if they are generated by the sensors that are located in the same room. This can be easily done by TAG because TAG uses SQL-like query, and the layouts of the SQL results have the same attributes if they are generated by the same query. Checking the attribute that is specified in the GROUP BY clause, sensors know whether or not to aggregate that data in different packets.

Because of in-network aggregation, TAG reduces the required bandwidth and number of message transmissions to save energy. The in-network aggregation is very efficient because TAG uses a simple SQL-like query interface which results in the same layout of the data. These properties make TAG a suitable aggregation service for low-power, distributed wireless sensor networks.

5 Greedy Aggregation on Directed Diffusion

In [7], the authors propose a more energy efficient aggregation protocol based on directed diffusion, named *Greedy Aggregation*. *Greedy Aggregation* increases the energy saving by increasing the *path sharing* among different sources. The number of aggregations increases because the length of shared path increases, thus achieving better energy conservation.

In directed diffusion [1], the sink selects preferred paths by reinforcing the paths with lower delay or better packet delivery ration. Packets are aggregated opportunistically along the paths while being forwarded to the sink. Using this approach, packets from two sources may not share the same path even if they are close. This reduces the possibility of aggregation because packets are forwarded on different routes. Even if sources share some paths, there may be only few instances of aggregation because aggregation happens opportunistically. This approach favors paths with lower delay.

Greedy Aggregation, on the other hand, favors minimization of energy consumption over reducing latency by increasing path sharing. As illustrated in Figure 4, the path sharing number in (*b*) is higher than (*a*). This has the benefit of reducing overall transmitting power consumption if packets can be aggregated when the routes merge into one path.

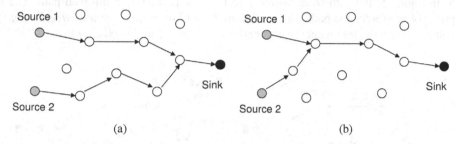

Fig. 4. Increasing path sharing reduces the number of transmissions. Assume packets are always aggregated at the merging node. (a) requires eight transmissions while (b) requires only six transmissions.

Like directed diffusion, the sink floods its interests to all nodes in the beginning, and nodes construct the *gradients* when the interests are propagated across the network. When sources detect an event os interest, they send the data back to the sink along the gradient paths. In addition to the original attributes that the sink is interested in, the packets contain an extra attribute E, representing the energy cost of forwarding the packet from source to current nodes. Every time a node receives an unseen event packet, it adds the cost for forwarding that packet to attribute E. The energy cost can be the real estimated energy consumption, or just the number of hops the packet has been forwarded so far. Therefore when the sink receives the packets, the energy cost of forwarding the interests along different paths can be collected, and the path with minimum energy cost is reinforced.

Once a reinforced path is constructed, the protocol tries to increase path sharing by letting other sources use this path to forward packets, i.e., constructs a tree such that all sources are connected to the reinforced path using the shortest path in terms of energy cost. The protocol uses *incremental cost messages* to achieve this goal.

When nodes on the tree (initially the tree contains only nodes on the reinforced path) receive an unseen event from other sources, it generates an *incremental cost message* that contains the message *id* corresponding to that event and the additional energy cost C required for transmitting the event to the tree. The *incremental cost message* is only sent along the reinforced path. When a node receives the message, it searches the packets of corresponding events from its message cache and compares the energy cost E of the cached packet with C. The node updates C of the message to the minimum value of C or E, and sends the updated incremental cost message to the next node.

After receiving the incremental cost message, the sink reinforces the neighbors that send packets with minimum of E or C. When the neighboring node receives the reinforcement, it reinforces its upstream nodes that send packets with minimum of E or C. Therefore, a greedy incremental tree can be constructed, allowing nodes to forward packets to the closest path using minimum energy. The reinforcement of minimum energy cost to construct a greedy incremental tree is illustrated in Figure 5. In Figure 5, the path from *Source 1* to the sink is the first reinforced path. The protocol reinforces the path with minimum E or C of packets from *Source 2*, thus constructing a minimum energy cost path from *Source 2* to the existing tree.

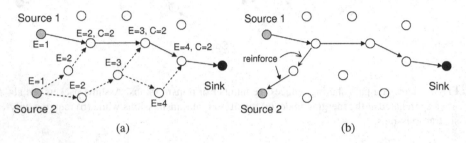

(a)   (b)

Fig. 5. The path with minimum incremental energy cost is reinforced.

In directed diffusion, multiple paths can be reinforced. Therefore, the sink or the intermediate nodes may receive an aggregated packet containing the event transmitted by the same source from multiple reinforced paths. If we can reduce the duplication, we can reduce the number of transmissions to save energy. However, this is like a set-covering problem, which is an NP-hard problem [13]. For example, as shown in Figure 6, The sink receives data A_1, B_1, C_1 from multiple paths via nodes D, E, and F. The sink can get A_1, B_1, C_1 from D and F only, without packets from E. Therefore, by truncating the path from E, more energy can be saved.

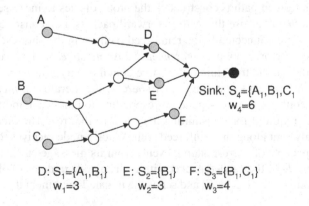

Fig. 6. The weighted set-covering problem.

The problem is the weighted set-covering problem (The regular set-covering problem is a special case of the weighted set-covering problem with all weights equal to 1). Each incoming packet is associated with a weight, i.e., energy cost. To find a set of paths that transmit packets from all sources with minimum energy cost is to find the covering set with minimum weight.

The protocol uses a greedy heuristic method to find an energy inefficient path, and uses negative reinforcement to truncate them. The greedy heuristic is to select a subset that covers uncovered elements with the lowest cost ratio, or the cost per element, until all elements are covered. As in Figure 6, nodes D, E, and F have aggregated packets containing A_1, B_1, B_1, and B_1, C_1, and their weights are 3, 3, 4 respectively. The greedy approach first calculates the cost ratio for each set. Therefore the cost ratio for set S_1 is $w_1/|S_1| = 1.5$, for set S_2 is $w_2/|S_2| = 3$, and for set S_3 is $w_3/|S_3| = 2$. Therefore the greedy heuristic selects set S_1 first. At second step, because B_1 is already covered, the uncovered elements in set S_2 is 0, therefore the cost ratio for S_2 is ∞ (actually we can eliminate sets with 0 uncovered elements immediately since including them does not increase the covered elements). The uncovered elements in set S_3 is only C_1, and cost ratio for set S_3 is $4/1 = 4$. Therefore S_3 is selected at the second step, and all elements are covered.

After the covering sets are decided, the node sends the negative reinforcement to the nodes whose sets are not selected. Nodes receiving the negative reinforcement delete the gradients to that node from which the negative reinforcement is received, therefore they stop sending packets to that node.

6 DCTC

DCTC [8] is a dynamic convey tree collaboration framework that takes advantage of node collaboration for target tracking. Nodes construct a tree, named a *convey tree*, to collect sensing report and collaboratively convey these reports to the root to provide robust and reliable data. While a target is moving, some nodes may be farther away from the original root and the energy cost of forwarding the packet to the root increases. Therefore the convey tree is reconfigured in an efficient way to reduce the energy consumption.

When a target enters the sensing range of the sensor networks, there may be multiple sensor nodes detecting the target. If every node generates the report and sends the data to the sink directly, the network will be flooded by many concurrent traffic flows, which is not only energy inefficient, but may also increase the detection delay and reduce the packet delivery ratio. DCTC avoids this problem by constructing a convey tree that aggregates concurrent sensing reports and collects these reports at the convey tree root. As Figure 7 shows, nodes in the sensing range construct the convey tree, and nodes send data to the sink by forwarding packets to their parent. Parent nodes wait for their children's packets before forwarding their own packets, therefore packets can be aggregated hop by hop along the path to the root.

In DCTC, nodes are divided into grids just like GAF. Only one node in each grid, i.e., the grid head, is required to remain awake, and other nodes go to sleep and wake

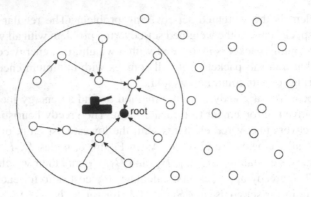

Fig. 7. Convey Tree rooted at the center of the event.

up periodically to save energy. When a target enters the sensing range, the grid head will wake up all nodes in its grid and nodes start to track the target and send the sensing report.

The processes in DCTC can be categorized into three operations: *Initial Tree Construction, Tree Expansion and Pruning*, and *Tree Reconfiguration*. These operations are described below:

- **Initial Tree Construction:** When a target first enters the sensing range of a sensor network, the nodes that detect the target will construct the initial convey tree. The first step is to select a root of the tree. Many leader election algorithms, such as those described in [10] and [11], can be used. To simplify the description of tree construction, we select the node that is closest to the target as the root (assume that nodes have the ability to detect the distance between the target and themselves). Each node broadcasts its (id, d) where id is node id and d is the distance to the target. If a node does not receive packets with smaller d, it becomes the root candidate, otherwise, it selects the node with the smallest d among its neighbors as its parent in the convey tree. There may be multiple root candidates in the network after the election. These root candidates flood their (id, d) to the nodes sensing the event. The node with the smallest d becomes the root, and other candidates create a route to the node flooding the packet with smallest d. Therefore, the initial convey tree is constructed.
- **Tree Expansion and Pruning:** When the target is moving, there will be new nodes joining the convey tree while detecting the target. Also there will be some nodes in the tree being removed because the target is moving out of those nodes' sensing range. A conservative scheme or a prediction-based scheme can be used. In a conservative scheme, the root calculates the possible nodes that may detect the target within time t, where t is the duration to execute the tree expansion and pruning process. As shown in Figure 8(a), based on the current target moving velocity v_t and the sensing radius d_s, the root knows which nodes should be included in the tree, and which nodes should be removed. The d_c in Figure 8(a)

is the maximum range of nodes that may sense the target after time t, and $d_c = (v_t + \beta) \times t + d_s$ where $v_t + \beta$ is expected maximum velocity of the target.

The prediction-based scheme uses some movement prediction techniques, such as [12], to predict the next location of the target. As shown in Figure 8(b), only nodes in the predicted area need to join the tree.

After deciding which node should join the tree, the root sends a notification message to the grid head of the grid containing those nodes. When the grid head receives the notification, it wakes up all nodes in the grid, and nodes can join the convey tree. If some nodes need to be pruned, the root sends a prune message to the grid head of the grid in which all nodes should be removed. The grid head receiving the prune message broadcasts it to nodes in its grid immediately, and those nodes can leave the tree and go to sleep.

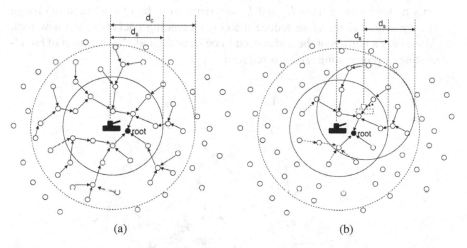

(a)   (b)

Fig. 8. Tree expansion and pruning. (a) The conservative scheme. (b) The prediction-based scheme.

- **Tree Reconfiguration:** While the target keeps moving, it may move far away from the root of the initial convey tree. If nodes keep forwarding sensing data to the root of the original tree, packets have to be forwarded throughout multiple hops, and will consume more energy while the target moves farther away. Therefore reconstructing a tree to achieve more energy efficient aggregation is desired.

DCTC triggers the tree reconfiguration when the distance between the root and the target exceeds a threshold. When the distance exceeds a threshold, one of the nodes that is closest to the target is selected randomly, and the current root sends a *migration request* to the new root.

After receiving the migration request, the new root broadcasts the *reconf* message. A node receiving the *reconf* message re-broadcasts the message and attaches its location and the cost of sending a packet to the new root. Nodes receiving the *reconf* message change their parent to the node with minimum energy cost of sending a packet to the new root.

DCTC can also use other reconfiguration schemes to reduce the broadcasting overhead in reconfiguration. The first one is based on grid structure. Instead of flooding the *reconf* messages, the *reconf* message are only broadcast within the grid, and are sent to neighboring grid heads. The neighboring grid heads broadcast the *reconf* to their grids, and forward it to their neighboring grid heads. The *reconf* message sent to neighboring grid heads contains the location and cost of each node in the current grid. Nodes receiving the broadcast *reconf* message find the parent according to this information, and therefore can construct a minimized cost tree to the new root.

The second approach is used when only some nodes in the tree need to be reconfigured [9], named interception-based reconfiguration. As shown in Figure 9, only nodes between lines L_1 and L_2 are required to be reconfigured to change their parent, and therefore reduce the cost of sending packets to the new root. Since only a portion of the nodes need to be reconfigured, the overhead of broadcasting or propagating *reconf* is reduced.

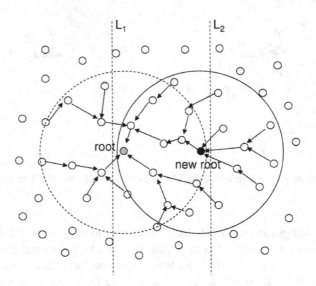

Fig. 9. Interception-based reconfiguration.

7 Gateway Placement

For data gathering in wireless sensor networks, one way is to place multiple gateways in the network to reduce the traversing hops of data. Sensor nodes send data packets to their nearest gateways, and the data are gathered from these gateways through wired lines to a data center. The issue involved in this data gathering model is how to optimize the placement of gateways.

In [14], J. Wong *et al.* use integer linear programming (ILP) to calculate the optimal gateway placement under the assumption of known node positions and communication range.

First the possible positions to place the gateways are found by identifying competitive regions (CRegions). A region here is defined as the overlapping communication ranges of a set of nodes. Thus if a gateway is placed in this region, it can communicate with these nodes in one hop.

Then breadth-first search is used to determine the number of communication hops needed between each node and potential gateway position pair.

Next, the network size is examined to determine the algorithm used. If the network is of a reasonable size, then ILP is used to find the optimal solution, else a heuristic approach is used to determine the approximately best placement.

There are four common optimization scenarios:

1. For a given bound on the number of communication hops for each sensor node to reach at least one gateway, minimize the number of gateways.

   Suppose there are N nodes and at most R CRegions. Let A be an $R \times N$ binary matrix whose element a_{ij} is set if node N_j can communicate with CRegion i in less than or equal to M_{hops} hops specified beforehand. Let x be an $R \times 1$ vector, and 1 be the identity vector (all elements are set to 1). Then the objective is to minimize the number of 1's in x, which is translated into objective function

$$Y = MIN(1'x).$$

   The only constraint is to ensure that each sensor node can communicate with at least one gateway, which is expressed as

$$Ax \geq 1.$$

2. For a given bound k on the number of gateways, minimize the worst-case number of communication hops for any node to reach a gateway.

   To solve this problem, a virtual graph V is constructed over two vertex sets. One is the set of all sensor nodes, and another is the set of all possible CRegions. Each sensor node and each CRegion are connected by an edge with the communication hop as the edge weight. The goal is to select at most K CRegion vertices such that

   a) all sensor nodes are connected to at least one CRegion in graph V.

   b) the maximum (worst-case) weight of selected edges in V is minimized.

   Using the same symbols as the first problem, let x' be the complement value of x (thus $x + x' = 1$), min_j be the minimum hop to reach a CRegion for node N_j, m be the maximum of min_j for $j = 1, 2, \ldots, N$, and $R \times N$ matrix H with element h_{ij} records the number of hop counts for node N_j to reach CRegions i. Then the constraints are

   a) At least one and no more than K CRegions are selected:

$$1'x \geq 1,$$
$$1'x \leq k.$$

b) Each sensor node must be connected with at least one CRegion:

$$Ax \geq 1.$$

c) If CRegion i is selected, min_j should be less than or equal to $h_{ij}x_i$. To formulate this, it must be ensured that when CRegion i is not selected, min_j should not be set to 0. Thus the constraint is

$$min_j \leq h_{ij}x_i + mx_i'$$

where m is a constant larger than the maximum of h_{ij}'s.

Since m is the maximum of all min_j's, the objective function is

$$Y = MIN(1'm).$$

3. For a given bound m_{total_hops} on the total communication hops for all nodes to reach their closest selected CRegions, minimize the number of gateways. The formulation is the same as in the previous question except that the constraint $1x \leq k$ is replaced by

$$1'min \leq m_{total_hops}$$

where $min = (min_1, min_2, \ldots, min_N)'$.
The objective function is also changed to

$$Y = MIN(1'x).$$

4. For a given maximum number of gateways, find a placement such that the total number of communication hops for all sensor nodes to reach their closest selected gateways.
   Based on the problem formulation of Problem 2, the constraint of m is removed since the total number of hops are concerned instead of the maximum. Thus the objective function is also changed to

$$Y = MIN(1'min).$$

8 Summary

Data Aggregation is an efficient mechanism as it not only reduces the energy consumption of packet transmissions but also lowers the traffic load and therefore reduces the contentions and collisions. It is especially useful for sensor networks that collect statistical data, such as sum, count, average, max/min...etc. Some approaches have also been proposed to approximate the sensing data that can not be simply obtained by one aggregated message, such as the median and histogram [15]. Image processing that compresses pictures or video streams is another form of aggregation that is different from the aggregation paradigms described above.

Therefore, data aggregation is highly application dependent. Different applications require different aggregation approaches if the aggregation properties are different. The challenge of designing a data aggregation protocol is to find a suitable data reduction technique, and to design the in-network aggregation approach based on the characters of that technique. Once the data aggregation mechanism is deployed, the energy consumption will be reduced and the network lifetime can be extended.

References

1. Chalermek Intanagonwiwat, Ramesh Govindan, and Deborah Estrin, *Directed diffusion: a scalable and robust communication paradigm for sensor networks*, (MobiCom 2000) pp 56-67.
2. Wendi B. Heinzelman, Anantha Chandrakasan, and Hari Balakrishnan, *Energy Efficient Communication Protocol for Wireless Microsensor Networks*, (33rd Hawaii International Conference on System Sciences, 2000).
3. Wendi B. Heinzelman, Anantha Chandrakasan, and Hari Balakrishnan, *An Application-Specific Protocol Architecture for Wireless Microsensor Networks*, (IEEE Transactions on Wireless Communications, Vol. 1, No. 4, 2002) pp 660-670.
4. Timothy J. Shepard, *A channel access scheme for large dense packet radio networks*, (SIG-COMM 96) pp 219-230
5. S. Lindsey, C. S. Raghavendra, *PEGASIS: Power Efficient GAthering in Sensor Information Systems*, (IEEE Aerospace Conference 2002), pp 1-6.
6. Samuel Madden, Michael J. Franklin, Joseph M. Hellerstein, and Wei Hong, *TAG: A Tiny AGgregation Service for Ad-Hoc Sensor Networks*, (ACM SIGOPS Operating Systems Review 2002) pp 131-146.
7. Chalermek Intanagonwiwat, Deborah Estrin, Ramesh Govindan, and John Heidemann, *Impact of Network Density on Data Aggregation in Wireless Sensor Networks*, (ICDCS 2002).
8. Wensheng Zhang and Guohong Cao, *DCTC: dynamic convoy tree-based collaboration for target tracking in sensor networks*, (IEEE Transactions on Wireless Communications, Volume 3, Issue 5, Sept. 2004) pp 1689-1701.
9. Wensheng Zhang and Guohong Cao, *Optimizing Tree Reconfiguration for Mobile Target Tracking in Sensor Networks*, (INFOCOM 2004)
10. Gerard Tel, *Introduction to Distributed Algorithm*, (Cambridge Univ. Press, 2000)
11. Nancy Lynch, *Distributed Algorithms*, (Morgan Kaufmann Publishers, Inc. 1996)
12. A. Aljadhai and T. Znati, *Predictive mobility support for QoS provisioning in mobile wireless environments*, (IEEE J-SAC, Vol. 19, 2001)
13. Michael R. Garey and Davis S. Johnson, *Computers and Intractability, a Guide to the Theory of NP-Completeness*, (W. H. Freeman and Company, 1991)
14. Jennifer L. Wong, Roozbeh Jafari, and Miodrag Potkonjak, *Gateway Placement for Latency and Energy Efficient Data Aggregation*, (29th Annual IEEE International Conference on Local Computer Networks, 2004) pp. 490-497
15. Nisheeth Shrivastava, Chiranjeeb Buragohain, Divyakant Agrawal, and Subhash Suri, *Medians and beyond: new aggregation techniques for sensor networks*, (Sensys 2004)

Chapter 14
Performance Comparison of Clustering Schemes in Sensor Networks

Yadi Ma and Maggie Cheng

Computer Science Department
University of Missouri, Rolla, MO 65401
{ym95d,chengm}@umr.edu

1 Introduction

Recent advances in microelectro-mechanical systems and wireless communications have enabled the development of distributed, wireless networks of small, inexpensive, low power sensors. These sensors, which possess sensing, data processing and short range communication capabilities, can be deployed in diverse environments to collect useful information. Large numbers of such inexpensive sensors form ad hoc wireless networks which can be used in a variety of commercial and military applications.

As sensors become inexpensive and widely available, sensor networks can be deployed in larger scales. One of the issues arising consequently is scalability. A flat structure of a large number of sensors often provides low scalability and makes network-wide coordination difficult. To solve this problem, hierarchical architectures (clusters) have been proposed to solve the scalability problem. Appropriate clustering can reduce the need for global coordination and restrict most of the sensing, data processing and communication activities within clusters, thus can improve resource efficiency and prolong network lifetime ([1], [2], [3], [4] and [5]). Clustering can also provide load balancing if appropriately configured.

The salient advantage of using clusters in a sensor network comes from in-network data aggregation. Data aggregation has emerged as a basic tenet in sensor networks ([6], [7] and [8]). The key idea is to combine data from different sensors to eliminate redundant transmissions. With clustering, sensor nodes transmit their local information to their clusterheads, and clusterheads aggregate the received information and forward it to the base station. Periodic re-clustering can select nodes with higher residual energy to act as clusterheads. Network lifetime is prolonged by (1) reducing the number of nodes contending for channel access (2) summarizing network state information and updates at clusterheads through intra-cluster coordination, and (3) routing through an overlay among clusterheads with relatively small network diameters [9].

In this article, we propose a new clustering scheme, *Forest*, and compare it with two other clustering schemes, LEACH (Low-Energy Adaptive Clustering Hierarchy [10]) and Max-Min D-cluster ([2]). The three schemes each represent a different category of clustering method. We compare them in energy efficiency, control message overhead, cluster distribution, i.e., the average cluster size and the variation of cluster sizes, as well as stability in the presence of node mobility.

Energy-efficiency is an important metric. Sensor nodes are typically densely deployed and highly energy-constrained. Further, recharging or replacing batteries on hundreds or thousands of nodes in possibly hostile environment is infeasible ([8], [9] and [1]). The key challenge in such a system is conserving sensor energy, thus maximizing network lifetime. Among many other activities, to gather the sensory data periodically and transmit it to the base station is the most energy consuming. Clustering plays a significant role in energy conservation.

Message overhead is another important metric for comparing clustering schemes, as it measures the scalability of a clustering scheme, the degree to which it will function in a congested or low-bandwidth environment, and its efficiency in terms of consuming battery power. We evaluated the number of control messages used by each scheme during cluster formations.

In sensor networks, the size of clusters and the number of clusterheads as well as the stability of clusters are of considerable importance to the higher layer protocols [11]. Since each clusterhead needs to keep track of the routing information of other clusterheads in the system, the larger the number of clusterheads, the larger will be the overhead in sharing the routing information. However, too few clusterheads will be overloaded with too many members. We measure the average number of clusters, the average cluster size and the standard deviation of cluster sizes, which indicate the load distribution of clusterheads. Stability is also important in a mobile network. High stability can reduce communication overheads during transition.

The remainder of this article is organized as follows. In Section 2, we review some previous work related to clustering in sensor networks. Section 3 provides details of the *Forest* clustering scheme as well as the two other clustering schemes that we used for comparison. Section 4 presents network model for simulation, performance metrics, and analytical and simulation results of the three schemes. Finally, we summarize the main results of the chapter and outline the possible directions of future work in Section 5.

2 Related Work

There are several applications of clustering schemes for wireless ad hoc networks in the literature. For example, Amis et al. proposed a *Max-Min D-*

Cluster formation heuristic to form *d*-clusters in a wireless ad hoc network [2]. Chatterjee et. al proposed a weighted, distributed clustering algorithm ,WCA, for mobile ad hoc networks in [12]. Clustering is particularly useful in sensor networks that require scalability to hundreds or thousands of nodes. Prolonged network lifetime, scalability, and load balancing are important requirements for many sensor network applications. By exploit clustering techniques, several applications and protocols are proved to have increased scalability, reduced delays and prolonged lifetime. Examples include [13], [10] and [14], etc. Most clustering schemes in the literature fall into the following three categories:

1. identifier-based clustering
2. topology-based clustering
3. energy-based clustering

In the following, we will explore the common features of each category of clustering scheme, and provide some insightful observations on their performance aspects.

2.1 Identifier-based Heuristic

Baker and Ephremides [15] devised one of the earliest clustering algorithms for ad hoc networks, the *Linked Cluster Algorithm*, which originated the identifier-based heuristic. This heuristic assigns a unique logic ID to each node and chooses the node with the minimum/maximum id as a clusterhead. Thus, the IDs of the neighbors of the clusterhead will be higher/lower than that of the clusterhead. The Max-Min D-Cluster [2] scheme belongs to this category, in which clusters are formed by diffusing node identities along wireless links.

A logic ID-based clustering heuristic provides a simple means to form clusters. However, this clustering scheme is biased towards certain nodes on their identifiers, which results in non-uniform load distribution and leads to the battery drainage of certain nodes [11]. One might think that this problem could be fixed by renumbering the node IDs from time to time, which is however non-trivial [12]. In general, ID-based schemes have better throughput in mobile environments than the topology-based schemes, since it is unlikely that node degrees will remain stable, and a topology-based scheme would require frequent cluster head updates.

2.2 Topology-based Heuristic

The topology-based clustering was originally proposed in [16]. Each node broadcasts its ID to the nodes that are within its transmission range. Two nodes are considered to be a neighbor of each other if one node lies within the transmission range of the other node. The node with maximum number of neighbors (i.e., maximum degree) is chosen as a clusterhead. The neighbors of a clusterhead become members of that cluster and can no longer participate in the election process. Since no clusterheads are directly linked, only one clusterhead is allowed per cluster. Any two nodes in a cluster are at most two-hops away since the clusterhead is directly linked to each of its neighbors in the cluster. Basically, each node either becomes a clusterhead or remains a neighbor of a clusterhead.

The performance of a topology-based scheme like WCA ([12]) is largely dependent on the network stability. When nodes move around, the number of nodes in a cluster will change. As the number of nodes in a cluster is increased, the throughput drops and hence a gradual degradation in the system performance is observed. The reaffiliation of nodes is quite often due to node movements and as a result, the current clusterhead may not be re-elected to be a clusterhead. All these drawbacks occur because this approach does not have any restriction on the number of nodes in a cluster. In this chapter, we present a new topology-based heuristic, *Forest* scheme, in which clusters are formed as disjointed trees and the clusterheads are roots of trees. To solve these problems, we add restrictions on the cluster size in the Forest scheme.

2.3 Energy-based Heuristic

With the rapid development of sensor networks, many energy-based heuristics have been proposed ([10], [13], [17], [9], [14] and [1]). LEACH([10]) is a well-known representative in this category and will be discussed in detail in Section 3. HEED (Hybrid Energy-Efficient Distributed clustering) ([14]) periodically selects clusterheads based on the hybrid of their residual energy and a secondary parameter, such as node proximity to its neighbors or node degree. In general, the energy-based heuristics have lower energy dissipation and longer system lifetime than other schemes.

3 Overview of Algorithms

In this section, we will first provide an overview of the schemes to be compared: LEACH, Max-Min D-cluster and a new scheme, *Forest*. Each of the three schemes is a representative of energy-based, ID-based and topology-based clustering schemes respectively. We briefly describe the key features of each scheme and the key control parameters in the implementation.

3.1 LEACH: Low-Energy Adaptive Clustering Hierarchy

In conventional clustering algorithms, clusterheads are chosen a priori and fixed throughout the system lifetime. It is obvious that sensors chosen to be clusterheads would consume more energy, because they have more communication load. Thus, these clusterheads will die quickly and the overall system lifetime may be reduced. LEACH [10] addressed this problem by using randomized rotation of the "clusterheads" and the corresponding clusters, which can distribute the work load evenly among sensors in the network.

The operation of LEACH is broken up into rounds. Each round includes two phases, a set-up phase, during which the clusters are formed, and a steady-state phase, during which data is transmitted to the base stations.

Initially, each sensor node decides whether to become a clusterhead or not based on the suggested percentage of clusterheads in the sensor network, and the number of times the node has been a clusterhead so far. Each node randomly chooses a number between 0 and 1. If the number is less than the threshold $T(n)$, the node becomes a clusterhead for the current round. The threshold is computed as

$$T(n) = \begin{cases} \dfrac{P}{1 - P \times (r \bmod \frac{1}{P})} & \text{if } n \in G, \\ 0 & \text{otherwise.} \end{cases}$$

where P is the percentage of clusterheads given as an input, r is the current round, and G is the set of nodes that have not been clusterheads in the last $\frac{1}{P}$ rounds.

Each node that has elected itself a clusterhead for the current round will broadcast an advertisement message to the rest of the nodes. Each non-clusterhead node decides which node to be its clusterhead for this round based on the received signal strength of the advertisements. It then informs the clusterhead that it will join the cluster. When the clusterhead receives all the messages, it will broadcast a schedule telling each node in the cluster when to transmit data. Only during data transmission phase can nodes send data to the clusterhead. When all the data has been received, the clusterhead will compress the data into a single stream and send it to the base station. After a specified period of time, the next round begins with the set-up phase and goes on as described above.

This scheme has relatively low message overhead, and is energy efficient, as we will see in the simulation. However, it only has a loose control over the percentage of clusterheads: it guarantees that within every $\frac{1}{P}$ rounds, every node has a chance to be a clusterhead, but it has no tight control over the number of clusterheads and the distance from a sensor to its head in each round.

3.2 Max-Min D-Cluster Formation

[2] used the concept of minimum d-hop dominating set to construct clusters. It is proved that the minimum d-hop dominating set problem is NP-complete. [2] presented a heuristic to form d-clusters in a wireless ad hoc network where each sensor node is at most d hops away from its cluster head. Clusters are formed by diffusing node identities along the wireless links. The heuristic has four logical stages: first the propagation of larger node *ids* via *floodmax*, second the propagation of smaller node *ids* via *floodmin*, third the determination of clusterheads, and fourth the linking of clusters.

The first stage uses d rounds of *floodmax* to propagate the largest node *id* in each node's d-neighborhood. At the conclusion of the *floodmax*, the surviving node *ids* are the elected cluster heads in the network. The second stage uses d rounds of *floodmin* to propagate the smaller node *ids* that have not been overtaken, using the values that exist at each node after the first d rounds. At the conclusion of the *floodmin*, each node evaluates the round's WINNERs to best determine its clusterhead. At the third stage, three rules are applied to decide the clusterheads. When the heuristic terminates, a node either becomes a clusterhead, or is at most d hops away from its cluster head. The value of d is an input parameter.

This scheme can precisely control the maximum number of hops from a sensor node to its head, but the performance largely relies on the distribution of node *ids*. The optimal case is when the largest node *ids* are spaced d distance apart, and the worst case is when the largest node *ids* are located at close proximity (one hop away from one another). When nodes with the largest ids move or die, a large number of clusters need to be reconstructed.

3.3 Forest Approach

The LEACH approach has a random process that makes it have no control over the number of clusterheads and the sizes of clusters in each round; the Max-Min D-Cluster has the limitation that the performance relies on the distribution of node IDs. Having observed the limitations of the two schemes, we propose a new clustering scheme *Forest*, which outperforms the above two schemes in these two aspects, and is more energy efficient in data transmission.

In the Forest Approach, clusters are formed in two stages. First, we compute a Minimum Dominating Set (MDS) of the sensor network using the distributed implementation of a greedy algorithm from [18]. At the end of the first stage, some nodes are elected dominators, others are non-dominators located at most one hop away from dominators; dominators are 1, 2, or 3 hops away from each other. The dominators form a virtual graph with link cost equal to the number of hops between each other. In the second stage, a distributed algorithm will run on the virtual graph to form super clusters.

At the beginning of the second stage, all the black nodes are clusterheads, and the level of the clusters is zero. To meet the size requirement, clusters are further joined or split through multiple rounds (splitting is rarely used at the beginning of the second stage, except in extremely dense networks). At each round, the nodes in each cluster collaboratively select a minimum weight outgoing edge and try to merge with the cluster at the other end of the edge. This procedure is repeated until there is only one cluster left or the size of the cluster has reached the limit. Each round can take as many as five steps if it is a cluster with $Level > 0$, or two steps if it is a cluster of $Level = 0$.

After a cluster has selected its best outgoing edge, it sends a CONNECT request to the other side of the edge. Two clusters join together when (1) Two clusters of Level L merge into one cluster of Level $L + 1$; (2) a cluster of lower level L_L is absorbed by another cluster of higher level L_H. In the first case, the new clusterhead will be one of the two nodes connected to the merging edge; in the second case, the final cluster level will remain at L_H, and the cluster head will remain the same. In both cases, if a join occurs, the previous cluster head(s) will update the new cluster head with the list of members, so the cluster head always has the most recent information.

A *join* attempt will fail if the cluster receiving the CONNECT request has a lower level, or it has chosen a different edge to merge over, or it has stopped clustering due to its size.

The clustering algorithm is terminated when all nodes in a cluster have no outgoing edge or the cluster size n hits the limit $2(1-\alpha)N$, where N is the desired cluster size and $0 < \alpha < 0.5$. Upon termination of the clustering algorithm, it is possible that a small number of clusters are undersized. One remedy for this is to split the cluster from the most recent merging edge and re-cluster each fragment with other clusters in the neighborhood. Re-clustering can be done recursively until there is no small fragment left. The two control parameters are N and α.

4 Performance Comparison

4.1 Network Model

The overall goal of the simulation is to compare the three clustering schemes in a sensor network environment. We simulate sensor networks on a $150m \times 150m$ region. Sensor nodes are randomly deployed with different levels of density. The communication range of each sensor is set to 20 meters. Two nodes have a wireless link between them if they are within the communication range of each other.

Initially, each node was assigned a unique id, random x, y coordinates within the region and $0.5J$ of energy. Then we run the three schemes separately. For each simulation run, some important statistics were measured.

We assume the same radio model as in [10], where the radio dissipates $E_{elec} = 50nJ/bit$ to run the transmitter or receiver circuitry and $\epsilon_{amp} = 100pJ/bit/m^2$ for the transmit amplifier. We also assume an r^2 energy loss due to channel transmission, where r is the transmission distance. Thus, to transmit a k-bit message over a distance of d meters using our radio model, the radio expends

$$E_{Tx}(k,d) = E_{Tx-elec}(k) + E_{Tx-amp}(k,d)$$
$$= E_{elec} \times k + \epsilon_{amp} \times k \times d^2$$

and to receive this message, the radio expends:

$$E_{Rx}(k) = E_{Rx-elec}(k)$$
$$= E_{elec} \times k.$$

4.2 Performance Metrics

The performance metrics we used are: message overhead, cluster size, energy efficiency and cluster stability in a mobile environment.

- Message Overhead: The total number of control messages used during the cluster formation. This is an important metric for scalability.
- Energy Efficiency: Energy dissipation on data transmission after the clusters are established.
- Cluster Size: The number of clusters, the average cluster size and the standard deviation of cluster sizes. These are important measures of load distribution.
- Stability in Mobile Environments: The percentage of nodes that change their cluster membership in the sensor network when some node moves. This metric reflects the stability of the network. Because clusters are used as a lower layer infrastructure to support upper layer operations such as routing or data gathering, the stability of a cluster itself is very important.

4.3 Simulation Results

Message Overhead

In the simulation study, we define the message overhead as the total number of control messages used during clustering formation. We assume the total number of nodes in the network is n, and the maximum node degree is Δ.

In LEACH, each node has a probability 1 to become a cluster head for every $\frac{1}{P}$ rounds. So there will be Pn cluster heads per round on average. Each node that has elected itself a clusterhead for the current round will broadcast an advertisement message to the rest of the nodes within its communication range. The message overhead will be Pn in this phase. After that, when a node decides which cluster to join, it will inform the clusterhead which will then broadcast the transmission schedule of all its children. The message overhead during this phase will be n. The total message overhead will be $(Pn + n)$ in each round.

In Max-Min, each node propagates node ids for $2d$ rounds to elect clusterheads. A converge-cast is then initiated to inform the clusterheads of their children. Since no node is more than d hops away from its clusterhead, the converge-cast will be at most d rounds of messages. Altogether, the total message overhead will be $3dn$.

In Forest, during the stage of computing a MDS, each node keeps exchanging its state information within its 2-hop neighborhood. This would require each node to broadcast its own information to its one-hop neighbors and relay information for all its one-hop neighbors. This amounts to $(n(\Delta+1))$ messages per round ([18]). After the MDS algorithm terminates, the black nodes form a virtual graph, then we run the clustering algorithm on the virtual graph.

Each "join" will take as many as five steps if it is a cluster with $level > 0$, or two steps if it is a cluster of $level = 0$. For a graph of $|V|$ nodes and $|E|$ edges, the number of messages used is $5|V| \log_2 |V| + 2|E|$ ([19]). Therefore the message overhead in the second phase is $5|V| \log_2 |V| + 6|E|$, where $|V|$ is the number of black nodes and $|E|$ is the number of edges on the virtual graph, and each of the $|E|$ virtual edges is at most three wireless hops.

LEACH uses the fewest number of messages on cluster formation. Forest and Max-Min both have a sharp increase when the number of nodes grows, and Forest also increases with node degree. Fortunately, Forest is the most stable one, as we can see from the next simulation, so the cluster formation won't be a frequent operation; and Forest also consumes the least energy in data transmission due to the optimality of using the minimum weight edges, so the cost of using Forest during cluster formation is paid off in the data transmission.

Cluster Size

In this simulation, we observe the average number of clusters, the average cluster size and the standard deviation of cluster sizes for the three schemes with different network density.

The average number of clusters in a network is an indicator of load distribution. It is not good to have too few or too many clusters. Having too few clusters will overload the clusterheads with too many children. While having too many clusterheads, the energy dissipation will be increased, as the clusterheads need to keep track of the routing information of each other.

The average cluster size is inversely proportional to the average number of clusters. If the clusters are too large, their clusterheads will be overloaded. On the contrary, too small clusters will have clusterheads idle a good part of time.

The standard deviation of cluster sizes reflects the load distribution from another perspective. If the standard deviation of cluster sizes in a network is small enough, the load will be distributed evenly among clusterheads. This will help to reduce the load disparity and prolong the overall system lifetime.

In our simulation, we run LEACH, Max-Min and Forest schemes for 100 rounds and the average results are shown in Figure 1.

As shown in Figure 1(a) and Figure 1(b), the average number of clusters is inversely proportional to the average cluster size.

In LEACH simulation, the percentage of clusterheads P is set to 0.05. The simulation shows that the average number of clusters in LEACH is exactly 0.05 times the number of nodes. When the number of nodes increases, the average cluster size slightly decreases in Max-Min D Cluster. As the network density increases, there are more nodes in a node's d neighborhood (d is set to 3 in our simulation), thus Max-Min has fewer clusters and larger cluster sizes. In Forest, we set the desired cluster size equal to the square root of the number of nodes. It shows from the simulation that Forest's average cluster

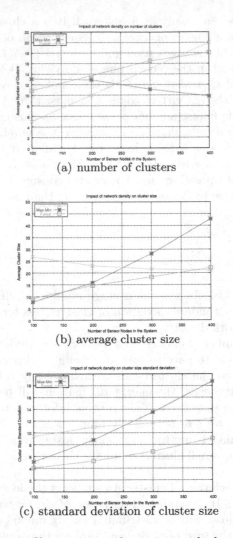

(a) number of clusters

(b) average cluster size

(c) standard deviation of cluster size

Fig. 1. Cluster sizes under various node density.

size is close to the square root of node sizes in all settings. Forest has a size control mechanism, preventing each cluster from getting too large, the simulation results having confirmed that it is indeed effective.

The simulation result in Figure 1(c) shows that Forest's clusters are distributed more evenly among nodes in the whole network than the other two schemes. The standard deviation of cluster sizes in LEACH doesn't change too much as the number of nodes increases, while in Max-Min, it is almost proportional to the number of nodes, which is not a desired property.

Energy Efficiency

We consider the scenario where sensor nodes in a cluster periodically transmit data to the cluster head. After receiving data from all its children, a cluster head performs local data aggregation before finally sending data to the base station. Because the location of the base station has greater impact on the overall energy dissipation than the other factors, such as which one acts as clusterhead and how many nodes are in a cluster etc., inclusion of the energy consumption from clusterheads to the base station will make it hard to illustrate the subtle difference in the clustering schemes. Therefore we only consider the energy dissipation of data transmission from children to their clusterheads and do not count the energy consumption from clusterheads to the base station.

We ran LEACH, Max-Min and Forest for 100 rounds over the randomly deployed 100, 200, 300 and 400-node networks (assume each node has sufficient energy and no node will die during this period) and measure the energy dissipation for data gathering from sensor nodes to clusterheads. We assume the size of a data packet from a sensor node to its cluster head is 2000 bits and compute the transmission energy using the formula in Section 4.1. LEACH has different energy consumption each round, therefore we take the average value. For the other two schemes, with a fixed cluster structure, the energy consumption is the same in each round.

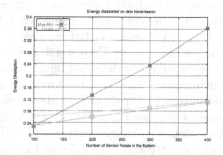

Fig. 2. Average energy dissipation in data transmission per round.

Figure 2 shows that as the number of nodes increases, the energy dissipation is increased in all three schemes. However, the differences among them are significant. Max-Min has a sharp increase as the number of nodes increases. Forest is the most energy efficient among all three schemes. LEACH consumes twice as much energy as Forest does when the network size is 100 nodes, and gradually gets close to Forest as the network size increases.

Stability in Mobile Environments

In this simulation, we randomly choose a node and make it move around, then we observe how the cluster structure will change accordingly. We assume a node moves at a speed of $2m/s$ from one corner (75, 150) of the region toward the opposite corner, as shown in Figure 3. We also assume the three schemes run automatically after the node moves. We measure the status of clusters once every $5s$ for $100s$, as the node approaches the opposite corner. The size of the network is 100 nodes.

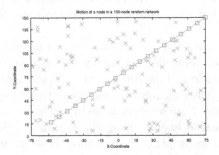

Fig. 3. Motion of a node in a 100-node network.

Our experiments show that LEACH elects new clusterheads periodically no matter whether there is a moving node or not. Therefore the percentage of nodes that change their clusterheads is 100 %. This is because in LEACH each node uses a random number to decide if it will be a clusterhead, which is independent of the node location. On the other hand, the clusters of Max-Min and Forest remain unchanged until there is a topology change. Specifically, a change of affiliation occurs in Forest only if the local topology has been changed in the vicinity of the moving node. In Max-Min, a change occurs only if the moving node causes a change of largest *id* within d hops.

We measure the cluster structure every $5s$ and count the total number of nodes that have changed clusters during the first $100s$ period, so there are a total of 2000 measures for 100 nodes. As shown in Table 1, nodes in LEACH change their clusters all the time, while the other two schemes are more stable. We also observed that Max-Min greatly depends on the ID of the moving node. A large ID always causes more changes, while Forest is not sensitive to node ID at all. When node 50 moves, 23 of them reported changes in Max-Min, and 47 of them reported changes in Forest, which is 1.15 % and 2.35 % respectively. When node 98 moves, the reported changes are 84 in Max-Min and 48 in Forest.

Table 1. Total number of changes when a node moves

mobile node ID=50		
	Total changes	Percentage(%)
LEACH	2000	100
Max-Min	23	1.15
Forest	47	2.35
mobile node ID=98		
	Total changes	Percentage(%)
LEACH	2000	100
Max-Min	84	4.2
Forest	48	2.4

5 Conclusion

The area of sensor networks has been receiving increasing attention among researchers in recent years, as available microelectro-mechanical systems and wireless communications are now capable of supporting this technology. Over the past few years, a variety of clustering schemes targeted specifically at the sensor network have been proposed. But no detailed performance comparison between these schemes is available.

In this chapter, we propose *Forest*, a new clustering scheme, and compare its performance with two other well-known clustering schemes, LEACH and Max-Min D-Cluster. Each of these three algorithms represents a category of clustering schemes, i.e., energy-based clustering, identifier-based clustering and topology-based clustering. Each of the three schemes performs well in some aspects and has certain drawbacks in others. LEACH performs well with small energy dissipation and appropriate cluster sizes. Yet, LEACH's clusters are not distributed as evenly as Forests does and it doesn't perform well in presence of node mobility. Max-Min D-Cluster performs well only when the node density of the network is small. Forest performs pretty well with the least intra cluster energy dissipation in data transmission, the most uniform cluster distribution and high stability in mobile environment. The only significant drawback is the high message overhead. However, the cluster formation consumes much less energy than the regular data transmission, and it is done less frequently. The benefit of using Forest can be observed over a long term.

When the network is static, the structure of Max-Min clusters and Forest clusters will not change. In many scenarios, sensor nodes will be static, so clusterheads will continue to be clusterheads until they are depleted of energy. These nodes will die out quickly, which may cause more nodes to die. We will improve the ID based and the topology based schemes by re-electing clusterheads at proper times. The current Forest scheme does not precisely consider the remaining energy of a node when choosing clusterheads. Being clusterheads will not consume the same amount of energy as others, so a threshold related to the residual energy may contribute to prolonging the system lifetime. We will improve Forest to include this.

Future work will be conducted to extend the network simulator $ns2$ using LEACH, Max-Min and Forest to support upper layer protocols in data gathering and dissemination. The integrated simulation environment will provide more detailed comparison on their performance.

References

1. O. Younis and S. Fahmy, "Distributed clustering for scalable, long-lived sensor networks," in *Mobicom 2003(poster)*, 2003. [Online]. Available: citeseer.ist.psu.edu/641340.html
2. A. D. Amis, R. Prakash, D. Huynh, and T. Vuong, "Max-min d-cluster formation in wireless ad hoc networks," in *INFOCOM (1)*, 2000, pp. 32–41. [Online]. Available: citeseer.ist.psu.edu/amis00maxmin.html
3. A. Karnik and A. Kumar, "Distributed optimal self-organisation in a class of wireless sensor networks," in *INFOCOM 2004*, vol. 1, 2004, pp. 536–547. [Online]. Available: citeseer.ist.psu.edu/695226.html
4. Y. P. Chen, A. L. Liestman, and J. Liu, "Clustering algorithms for ad hoc wireless networks." [Online]. Available: citeseer.ist.psu.edu/677953.html
5. C. R. Lin and M. Gerla, "Adaptive clustering for mobile wireless networks," *IEEE Journal of Selected Areas in Communications*, vol. 15, no. 7, pp. 1265–1275, 1997. [Online]. Available: citeseer.ist.psu.edu/lin97adaptive.html
6. K. Kalpakis, K. Dasgupta, and P. Namjoshi, "Efficient algorithms for maximum lifetime data gathering and aggregation in wireless sensor networks," *Computer Networks*, vol. 42, no. 6, pp. 697–716, August 2003. [Online]. Available: citeseer.ist.psu.edu/kalpakis02efficient.html
7. A. Joshi, R. Batta, and R. Nagi, "Ad hoc sensor network topology design for distributed fusion: A mathematical programming approach," in *Proc. of the 7th Int. Conf. on Information Fusion, Stickholm*, 2004, pp. 836–841. [Online]. Available: citeseer.ist.psu.edu/696672.html
8. K. Dasgupta, K. Kalpakis, and P. Namjoshi, "An efficient clustering-based heuristic for data gathering and aggregation in sensor networks," in *IEEE Wireless Comunications and Networking(WCNC)*, vol. 3, 2003, pp. 1948–1953. [Online]. Available: citeseer.ist.psu.edu/575548.html
9. O. Younis and S. Fahmy, "Distributed clustering in ad-hoc sensor networks: A hybrid energy-efficient approach," in *INFOCOM 2004*, vol. 1, 2004, pp. 629–640. [Online]. Available: citeseer.ist.psu.edu/697086.html
10. W. R. Heinzelman, A. Chandrakasan, and H. Balakrishnan, "Energy-efficient communication protocol for wireless microsensor networks," in *Proceedings of the 33rd Annual Hawaii International Conference on System Sciences(HICSS)*, January 2000, pp. 3005–3014. [Online]. Available: citeseer.ist.psu.edu/rabinerheinzelman00energyefficient.html
11. A. Siddiqui and R. Prakash, "Modeling, performance measurement, and control of clustering mechanisms for multi-cluster mobile ad hoc networks." [Online]. Available: citeseer.ist.psu.edu/488604.html

12. M. Chatterjee, S. Das, and D. Turgut, "Wca: A weighted clustering algorithm for mobile ad hoc networks," *Journal of Cluster Computing(Special Issue on Mobile Ad hoc Networks)*, vol. 5, pp. 193–204, April 2002. [Online]. Available: citeseer.ist.psu.edu/chatterjee02wca.html

13. S. Bandyopadhyay and E. Coyle, "An energy efficient hierarchical clustering algorithm for wireless sensor networks," in *INFOCOM 2003*, vol. 3, 2003, pp. 1713–1723. [Online]. Available: citeseer.ist.psu.edu/bandyopadhyay03energy.html

14. O. Younis and S. Fahmy, "Heed: a hybrid, energy-efficient, distributed clustering approach for ad hoc sensor networks," *IEEE Transactions on Mobile Computing*, vol. 3, no. 4, pp. 366–379, 2004. [Online]. Available: citeseer.ist.psu.edu/698974.html

15. D. Baker and A. Ephremides, "A distributed algorithm for organizing mobile radio telecommunication networks," in *Proceedings of the 2nd International Conference on Distributed Computer Systems*, 1981, pp. 476–483.

16. A. K. Parekh, "Selecting routers in ad-hoc networks," in *In Proceedings of the SBT/IEEE International Telecommunications Symposium*, 1994.

17. M. Handy, M. Haase, and D. Timmermann, "Low energy adaptive clustering hierarchy with deterministic cluster-head selection," in *IEEE International Conference on Mobile and Wireless Communications Networks, Stockholm, 2002.*, 2002, pp. 368–372. [Online]. Available: citeseer.ist.psu.edu/handy02low.html

18. M. X. Cheng, D.-Z. Du, and D. H.-C. Du, "Location management in mobile ad hoc wireless networks using quorums and clusters," *Wireless Communications and Mobile Computing*, 2005, to appear.

19. R. G. Gallager, P. A. Humblet, and P. M. Spira, "A distributed algorithm for minimum-weight spanning trees," *ACM Transactions on Programming Languages and Systems*, vol. 5, no. 1, pp. 66–77, 1983.

Chapter 15
Reliable and Efficient Information Forwarding and Traffic Engineering in Wireless Sensor Networks

Fernand S. Cohen, Joshua Goldberg, and Jaudelice C. de Oliveira

Electrical and Computer Engineering Department
Drexel University, Philadelphia, PA 19103
{fscohen@coe, jbg25@, jau@coe.}drexel.edu

1 Introduction

Sensor nodes often transmit via a wireless medium in which the power required to send data is proportional to the square of the distance between the source and the destination. This problem is compounded by the fact that the sink (node which collects the sensed data) can be far removed from any given node. In many situations, it is likely that most nodes will not be able to have a direct connection with the sink. In order to address these issues, a multi-hop distributed routing protocol needs to be implemented to relay the information in a quick and power efficient manner.

Routing protocols have been extensively studied in traditional areas of wireless voice and data communication networks. Wireless networks are classified as either ad hoc or infrastructured. Infrastructured wireless networks have a central manager (base station or access point) controlling the communications. In such networks, each node first communicates with the manager regardless of whom the node is trying to contact. The base station acts as a traffic controller and also as a gateway to other infrastructured networks. The characteristics of infrastructured networks differ considerably from those of wireless sensor networks. For instance, sensor networks usually have a much larger number of nodes, the nodes have much more limited processing capability, and are very prone to failures. The nodes in a wireless sensor network need to be able to communicate information efficiently with their neighbors without a centralized communication mechanism. In ad hoc wireless networks, nodes talk to each other without the use of a centralized infrastructure, which is similar to a sensor network scenario. The existing ad hoc routing protocols provide an excellent basis from which to start working on the design of efficient routing protocols for sensor networks. However, several aspects exist that prevent their direct application to sensor networks. In existing ad hoc wireless networks it is often assumed that the number of nodes is not large, and that the topology, although temporal, is relatively slow-changing in comparison to sensor networks. Sensor networks have dense topologies of nodes numbering in the thousands or even millions. These nodes are not meant to stay active for long periods of time and are expected to eventually die out. Nonetheless, the ad hoc routing protocols are based on many of the same constraints as sensor network protocols and thus can be used as a platform for the design of suitable protocols for wireless sensor networks.

In this chapter, routing protocols for sensor networks are surveyed, with an emphasis on trajectory-centric routing mechanisms. Existing routing protocols are classified and their advantage and disadvantages are compared. Design trade-offs between constrained and unconstrained routing with regards to efficiency, speed of routing, and computational complexity are discussed. Finally, a new trajectory-centric routing mechanism, called Traffic Engineering Routing (TE-Routing or TER), is described and analyzed. With the objective of securely forwarding data in a sensor network, in TE-Routing, a preferred trajectory is traced a priori. This is particularly needed in problems where obstacle avoidance is necessary. In these scenarios, the network needs to be supplied with a trajectory that would serve as a "nominal" trajectory that the routing protocol will try to adhere to, taking into account its own constraints, such as node power depletion. The use of a computer aided design (CAD) tool is proposed to allow an expert to enter a set of ordered coordinate points and have the CAD design come up with a compact description of the "nominal" trajectory, adapting it to the given constraints. Simulation results are discussed and a comparison with existing mechanisms is also given.

2 Routing in Ad Hoc Networks

Routing protocols in ad hoc networks can be grouped into two categories: proactive and reactive protocols. Several protocols have been proposed in the literature and many of them have served as mimicking models importable to sensor networks. In this section, a brief description of both categories, their advantages and disadvantages is given.

2.1 Proactive Routing

Many routing protocols fall under the category of proactive based routing. Proactive protocols set up and update routing tables regardless of whether communication is needed. Destination Sequence Distance Vector (DSDV) [17] is a classical example of this group. DSDV is based on the Bellman–Ford algorithm which ensures that no loops are formed in the routing tables. Every node in the network stores information about the next hop and distance to every other node in the network. Routing table updates are periodically transmitted through the network to keep the nodes updated with the same information. The Link State Routing (LSR) is another example of proactive protocol. Every node floods the network with the cost of all the links to which it is connected. Upon receiving the flooded information, every node calculates the shortest distance to every other node.

A general advantage of proactive protocols is that they can give QoS guarantees related to latency, connection setup, and other real-time requirements. The routing tables are updated frequently and therefore, as long as the topology does not change very fast, they reflect the current topology with a certain confidence. On the other hand, proactive protocols have a big disadvantage which is related to excessive signaling overhead in lightly loaded networks. In a light load scenario, the frequent updates on the routing tables still take place, regardless of the actual need for communication, resulting in critical energy being wasted.

2.2 Reactive (On-demand) Routing

One way of dealing with routing in the presence of a fast changing topology of an ad hoc network is by using a reactive protocol or on-demand routing. Unlike proactive routing, on-demand routing waits for a data packet before the node attempts to find the next hop. This allows for the path to be calculated step by step. This method can guarantee the path only on a hop-by-hop basis, but cannot guarantee an end-to-end path. Most of these protocols include adaptive algorithms to get around obstacles or dynamically back track and try a different set of nodes. Ad-Hoc on-demand Distance Vector Routing (AODV) [18] is a classical example of a protocol designed to set up temporary paths in an on-demand fashion. AODV is an on-demand version of DSDV. Instead of setting up routing paths to every node in the network, a node in AODV only initiates a path when it becomes necessary. Once a node needs to transmit data, a route request message is broadcast with a unique ID. When a receiving node has a path to the destination in its routing table with a higher ID than the route request's ID, it broadcasts a route reply. Otherwise it broadcasts the route request packet to its neighbors and increments the hop count.

On-demand routing also has disadvantages. In situations where the data is time critical, each node does not have time to query its neighbors for the information necessary to decide on the next hop. This infers that the node already has the information necessary to figure out an optimum next hop. The information could be stored and transmitted with periodic local broadcasts. These periodic transmissions are overhead because several of the transmitting nodes may not be used in a routing path. When the data is not time-critical, this approach is very efficient, unless the path needs to back track from a dead end. On-demand routing is very robust to a fast changing topology but offers little in guaranteeing a complete path from the source to the destination.

3 Routing in Sensor Networks

There are several ways to classify the different approaches to routing in sensor networks. In this section, four separate classes are described: data-centric, hierarchy-centric, location-centric and trajectory-centric routing.

3.1 Data-Centric Routing

A sensor network's ultimate purpose is to sense data and relay it to the sink. Unlike end-to-end routing problems faced in ad hoc wireless networks, sensor networks need to aggregate several sources of information into energy efficient transmissions [27]. In data-centric routing protocols, data from several sources can be combined en route to the sink. This reduces the size of the total data, the number of transmissions, and thus the total energy consumed.

Data-centric routing differs from the traditional address-based routing where routes are created between nodes that are addressable. In data-centric protocols, the sink sends queries to request data, and therefore attribute-based naming is used to specify data characteristics. Data-centric protocols need to optimize the aggregation of data along the route instead of finding optimal routes using typical routing metrics. Data-centric protocols are very useful in situations where data redundancy is present. When the data being transmitted is redundant in all or part of the transmitting nodes, data can be aggregated. The intermediate nodes can sequentially fuse (aggregate) the data as it is routed to the sink. Data-centric protocols inherently introduce a latency into the transmissions by avoiding the optimal route to pursue data fusion, but the tradeoff in energy savings is more than justified.

Sensor Protocols for Information via Negotiation (SPIN) [5] is the first data-centric protocol which considered interest negotiation before the actual data forwarding in order to eliminate redundant data and save energy. In SPIN, data is named with high-level descriptors or meta-data. SPIN uses meta-data negotiation where each node that receives new data advertises it to its neighbors (rather than sending the actual data) and waits to hear their interest in the data before forwarding it. This procedure solves the problems of the classical flooding mechanism in which each node forwards the data to all of its neighbors. SPIN avoids data redundancy and resource blindness, thus achieving significant energy savings.

Directed Diffusion [7], Energy Aware Routing (EAR) [23], Rumor Routing [1], Gradient Based Routing [22], Constrained Anisotropic Diffused Routing [2], COUGAR [28], and ACQUIRE [21] are other examples of data centric protocols.

3.2 Hierarchy-Centric Routing

Borrowing ideas from infrastructured networks, hierarchical based routing schemes take the large number of nodes and organize them into clusters, and a clusterhead is elected. The clusterheads represent the entire cluster to the rest of the network, and are chosen periodically according to different algorithms. This allows the routing algorithms to break the routing process into separate subsections, similar to IP based routing, regardless of how many nodes actually exist in the ad hoc network. This scheme is very flexible and allows for scalability. These algorithms must be carefully tuned to make sure that the nodes inside the clusters can efficiently communicate with the clusterhead and that the clusterhead can in turn communicate efficiently with the other clusterheads. Since the clusterhead may not be chosen based on its geographic distance from the other clusters, one cannot guarantee that a cluster can always directly communicate with another cluster efficiently. In effect, the extra layer of abstraction takes away from the precision of the routing algorithms which works on top of the hierarchy. Hierarchical based protocols are still an excellent tool in the design of a sensor network. The hierarchy concept is very robust and has many applications in sensor networks besides routing, for instance to minimize interference and deploy frequency reuse.

Low Energy Adaptive Clustering Hierarchy (LEACH) [19] is a classical hierarchical protocol designed specifically for sensor networks. LEACH assumes that all nodes are within the transmission distance of the sink. Clustering is utilized to allow for scalability and a rotation of clusterheads is configured to distribute the load. Data from within a cluster is forwarded to the clusterhead according to a Time Division Multiple Access (TDMA) schedule maintained by the clusterhead. The clusterhead will aggregate all of the data and forward it to the sink after compression. The clusterheads are chosen according to equation 1 or 2, where P is the number of nodes desired per cluster, r is the round number, r_s is the successive amount of rounds in which the node has not been a clusterhead, E_{n_max} is the maximum energy available to a node, and $E_{n\_current}$ is the current energy available to a node.

$$T(n) = \frac{P}{1 - P(r \bmod \frac{1}{P})}, \tag{1}$$

$$T(n) = \frac{P}{1 - P(r \bmod \frac{1}{P})} \left[\frac{E_{n\_current}}{E_{n\_max}} + \left(\frac{r_s}{\frac{1}{P}} \right) \left(1 - \frac{E_{n\_current}}{E_{n\_max}} \right) \right]. \tag{2}$$

Equation 1 is a stochastic threshold, which decreases as the amount of successively-failed selection rounds pass [19]. Equation 1, starting at P, gradually increases the threshold every round until it reaches 1. The threshold will reach 1 every $1/P$ rounds. In the last round, before the threshold wraps back to P, every node that has not been chosen as a cluster head in the last $1/P$ rounds will now be a clusterhead.

Equation 2 is a deterministic threshold, which decreases according to Equation 1 but also takes into account the energy available at the node [4]. Equation 1 tries to stochastically distribute which nodes are clusterheads every round, effectively distributing the workload. The problem is that the workload might not be distributed evenly since some nodes might lie very far from the sink and some might be very close, or even a few adjacent nodes could become clusterheads. To more evenly distribute the power consumption of the network, in Equation 2 the threshold for each node is scaled by the proportion of residual energy in a node. This scaling can lead to cases where the threshold is too small and no clusterhead will be chosen. To avoid this situation an additional term is added to increase the fraction of the threshold according to the number of rounds in which the individual node has not yet been chosen as a clusterhead.

In every round, the nodes generate a random number between 0 and 1 and compare it to the threshold. A random number above the threshold means that the node will become a clusterhead. Once a node decides to be a clusterhead, an advertisement is broadcast to the the rest of the nodes. Nodes which have not decided to become clusterheads choose a clusterhead according to the received signal strength. Since all nodes are within transmission distance of the sink, the transmitting clusterheads are cycled evenly and the energy consumption is evenly distributed. This protocol is very scalable but requires some additional work to maintain an efficient route to the sink if the clusterheads are not within transmission range.

TEEN [12], APTEEN [13], PEGASIS [11], Energy Aware Routing (EAR) for Cluster-Based Sensor Networks [29], and self-organizing protocol [25] are other examples of hierarchical protocols.

3.3 Location-Centric: Geographical Routing

A problem with using IP based routing in sensor networks comes from the fact that the nodes are randomly distributed over a region. The IP address assigned to a specific node is constant and has no relation to its actual physical location. When a node moves or dies its IP address loses significance since it does not offer any help in actually finding the node. To address this issue, the concept of geographical routing, where each node can dynamically determine its location, was developed. The problem of finding a node's position relative to the other nodes is called *localization*. Each node can be equipped with a GPS capable of supplying the node with its longitude and latitude. Transmitting to the node which is in the same direction as the destination will be a great start to any routing protocol in which the nodes are aware of their position. The geographic coordinates of the nodes is not always available or desirable. In the case where GPS is not available, localization can be very costly in terms of power, sometimes more than the actual routing. Although it has been shown in [9] that routing protocols that do not use geographical location information are not scalable (e.g., traditional ad hoc protocols such as DSR and AODV), the number of proposed energy-aware location based protocols is still quite small.

Greedy Perimeter Stateless Routing (GPSR) [8] is a classical geographic routing protocol. GPSR routes traffic greedily in a direct geographic line from the source to the destination. A route is not always guaranteed to be found as, at any given node, there is a possibility that there is no neighboring node in the direction of the destination. The routing is done on-demand where the nodes only need to know the geographic location of their neighbors. At every hop the routing node determines the best next hop by finding its neighboring node which is closest to the destination, using the Euclidean distance as the deciding metric. If no such neighbor is found, the node begins a search. The search progresses as the node forwards the packet via the right-hand rule. The right-hand rule states that the next hop is located counter clock-wise to the edge created between the previous hop and the current hop. A visual representation of this is shown in Figure 1.

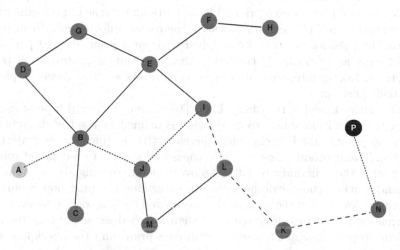

Fig. 1. GPSR Algorithm: Light gray dashed lines represent greedy routing. Dark dashed lines represent perimeter routing.

Every node receives its geographical position from a GPS or a localization algorithm. This information is shared whenever a packet is forwarded and during periodic transmissions. GPSR uses an absence of these periodic messages as a flag that a neighboring node has either moved away or gone to sleep. This method has been designed with scalability in mind. Regardless of how many nodes are in the network or how many source-destination pairs exist, the nodes only need the position of their neighbors to successfully route data. Since forwarded packets also transmit position information, the number of packets required to keep the routing information up to date is limited.

In the case of sensor networks, since the destination, or sink, is often stationary, the destination node (sink) is set and only the source nodes change. Therefore, routes to the sink will have many common nodes in the neighborhood of the sink node. These nodes will be used often for routing and therefore may die out faster than other nodes, causing routing to be switched to alternate neighboring nodes. Nodes which are farther from the sink and are not a source of data will be less likely to be included in a data path. Regardless of the position or frequency of use of a node, all nodes in the network will keep up to date information about location received either when packets are forwarded or from the periodic updates. Thus, for the nodes which are not often used as relays, this information can be considered an unnecessary overhead.

MECN [20], SMECN [10], GAF [32], and GEAR [30] are other examples of location-centric protocols.

3.4 Trajectory-Centric Routing

With the objective of securely forwarding data in a sensor network, a preferred trajectory could be traced a priori. This is particularly true in problems where obstacle avoidance is necessary to secure the routed information. In such scenarios, the network needs to be supplied with an a priori desired path that would serve as a "nominal" trajectory that the routing protocol will try to adhere to, taking into account its own constraints such as power depletion and node position.

Trajectory Based Forwarding (TBF) [16] is an on-demand type of routing where the path from source to destination is defined by a set of discrete geographical points called checkpoints (therefore the classification as trajectory-centric). This method offers the robustness and speed of on-demand routing along with the reliability of path discovery based routing. In terms of on-demand routing, the metric necessary to determine the next hop is only the geographic location of the surrounding nodes and their associated power. This information can be broadcast once and then re-broadcast every time the node goes to sleep or moves. The path is defined a priori and the checkpoints are broadcast from the sink.

Trajectory-centric protocols have very interesting features that can bring benefits to dense sensor networks. Forwarding based on trajectories decouples the path name from the path itself [16]. Route maintenance is virtually free and unaffected by mobility, node failure, or sleep modes as the path is independent of the names of nodes involved in the forwarding. Flooding, discovery and multicast can be implemented easily. It can work even without the availability of a GPS on the nodes since a coordinate system with respect to the source can be defined by locating only nodes in the neighborhood of the intended trajectory. Finally, the use of alternate routes is inexpensive (for multipath routing purposes) since it only implies adding another trajectory [16]. All of these reasons make a very strong argument for the success of trajectory-centric routing protocols.

Trajectory Based Forwarding [16] was originally proposed as a source routing scheme. A continuous trajectory is determined by a source node and then distributed as overhead in the forwarded packets. The continuous path is parametrically defined, where the parameter corresponds to the sequential forwarding of a packet. A continuous path described by a parametric equation is extended to a recursive form to implement multi-cast or multi-path routing. Sequential hops along the route are determined according to several cost functions. Every node analyzes the curve in its neighborhood. The neighborhood of a node is defined by a circle of radius r_0. The node will approximate the curve as discrete points within its neighborhood and calculate the residuals of the neighboring nodes. The residuals are defined as the parameter value corresponding to the point which is closest to a node. Using these residuals as a metric, the algorithm proposes several cost functions. These cost functions vary and differ depending on application. For example, when the trajectory is designed to avoid insecure transmission zones, a cost function which minimizes the deviation from the curve would be optimal. In a general case of sensor networks where power is paramount, a cost function that selects the nodes with the highest power would be selected. Every cost function should be sure to select a node whose residual corresponds to a forward traversal of the trajectory. Although the proposed mechanisms are very interesting, the computation complexity of the method can be improved.

4 TE-Routing

Taking advantage of the preliminary ideas proposed in [16] as base for our work and extending it, we proposed Traffic Engineering Routing (TE-Routing or TER). As mentioned in [16], the trajectory should be designed by a trajectory mapping service to guarantee that all of the aspects of the landscape are considered. To optimize the usefulness of this algorithm, we propose that the trajectory be defined by an expert using a computer aided design (CAD) tool. Note that all the expert is required to do is to enter/click a few points which will be used to define the curve that the routing mechanism will try to follow. For instance, suppose that sensor nodes are spread on a large field collecting data, and enemy camps are part of the field. For security reasons, the engineers might decide that the traffic should be routed away from these regions, and therefore, the expert would click on the map and enter points that the routing mechanism must follow, avoiding the unwanted region. Figure 2 illustrates our example. Note also that the expert does not need to know the position of the nodes in the field. He or she only needs to enter a set of points that will be automatically translated to a curve that the routing path must follow. We propose to use a B-Spline [3, 6] curve which will pass through all of the points. The B-Spline is later segmented into checkpoints to be distributed to the nodes. A discrete set of points is chosen to avoid the computation necessary to approximate the trajectory at the individual nodes, therefore simplifying the calculations needed in TBF. Since the trajectory is intended to be distributed one time by a high power sink, the overhead introduced is minimal.

For a complicated continuous trajectory, the residues proposed in [16] are inefficient to calculate. Complicated trajectories can be considered as those

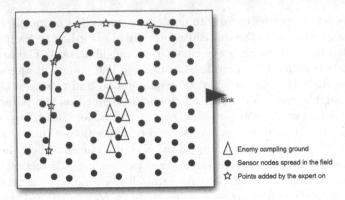

Fig. 2. (a) A sensor field where an enemy camping area needs to be avoided. The figure shows the points entered on the CAD system and the curve generated. The routing path will be chosen to follow the curve as closely as possible given the residual energy constraint of the nodes.

with loops or many turns. In this case, the algorithm will correctly select nodes farther on the trajectory but will have skipped entire portions. Discrete points along with the corresponding indexes can be used to correctly route in loops. The optimal distance between the discrete points and a method to traverse the discrete path, is needed. The calculation of the residual for every node within a region given a set of points, as in TBF, can be computation intensive and unnecessary.

TE-Routing attempts at finding the closest node from a set of nodes that fall within a desirable area to a checkpoint. This diminishes the number of nodes which are considered. The desirable area is referred as the search window. In a best case scenario, a directional antenna would turn to face the direction of the next checkpoint. This would force the node to only consider neighbors within the search window and also eliminate all calculations necessary to do so. When a directional antenna is not available, the search window is defined as a function of the checkpoints in the shape of a triangle. The aperture of the triangle opens in the direction of the curve and osculates along the curve trajectory. The construction of the triangle is done as follows:

- A line L_1 connecting the current checkpoint (C_1) and next checkpoint (C_2) is drawn.
- A line L_2 perpendicular to L_1 which passes through C_2 is drawn.
- A line L_3 parallel to L_1 which passes through the current node (N_1) is drawn.
- The intersection of L_3 and L_1 is defined as the midpoint M.
- Two lines that form an angle θ with L_3 are calculated. The intersection of these two lines with L_1 are two of the vertices for the search window, T_2 and T_3. N_1 is the other vertex of the search window.

An algorithm is needed to select the nodes which are within this search window. This problem is faced in computer graphics in relation to ray-tracing [24]. The solution is to represent a node's position as a vector from the origin and then decompose the vector into two directions with an offset. The first direction is taken as the vector V_1 going from N_1 to T_2, the other direction is the vector V_2 going from T_2 to T_3. The important terms of the decomposition are the multiplying factors of the two direction vectors, p_1 and p_2 respectively. If p_1 or p_2 is greater than 1 or less than 0, then the point lies outside of the triangle. The other discriminating condition is if p_2 is greater than p_1. Let X be the node that is being tested, then:

$$[X] = [N_1] + p_1[(T_2 - N_1)] + p_2[(T_3 - T_2)], \qquad (3)$$

$$[(T_3 - T_2)\,(T_2 - N_1)]^{-1}\,[(X - N_1)] = \begin{bmatrix} p_1 \\ p_2 \end{bmatrix}. \qquad (4)$$

The matrix $[(T_3 - T_2)\,(T_2 - N_1)]^{-1}$ is a function of the triangle and only needs to be calculated once. Once a neighboring node is found to be within the search window, the next hop can be chosen according to their distance from the current checkpoint.

The triangle can be counterproductive if the current checkpoint is close to the current node. At this point, the triangle area will be very small and the chances to find a node decreases significantly. A similar situation occurs when the angle θ is too small. To address these cases, the nodes will resize their search window in two ways. First the node will increase the angle θ, and if this also fails, it will select the checkpoint after the next checkpoint as C_2. If the next checkpoint is changed, the window angle can be reset to the default or left at the maximum value, depending on the application. If the checkpoints are given too close together, this algorithm gives the nodes the option of re-sampling dynamically.

The algorithm terminates when the destination node is within the search window, or a next hop neighbor cannot be found. Depending on the application, the final node in a failed attempt may still forward the data to the destination node if the destination is in transmission range.

4.1 CAD Trajectory Design

To present the most flexible and easy to use tool to the expert who is charged with tracing the desired trajectory or map road, a CAD system with a virtual road map of the environment where the sensors are deployed is considered. The expert is asked to input a sequence of points in order (versus scattered) as to where the nominal trajectory will follow. These ordered points can be considered as data points to which a parameter set describing the trajectory will be found by fitting a B-spline model to the data as in [26]. There are many reasons why B-splines are attractive structures:

- Smoothness and continuity which allows any curve to consist of a con-
  catenation of curve segments, yet be treated as a single unit that can be
  described at any desired resolution (infinite resolution);
- Built-in boundedness, a property which is lacking in both the implicit or
  explicit polynomial representation, whose zero set can shoot to infinity
  [31]. A B-spline is bounded by the polygon formed by the B-spline control
  points;
- The ease of specifying the range of a multi-valued curve;
- The decoupling of x and y (and z in 3D) coordinates, with each having its
  parametric representation;
- Local controllability, which implies that local changes in shape are only
  confined to the B-spline parameters local to that change.

4.2 B-Spline Curves

The B-splines are piecewise polynomial functions that provide local approximations to contours/surfaces using a small number of parameters (control
points). A pth order B-spline is C^{p-1} continuous, i.e., is continuous and has
$(p-1)$ continuous derivatives. A pth order closed B-spline with $n+1$ parameters $P_0, P_1, \ldots, P_n$ (control points) consists of $n+1$ connected curve segments
$r_i(t) = (x_i(t), y_i(t))$, each of which is a linear combination of $(p+1)$ polyno-
mials of order p in the parameter t, where t is normalized between 0 and 1,
$(0 \le t \le 1)$. The parameter t may be thought of as time and the curve may
be thought of as the trajectory of a particle moving in 2-D or 3-D space with
a speed of $\|dr_i(t)/dt\|$.

The recursive equations of the B-Spline basis function are shown in equations 5 and 6, and Figure 3, where P_i are the control points, U is the knot
vector, and p is the B-Spline order.

$$R(t) = \sum_{i=0}^{n} N_{i,p}(t) P_i, \quad 0 \le t \le 1, \qquad (5)$$

$$N_{i,p}(t) = \frac{t - U_i}{U_{i+p} - U_i} N_{i,p-1}(t) + \frac{U_{i+p+1} - t}{U_{i+p+1} - U_{i+1}} N_{i+1,p-1}(t), \qquad (6)$$

$$N_{i,0}(t) = \begin{cases} 1 \ U_i \le t < U_{i+1}, \\ 0 \ \text{otherwise}. \end{cases}$$

The control points for the B-Spline are chosen such that the resulting curve
is an intuitive fit to the expert's data points. A B-Spline order of 3 proved
to be sufficient to exceed the requirements of the CAD and the trajectory.
The method used to form the B-Spline can be found in detail at [26]. The
algorithm used generates a set of control points. The corresponding B-Spline
passes through all of the data points and the velocity is equal at the knot
points and the middle points between the knots. This does not guarantee that

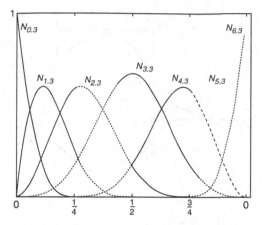

Fig. 3. B-Spline Basis Functions For $p = 3$ and $n = 6$.

the velocity is constant throughout the curve but it approximates it very well. We select all the data points as control points and then generate two new control points between each of the data points. Equation 7 can be used to calculate the extra control points, where Q_k are the data points and T_k are the tangent vectors.

$$P_{1,k} = Q_k + \tfrac{1}{3}\alpha T_k,$$
$$P_{2,k} = Q_{k+1} - \tfrac{1}{3}\alpha T_{k+1}. \tag{7}$$

An example of a B-Spline trajectory generated from the set of control points is shown in Figure 4. For every data point, except the first and last, two extra checkpoints are generated on the line tangent to the B-Spline at the data point. For the first and last, only one extra control point is generated. Since this is done before the actual B-Spline is generated, the tangent vectors need to be approximated using the surrounding data points. A 5-point method is used to approximate the tangent vectors and the positions of the extra control points on the vector as in [26].

4.3 Simulation and Experimental Results

The algorithm starts by using the Computer Aided Design (CAD) tool and selecting the checkpoints. The CAD tool has been designed to accept node positions from a file or by individual input from the expert. Once a source node and destination node have been specified, the power is dynamically assigned to the nodes. The assumption is that the source node spent a large portion of its energy communicating with its neighbors before deciding to transmit to the destination. The source node and its neighbors should be relatively low on power but the power available to the nodes should increase as the distance from the source increases. In the CAD tool, the power is displayed as a color gradient from a low power color to a high power color. This color

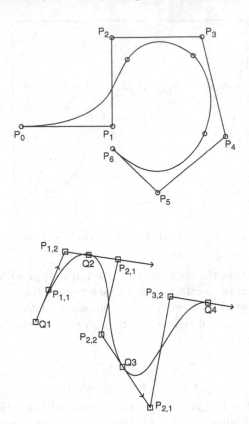

Fig. 4. (a) A B-Spline generated using the data points as control points.(b) A B-Spline interpolated from the data points. Extra Control points are shown.

arrangement is configurable. The data points are entered by mouse clicks and the corresponding B-Spline is shown when the expert is done entering data points. When the simulation is run, the search windows are shown and if a path can be completed to the destination, a solid line is drawn. The line represents the actual path traversed. The node IDs are shown along with the nodes' power. The window angle, the transmission distance, and the distance between checkpoints are input to the CAD tool system.

To test the algorithm, two metrics were considered: the success rate versus node densities, and hop count versus checkpoint distances. The success rate is extremely important to be certain that the algorithm is viable for a given application node density. The checkpoint distances determine how well the traversed path follows the designed trajectory, how many resizes occur, and whether or not the algorithm will succeed. The simulation runs 1000 tests for each node density per checkpoint distance. The area is 200 by 150 units and the transmit distance is 56 units. This corresponds to the configuration that is used for the testbed of mica2 sensor nodes. In terms of physical distance, the values are about 10 inches for the radio distance in an area 3 ft. by 2.3 ft. The nodes were uniformly distributed over the area with the source and destination at fixed positions. The same curve was used in each test.

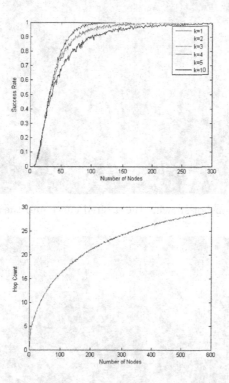

Fig. 5. (a) Success vs. node count for various checkpoint distances. (b) Hops vs. node count for $k = 10$.

In Figure 5(a), $\frac{1}{k}$ is the fraction of the radio range used as the distance between checkpoints. The success rates rise rapidly and give a good sense of the algorithm's reliability. A more interesting relation can be seen by analyzing the number of hops traversed. The nodes skip checkpoints if the algorithm fails to locate a next hop, and so the hop count is variable. The plot shows a strong correlation between node density and hop count. This can be used to determine the granularity or resolution of the trajectory that the nodes will be able to follow. The plot shown is only for the run when $k = 10$. The other runs reached the maximum hops available very fast and did not reveal information of much interest.

For trajectory based forwarding to be useful, the trajectory seen by the expert and the path traversed by the nodes need to be close. Figure 5(b) can

Fig. 6. CAD snapshot showing the desired curve and the selected nodes.

Fig. 7. CAD snapshot zoom.

be used to estimate an optimal resolution for the checkpoints that the nodes will be able to follow.

Figures 6 and 7 show a snap shot of the CAD and a zoom into the picture, respectively. The CAD trajectory is shown in white, the available sensor nodes are shown as white dots, and the estimated routing path found by the algorithm is shown in black. As we can see from the simulation results on that snap shot, the estimated path follows very closely that of the CAD trajectory. In the same figure, we can also see the osculating search window (triangle) as it navigates from source to destination node.

Similar results are shown with real sensors in Figure 8. Here, the desired trajectory is shown in thick white whereas the estimated and followed routing path is shown in a slim black line. The routing path is found in real time.

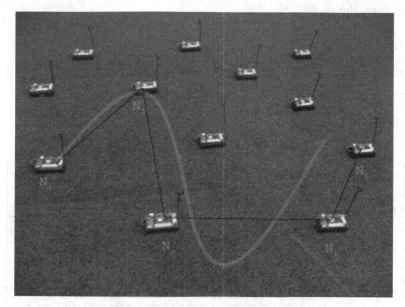

Fig. 8. Mica2 Sensor Node Test Bed. Maximum Radio Transmission range set to 10cm. at a radio power of -19dBm. The processor is an ATmega128 powered by two AA batteries. The radio is a CC1000 chip. The node draws $17\mu A$ of current during sleep mode. Application of TE-Routing utilizes a simple CRC transmission component, the routing protocol, and a test application which transmits the source's battery power.

4.4 Related Work

Niculescu and Nath were the first to introduce trajectory-based routing, discussing its basic features in [14, 15, 16]. Our contributions are to how the trajectory is encoded (B-Spline and checkpoints) and to the reduced computation on each participating node by introduction of the adaptive search window.

In [31], the authors propose the use of a Bezier parametric curve for a trajectory-based source routing in ad hoc networks. However, crucial issues particular to sensor networks were not taken into account, such as power constraints and low complexity. Moreover, the problem of finding the nodes that are the closest to the trajectory is highly nonlinear and becomes computationally intensive and even prohibitive considering Bezier curves with higher order than cubic, which is the realistic scenario. Therefore, our encoding technique is much simpler and suitable for deployment in actual sensor networks.

Table 1 summarizes the differences between our proposed algorithm (TER) and the algorithm described in [14, 15, 16]. The following conclusions can be drawn from the table:

Table 1. Comparison between TBF and TE Routing (TER) mechanisms.

Metric	TBF	TER	Comparison-TBF	Comparison-TER
Path Definition	Source-Defined. Continuous parametric function.	Sink-Defined. Arbitrary function defined by the expert.	Dynamic Curve Definition. Lack of Curve Complexity. Packet Overhead.	Initial point distribution overhead. Expert defined curve. Fixed curve granularity.
Curve Breakdown	Every hop breaks the curve down into discrete points. Calculation done for each neighborhood node.	Sink breaks the entire curve down into discrete points. The sink distributes all of the points to the nodes.	Static breakdown at the sink.	Dynamic breakdown at nodes. Energy can be an issue.
Closeness to Curve	Curves which form loops will skip sections.	Global discrete breakdown enumerates all the points. The traveresed path will pass over every discrete point when possible.	Lacks support for a specific curve type.	Supports accurate following of the specified curve.
Success Rate	Best possible success rate given one-hop neighbor information available.	Sub-optimal performance since only a portion of single hop neighbors are considered.	All available information is used to complete the message path.	The search window limits which of the neighboring nodes will be considered.
Computation Complexity	P points per hop: P function evaluations. M nodes in the neighborhood. P distance calculations : $P*M*(2MULT+1ADD/SUB)$.	Define the search window per hop: $16ADD/SUB+17MULT$. N nodes in the search window. N distance calculations : $N*(2MULT+1ADD/SUB)$.	Depending on how the next hop is chosen, P can be small.	N will be smaller than P*M. The search window is only calculated once and is comparable to P function evaluations.

- TBF requires the source to define the path as a continuous function in t, while in TER the path is defined, regardless of complexity, at the sink and distributed as a set of discrete points to the nodes. TBF may allow for a different path to be used for every packet. This comes at the cost of overhead and lack of support for complex curves.
- TBF requires that every node discretizes the curve within its neighborhood. The number of calculations is dependent on dt and the complexity of the curve function. In TER, the curve is discretized a priori. The curve only needs to be discritized once in either case, but discretizing it at the sink saves power and allows for more complex curves.
- TBF requires floating point calculations to discretize the curve. In TER, as long as the coordinates of the nodes is kept as integers, no floating

point calculations are needed. Floating point processors are expensive to implement in hardware and are usually implemented as a set of instructions using the integer arithmetic logic unit. In the case where floating point is done as an algorithm, it takes many more instructions/cpu time to compute than integer calculation.

- With TBF, entire sections of the curve may be skipped if it has sections which backtrack along previous sections of the curve. TER uses discrete indexes for each point and does not encounter this problem.
- Finally, at the cost of complexity, TBF's success rate is the best found using only single-hop neighbors and path information. TER may yield a sub-optimal solution as some of the nodes may not lie in the search window (this is addressed by varying the size of the window).

5 Conclusions and Research Directions

In this chapter we presented a host of routing protocols and have proposed and suggested a new one that combines expert CAD trajectory with directional antenna/osculating window search to arrive at a route from source to destination nodes taking into account both the proximity to the CAD trajectory as well as the power constraints inherent in the sensor nodes. The introduction of the CAD design, coupled with osculating window search have a double advantage in terms of limiting the forward path to a subset of the nodes in the network that are in the vicinity of the CAD trajectory, as well as distributing the routing load so that the power is not depleted when information is needed to be sent to the destination node (the sink). This has a direct impact on the speed of communication. In addition, such a coupling allows for minimal information that the sensor nodes need to carry about their environment and the other nodes in the network.

Interesting research points need still to be addressed ranging from the desired resolution of the trajectory and how it relates to the density of nodes in the sensor network, to ways of guaranteeing that the information is sent under various node topologies. Partial answers to these questions were proposed and implemented but further investigation is needed.

References

1. D. Braginsky and D. Estrin, "Rumor Routing Algorithm for Sensor Networks," in the Proceedings of the *First Workshop on Sensor Networks and Applications* (WSNA), Atlanta, GA, October 2002.
2. M. Chu, H. Haussecker, and F. Zhao, "Scalable Information-Driven Sensor Querying and Routing for ad hoc Heterogeneous Sensor Networks," *The International Journal of High Performance Computing Applications*, Vol. 16, No. 3, August 2002.

3. F. S. Cohen, Z. Yang, Z. Huang, and Y. Nissanov, "Computer Matching of Histological Rat Brain Sections," *IEEE Trans. on Biomedical Engineering*, Vol. 45, No. 5, pp. 642–649, May 1998.
4. M. Handy, M. Haase and D. Timmermann. "Low-Energy Adaptive Clustering Hierarchy With Deterministic Clusterhead Selection," in the Proceedings of IEEE *Int. Conference on Mobile and Wireless Communications Networks*, Stockholm, September 2002.
5. W. Heinzelman, J. Kulik, and H. Balakrishnan, "Adaptive Protocols for Information Dissemination in Wireless Sensor Networks," in the Proceedings of the *5th ACM/IEEE Mobicom Conference* (MobiCom '99), Seattle, WA, August, 1999.
6. Z. Huang and F. S. Cohen, "Affine-Invariant Moments and B-Splines for Object Recognition from Image Curves," *IEEE Trans. on Image Processing*, Vol. 5, No. 10, pp. 1473–1480, October 1996.
7. C. Intanagonwiwat, R. Govindan and D. Estrin, "Directed Diffusion: A Scalable and Robust Communication Paradigm for Sensor Networks," In the Proceedings of the *Sixth Annual International Conference on Mobile Computing and Networks (MobiCOM 2000)*, Boston, Massachusetts, August 2000.
8. B. Karp and H. T. Kung, "GPSR: greedy perimeter stateless routing for wireless networks," in the Proceedings of *ACM MOBICOM 2000*, pp. 243–254.
9. J. Li, J. Jannotti, D. De Couto, D. Karger, and R. Morris, "A Scalable Location Service for Geographic Ad Hoc Routing," in the Proceedings of *IEEE/ACM Mobicom 2000*, pp. 120–30.
10. L. Li and J. Y Halpern, "Minimum energy mobile wireless networks revisited," in the Proceedings of *IEEE International Conference on Communications* (ICC01), Helsinki, Finland, June 2001.
11. S. Lindsey and C. S. Raghavendra, "PEGASIS: Power Efficient Gathering in Sensor Information Systems," in the Proceedings of the *IEEE Aerospace Conference*, Big Sky, Montana, March 2002.
12. A. Manjeshwar and D. P. Agrawal, "TEEN: A Protocol for Enhanced Efficiency in Wireless Sensor Networks," in the Proceedings of the *1st International Workshop on Parallel and Distributed Computing Issues in Wireless Networks and Mobile Computing*, San Francisco, CA, April 2001.
13. A. Manjeshwar and D. P. Agrawal, "APTEEN: A Hybrid Protocol for Efficient Routing and Comprehensive Information Retrieval in Wireless Sensor Networks, in the Proceedings of the *2nd International Workshop on Parallel and Distributed Computing Issues in Wireless Networks and Mobile computing*, Ft. Lauderdale, FL, April 2002.
14. B. Nath and D. Niculescu, "Routing on a Curve," in Proceedings of ACM HOTNETS-I 2002 and SIGCOMM Computer Communication Review, January 2003.
15. D. Niculescu and B. Nath, "Localized positioning in ad hoc networks," in Proceedings of the First IEEE *International Workshop on Sensor Network Protocols and Applications*, Anchorage, AK, USA, May 2003.
16. D. Niculescu and B. Nath, "Trajectory Based Forwarding and Its Applications," in Proceedings of *ACM MOBICOM 2003*, San Diego, CA, USA, September 2003.
17. C. Perkins and P. Bhagwat. "Highly Dynamic Destination-Sequenced Distance-Vector Routing (DSDV) for Mobile Computers," in Proceedings of the *ACM SIGCOMM*, October 1994.
18. C. Perkins. "Ad Hoc On Demand Distance Vector (AODV) Routing," IETF, Internet Draft, *draft-ietf-manet-aodv-00.txt*, November 1997.

19. W. R. Heinzelman, A. Chandrakasan, and H. Balakrishnan, "Energy-Efficient Communication Protocol for Wireless Microsensor Networks," in the Proceedings of *HICSS* 2000.

20. V. Rodoplu and T.H. Ming, "Minimum energy mobile wireless networks," *IEEE Journal of Selected Areas in Communications*, Vol. 17, No. 8, pp. 1333–1344, 1999.

21. N. Sadagopan, B. Krishnamachari, A. Helmy, "The ACQUIRE Mechanism for Efficient Querying in Sensor Networks," First *IEEE International Workshop on Sensor Network Protocols and Applications (SNPA)*, in conjunction with IEEE ICC 2003, May 2003, Anchorage, AK, USA.

22. C. Schurgers and M.B. Srivastava, "Energy efficient routing in wireless sensor networks," in the *MILCOM Proceedings on Communications for Network-Centric Operations: Creating the Information Force*, McLean, VA, 2001.

23. R. Shah and J. Rabaey, "Energy Aware Routing for Low Energy Ad Hoc Sensor Networks," in the Proceedings of the *IEEE Wireless Communications and Networking Conference (WCNC)*, Orlando, FL, March 2002.

24. O. J. A. Smith, "Ray-Tracing With Affine Transforms," *MathVISION Inc*, June 1995.

25. L. Subramanian and R. H. Katz, "An Architecture for Building Self Configurable Systems," in the Proceedings of *IEEE/ACM Workshop on Mobile Ad Hoc Networking and Computing*, Boston, MA, August 2000.

26. Les Piegl, Wayne Tiller, "The NURBS Book Monographs in Visual Communication," Berlin: Springer, 1997.

27. B. Krishnamachari, D. Estrin, and S. Wicker, "Modelling Data-Centric Routing in Wireless Sensor Networks," in the Proceedings of *IEEE INFOCOM*, New York, NY, USA, 2002.

28. Y. Yao and J. Gehrke, "The cougar approach to in-network query processing in sensor networks," in *SIGMOD Record*, September 2002.

29. M. Younis, M. Youssef and K. Arisha, "Energy-Aware Routing in Cluster-Based Sensor Networks," in the Proceedings of the 10th *IEEE/ACM International Symposium on Modeling, Analysis and Simulation of Computer and Telecommunication Systems* (MASCOTS2002), Fort Worth, TX, October 2002.

30. Y. Yu, D. Estrin, and R. Govindan, "Geographical and Energy-Aware Routing: A Recursive Data Dissemination Protocol for Wireless Sensor Networks," *UCLA Computer Science Department Technical Report*, UCLA-CSD TR-01-0023, May 2001.

31. M. Yuksel, R. Pradhan and S. Kalyanaraman, "An Implementation Framework for Trajectory-Based Forwarding in Ad Hoc Networks," in the Proceedings of *Wireless Networking Symposium part of IEEE International Conference on Communications (ICC)*, Paris, France, June, 2004.

32. Y. Xu, J. Heidemann, and D. Estrin, "Geography-informed energy conservation for ad hoc routing," in the Proceedings of the 7th Annual *ACM/IEEE International Conference on Mobile Computing and Networking* (MobiCom01), Rome, Italy, July 2001.

Chapter 16
Modeling Data Gathering in Wireless Sensor Networks

Bhaskar Krishnamachari

Department of Electrical Engineering-Systems
Viterbi School of Engineering, University of Southern California, Los Angeles, CA 90089
bkrishna@usc.edu

1 Introduction

The predominant protocol development methodology in the area of wireless sensor networks today can be characterized as being one of *design-by-intuition/validate-through-simulation*. However, a concurrent development of complementary theoretical models for these protocols is essential for the rapid advancement of this technology. This is because the severe resource constraints on energy, computation, and storage that are characteristic of these networks make it crucial to optimize protocols, in order to maximize network lifetime while providing an acceptable quality of sensed information.

We survey in this chapter some examples drawn from recent studies pertaining to data gathering in sensor networks. These examples demonstrate the importance of optimizing protocol parameters carefully to maximize performance. We emphasize the use of a *first-order mathematical modeling approach*. The optimizations are all based on simple expressions that are intended to capture the impact of essential environmental and protocol parameters. This approach is motivated by the desire to understand easily the key design trade-offs that are involved in each context. As we shall see, even such simple models can yield fundamental design insights to improve the performance of practical protocols.

This style of modeling is nicely described in an essay written by the noted economist, Prof. Hal Varian, titled "How to build an economic model in your spare time" [1]:

> "The critical advice here is KISS: keep it simple, stupid. Write down the simplest model you can think of, and see if it still exhibits some interesting behavior. If it does, then make it even simpler.
> ... keep at it till it gets simple. The whole point of a model is to give a simplified representation of reality. Einstein once said 'Everything

should be as simple as possible... but no simpler.' A model is supposed
to reveal the essence of what is going on: your model should be reduced
to just those pieces that are required to make it work."

The methodology employed in these studies can be summarized as follows:

1. Identify the unique functionality of the protocol to be modeled. What
   exactly does it do — does it provide for routing with data aggregation
   from a set of sources to a common sink, or is it for gathering information
   from the network to resolve a query for a specific named attribute?
2. Identify the primary performance metric of interest in analyzing this protocol. For battery-constrained sensor networks this often translates to
   minimizing the total number of transmissions required to accomplish the
   specified networking task. This is because under the assumption that idle
   listening and overhearing can be minimized through appropriate MAC-
   level scheduling, transmissions of packets (and their corresponding recep-
   tions) are the primary source of energy consumption.
3. Identify the building blocks of the model. It is typical in these models to
   assume some simple topology such as uniform random placement with a
   fixed radius for connectivity, or a carefully placed grid of sensors, each
   communicating with just their four cardinal neighbors. Other significant
   building blocks for the model are the environmental and protocol parameters that have an significant impact on performance. As we are aiming
   to build an abstracted, simplified model of reality, this need not be an
   exhaustive list, but should include key parameters. This is more of an art
   than a science in many respects, and often entails an iterative process to
   refine the components of the model.
4. Derive a simple mathematical expression that gives the performance metric for that protocol, as a function of the variables corresponding to key
   environmental, network, and protocol parameters. Along with the previous step, this is part of the core work of building the model.
5. Refine the model, by adding, discarding, or modifying variables corresponding to environmental, protocol or network settings. The goal is to
   obtain an expression for the protocol performance metric that illustrates
   the core tradeoff.
6. Solve for the value of the protocol parameter which optimizes the performance metric of interest. There are often opposite trends in different
   components of the model that are in tension with each other. As a result,
   performance loss may be incurred in setting a key protocol parameter to
   too low a value or too high a value. In most cases, determining the optimum parameter setting requires just finding the zero of the derivative
   of the metric with respect to the parameter in question. The obtained
   result reveals how the optimal protocol parameter setting depends upon
   environmental and network conditions.

In the following sections, we shall present models for three specific problems pertaining to data gathering in wireless sensor networks. In the first case

study, we optimize the look-ahead parameter for an active querying mechanism that provides a tunable tradeoff between trajectory-based and flooding-based querying. In the second case study, we optimize the cluster size for joint routing and compression that minimizes the total transmitted information for a prescribed level of correlation between the sources. Finally, in the third case study, we look at a problem of querying for replicated information and identify the optimal number of replicas that minimizes the total energy cost involved.

2 Active Querying with Look-Ahead

The ACQUIRE mechanism [2] is an active querying technique designed for sensor networks. In essence, it consists of the following repeated sequence of steps: (i) An active node which receives the query checks its local cache to see if it contains the information requested. (ii) If the information in the local cache is not fresh, the active node sends a controlled flood of the query to all nodes within d hops of it to obtain a fresh update of the information. (iii) If the query is still not resolved, the query is forwarded to a succeeding active node that is $2d$ hops away along a trajectory (which could be random or guided in some way). Finally, when the information being sought is obtained, the query response is routed back to the original querying node. This is illustrated in Figure 1.

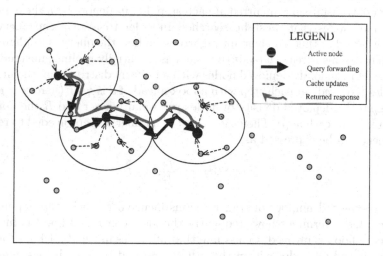

Fig. 1. Illustration of ACQUIRE.

One interesting observation about the ACQUIRE querying mechanism is that the look-ahead parameter d essentially allows for tuning across a wide range of behaviors. When $d = 0$, then the query is simply forwarded along some path until it is resolved (e.g., a random walk query, or a geographic trajectory based query). When d is large enough to be the diameter of the network, then the query is essentially performed as a network-wide cache-based flooding.

A key question in this setting that we shall address with first-order analysis is what should determine the optimal setting of this look-ahead parameter d. It turns out that, since caching is employed, this is affected primarily by the ratio of updates to queries, which we denote by c. (When $c = 0.01$, for example, on average one update is requested every 100 queries. Alternately, we could say that the cache at each active node remains valid on average for 100 queries). This parameter quantifies the level of dynamics in the environment relative to the rate at which queries are posed.

We will use, as the metric of interest, the average total number of transmissions required to resolve a query. For ACQUIRE this is essentially the product of two factors, the expected number of steps (i.e., the number of active query nodes visited in the trajectory), and the expected total number of transmissions incurred at each step. Interestingly, each of these factors depends in a different manner on the look-ahead parameter d. The expected number of steps is smaller when the look-ahead parameter is large, because each step would cover a larger portion of the network and make it more likely that the query is resolved in fewer steps. However, with a larger look-ahead parameter, the expected number of transmissions incurred at each step is larger as the controlled flood has to reach a larger number of nodes.

Let $S(d)$ be the expected number of steps, and $T(d)$ be the expected number of transmissions incurred at each step. Let us denote by η the expected number of nodes that must be searched in order to resolve the query (we assume here that this is a constant regardless of how the query is implemented in practice. This is reasonable if the query is essentially a blind, unstructured search). For randomly deployed nodes with a uniform distribution, the number of nodes "covered" at each step with a look-ahead of d is $\gamma \cdot d^2$ (here $\gamma = \rho \pi R^2$, where ρ is the deployed density of nodes per square meter and R the nominal radio range for each hop). Then the expected number of steps needed to resolve the query can be expressed as:

$$S(d) = \frac{\eta}{\gamma d^2}. \tag{1}$$

The expected number of transmissions incurred at each step depends on c, since this determines how frequently the local controlled flood is invoked. When the flood is invoked, we assume that all nodes in the $d-1$ hops forward the flood, and all nodes within the d hops respond back with messages providing their respective information. The expected number of nodes at hop i is $\gamma i^2 - \gamma(i-1)^2 = \gamma \cdot (2i-1)$. These must all send their information back to the active node through i transmissions. The expected number of transmissions at each step is therefore:

$$T(d) = c(\gamma(d-1)^2 + \gamma \sum_{i=1}^{d}(2i-1)i) = c\gamma((d-1)^2 + \frac{1}{3}d(d^2-1)). \qquad (2)$$

Now taking into account that the resolved response to the query must then be returned to the original querying node by incurring about $S(d) * 2d$ additional transmissions (assuming $S(d) > 1$, else it would be 0), we have the total expected number of transmissions $N(d)$ required by ACQUIRE with a look-ahead setting of d to be as follows:

$$N(d) = S(d)(T(d) + 2d) = \frac{\eta}{\gamma d^2}(c\gamma((d-1)^2 + \frac{1}{3}d(d^2-1)) + 2d). \qquad (3)$$

This expression is plotted in Figure 2(a) for different values of c (assuming $\eta = 400, \gamma = 10\pi$). We can see that for a fixed value of c, the optimal setting of the look-ahead parameter that minimizes the total number of transmissions varies. We can determine the optimal d by taking the derivative of the above expression with respect to d and setting it to zero (the resulting real value is then rounded to the nearest integer). The numerical solution for the optimal d is plotted as a function of c in Figure 2(b). This figures quantifies the insight that a smaller look-ahead (corresponding to a trajectory based search) is favored when the environmental dynamics are so high that caching is not effective (high c), whereas a larger look-ahead (resembling flooding) is favored when caches can be used with high frequency (low c).

3 Cluster-Based Joint Routing and Compression

Because of their application-specificity, sensor networks are capable of performing data-centric routing, which allows for in-network processing of information. In particular, to reduce total energy consumption, data from correlated sensors can be compressed at intermediate nodes even as they are routed. We examine now how the appropriate joint routing and compression strategy can depend on the degree of correlation between the sources.

We first need a model to quantify the amount of information generated by a set of sources. We use here a simple model that has been previously validated with some real data [3]. In this model, there is a tunable parameter δ which varies from 0 to 1 and provides an indicator of the level of correlation between the sources. We use the joint entropy H_n of the sources as the measure of the total information they generate, assuming that each individual source has an identical entropy of H_1:

$$H_n(\delta) = H_1(1 + \delta(n-1)). \qquad (4)$$

Thus, when $\delta = 0$, the correlation is the highest (the sources sensing identical readings), resulting in a joint entropy that is equal to the entropy

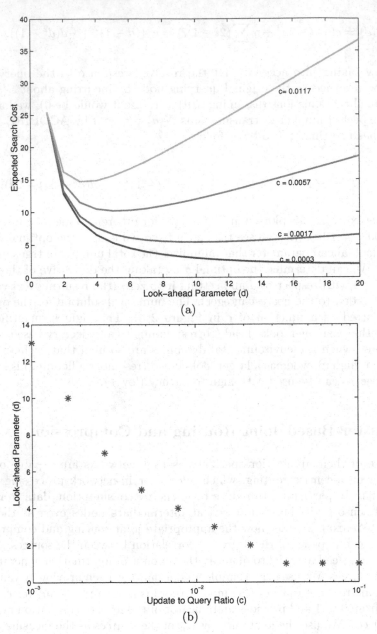

Fig. 2. Performance of ACQUIRE.

of a single source. On the other extreme, when $\delta = 1$, there is no correlation at all, with a joint entropy that is equal to the sum of the entropies of each source.

To illustrate the tradeoffs involved in joint routing and compression, we consider a simple network scenario illustrated in Figure 3. The n sources are equally spaced, each having D additional intermediate nodes between them and the sink. The way the information is routed from each source to the sink is as follows.

First the set of sources is divided into clusters of s nodes. Within each cluster, the data is routed sequentially from node to node, with compression at each successive step. Thus the H_1 bits of data from the first sensor move to the second sensor, where they are compressed jointly with the data at that node (we assume an idealized entropy coding that achieves the maximum compression possible); then H_2 bits are transmitted from the second sensor to the third, and so on till the last node within the cluster. Then the jointly compressed H_s bits of data from each cluster are routed to the sink along the shortest path. Thus we have a family of cluster-based joint routing and compression strategies that span from one extreme ($s = 0$) where no compression is performed and each node routes its information along the shortest path to the sink, to the other extreme ($s = n$) where the data from every source is compressed sequentially before routing to the sink.

The key question we address in this modeling effort is: what is the correct setting of the cluster size? The energy metric we use is the total number of bits that are transmitted over the air to deliver sensed data from all sources to the sink. We can intuit the tradeoff that is involved here: a strategy that uses a small cluster size favoring shortest path routing may perform best when the correlation is low (high δ), while a strategy using a large cluster size may perform best when the correlation is high (low δ). This is because when the correlation is high, the savings due to compression of data near the sources outweigh the benefits of shortest-path routing.

We need to consider the two components of the cost in terms of the total number of bits required to transport information from all sensors to the sink. Within each cluster the cost is $\sum_{i=1}^{s} H_i(\delta)$. To carry the combined information from each cluster to the sink requires a cost of another $H_s D$, and there are n/s clusters in all. Therefore the total cost for first compressing within clusters of size s and then transporting the information to the sink is given by the following expression:

$$C_{total}(s, \delta) = \frac{n}{s} \left(\sum_{i=1}^{s} H_i(\delta) + H_s D \right) \tag{5}$$

$$= n H_1 \frac{(s - s\delta + \delta s(s-1)/2 + D + D\delta(s-1))}{s} \tag{6}$$

$$= n H_1 (1 - \delta + D\delta + (s-1)\delta/2 + D(1-\delta)/s). \tag{7}$$

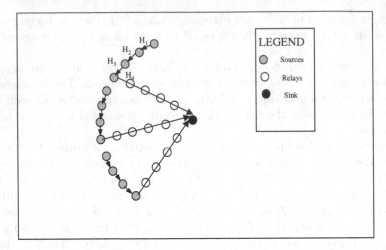

Fig. 3. Illustrative Scenario for Cluster-based Routing with Compression.

The minimization of the above expression for the total cost yields the optimal cluster size to be

$$s_{opt}(\delta) = \sqrt{2D\frac{1-\delta}{\delta}}. \tag{8}$$

The above applies for all intermediate values of δ in $(0,1)$. For the two extreme cases, we get that when $\delta = 0$, $s_{opt}(0) = n$ and when $\delta = 1, s_{opt} = 1$. Figure 4(a) shows the performance for different cluster sizes as a function of the correlation level, for a scenario with $n = 100, D = 100$. Figure 4(b) shows the optimal cluster size s_{opt} decreasing with δ. This quantifies the tradeoff mentioned above, that a high correlation favors large clusters, while low correlations favor small clusters.

In [3], this analysis is validated for more general topologies through simulations involving random placement of sensors in a 2D region. Another interesting finding of that study is that while the optimal cluster size is indeed a function of the level of correlation, it is also possible to use a static cluster size that provides near-optimal performance regardless of the correlation. While we do not go into the analysis of the near-optimal clustering here, it is interesting to note that Figure 4(a) suggests such a result — the cluster size of 20 provides good performance for all correlation levels.

4 Joint Search and Replication

As a third case study to illustrate first-order modeling, we examine the problem of querying a sensor network for information that can be replicated.

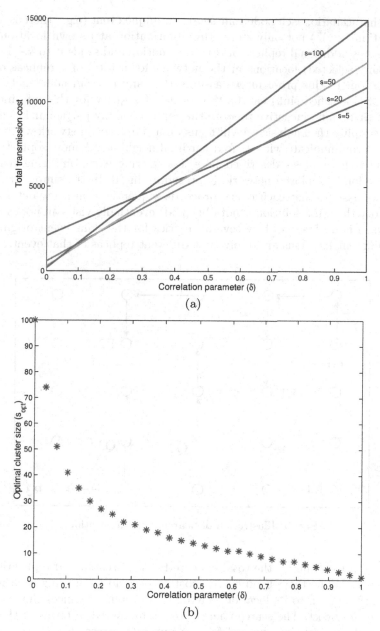

Fig. 4. Performance of Clustering.

In this scenario, each node that senses a unique event (e.g. "there is a bird at location (x,y)") not only stores this information at its own location, but also creates additional replicas of this information and sends it to $k-1$ other (randomly selected) locations in the network for a total of k replicas of the information. In this problem, we assume that any random node (not just a single pre-identified sink) can be the source of a query for this information, so that there is no incentive to store the replicas in any particular locations.

To simplify the analysis we will focus on a simple grid network where each node can communicate with its four cardinal neighbors. A more sophisticated version of the analysis described here, considering expanding ring searches for a randomly deployed network, is presented in [4]. In the simple grid network, we assume that each query proceeds sequentially in a pre-determined trajectory that (if a solution is not obtained) eventually visits all nodes in the network. Figure 5 shows how several queries for the same event originating from different locations are resolved at different replicas of that event.

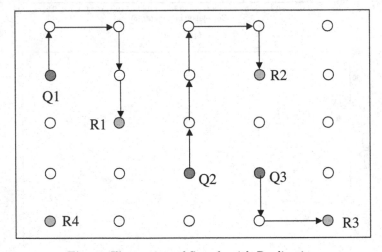

Fig. 5. Illustration of Search with Replication.

We aim to minimize the total expected cost of search and replication for each event. While there is an energy cost to be paid for moving each replica of the information to its location, having more replicas reduces the expected search energy cost. The search energy cost is measured in terms of the total number of transmissions needed for the query to locate the nearest replica. We could also account for the number of transmissions needed to return the response back to the querier by doubling this number, assuming that the response is returned along the reverse path.

Let us first consider the cost of replication. The expected number of transmissions required to place each replica at a randomly selected location is the expected Manhattan distance (i.e., the L_1 distance, measured as the sum of the absolute distance in the x-coordinate and the absolute distance in the y-coordinate) between any pair of nodes in the $n \times n$ grid. The expected x-distance is $n/3$ and the expected y-distance is $n/3$, hence $2n/3$ transmissions are required on average to place each replica. To place $k-1$ replicas, this cost is then:

$$C_{replication} = \frac{2}{3}n(k-1). \tag{9}$$

We now look at the search cost. The expected number of nodes visited on the trajectory till the nearest replica is obtained is the expected value of the minimum of k discrete random variables chosen from values between 1 and n^2 without replacement. A good approximation for this minimum is $n^2/(k+1)$ (which can be obtained, for instance, by considering a continuous distribution and using an integral to compute the corresponding integral expression for the expected value). Taking into account the same cost for the returned response, the expected search energy cost is therefore

$$C_{search} = 2\frac{n^2}{k+1}. \tag{10}$$

Combining the two components with variables f_e and f_q to denote, respectively, the frequency with which the event is generated (we can assume that an update of each replica occurs whenever new information is obtained about that event) and the frequency with which a query for the event is sent, we have:

$$C_{total}(k) = 2f_q\frac{n^2}{k+1} + \frac{2}{3}f_e(k-1)n. \tag{11}$$

The combined cost of search and replication for different values of the query frequency f_q (assuming $f_e = 1$) is shown in Figure 6(a) for a 100×100 grid. The optimal replication size can be determined from the above expression as

$$k_{opt} = \sqrt{\frac{3f_q}{f_e}n} . \tag{12}$$

The variation of the optimal replication size with respect to the ratio of query frequency to event frequency is shown in figure 6(b).

5 Conclusions

We have shown several examples of first-order analysis for data gathering mechanisms in sensor networks. Such modeling can provide a clear understanding of the key design tradeoffs underlying such mechanisms, and give an insight into how protocol parameters should be optimized to provide efficiency in terms of energy savings or latency improvements, or other relevant metrics.

We should caution, however, that the first order protocol analysis methodology, which emphasizes tractability, abstraction, and simplicity, is by no

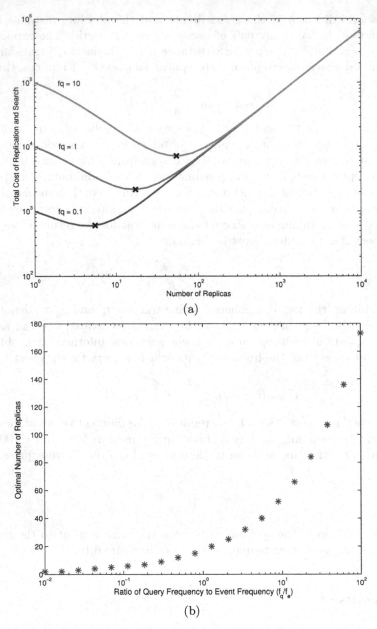

Fig. 6. Performance of Search with Replication.

means a complete substitute for other analytical and experimental tools which emphasize detail, realism, and sophistication. While such modeling provides a good starting point for understanding the key design tradeoffs involved in parameter selection, it is entirely complementary to other approaches. The translation of the insights obtained through mathematical analysis into practical protocols will certainly involve further evaluation through more detailed simulations, as well as through experiments on a test-bed and real-world implementations.

6 Acknowledgement

This work has been supported in part by the following grants from the National Science Foundation: CNS-0435505 (NeTS-NOSS), CNS-0347621 (CAREER), CCF-0430061, and CNS-0325875 (ITR). The author would like to acknowledge the input of several colleagues and students in the original development of the models described in this chapter, including Narayanan Sadagopan, Ramesh Govindan, Sundeep Pattem, Joon Ahn, and Ahmed Helmy. More details regarding these models can be found in the corresponding papers listed as references.

References

1. Hal R. Varian, "How to Build an Economic Model in your Spare Time," *Passion and Craft: Economists at Work*, Ed. M. Szenberg, University of Michigan Press, 1997.
2. Narayanan Sadagopan, Bhaskar Krishnamachari, and Ahmed Helmy, "Active Query Forwarding in Sensor Networks (ACQUIRE)", *Ad Hoc Networks Journal-Elsevier Science*, Vol. 3, No. 1, pp. 91–113, January 2005.
3. Sundeep Pattem, Bhaskar Krishnamachari, and Ramesh Govindan, "The Impact of Spatial Correlation on Routing with Compression in Wireless Sensor Networks," *ACM/IEEE International Symposium on Information Processing in Sensor Networks (IPSN)*, April 26-27, Berkeley, CA 2004.
4. Bhaskar Krishnamachari and Joon Ahn, "Optimizing Data Replication for Expanding Ring-based Queries in Wireless Sensor Networks," *USC Computer Engineering Technical Report CENG-05-14*, October 2005.

SECTION IV
SECURITY

Chapter 17
A Survey on Sensor Network Security

Xiaojiang Du[1] and Yang Xiao[2]

[1] Department of Computer Science
North Dakota State University, Fargo, ND 58105
Xiaojiang.Du@ndsu.edu
[2] Department of Computer Science
The University of Memphis Memphis, TN 38152
yangxiao@ieee.org

1 Introduction

1.1 Abstract

Recent advances in electronics and wireless communication technologies have enabled the development of large-scale sensor networks that consist of many low-power, low-cost, and small-sized sensor nodes. Sensor networks hold the promise of facilitating large-scale and real-time data processing in complex environments. Security is very important for many sensor network applications, such as military target tracking and security monitoring. Providing security to small sensor nodes is challenging, due to the limited capabilities of sensor nodes in terms of computation, communication, and energy. In this chapter, we present the current state-of-art of research on sensor network security. In particular, we discuss several important security issues in sensor networks: typical attacks, security objectives, key management, and secure routing.

1.2 Main Introduction

Large-scale sensor networks have been deployed due to recent advances in electronics and wireless communication technologies. In one such sensor network, many low-power and low-cost small sensor nodes are distributed over a vast field to obtain fine-grained and high-precision sensing data. These tiny sensor nodes consist of sensing, data processing, and communicating components, and leverage the idea of sensor networks. Sensor nodes are typically powered by batteries, communicate through wireless channels, and are usually scattered densely and statically. Sensor networks have a broad range of applications in military, homeland security, health care, environment, agriculture, manufacturing, and so on.

One can envision in the future the deployment of large-scale sensor networks where hundreds and thousands of small sensor nodes form self-organizing wireless networks. Providing security in sensor networks is not an easy task. Compared with conventional desktop computers, severe challenges exist since sensor nodes have limited processing capability, storage, and energy, and wireless links have limited bandwidth. Despite the above challenges, security is important and even critical for many applications of sensor networks, such as military and homeland security applications. Several recent works have addressed security issues in sensor networks [1-18]. However, the privacy and security issues posed by sensor networks still represent a rich field of research problems.

In this survey, we first summarize typical attacks on sensor networks. We then present the security objectives of sensor networks. Finally, we particularly discuss two important security issues in sensor networks: key management and secure routing. To achieve security in wireless sensor networks, it is important to be able to perform various cryptographic operations, including encryption, authentication, etc. Keys for these cryptographic operations must be set up by communicating nodes before they can exchange information securely. A key management scheme is to establish various cryptographic keys in a network, and it is an essential cryptographic primitive upon which other security primitives are built. Most security requirements, such as privacy, authenticity, and integrity, can be addressed by building upon a solid key management framework. In fact, a secure key management scheme is the prerequisite for the security of other primitives, and thus essential to achieving secure infrastructure in sensor networks.

The primary functionality of wireless sensor networks is to sense the environment and transmit the acquired information to base stations for further processing. Thus, routing (data dissemination) is a fundamental and very important operation for sensor networks. Efficient and secure data dissemination is challenging and critical for the successful operation of many sensor networks. Some recent works (e.g., [3, 31]) have considered the security routing issue in sensor networks. However, most of the proposed approaches try to add security features to existing routing protocols. They either do not address security very well, or dramatically degrade routing performance. Few existing works consider security issues during the design time of the routing protocol. Although one may add security features to existing routing protocols, the best way is to consider security at the protocol design time [13].

Past researches on sensor network routing have been focused on efficiency and effectiveness of data dissemination, and many routing protocols have been proposed for sensor networks, such as Directed Diffusion [21], TTDD [20], LEACH [24], Mesh [19], etc. Since most existing routing protocols have not been designed with security as a goal, these routing protocols are vulnerable to many attacks. However, it is non-trivial to fix the above problem since it is unlikely that a routing protocol in a sensor network can be made secure by incorporating security mechanisms after the design has completed. Studies and experiences have shown that considering security during design time is the best way to provide security for sensor network routing.

In this chapter, we present the current state-of-art of research on sensor network security. The rest of the chapter is organized as follows. We discuss various attacks on sensor networks in Section 2. We present typical assumptions and security objectives of sensor networks in Section 3. In Section 4, we present a survey of key management schemes designed for sensor networks. Secure routing issue is discussed in Section 5. Finally, we conclude this article in Section 6.

2 Attacks on Sensor Networks

A large-scale sensor network consists of thousands of sensor nodes and may be dispersed over a large area. Typical sensor nodes are small with limited communication and computing capabilities, and are powered by batteries. These small sensor nodes are susceptible to many kinds of attacks. For a large-scale sensor network, it is impractical to monitor and protect each individual sensor from physical or logical attack. Attacks on sensor networks can be classified based on layers, including attacks on physical, link (medium access control), network, transportation, and application layers. Attacks can also be classified based on the capability of the attacker, like sensor-level attacker and laptop-level attacker, etc. A powerful laptop-level adversary can do much more harm to the network than a malicious sensor node, since it has much better power supply, as well as large computation and communication capabilities than a sensor node. Attacks can be also classified into outside attacks and inside attacks. An outside attacker has no access to most cryptographic materials in the sensor network. While an inside attacker may have partial key materials and have the trust from other sensor nodes. Insider attacks are much harder to detect and defense. In [13], Wood and Stankovic have classified various Denial of Service (DoS) attacks on sensor networks according to network layers. We summarize typical attacks on sensor networks and possible defense techniques in Figure 1. The attacks in Figure 1 are listed according to network layers, and include most DoS attacks in [13] and several other attacks identified in other literatures [3, 12].

In the following, we describe the various attacks in more detail.

2.1 Physical Layer Attacks

Jamming

Jamming is a well-known attack on wireless communication, and it interferes with the radio frequencies that are used by nodes in a network. A small number of randomly distributed jamming nodes can disrupt the entire network, and

406 Xiaojiang Du and Yang Xiao

Network layer	Attacks	Possible Defense Techniques
Physical	Jamming	Spread-spectrum, lower duty cycle
	Tampering	Tamper-proofing, effective key management schemes
Link	Collision	Error-correcting code
	Exhaustion	Rate limitation
Network and routing	Manipulating routing information	Authentication, encryption
	Selective forwarding attack	Redundancy, probing
	The Sybil Attack	Authentication
	Sinkhole (blackhole) Attack	Authorization, monitoring, redundancy
	Wormhole Attack	Monitoring, flexible route selection
	Hello Flood (Unidirectional) Attack	Two-way authentication, three-way handshake
Transport	Flooding	Limiting connection numbers, client puzzles
Other attacks	Clone Attack	Unique pairwise keys

Fig. 1. Typical Attacks on Sensor Networks.

cause all the nodes in the network to be out of service. There are many low-cost devices available in the market which can be used for jamming purpose. For sensor networks using single radio frequency, the jamming attack is simple and effective.

The standard defense against jamming involves various forms of spread-spectrum communication. To attack frequency hoppers, the adversary must be able either to follow the precise hopping sequence or to jam a wide section of the band. Mobile-phone networks commonly use code spreading as a defense against jamming. Since spread-spectrum communication requires greater design complexity and more power, low-cost, low-power sensor nodes may not be able to use this technique. Sensor nodes can defend intermittent jamming attacks by switching to a lower duty cycle and conserving as much power as possible. Periodically, the nodes can wake up and check whether the jamming has ended. By spending energy frugally, the nodes may be able to outlive an adversary, who must continue to jam at greater expense [13].

Tampering

A large-scale sensor network may consist of thousands of sensor nodes and may be dispersed over a large area. It is impractical to assume that we can monitor and protect each individual sensor from attacks. An adversary can capture a sensor node and tamper with nodes physically. If the adversary compromises a node, she can extract all key material, data, and code stored on that node. The adversary can also re-program the captured node, or clone several illegal nodes from the captured node. A variety of attacks can be launched after obtaining cryptographic keys and code, such as eavesdropping, selective forwarding, etc.

One defense technique is to use tamper-resistant hardware in sensor nodes. With tamper-resistant hardware, a tampering can be detected and crypto-graphic keys and sensitive data can be erased from the sensor node. However, the cost of current tamper-resistant hardware is too high to be installed in each sensor node.

Thus, in most sensor security papers, a general assumption is that sensor nodes are not equipped with tamper-resistant hardware due to cost constraints. If a globally shared key is used in the network for encryption, then tampering with one sensor node will render the whole network unsecured. Effective key management schemes can reduce the damage of node tampering. For example, each node can use a unique key to communicate with the base station, and each pair of nodes can share a unique pairwise key with each other for communication. In such a case, when a node is compromised and the stored keys are extracted, the damage is limited to the local area (e.g., the neighbors of the compromised node). Several effective key management schemes have been proposed, such as LEAP [10], SPINS [14], etc., and these schemes can provide unique pairwise keys for each pair of nodes. However, the cost is to have many keys to handle and manage.

2.2 Attacks on Link Layer

The link or medium access control (MAC) layer provides channel arbitration for neighbor-to-neighbor communication. Contention-based MAC protocols that rely on carrier sense, which let nodes detect if other nodes are transmitting, are particularly vulnerable to several attacks. Some of the typical attacks on the link layer are listed below.

Collision

Sensor nodes communicate with each other through a shared wireless channel. An adversary can cause a collision by concurrently transmitting a packet within the interference range. One byte of collision can corrupt an entire frame. A corrupted routing packet or MAC control frame may cause large protocol overhead. For example, a corrupted acknowledgement message could induce costly back-off in some MAC protocols, e.g., IEEE 802.11 MAC [40]. Error-correcting codes can be used to provide certain defense to the collision attack. However, error-correcting codes would not work if lots of bits received are corrupted. Other efficient security mechanisms need to be designed to defend against the collision attack.

Exhaustion

If a contention-based MAC protocol is used in the network, an adversary may attempt transmission repeatedly, and this renders neighbor sensor nodes unable to transmit any frame. For example, IEEE 802.11-based MAC protocols [40] use Request-To-Send (RTS), Clear-To-Send (CTS), and Data/Ack messages to reserve channel access and transmit data. An adversary could repeatedly request channel access with RTS, eliciting a CTS response from the targeted neighbor. If the adversary is a powerful node (e.g., a laptop with long transmission range and rechargeable energy supply), the adversary could block sensor transmissions in a large area and could exhaust the energy of targeted sensor nodes. Possible solutions include limiting the MAC admission control rate of each node, or using MAC protocols that combine time-slotted mechanisms (like TDMA) and contention-based mechanisms.

2.3 Attacks on Routing

Many sensor network routing protocols are quite simple, and for this reason are susceptible to several kinds of attacks. Attacks on sensor networks have been discussed in several papers [3, 12, 13, 14]. Most network layer attacks against sensor networks fall into one of the following categories: manipulating routing information; selective forwarding; Sybil [16]; sinkhole; wormhole [15]; and Hello flooding (unidirectional) attacks [3]. The secure routing protocol presented in [5] can defend against all the above attacks on routing. We briefly describe the attacks on sensor network routing in the following.

Manipulating Routing Information

The most direct attack against a routing protocol is to target the routing information exchanged among nodes [3]. By spoofing, altering, or replaying routing information, adversaries may be able to create routing loops, attract or repel network traffic, extend or shorten source routes, generate false error messages, partition the network, increase end-to-end latency, etc.

Selective Forwarding Attack

Many sensor network routing protocols are based on the assumption that participating nodes will faithfully forward received packets. In a selective forwarding attack [13], compromised or malicious nodes may selectively forward some packets while dropping other packets. An adversary interested in suppressing or modifying packets originated from some selected nodes can reliably forward the remaining traffic and limit suspicion of her misbehaviors. Selective forwarding attacks are typically most effective when the attacker is explicitly included on the path of a data flow.

The Sybil Attack

In a Sybil attack [16], a single node presents multiple identities to other nodes in the network. The Sybil attack can significantly reduce the effectiveness of fault-tolerant schemes such as distributed storage, multi-path routing, and topology maintenance. Storage partitions or multi-path routes believed to be using disjoint nodes could in actuality be using a single adversary presenting multiple identities. Sybil attacks also pose a significant threat to geographic routing protocols. Location aware routing often requires nodes to exchange coordinate information with their neighbors to efficiently route geographically addressed packets. It is only reasonable to expect a node to accept a single set of coordinates from each of its neighbors, but by using the Sybil attack, an adversary can "be in more than one place at once".

Sinkhole Attack

In a sinkhole attack [3], the adversary's goal is to lure nearly all the traffic from a particular area through a compromised node, creating a metaphorical sinkhole with the adversary at the center. Sinkhole attacks can enable many other attacks such as selective forwarding. Sinkhole attacks typically work by making a compromised node look especially attractive to surrounding nodes with respect to the routing algorithm. For instance, an adversary could spoof or replay an advertisement for an extremely high quality route to a base station. Some protocols might actually try to verify the quality of route with end-to-end acknowledgements containing reliability or latency information. In this case, a laptop-class adversary with a powerful transmitter can actually provide a high quality route by transmitting with enough power to reach the base station in a single hop. Due to either the real or imagined high quality route through the compromised node, it is likely each neighboring node of the adversary will forward packets destined for a base station through the adversary, and also propagate the attractiveness of the route to its neighbors.

Wormhole Attack

In the wormhole attack [15], an adversary tunnels messages received in one part of the network over a low latency link and replays them in a different part. Wormhole attacks usually involve two distant malicious nodes colluding to understate their distance from each other by relaying packets along an out-of-bound channel available only to the attacker. An adversary situated close to a base station may be able to completely disrupt routing by creating a well-placed wormhole. An adversary could convince nodes that would normally be multiple hops from a base station that they are only one or two hops away via the wormhole. Wormhole attacks would likely be used in combination with selective forwarding or eavesdropping. Detection is potentially difficult when used in conjunction with the Sybil attack.

Hello Flood (Unidirectional) Attack

In [3], the authors introduced a novel attack against sensor networks: the Hello flood attack. It is an attack by utilizing unidirectional connections between nodes. We also refer to this attack as unidirectional attack. Many protocols require nodes to broadcast Hello packets to announce themselves to their neighbors, and a node receiving such a packet may assume that it is within (normal) radio range of the sender. This assumption may be false because of the well-known unidirectional problem in ad hoc networks. For example, a powerful attacker (e.g., a laptop) broadcasting routing or other information with large enough transmission power could convince many sensor nodes in the network that the adversary is one of their neighbors. But those sensor nodes sufficiently far away from the adversary can not send packets to the attacker directly, and they would send packets into oblivion. The network is left in a state of confusion. A node realizing the link to the adversary is false could be left with few options: all its neighbors might be attempting to forward packets to the adversary as well.

2.4 Other Attacks

Clone Attack

In a clone attack [41], an attacker loads its own nodes with the keys of a compromised node, and then deploys these cloned nodes in different locations of the sensor network. These cloned nodes then try to establish pairwise keys with their neighbors. Once they are accepted by their neighbors, they can launch various insider attacks such as injecting false data packets. Consequently, an attacker might only need to compromise a few sensor nodes to bring down the entire network due to the unattended nature of a sensor network.

Attacks on Transport Layer - Flooding Attack

The transport layer manages end-to-end connections. Typical transport layer protocols used in computer networks and Internet are UDP and various versions of TCP. In [36], Stann and Heidemann present RMST — a transport protocol specifically designed for sensor networks. One possible attack on the transport layer is the flooding attack. Transport protocols that maintain states at either end are vulnerable to the flooding attack which can exhaust memory in nodes. A powerful adversary (e.g., a laptop) can send many connection-establishment requests to a sensor node, and each request causes sensor nodes to allocate memory to maintain the connection states. A sensor node has limited memory, and its memory will be exhausted under the flooding attack.

One defense against flooding attack is to limit the number of connections that a node can request (in a period of time). In [37], the authors propose to use client puzzles to defend against DoS attack. Considering a client / server connection scenario, a client needs to demonstrate the commitment of its own resource to each connection by solving the client puzzles, which are created and verified by the server. The server distributes the puzzles, and clients wishing to connect must solve them and present them to the server before establishing a connection. Thus, the number of connections can be limited by the available knowledge to solve the puzzles.

3 Security Objectives for Sensor Networks

Wireless sensor networks have many unique features that differ from mobile ad hoc networks and other wireless (and wired) networks. When considering security in sensor networks, we need to state assumptions on the network. Some typical assumptions made in existing literatures are listed below.

3.1 Typical Assumptions

Since sensor nodes use wireless communications, radio links are generally insecure. Eavesdropping, injection, replay, and other attacks can be placed on the network. The adversary is able to deploy malicious nodes in the network, or compromises some legitimate nodes. Most existing papers in the literature on sensor network security do not assume that sensor nodes are tamper resistant since the corresponding investment adds significant per-unit cost to sensor nodes.

A typical assumption is to assume that base stations are well protected and trusted. Since a base station is the gateway for sensor nodes to communicate with the outside world, compromising the base station could render the entire sensor network useless. Thus, base stations in sensor networks are assumed to be secure.

Other typical assumptions on sensor networks are listed as follows: (1) sensor nodes are densely and statically deployed in the network; (2) sensor nodes are aware of their own locations. Location awareness is a basic requirement for sensor nodes in many sensor networks, since most sensing data must be associated with the locations where data is generated. The network can use location services such as [22] and [23] to estimate the locations of individual nodes, and no GPS receiver is required at each sensor.

There are other particular assumptions made in some work, which may limit the applicability of the proposed schemes. We do not discuss these particular assumptions in this chapter.

3.2 Security Objectives

The ultimate security objective is to provide confidentiality, integrity, authenticity, and availability of all messages in the presence of resourceful adversaries. Every eligible receiver should receive all messages intended for it and be able to verify the integrity of every message as well as the identity of the sender. Adversaries should not be able to infer the contents of any message. In conventional computer networks, the primary security goal is reliable delivery of messages, i.e., protection against denial of service attack. Message authenticity, integrity, and confidentiality are usually achieved by an end-to-end security mechanism such as SSH or SSL. The reason is because the dominating traffic pattern is end-to-end communication, where it is neither necessary nor desirable for the contents of the message (beyond the necessary headers) to be available to the intermediate routers.

However, the dominant traffic pattern in sensor networks is many-to-one, with many sensor nodes sending data to a base station. In-network processing such as data aggregation, duplicate elimination, or data compression is very important for sensor networks to run in an energy-efficient manner. Since in-network processing requires intermediate nodes to access, modify, and possibly suppress the contents of messages, it is highly unlikely that end-to-end security mechanisms between a sensor node and a base station can be used to guarantee integrity, authenticity, and confidentiality of such messages.

In the presence of insider adversaries, link layer security is not enough to protect the network, since an insider has complete access to any message routed through it and it can modify, suppress or even discard the message. In such a case, one might not be able to provide confidentiality, integrity, authenticity, and availability to every message. Thus, in the presence of insider attackers, the security objective should be to ensure that the sensor network can provide the basic functionality (i.e., performing sensing tasks and transmitting data to the base station) with minimum degradation.

In the following, we discuss two important security issues in sensor networks — key management and secure routing.

4 Key Management in Sensor Networks

To achieve security in wireless sensor networks, it is important to be able to perform various cryptographic operations, such as encryption, authentication, etc. Keys for these cryptographic operations must be set up by communicating nodes before they can exchange information securely. Key management schemes are mechanisms used to establish various kinds of cryptographic keys in the network, like individual keys, pairwise keys, group keys, etc. Key management is an essential cryptographic primitive upon which other security primitives are built. Most security requirements, such as privacy, authenticity and integrity, can be addressed by building upon a solid key management framework. In fact, a secure key management scheme is the prerequisite for the security of these primitives, and thus essential to achieving secure infrastructure in sensor networks.

Due to resource constraints, achieving such key agreement in wireless sensor networks is non-trivial. The challenge of designing key management protocols for sensor networks lies in establishing a secure communication infrastructure, before any routing fabric has been established and either with or without the presence of any trusted authority or fixed server, from a collection of sensor nodes which have no prior contact with each other.

Some cryptographic information is normally preloaded in sensor nodes before deployment, and allows sensor nodes to perform secure communications with each other. Most schemes do not assume prior knowledge of the network deployment topology and allow nodes to be added to the network after deployment. The schemes must be low computational and have low storage requirements.

There are three types of general key agreement schemes: trusted-server scheme, self-enforcing scheme, and key pre-distribution scheme. We explain these schemes in details in the following subsections.

4.1 Trusted-server Scheme

The trusted-server scheme depends on a trusted and secure server such as the base station for key agreement between nodes, e.g., Kerberos [32]. The server can be treated as the Key Distribution Center (KDC). For example, assume that two sensor nodes plan to make a secure connection. In a typical case, a symmetric key is generated for each node in the sensor network before deployment and is embedded in each sensor node's memory. This embedded key is used for the two sensors to authenticate themselves to the base station. Then the base station generates a link key or a session key and sends it securely to both sensor nodes via a single-hop or multi-hops. This is exactly part of the approach proposed in SPINS [14].

In the trusted-server scheme, the base station is the most appropriate choice for the server, and each sensor node stores only an embedded key so that a compromising/captured node cannot reveal much security information of the sensor network.

The drawback of the trusted-server scheme is that if the server is compromised, the network is totally unsecured. However, we usually assume that the base station where the server runs is secured.

4.2 Self-enforcing Scheme

The self-enforcing scheme depends on asymmetric cryptography, such as key agreement using public key certificates. If the sensor node can support the computationally intensive asymmetric cryptographic operations, key distribution via asymmetric cryptography is a favored scheme. Sensor nodes conduct exchanges of public keys and master key signatures after deployment. A sensor node is legitimate if the master key's signature is verified using the master public key. A symmetric session key for a sensor node can be generated and sent using the sensor node's public key.

In the self-enforcing scheme, a compromising sensor node reveals no security information about other keys in the network except current on-going session keys.

However, limited computation and energy resources of sensor nodes make it undesirable to use public key algorithms, such as the Diffie–Hellman key agreement [33] or RSA [34]. Some recent work proposed to use public key schemes in sensor networks can be founded in [42].

4.3 Key Pre-distribution Scheme

The third type of key agreement scheme is key pre-distribution, where key information is distributed among all sensor nodes prior to deployment. Recent research on sensor networks suggests that key pre-distribution schemes are a promising practical option for scenarios where the network topology is not known prior to deployment.

Eschenauer and Gligor [11] first present a key management scheme for sensor networks based on probabilistic key pre-distribution. Chan et al [9] extend this scheme and present three mechanisms for key establishment. Liu and Ning [8] propose a key management scheme based on key pre-distribution approach to establish pairwise keys in sensor networks. A common assumption made by these random key pre-distribution schemes is that no deployment knowledge is available. In [1], Du et al. present an effective random key pre-distribution scheme for wireless sensor networks that utilizes sensor deployment knowledge. With such knowledge, each node only needs to carry a portion of the keys required by the key pre-distribution schemes in [11] and [10] while achieving the same level of connectivity. In [1], the authors show via both theoretic analysis and simulations that the performance (e.g., connectivity, memory usage, and network resilience against node capture) of sensor networks can be substantially improved with the use of sensor deployment knowledge.

In [14], Perrig et al. propose SPINS — a suite of security building blocks for sensor networks. SPINS uses the base station to help establish a pairwise key between two nodes. In particular, SPINS includes SNEP, a protocol for data confidentiality and two-party data authentication, and TESLA, a protocol for broadcast data authentication. However, the SPINS scheme relies on the base station for pairwise key establishment, and this limits its scalability and leaves it subject to Sybil attacks [16].

Zhu et al. present a distributed key management protocol for sensor networks — LEAP [10]. They assume there is a lower bound on the time interval - T_{min} that for an adversary to compromise a sensor node, and a globally shared key is used before T_{min} to establish pairwise keys between each sensor and its neighbors.

Karlof et al. [17] describe TinySec, a link layer security mechanism using a single preloaded fixed group key for both encryption and authentication, assuming no node compromises. They also discuss the impact of different keying mechanisms on the effectiveness of in-network processing in sensor networks. Deng et al. [2] discuss several security mechanisms for supporting in-network processing in hierarchical sensor networks.

Several interesting key pre-distribution schemes are classified and reviewed in the following subsections.

Fully Pairwise Key Scheme

In the fully pairwise key scheme, each sensor node has a symmetric key with each other sensor node, i.e., there are a total of $n(n + 1)/2$ symmetric keys called pairwise keys, in the network, where n is the number of sensor nodes in the network. Each sensor node is preloaded with $n - 1$ symmetric keys.

In the fully pairwise key scheme, a compromising/captured sensor node does not reveal other security information except the $n - 1$ pairwise keys within itself, where $n - 1 = O(n)$. One drawback of this scheme is that the scheme requires a large amount of memory storage space for $n - 1$ symmetric keys, when n is large. Furthermore, most of the keys may never be used.

λ-secure Key Scheme

A trade-off between security and memory space in the fully pairwise key scheme can be parameterized with the λ-secure key scheme introduced in [18]. The λ-secure property is that if the number of compromising sensor nodes is smaller than λ among n sensor nodes, these comprising sensor nodes reveal no security information about any pairwise key between any two non-compromised sensor nodes [38, 39]. In [38, 39], each node among n nodes stores a secret vector of length $\lambda + 1$, where the secret vector is multiplied to a publicly known $(\lambda + 1) \times n$ matrix to compute a symmetric key with another node. Du et al. [18] adopt a similar method so that only $O(\lambda)$ keys are needed per node. Note that the fully pairwise key scheme is a special case of the λ-secure key scheme, where $\lambda = n$. However, the number of keys saved per node may be still large since λ must increase with n, and if the number of compromised nodes reach λ, the network is totally unsecured.

p-probabilistic Key Pre-distribution Scheme

Eschenauer and Gligor [11] present a p-probabilistic key pre-distribution scheme in which m random keys out of a pool of total of M keys are stored in a sensor node. All the sensor nodes choose keys from the same pool of the M keys, and the pool of the M keys is designed in such a way that two random subsets of size m in the pool at least have one key with probability p, which should be chosen to be related to node density. Therefore, two sensor nodes can share a common key to communicate with probability p after performing a challenge-response key discovery.

The p-probabilistic key pre-distribution scheme is a trade-off scheme between using a single key and using a large number of pairwise keys, i.e., a tradeoff of security and memory space. However, the p-probabilistic key pre-distribution scheme may be difficult to provide guaranteed connectivity under non-uniform/sparse deployment. Since all sensor nodes choose m keys randomly from the same key pool, the network security becomes weaker after an attacker compromises more nodes.

q-composite Key Pre-distribution Scheme

Chan et al. [9] propose a q-composite key pre-distribution scheme to improve the p-probabilistic key pre-distribution scheme. In the q-composite key pre-distribution scheme, any two sensor nodes have probability p of sharing at least q different keys, where these q keys are used in the generation of the communication key. The q-composite key pre-distribution scheme improves the p-probabilistic key pre-distribution scheme, since an adversary by eavesdropping has to compromise all q keys instead of one key to compromise the communication key. However, this scheme should have a larger key pool to be secure.

Random Pairwise Key Scheme

Chan et al. [9] propose the Random Pairwise Key scheme in which, $m(<< n)$ pairwise keys from each node are preloaded so that these m keys provide some sufficient probability p of enabling any two neighboring sensor nodes to establish a secure link.

Multi-space Key Scheme

Liu and Ning [6] and Du et al. [18] propose multi-space key schemes, in which each node randomly selects a subset of key spaces from the pool of key spaces such that any two nodes have some common key space with probability p, and the common key space is used to perform the relevant λ-secure $n \times n$ key establishment scheme to generate a secure session key, where each key space is an instance of a different λ-secure $n \times n$ key scheme. Such a scheme is a hybrid between key-pool-based random key distribution and the λ-secure $n \times n$ key scheme, and compromised sensor nodes reveal much less information to the adversary, but, the scheme has no guaranteed connectivity

5 Secure Routing in Sensor Networks

The primary functionality of wireless sensor networks is to sense the environment and transmit the acquired information to base stations for further processing. Thus, routing (data dissemination) is a fundamental and very important operation for sensor networks. Efficient and secure data dissemination is challenging and critical for the successful operation of many sensor networks.

Past researches on sensor network routing have been focused on efficiency and effectiveness of data dissemination, and many routing protocols have been proposed for sensor networks, such as Directed Diffusion [21], TTDD [20], LEACH [24], Mesh [19], etc. However, not many works have been published on secure routing in sensor networks.

Secure routing in Mobile Ad Hoc Networks (MANETs) has been well studied, and several secure routing protocols have been proposed for MANETs. Some of the secure routing protocols are based on public key cryptography, (e.g., [25], [26], [27]). However, public key cryptography is too expensive in terms of computation and communication for sensor nodes. Therefore, security protocols for sensor networks must rely exclusively on efficient symmetric key cryptography. There are several MANET secure routing protocols which are based on symmetric key cryptography, (e.g., [28], [29], [30]). These protocols are based on source routing or distance vector protocols and are unsuitable for sensor networks. They are too expensive in terms of node state and packet overhead, and are designed to find and establish routes between any pair of nodes — which is different from a many-to-one traffic pattern dominant in sensor networks, i.e., a large number of sensor nodes send data to one (or a small number) of base stations.

Sensor networks have many unique features that make them quite different from MANETs. For example, sensor nodes (e.g., Mica2 sensor nodes [35]) have very limited processing capability, storage, and energy, compared to typical nodes (e.g., PDAs, laptops) in MANETs. Furthermore, in sensor networks, the many-to-one communication pattern is dominant. Due to these unique features of sensor networks, the existing secure routing protocols for MANETs [25-30] can not be directly applied to sensor networks.

In [13], Wood and Stankovic identify a number of DoS attacks in sensor networks. Many of these DoS attacks are on sensor network routing. In [3], Karlof and Wagner describe several security attacks on routing protocols in sensor networks. They also analyze the possible attacks on several existing routing protocols, including Directed Diffusion and LEACH. However, Karlof and Wagner did not present any secure routing protocol for sensor networks in [3].

Several recent works [1-18] have addressed security issues in sensor networks. However, most works on sensor networks consider the designs of routing protocols and security schemes (like key management, authentication) separately. Few works consider security issues during the design time of the routing protocol. Since most existing routing protocols have not been designed with security as a goal, it is unsurprising that they are vulnerable to many attacks. However, it is non-trivial to fix the problem since it is unlikely that a sensor network routing protocol can be made secure by incorporating security mechanisms after the design has completed. Studies and experiences have shown that considering security during design time is the best way to provide security for sensor network routing.

Although one may be able to add security features to the existing routing protocols, certain security schemes may not work efficiently or even correctly with certain routing protocols. Often the routing protocols and /or security schemes have to be modified to fit with each other, which can cause the degradation of routing performance. Thus, the best way to provide secure and efficient routing in sensor networks is to consider security during the design time of the routing protocol.

In [5], Du and Xiao present an efficient key management scheme and a secure routing protocol - Secure Cell Relay (SCR) for sensor networks. The authors consider security during the design time of the routing protocol. In the SCR, the routing area is divided into several small cells. Based on the locations of the source node and the base station, packets are forwarded by cells along the direction from source to base station. After deployment, each sensor uses a three-way handshake protocol to discover neighbor sensor nodes and establish pairwise keys. The three-way handshake can defend against the Hello flood attack. The nature of the SCR routing (relaying packets via certain cells) makes it resistant to spoofed routing information, selective forwarding, sinkhole attack, and wormhole attack. The SCR can also defend against the Sybil attack and clone attack.

Deng et al. [31] present an intrusion-tolerant routing protocol for wireless sensor networks — INSENS. INSENS does not rely on detecting intrusions, but rather tolerates intrusions by bypassing the malicious nodes using redundant multi-path routing. The idea of INSENS is that an intruder may compromise a small number of nodes in the network, but the damage is limited and does not spread in the network.

In [7], Ye et al. consider how to efficiently detect false data injected by compromised nodes. They present a Statistical En-route Filtering (SEF) mechanism that can detect and drop false data reports. The idea is to require that each sensing report be attached with a message authentication code and be validated by several nodes that detect the same event. As the report is forwarded to the base station, each sensor in the route verifies the correctness of the message authentication code. Their analysis and simulation show that with a small overhead, the SEF is able to drop most of the injected false reports.

The development of secure routing protocols for sensor networks is a challenging effort because sensor nodes have limited resources in terms of computation, communication, energy supply, storage, etc. So far, only few secure routing protocols (which consider security during the protocol design time) have been proposed for sensor networks. Secure routing in sensor networks remains a largely unexplored issue and this topic has started to attract more and more researchers.

6 Conclusions

Security is very important for many sensor networks. Due to the limited capabilities of sensor nodes, providing security to sensor networks is a challenging task. In this chapter, we summarize typical attacks on sensor networks, and we present the current state-of-art of research on sensor network security. We focus on two important security issues in sensor networks — key management and secure routing. Many key management schemes have been proposed for sensor networks. Recent research suggests that key pre-distribution scheme is a promising practical option for key management in sensor networks. Efficient and secure routing is critical for the successful operation of many sensor networks. So far, not many works have been done on secure routing in sensor networks. We expect to see more researchers working on this topic.

References

1. Wenliang Du, Jing Deng., Yunghsiang S. Han, Shigang Chen, and Pramod K. Varshney, A Key Management Scheme for Wireless Sensor Networks Using Deployment Knowledge, *Proc. of IEEE INFOCOM 2004.*
2. J. Deng, R. Han, and S. Mishra, Security support for in-network processing in wireless sensor networks, *Proc. of First ACM Workshop on the Security of Ad Hoc and Sensor Networks (SASN'03 2003).*
3. C. Karlof and D. Wagner, Secure Routing in Sensor Networks: Attacks and Countermeasures, *Proc. of First IEEE International Workshop on Sensor Network Protocols and Applications, 2003.*
4. H. Chan and A. Perrig, PIKE: Peer Intermediaries for Key Establishment in Sensor Networks, *Proc. of IEEE INFOCOM 2005.*
5. X. Du and Y. Xiao, Secure Cell Relay Routing Protocol for Sensor Networks, Submitted to *Wireless Communications and Mobile Computing (WCMC) Journal, Special Issue on Wireless Network Security.*
6. D. Liu, P. Ning, Establishing Pairwise Keys in Distributed Sensor Networks, *Proc. of the 10th ACM Conference on Computer and Communications Security (CCS '03).*
7. F. Ye, H. Luo, S. Lu, and L. Zhang, Statistical En-route Detection and Filtering of Injected False Data in Sensor Networks, *Proc. of IEEE INFOCOM 2004.*

8. D. Liu and P. Ning, Establishing pairwise keys in distributed sensor networks, *Proc. of the 10th ACM Conference on Computer and Communications Security (CCS '03), pp. 52-61.*

9. H. Chan, A. Perrig, D. Song, Random Key Predistribution Schemes for Sensor Networks, *Proc. of the 2003 IEEE Symposium on Security and Privacy, May 11-14, 197 - 213.*

10. S. Zhu, S. Setia and S. Jajodia, LEAP: Efficient Security Mechanisms for Large-Scale Distributed Sensor Networks, *Proc. of the 10th ACM Conference on Computer and Communications Security (CCS '03).*

11. L. Eschenauer and V. D. Gligor, A key management scheme for distributed sensor networks, *Proc. of the 9th ACM Conference on Computer and Communication Security, pp. 41-47, Nov. 2002.*

12. H. Chan, A. Perrig, Security and privacy in sensor networks, *Computer, Vol. 36, No. 10, Oct. 2003, pp. 103 - 105.*

13. A.D., Wood, J.A., Stankovic, Denial of service in sensor networks, *Computer, Vol. 35, No. 10, Oct. 2002, Pages: 54 - 62.*

14. A. Perrig, et Al., SPINS: Security Protocols for Sensor Networks, *Proc. of MOBICOM 2001.*

15. Y.-C. Hu, A. Perrig, and D. B. Johnson, Wormhole detection in wireless ad hoc networks, *Department of Computer Science, Rice University, Tech. Rep. TR01-384.*

16. J. R. Douceur, The Sybil Attack, *Proc. of IPTPS '02.*

17. C. Karlof, N. Sastry, and D. Wagner, TinySec: A Link Layer Security Architecture for Wireless Sensor Networks, *Proc. of the Second ACM Conference on Embedded Networked Sensor Systems (SenSys 2004).*

18. W. Du, J. Deng, Y. Han, P. Varshney, A pairwise key pre-distribution scheme for wireless sensor networks, *Proc. of the 10th ACM Conference on Computer and Communi-cations Security (CCS), pp. 42-51, 2003.*

19. F. Ye, S. Lu, and L. Zhang, Gradient Broadcast: A Robust, Long lived Sensor Network, (http://irl.cs.ucla.edu/papers/grab-techreports.ps, 2001).

20. F. Ye, H. Luo, J. Cheng, S. Lu, and L. Zhang, A Two tier Data Dissemination Model for Large-scale Wireless Sensor Networks, *Proc. of ACM MOBICOM'02.*

21. C. Intanagonwiwat, R. Govindan and D. Estrin, Directed Diffusion: A Scalable and Robust Communication Paradigm for Sensor Networks, *Proc. of ACM MOBICOM'00.*

22. A. Savvides, C. Han, and M. Strivastava, Dynamic fine-grained localization in ad-hoc networks of sensors, *Proc. of ACM MOBICOM'01, pp 166-179.*

23. L. Doherty, L. El Ghaoui, and K. S. J. Pister, Convex position estimation in wireless sensor networks, *Proc. of IEEE INFOCOM 2001.*

24. W. Heinzelman, A. Chandrakasan, and H. Balakrishnan, Energy-Efficient Communication Protocols for Wireless Microsensor Networks, *Proc. of Hawaiians Int'l Conf. on Systems Science, Jan. 2000.*

25. J. Kong, P. Zerfos, H. Luo, S. Lu, and L. Zhang, Providing robust and ubiquitous security support for mobile ad-hoc networks, *Proc. of IEEE International Conference on Network Protocols (ICNP), pp. 251-260, 2001.*

26. K. Sanzgiri, B. Dahill, B. N. Levine, C. Shields, and E. Belding-Royer, A Secure Routing Protocol for Ad Hoc Networks, *Proc. of IEEE International Conference on Network Protocols (ICNP). Nov. 2002.*

27. J. Kong, H. Luo, K. Xu, D. L. Gu, M. Gerla, and S. Lu, Adaptive security for multi-layer ad-hoc networks, *Wireless Communications and Mobile Computing, 2002.*

28. Y.-C. Hu, D. B. Johnson, and A. Perrig, SEAD: Secure efficient distance vector routing for mobile wireless ad hoc networks, *Proc. of the 4th IEEE Workshop on Mobile Computing Systems and Applications (WMCSA), Jun. 2002, pp. 3–13.*

29. Y.-C. Hu, A. Perrig, and D. B. Johnson, Ariadne: A secure on-demand routing protocol for ad hoc networks, *Proc. of The 8th ACM International Conference on Mobile Computing and Networking, Sep. 2002.*

30. P. Papadimitratos and Z. Haas, Secure routing for mobile ad hoc networks, *Proc. of SCS Communication Networks and Distributed Systems Modeling and Simulation Conference (CNDS), Jan. 2002.*

31. J. Deng, R. Han, S. Mishra, INSENS: Intrusion-tolerant routing in wireless Sensor Networks, *Technical Report CU-CS-939-02, Department of Computer Science, University of Colorado, Nov. 2002.*

32. B. C. Neuman and T. Tso, Kerberos: An authentication service for computer networks, IEEE Communications, vol. 32, no. 9, pp. 33–38, Sep. 1994.

33. W. Diffie and M. E. Hellman, New Directions in Cryptography, *IEEE Transactions on Information Theory, vol. 22, pp. 644–654, Nov. 1976.*

34. R. L. Rivest, A. Shamir, and L. M. Adleman, A method for obtaining digital signatures and public-key cryptosystems, *Communications of the ACM, vol. 21, no. 2, pp. 120–126, 1978.*

35. Crossbow Technology Inc., *www.xbow.com.*

36. F. Stann and J. Heidemann, RMST: Reliable Data Transport in Sensor Networks, *Proc. of the First International Workshop on Sensor Net Protocols and Applications, pp. 102–112.*

37. T. Aura, P. Nikander, and J. Leiwo, DOS-Resistant Authentication with Client Puzzles, *Proc. of Security Protocols Workshop 2000, pp. 170–177.*

38. R. Blom, An optimal class of symmetric key generation systems, *In Advances in Cryptology: Proceedings of Eurocrypt '84, pages 335–338, 1984.*

39. C. Blundo, A. De Santis, A. Herzberg, S. Kutten, U. Vaccaro, and M. Yung, Perfectly secure key distribution for dynamic conferences, In Ernest F. Brickell, editor, *Advances in Cryptology - Crypto '92, pages 471–486, Berlin, 1992. Springer-Verlag. Lecture Notes in Computer Science Volume 740.*

40. LAN MAN Standards Committee of the IEEE Computer Society, Wireless LAN medium access control (MAC) and physical layer (PHY) specification, IEEE, New York, NY, USA, IEEE Std 802.11-1997 edition, 1997.

41. S. Zhu, S. Xu, S. Setia, and S. Jajodia, "LHAP: A Lightweight Hop-by-Hop Authentication Protocol For Ad-Hoc Networks," Proc. of the 23rd International Conference on Distributed Computing Systems Workshops (ICDCSW'03), May 2003, Providence, RI.

42. W. Du, R. Wang, and P. Ning. "An Efficient Scheme for Authenticating Public Keys in Sensor Networks," Proc. of the 6th ACM MobiHoc, May, 2005, UIUC.

Chapter 18
A Passive Approach to Unauthorized Sensor Node Identification

Cherita Corbett[1], John Copeland[1], and Raheem Beyah[2]

[1] Communications Systems Center
Georgia Institute of Technology
School of Electrical and Computer Engineering, Atlanta, GA 30332
{cherita, jcopeland}@ece.gatech.edu
[2] Department of Computer Science
Georgia State University, Atlanta, GA 30303
rbeyah@cs.gsu.edu

1 Introduction

As access to power becomes less of a concern [4] (solar powered devices, wind powered devices, longer battery life, AC), the desire for higher bandwidth communication, and a desire for easy deployment, sensor networks are increasingly using the 802.11 medium access control (MAC) protocol. Further, some sensor deployment schemes [3] are heterogeneous, using smaller low-powered sensors for traffic routing, but use higher-powered devices that use 802.11 to improve overall performance of the network. Accordingly, in this chapter we discuss security concerns that apply to sensor networks, but extend to any network using the 802.11 MAC, including wireless local area networks (WLANs) and ad hoc networks.

1.1 Security Concerns in 802.11 Networks

The shortcomings surrounding the security of 802.11 networks have been well documented [20, 19]. Expectedly, there are automated tools [18] that exploit these flaws to passively and actively attack wireless networks to gain unauthorized access. Unauthorized access could manifest itself as MAC address spoofing, as a man-in-the-middle attack, as a session-hijack or as message contamination.

1.2 802.11i in Sensor Networks

Reacting to the security weakness in 802.11, the IEEE 802.11 standards committee sought to provide additional security features with the 802.11i specification [2]. 802.11i primarily improves encryption via the Advanced Encryption Standard (AES), which requires significantly more computing power than the original standard. To be effective, 802.11i requires new hardware and must be commonly applied to all systems on the wireless network. An implementation of 802.11i in sensor networks would require each sensor to take the Supplicant, Authenticator, and Authentication Server roles to enforce its own security policy. Each sensor must authenticate each peer (even sensors that are functioning as relay nodes) and maintain a set of keys for each peer relationship. The required computing power coupled with the density and dynamically changing topology of sensor networks renders 802.11i an impractical solution. The 802.11i standard is better suited for non-transient, centralized networks with fixed infrastructure. Further, the 802.11i protocol works well against defending the nodes within the network from an outsider threat, but does little to protect authorized nodes from other authorized nodes.

1.3 Problems with Existing Approaches to Securing 802.11 Networks

Current intrusion detection strategies [17, 16] seek to address the problem of unauthorized access by monitoring the wireless network for a sequence of events that exhibit odd behavior or violate a security policy, such as jumps in sequence numbers or a station operating on a prohibited channel. This approach can be evaded by stealthy intrusions that do not use brute force to gain access or that do not behave out of profile. For example, an adversary can compromise or capture and reverse engineer a sensor node, which carries the necessary security information (i.e., encryption keys, authentication information). The adversary can then use this information to masquerade as an authorized node. In such a case, the adversary appears to have legitimate access and does not exhibit alarming behavior because it had the proper credentials. As this example demonstrates, a method of detecting unauthorized access (even by authorized nodes) is necessary. If a breach goes undetected, sensitive information can be stolen, network resources abused, or more sophisticated attacks targeting legitimate sensors can be launched. Detecting unauthorized access affords an opportunity to respond to the intrusion and curtail the potential damage to preserve the privacy and integrity of the sensor network.

1.4 Key Ideas and Outline

To address the problem of unauthorized access, we introduce a technique to identify an unauthorized node based on the composition of its radio interface (RI). Establishing an identity for valid types of RIs aids in detecting intruding systems that have a different type of RI. Though an attacker can use the same

RI, this technique adds another barrier for the attacker [1]. In this chapter, we show that differences in the composition of an RI influence data transmission patterns in a manner that is observable through traffic analysis. We extract subtle differences in the temporal behavior of a wireless stream to produce a spectral profile as the identity of an RI of a wireless sensor.

The remainder of the chapter is organized as follows. In Section 2, we present existing approaches to device identification. Sections 3 and 4 explore the organization of an RI and highlights factors that shape the behavior of wireless traffic. Sections 5 and 6 discuss rate switching as a viable attribute for identifying different types of RIs. In Section 7, we present our technique for passive RI identification. We conduct an experimental evaluation and present the results in Section 8. In Section 9, we give the conclusion and discuss future directions.

2 Related Work

Most current approaches to thwarting unauthorized access in 802.11 networks focus on wireless local area networks (WLANs). For this reason, our discussion of related work pertains to WLANs. However, it is important to note that these approaches will differ from those in sensor networks. Unlike sensor networks, WLANs have an access point that can enforce a uniform security policy across all wireless clients that communicate through the access point.

2.1 Wireless Security Approaches

WiMetrics [15] is a commercially available monitoring and intrusion protection system. It implements an identity profiling process that can preauthorize a user through a registration process or authorize on the fly by probing the wireless device to derive an identity profile based on the response. Probing wireless stations is intrusive and as the number of clients increases, the already constrained network becomes burdened with additional traffic imposed by the system. This approach has other drawbacks including the administrative overhead of the preauthorization process. In addition, a hacker could elude the system by crafting responses to the probe request to impersonate the identity of a legitimate user, reducing the effectiveness of this scheme. This method of establishing an identity profile is not applicable to sensor networks, particularly for dense sensor networks. The probing process burdens the constrained network with additional traffic and consumes valuable battery life at the sensor node. With nodes entering and exiting the network dynamically, the profiling process has to be repeated, further consuming limited resources.

IPass Inc. developed DeviceID [14] , a software-based authentication technology. DeviceID creates a digital fingerprint using random segments of serial

---

[1] As with any security system, if an attacker knows the technique/algorithm, the system can be evaded.

numbers for different hardware components within the device. It consists of two components, server and client software. The server encrypts and inventories the digital fingerprint in a database. The client resides on all end-point devices to establish secure sockets layer (SSL) connections for secure transmission of the device's fingerprint required for hardware authentication. This approach is intrusive and suffers from administrative overhead involved in distributing the client software and updating the database every time a hardware component changes in the device. Further, this approach generates traffic, placing additional strain on the wireless link.

Radio frequency (RF) fingerprinting captures the unique characteristics of the RF energy of a transceiver. When a radio transmitter is placed in transmit mode, a transient is generated by the frequency synthesizer whose function it is to generate the carrier frequency used for transmission. It has been determined that the turn-on transients generated are distinct enough that positive identification of the transmitter is possible. This technology was originally used in the cellular industry to identify fraudulent clones [13] . Researchers at Carleton University [12] have extended this approach to control access amongst BlueTooth wireless devices with future plans of including 802.11 transceivers. To implement this technology in a wireless sensor network, special equipment for processing RF signals would be required to overlay the coverage area of the sensor network. The cost of new equipment can become prohibitive especially for widespread sensors within a network. Also the deployment of specialized RF equipment is impractical in a sensor network. This was not of significant concern to the cellular industry because cellular towers are permanent fixed infrastructure that provide a monitoring and management point. Additionally, each tower services thousands of subscribers dissipating the cost of the equipment.

2.2 Host Fingerprinting

Kohno et al. [11] demonstrate a method for remotely fingerprinting a physical device by exploiting the implementation of the TCP protocol stack. When the TCP timestamp option is enabled, outgoing TCP packets reveal information about the sender's internal clock. The authors' technique exploits microscopic deviations in the clock skews to derive a clock cycle pattern as the identity for a device. For machines that do not enable the timestamp option by default, such as those running Windows 2000 and Windows XP, this approach becomes an active one. An active fingerprinting technique is needed to initiate a connection and trick the fingerprintee into using the timestamp option. The active approach must violate the TCP specification in order to execute the trick. The drawback to the active technique is that it is detectable to the fingerprinted device. Furthermore, the entire approach only applies to TCP traffic and can be evaded by spoofing the TCP timestamp field or setting it to an arbitrary value. Sensor networks utilize optimized, modified, lightweight protocols for data delivery. Pursuing a transport specific approach such as

Kohno's, requires developing a different technique for each transport delivery protocol.

3 Organization of a Radio Interface

An RI is responsible for carrying out the physical transmission of a packet over the air waves. To do so, the 802.11 specification requires the implementation of two layers: the physical layer (PHY) and the medium access control (MAC) layer. To support this implementation the RI is organized into hardware, firmware, and software (driver software and utility software). The functions of 802.11 PHY are entirely implemented in hardware. The firmware is a microprogram semi-permanently embedded into ROM to control the hardware. It works to communicate between the hardware and driver software. Driver software accepts generic I/O commands from the operating system (OS) of the host and then converts them into instructions the interface can understand. The utility software is used to configure parameters to change the overall behavior of the hardware and software. The 802.11 MAC is implemented by a combination of hardware and software.

4 Opportunities for Distinction

There are several attributes about an RI that offer opportunities for distinction. Below, we discuss how the architectural design, the implementation of the 802.11 standard, and the setting of configurable parameters contribute to the identification of a wireless system.

4.1 Software/Hardware Split

For the RI, an important performance factor is the amount of time it takes the interface to process a packet in its send queue and start the physical transmission over the airwaves, called the *packet servicing time*. Deciding how to split the implementation of the RI between hardware and software is at the discretion of the manufacturer and greatly impacts this parameter. Driver software makes it cheaper and easier to upgrade the functionality of the NIC, but it requires the resources of the host because it is embedded in the kernel space of the operating system (OS). An RI with dedicated hardware seeks to minimize intervention and utilization of the host which reduces the *packet servicing time*. In contrast, an architecture that relies on the resources of the host introduces additional latencies associated with the host, such as the overhead caused by interrupt handling and OS transitions to honor the requests of the RI. Consider the case where an RI uses a dedicated hardware engine to perform packet encryption instead of implementing it in software. The hardware encryption engine would have a shorter packet servicing time, because the software implementation would need to interrupt the host, transfer the packet to the host for encryption, allow the host to perform encryption, and retrieve the encrypted packet from host. While the CPU may very well be capable of handling the RI request in a timely fashion, the overhead of the OS raises concern regarding the split of the architecture between hardware and software. This decision directly impacts the *packet servicing time*, and based on how dependent the RI is on the host, the performance of the host may become the prominent factor in the packet servicing time. Capturing notable differences in *packet servicing time* contributes to the identification of a wireless system.

4.2 Implementation of 802.11 Services

The 802.11 standard [2] mandates a suite of services to which an RI must adhere to be in compliance with the standard for interoperability. However, the standard does not dictate how these services are to be implemented. This ambiguous mandate leads to the development of proprietary solutions among different manufacturers. To cope with the changing conditions of a wireless environment, these services may fragment packets, retransmit packets, adjust transmission rates, reserve the link, probe for a better network, or opt to poll for packets to conserve power. These events wield a certain behavior in the communication stream that can be observed and measured by parameters, such as the occurrence and duration of gaps between data packets, types of packets, and size of packets. Differences in the implementation of these services will cause a different influence on the behavior of the traffic that can be exploited to distinguish between RIs. We exploit this fact in our experimental evaluation (see Section 7).

4.3 Configuration of the Radio Interface

The 802.11 standard supports the dynamic configuration of the RI to tune its behavior to be conducive to a variety of environments. Examples of configurable parameters include request-to-send (RTS) threshold, fragmentation threshold, transmit power, and power save mode. Different settings of these parameters can alter the behavior of traffic. For example, the RTS threshold sets the data packet size for which to trigger the request-to-send/clear-to-send (RTS/CTS) handshake to reserve the wireless link prior to data transmission. The RTS/CTS handshake is overhead that widens the inter-arrival time between data packets. An RI with the RTS threshold set to a lower value will trigger the RTS/CTS handshake more frequently than an RTS threshold with a higher value. As a result, the packets' inter-arrival time would be larger and this phenomenon would occur more often than for the higher RTS threshold.

4.4 Acceleration Software/Hardware

In addition to the basic services specified in the 802.11 standard, manufacturers often include acceleration hardware and software to increase performance gains and to support future standards prior to ratification. Enhancement techniques currently deployed to improve data transmission rates include data compression, frame bursting, overhead management, and client-to-client transfer [5]. The use of proprietary enhancement techniques can help distinguish among devices. For example, the frame bursting technique, which is based on the proposed 802.11e standard, unpacks short data packets and rebundles them into a larger packet. An RI with frame bursting technology would exhibit different timing features by generating larger packets and less frequent management and control overhead traffic than an RI without frame bursting.

5 Using Rate Switching to Detect Unauthorized Nodes

To illustrate a technique for distinguishing among heterogeneous sensors, we focus on the implementation of the rate switching algorithm as an attribute within the RI. Rate switching is a service that is required by the 802.11 standard, but its implementation is unspecified. Additionally, it is not a configurable service and it would be difficult to conceal its influence on traffic without altering the hardware or driver software. By analyzing the differences in implementation of the rate switching algorithm we can establish an identity for the radio interface of a sensor. The 802.11 PHY provides multiple transmission rates. For example, 802.11b supports rates of 1, 2, 5.5, and 11 megabits per second. A rate switching algorithm aims to dynamically adapt the transmission rate per packet based on the channel conditions to optimize performance. During the period where a node undergoes rate switching, the behavior of the rate switching algorithm has a temporal impact on the transmission of each packet. How the algorithm responds to the transient and long-term changes to the condition of the wireless link will affect the transmission duration and inter-packet timing. The rate switching algorithm may also trigger other services such as the RTS/CTS handshake or retransmission, causing a greater impact on the behavior of the traffic. The actual rate switching algorithm implemented in the radio interface of a sensor is unknown, as it is considered sensitive proprietary property. However, [10] discusses algorithms that are speculated to be used in current products.

6 Empirical Analysis of Rate Switching

We have pinpointed rate switching as an opportunity for distinguishing between sensor nodes with RIs produced by different vendors. Before developing our approach, we conducted an empirical analysis to characterize the rate switching phenomenon. As a result of its accessibility and ease of node deployment, we used 802.11WLAN nodes to emulate a sensor network.

6.1 Experimental Setup

Analysis was conducted at a local hotspot on the campus of Georgia Institute of Technology. Over the course of seven days we captured all traffic on the wireless network. We used a Toshiba laptop with a Linksys WPC11 wireless card to collect traffic. We put the wireless card into monitor mode using the *wlanctl − ng* utility and stored the captured traffic using Ethereal. With the card in monitor mode we are able to detect the transmission rate associated with each packet collected, while Ethereal appends a timestamp to each packet. We used timing information and the transmission rate to generate statistics. Traffic was collected for a total of 13.3 hours over the course of seven days. During our observation period, there were a total of 61 wireless nodes that visited the hotspot.

6.2 Results

The results of our analysis show that rate switching is common at the hotspot. While this is definitely true for the hotspot we monitored, it is likely that RF interference occurs in most wireless environments. Therefore, rate switching is likely a widespread, common phenomenon. Figure 1 shows the transmission rate of each data frame transmitted by one of the nodes at the local hotspot. This particular node switched transmission rates 279 times. Overall, Figure

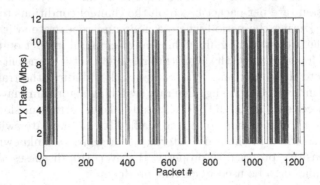

Fig. 1. Node at local hotspot invoking rate switching.

2(a) shows how often rate switching occurred for all wireless nodes over the entire observation period. Figure 2(b) shows that 67% of the clients performed rate switching, while 33% did not switch rates. Out of the nodes that did not perform rate switching, 85% sent less than nine packets (Figure 3). If we exclude the non-switching nodes that sent less than nine packets (assuming that these clients were never properly authenticated to the network), then the percent of nodes that perform rate switching becomes 92% (Figure 2(c)).

Examining only the wireless nodes that used rate switching, Figure 4 shows that 90% transmitted more than 37 packets and 88% were connected to network more than two minutes. Also, 85% of these nodes switched rates within the first three minutes of their connection.

We conclude that rate switching is a phenomenon that frequently occurs. Our results show that the longer a wireless node is a part of the network and the more packets it transmits, the more likely rate switching is to occur. Therefore, rate switching is a viable attribute within the RI for distinguishing between wireless nodes. This is a result of temporal and spatial interference, as well as the effect of collisions with link layer acknowledgements [1].

7 An Approach to Sensor Node Identification

Observing the impact of the rate switching algorithm on the temporal properties of a wireless stream is a passive way to identify sensors with different RIs. This approach is well suited for sensor networks because it does not inject traffic, does not require client software, operates independent of higher layer protocols and can work in the presence of encrypted traffic.

Given a trace of wireless traffic in which the rate switching algorithm has been invoked, we apply Fourier analysis to create a spectrum. The spectral features capture the temporal behavior of the trace influenced by the rate switching algorithm. We distinguish between RIs by comparing their spectral profiles.

7.1 Encoding Trace into Signal

Before we can apply spectral analysis, we must encode the traffic capture into a signal, a time series of events. Even with an encrypted payload, the 802.11 header offers a rich source of information, such as packet size, duration of payload, packet type, and retransmitted packets. Additionally, the traffic-capturing utility records a time stamp with each packet as it is collected. This information can be used to construct various types of signals.

Our goal is to construct a packet arrival timeseries from the wireless traffic stream. First we extract only data frames as indicated by the Subtype fields within the header. This step isolates the actual data transmission frames from other overhead communication to minimize the amount of noise in the frequency domain. Next, we use a sampling bin of s seconds and define the arrival process, $x(t)$, as the number of data packets that arrive in the bin$[t$, $t+s]$. Given a traffic capture T seconds long, we will have N=T/s samples. The maximum frequency that can be represented is $1/2s$ hertz.

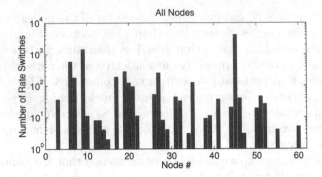

(a) Number of rate switches per node

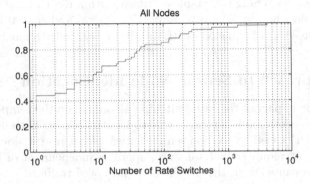

(b) CDF of rate switches for all clients

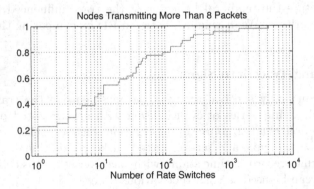

(c) CDF of rate switches excluding non-switching nodes that sent less than eight packets

Fig. 2. Rate switching nodes.

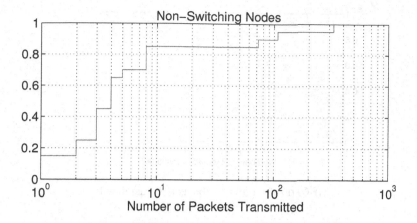

Fig. 3. CDF of number of packets transmitted by non-switching nodes.

7.2 Signal Processing

Signal processing has been previously applied to network research to detect and classify Denial of Service attacks [9], to map the flow of wireless traffic, and to extract information about protocol behavior in encrypted wireless traffic [8]. We apply signal processing to wireless streams to analyze the timing of packet arrival, particularly while the rate switching algorithm is invoked to distinguish between RIs with presumably different algorithms.

Given a signal $x(t)$ constructed using the process discussed above, we estimate the power spectral density (PSD) by computing the discrete-time Fourier transform of the samples of the process and taking the magnitude squared of the result. This estimate is called the periodogram [7]. The power spectral density, $\hat{P}_{xx}(f)$, of a process of length L is given in (1):

$$\hat{P}_{xx}(f) = \frac{\mid X_L(f) \mid^2}{f_s L},\tag{1}$$

where the discrete-time Fourier transform, X_L is given in (2):

$$X_L(f) = \sum_{n=0}^{L-1} x_L[n] e^{\frac{-2\pi j f n}{f_s}}.\tag{2}$$

8 Experimental Evaluation

In sensor networks, nodes typically have similar system configuration and end-user applications. Accordingly, the nodes in our experiments were completely

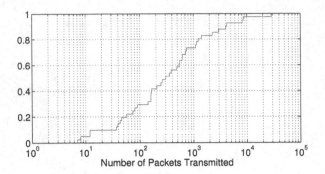

(a) CDF of number of packets transmitted

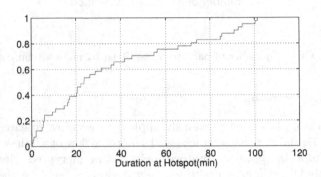

(b) CDF of duration at hotspot

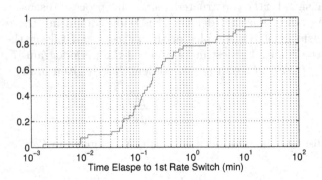

(c) CDF of time elapsed to 1st rate switch

Fig. 4. Rate switching nodes.

homogeneous, with the only variable being the RI. We again emulate a sensor network using an 802.11 WLAN, due to its ease of deployment.

8.1 Experimental Setup

The testbed is comprised of three nodes. A 1GHz Toshiba laptop functions as the source sensor node that generates wireless traffic. A Linksys 802.11b wireless router serves as a relay node to forward messages from the source to the sink node. A Dell desktop functions as the sink node. We should note that we are only concerned with the wireless segment from the source node to the relay node, thus the connection from the relay node to the sink is wired. We tested three types of RIs on the source sensor node: D-Link DWL-650, Linksys WPC11, and Lucent/Orinoco Gold. A fourth RI was used to capture traffic in promiscuous mode using tcpdump. We also used the iwconfig utility to record the transmission rate of the RI in one second intervals. For each experiment, the sensor source node sends data over the wireless link through the relay node to the sink. The test is repeated ten times for each RI.

We imposed a traffic load of 2.4Mbps. The load was light enough to not stress the node, but heavy enough to cause the RI to be the bottleneck in the sensor so that it is the primary factor influencing the behavior of the traffic. We used the sock [6] program to establish a user datagram protocol (UDP) connection carrying constant bit rate (CBR) traffic generating a 1470-byte packet every five milliseconds.

In a real environment, rate switching occurs due to the changes in channel conditions caused by noise. This noise may be caused by the network contention, interference from neighboring networks operating on the same channel, mobility of a wireless sensor, non-802.11 devices operating in the same frequency range, collisions with link layer acknowledgements, etc. During our experimental evaluation, we want to control the invoking of the rate switching algorithm. To emulate a real environment during our controlled experiments, we used an artificial noise source to alter the condition of the wireless link. In our experiments we started streaming data for 60 seconds, and then turned on the noise source causing an instant pulse of noise. After 60 seconds, the noise source was turned off and data continued streaming for another 60 seconds. We were able to trigger rate switching as seen in Figure 5.

8.2 Results

We analyzed the captures using the encoding process and periodogram estimation as discussed above. We partitioned the analysis into three parts: the interval before injecting noise, the interval with noise, and the interval after injecting noise. During our analysis we used a sampling bin of 2 ms, which represents a frequency range up to 250 Hz. We also removed the mean from the sampled signal prior to calculating the discrete-time Fourier transform to

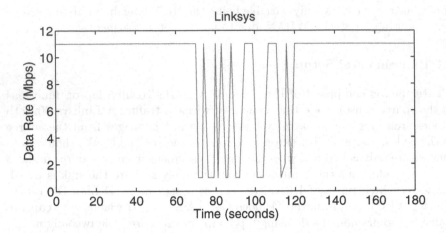

Fig. 5. Linksys card entering and exiting rate switching.

remove the DC bias from the signal. If not removed, the mean gives rise to significant power at 0Hz.

Our technique produces a spectrum that captures a view of the dynamic properties of a wireless stream. Because we filtered out all other frame types during the encoding process to only consider data frames, the spectrum captures the power or strength of the data transmission rate contained at a particular frequency. A similar analysis could be done to isolate the spectral content of management or control frames within a wireless stream or for a specific type of frame (i.e., retransmitted frames). Since the rate switching algorithm is only applied to data frames, we only encoded data frames.

Spectral analysis of the traffic trace prior to injecting noise generates a similar PSD for all three types of RIs as illustrated by Figure 6. The PSD also reveals that power is concentrated at discrete frequency points. Each RI has the most prominent peaks at 100Hz and 200Hz, confirming that the RIs behaved similarly in transmitting data frames when there is no rate switching (i.e., when the condition of the link is perceived as good).

During the interval in which noise was injected into the wireless environment, each RI generated a distinct PSD as shown in Figure 7. In contrast to the noiseless period, we also observed that prominent peaks are scattered throughout the frequency range, especially at the lower frequencies. For example, in Figure 7(a) the Lucent RI still has prominent peaks at 100Hz and 200Hz (that were seen before injecting noise), but new distinctive peaks are found at the lower frequencies ranges (0-10Hz and 50-60Hz). The spread of prominent peaks throughout the frequency range indicates that a host is transmitting data frames at several different rates. This type of behavior is expected while the RI is executing its rate switching algorithm. To address the stability of

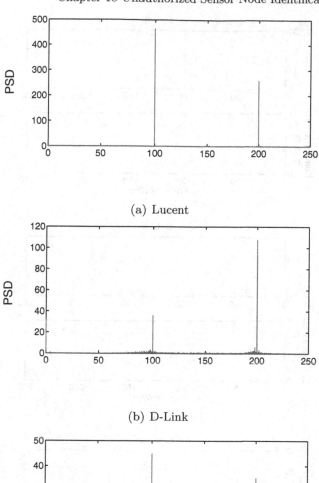

(a) Lucent

(b) D-Link

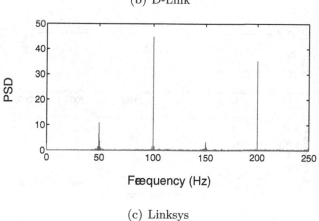

(c) Linksys

Fig. 6. PSD prior to injecting noise.

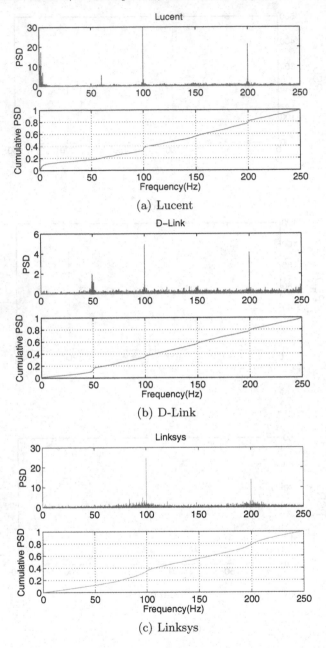

(a) Lucent

(b) D-Link

(c) Linksys

Fig. 7. PSD and cumulative PSD.

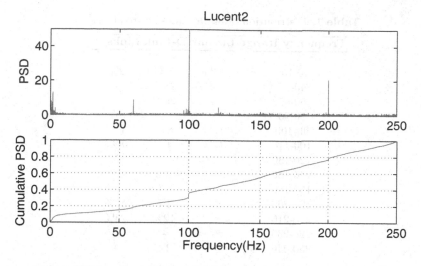

Fig. 8. PSD and cumulative PSD for repeated Lucent experiment.

the PSD, we repeated experiments with the same RI. The PSD for each RI, respectively, is similar. A comparison between Figure 7(a) and Figure 8 illustrates similarity among repeated experiments for the Lucent RI.

We also observed a distinction between RIs when comparing the normalized cumulative sum (NCS) of the spectrum during the noisy period. The slope of the NCS of the Linksys RI is almost linear with a modest variation in the slope over the range of 90Hz to 130Hz (and 190Hz to 210Hz), indicating that the power spreads (somewhat evenly) across this frequency range. DLink shows a concentration of power around 50Hz indicated by the strong rising slope in the NCS. The strong rising slope of the NCS for Lucent indicates a concentration of power around 10Hz (and 100 Hz).

To numerically compare the spectrum between RIs, we locate the frequency points that exhibit the greatest amount of power. These key frequency points estimate the most prevalent sending rates of the RI during rate switching. For our evaluation, we chose the top 50 frequency points to constitute a frequency set, $F = f1, f2, f50$, as the spectral profile of an RI. Table 1 displays the distribution of the set F for each RI. By examining the range where the majority (54% or more) of the set F is located, we can distinguish between RIs. A Lucent RI can be identified by 54% of frequencies concentrated between 0-10Hz. This indicates that a Lucent RI most often sends data frames at a rate of 100ms during rate switching. The concentration of F for the Linksys RI is over a broader range: 56% between 80-130Hz. A Linksys RI most often attempts to send data frames between 7.7ms and 12.5ms during rate switching. Whereas, DLink most often sends data frames between 17ms and 25ms, indicated by a concentration of 54% of the set F between 40–60Hz. The selection

Table 1. Distribution of 50 dominating frequencies.

Frequency Range	Lucent	D-Link	Linksys
0-10	54%	8%	2%
40-50	-	28%	-
50-60	4%	26%	-
80-90	-	-	10%
90-100	12%	8%	34%
100-110	10%	4%	8%
120-130	-	-	4%
140-150	-	2%	2%
150-160	-	6%	-
190-200	20%	4%	16%
200-210	-	12%	24%
220-230	-	-	-
230-240	-	2%	-

of 50 frequency points as a spectral profile proved to be adequate, because the distribution of the set F coincides with the observations made using NCS.

9 Conclusion

In this chapter we presented an approach for identifying unauthorized sensor nodes within a network. We identified the rate switching algorithm as an attribute of an RI as an opportunity for distinguishing between RIs manufactured by different vendors. We used signal processing to extract markedly different traffic characteristics among different RIs during rate switching.

An important aspect to explore is the stability of the spectral profile. We applied our technique and successfully tracked nodes in a real network. Other factors like the setting of the RI configuration parameters can be considered (i.e., RTS threshold, maximum retries, etc.). If the settings change the spectrum, then they become an essential part of the spectral profile. This could help distinguish between RIs manufactured by the same vendor. Heterogeneous sensor systems should also be considered. During our experiments we only used a single type of sensor. Sensors with different capacities may also affect the spectral profile. In this case the characterization may need to be broadened or restricted. The impact of these elements on the power spectrum may also require a technique other than establishing a set F of top frequencies to have a more robust comparison.

Also, other time attributes of a stream, such as the inter-packet delay and variations in inter-packet delay can be considered, as well as management and control frames. Considering more elements will improve the stability and robustness of the presented approach.

References

1. Sunwoong Choi, Kihong Park and Chong-kwon Kim, On the Performance Characteristics of WLANs: Revisited, ACM Sigmetrics, Banff, Alberta, Canada, 2005.
2. The 802.11i Standard, http://standards.ieee.org/ getieee802/download/802.11i-2004.pdf.
3. Intel, http://www.intel.com/research/exploratory/ heterogeneous.htm.
4. Chulsung Park, Qiang Xie and Pai H. Chou, DuraNode: Wi-Fi-based Sensor Node for Real-Time Structural Safety Monitoring, The Fourth International Conference on Information Processing in Sensor Networks (IPSN 2005), 2005.
5. Alefiya Hussain, John Heidemann and Christos Papadopoulos, Identification of repeated attacks using network traffic forensics, USC/Information Sciences Institute, ISI-TR-2003-577b, 2003.
6. W. Richard Stevens, Unix Network Programming, Prentice Hall, 1998.
7. A.V. Oppenheim and R.W. Schafer, Discrete-Time Signal Processing, Prentice-Hall, 1989.
8. C. Partridge, D. Cousins, A.W. Jackson, R. Krishan T. Saxena and T. Strayer, Using Signal Processing to Analyze Wireless Data Traffic, ACM Workshop on Wireless Security (WiSe), Atlanta, GA, 2002.
9. Chen-Mou Cheng, H.T. Kung and Koan-Sin Ta, Use of spectral analysis in defense against DoS attacks, IEEE GLOBECOM, 2002.
10. M. Lacage, M. Manshaei and T. Turletti, IEEE 802.11 Rate Adaption: A Practical Approach, ACM/IEEE MSWIM, Venice, Italy, 2004.
11. Tadayoshi Kohno, Andre Briodo and KC Claffy, Remote physical device fingerprinting, IEEE Transactions on Dependable and Secure Computing, vol.2 pp.93–108, 2005.
12. Jeyanthi Hall, Michel Barbeau and Evangelos Kranakis, Detection of Transient in Radio Frequency Fingerprinting using Signal Phase, Internet and Information Technology (CIIT), 2004.
13. www.decodesystems.com/mt/97dec/.
14. iPass, www.ipass.com/services/services_deviceid.html.
15. Wimetrics, www.wimetrics.com.
16. Joshua Wright, Detecting Wireless LAN MAC Address Spoofing, home.jwu.edu/jwright.
17. AirDefense, www.airdefense.net.
18. Slayer, The Definitive Guide To Wireless WarX'ing, teknik.ekitap.gen.tr/TDGTW-WarXing.html.
19. William A. Arbaugh, Narendar Shankar and Y.C. Justin Wan, Your 802.11 wireless network has no clothes, http://www.cs.umd.edu/ waa/wireless.pdf.
20. Nikita Borisov, Ian Golberg and David Wagner, Intercepting mobile communications: The insecurity of 802.11, MOBICOM, 2001.

SIGNALS AND COMMUNICATION TECHNOLOGY

(continued from page ii)